642 Delicious Recipes For On-the-Go Cooks

IT'S EASY to please your family with homemade, wholesome, delicious dishes every day of the week. Just rely on this ninth edition of the cookbook containing recipes from *Quick Cooking* and *Simple & Delicious* magazines.

2007 Quick Cooking Annual Recipes is a convenient collection of every fast-to-fix recipe published in *Quick Cooking* and *Simple & Delicious* during 2006—that's 642 recipes in all! This jam-packed cookbook also contains hundreds of gorgeous, full-color photos that show you exactly what your completed dish will look like when you set it on the table.

Here's what else you'll find inside:

Easy-to-Use Chapters. You can quickly locate the kinds of recipes you need in 21 big chapters, ranging from Breakfast & Brunch Favorites to Easy Half-Hour Entrees. (See page 3 for a complete list of chapters.)

For example, when you have just 10 minutes to spare in the kitchen, try Zesty Potato Cheese Soup, Pineapple Ham Pizzas, Guacamole Chicken Wraps, Cashew Pea Salad, Frosty Tiramisu or any of the 18 other super-fast dishes in the "10 Minutes to the Table" chapter.

Or, on hectic weeknights when your family is hungry for supper and you're watching the clock, see the "30 Minutes to Mealtime" chapter for 28 complete meals that go from start to finish in half an hour or less.

Weekly Meal Plans. The home economists in our Test Kitchen put together 6 full weeks of Monday-through-Friday dinners, complete with a shopping list for each week. Just follow their handy meal plans to enjoy weeks of stress-free suppers. (This chapter starts on page 110.)

Contest-Winning Recipes. You'll get all the rave-winning, sensational dishes that earned top honors in the six national recipe contests held last year: Main Dishes from Mixes, Make It in the Microwave, Fuss-Free Chicken, Easy Picnic Salads, 30-Minute Entrees and Simple Party Starters. Turn to page 4 to "meet" the Grand Prize winners and see where each standout recipe is located in this book.

Reader-Friendly Indexes. To make all 642 recipes easy to find, we've listed them in two indexes. (See page 316.) The general index lists every recipe by category and/or major food ingredient. The alphabetical listing is great for folks who are looking for a specific, family-favorite dish. In both indexes, you'll find a bold red checkmark (✓) in front of all recipes that use less fat, sugar or salt and include Nutrition Facts and Diabetic Exchanges.

Every fast-to-fix recipe and helpful hint in this *2007 Quick Cooking Annual Recipes* cookbook was specifically selected with on-the-go cooks in mind. You're sure to enjoy this indispensable treasury for years to come...and you'll be able to treat your loved ones to comforting, wholesome home cooking without spending all of your time in the kitchen.

2007 Quick Cooking
Annual Recipes

Editor: Michelle Bretl
Art Directors: Gretchen Trautman, Kathy Crawford
Vice President/Books: Heidi Reuter Lloyd
Senior Editor/Books: Mark Hagen
Associate Layout Designer: Julie Stone
Proofreaders: Linne Bruskewitz, Jean Steiner
Editorial Assistant: Barb Czysz

Taste of Home Books
©2007 Reiman Media Group, Inc.
5400 S. 60th St., Greendale WI 53129

International Standard Book Number (10):
0-89821-507-2
International Standard Book Number (13):
978-089821-507-6
International Standard Serial Number:
1522-6603

PICTURED ON THE COVER: Chocolate Mousse Torte (p. 24), Baked Potatoes with Topping (p. 262) and Flank Steak Pinwheels (p. 286).

To order additional copies of this book or any other Reiman Publications books, write: *Taste of Home* Books, P.O. Box 908, Greendale WI 53129; call toll-free 1-800/344-2560 to order with a credit card or visit our Web site at **www.reimanpub.com**.

TASTE OF HOME'S
simple&delicious

Editor: Mary Spencer
Associate Editors: Mary C. Hanson, John McMillan
Art Director: Brooke Luteyn
Associate Food Editors: Coleen Martin, Diane Werner RD
Senior Home Economist: Amy Welk-Thieding RD
Recipe Editors: Mary King, Sue A. Jurack, Christine Rukavena
Test Kitchen Home Economists: Tina Johnson, Peggy Fleming RD, Ann Liebergen, Marie Parker, Annie Rose, Karen Scales, Pat Schmeling, Wendy Stenman
Contributing Home Economist: Susan Guenther
Test Kitchen Assistants: Rita Krajcir, Kris Lehman, Sue Megonigle, Julie Meyers, Megan Taylor
Editorial Assistants: Ursula Maurer, Marilyn Iczkowski, Mary Ann Koebernik
Copy Editor: S.K. Enk
Graphic Art Associate: Ellen Lloyd
Contributing Designer: Monica Bergwall
Photographers: Rob Hagen (Senior), Dan Roberts, Jim Wieland
Associate Photographer: Lori Foy
Food Stylists: Joylyn Trickel (Senior), Sarah Thompson
Food Stylist Assistant: Kate Baumann
Set Stylist: Jennifer Bradley Vent
Set Stylists' Assistant: Melissa Haberman
Photo Studio Coordinator: Suzanne Kern
Contributing Food Stylists: Diane Armstrong, Suzanne Breckenridge, Sue Draheim, Mary Franz, Julie Herzfeldt, Jennifer Janz, Jim Rude
Contributing Set Stylists: Stephanie Marchese, Julie Ferron, Nancy Seaman, Grace Natoli Sheldon, Gail Engeldahl

President: Barbara Newton
Senior Vice President/Editor in Chief:
Catherine Cassidy
Creative Director: Ardyth Cope
Founder: Roy Reiman

⏱ Contents

Recipe Contests Yield Quick Winning Dishes

DURING the past year, busy cooks from across the country submitted their very best recipes for the national recipe contests in *Quick Cooking* and *Simple & Delicious* magazines.

Wondering which delicious, time-saving dishes were deemed tops in one of those contests? Simply check the special section here.

On these two pages, we've featured the six talented cooks who took home the Grand Prize in a 2006 contest. We've also let you know where to find their first-place recipes in this book, so you can turn to those celebrated dishes right away...and even prepare them for your family tonight!

Plus, we've added the 11 other recipes that were honored in each contest. You get a complete listing of dishes—all 72 of them—that were judged as contest winners during the past year.

Because we've included the page numbers for all of the runners-up, too, you'll easily be able to locate each rave-winning recipe in this book. Dozens of top-honor dishes are right at your fingertips!

From Super Salads to Snacks

The contest topics during the past year yielded a wide range of reader recipes. But all of those dishes have one thing in common—they're quick-to-fix foods that suit busy cooks' lifestyles.

In the "Main Dishes from Mixes" contest, readers found creative ways to speed up entrees using convenience products. And "Make It in the Microwave" yielded plenty of fabulous fare whipped up at the touch of a button.

Interested in top-choice chicken dishes? Glance at the main courses, snacks and more in "Fuss-Free Chicken." Or turn to "Easy Picnic Salads" and toss together something extra special for your next backyard barbecue or family meal.

On activity-packed nights during the week, "30-Minute Entrees" will get dinner on your table in only half an hour...or less. And "Simple Party Starters" are perfect when you'd like to entertain while keeping the fuss to a minimum.

Just choose your favorites among these prize-winning recipes—or plan to fit each one into an upcoming menu. Either way, you'll have standout sensations you and your family are sure to love.

Judges Chose Her Casserole from the Mix

A LONGTIME favorite recipe really paid off for Kathleen Grant of Swan Lake, Montana. When she submitted her delicious Sausage Spinach Bake for the "Main Dishes from Mixes" contest, our judges awarded it the Grand Prize.

"My husband, Richard, requests this casserole often because he likes all of the ingredients separately and loves how they come together in one hearty dish," says Kathleen. "Everyone who has tasted it seems to agree."

Main Dishes from Mixes Contest Winners

Sausage Spinach Bake *(Grand Prize)*	p. 80
Taco Casserole *(2nd Place)*	p. 80
Stuffed Cornish Hens *(3rd Place)*	p. 80
Easy Shrimp Creole *(4th Place)*	p. 81
Chicken Artichoke Pasta *(Runner-Up)*	p. 79
Golden Sea Bass *(Runner-Up)*	p. 82
Pecan-Crusted Chicken *(Runner-Up)*	p. 81
Italian Sausage Calzone *(Runner-Up)*	p. 82
Sausage Noodle Supper *(Runner-Up)*	p. 76
Tex-Mex Turkey Burgers *(Runner-Up)*	p. 82
Stuffed Pepper Soup *(Runner-Up)*	p. 83
Orient Express Chicken Salad *(Runner-Up)*	p. 83

Her In-the-Oven Dish Was Outstanding

FOR Vicki Ruiz of Twin Falls, Idaho, spending a day in the kitchen is a treat. But when this busy grandmother needs something speedy, she turns to her recipe file and pulls out Apricot Chicken—the first-place winner in our "Make It in the Microwave" contest.

"I created it using what I liked best from several different recipes," she relates. "People enjoy the apricot-flavored sauce, and I appreciate the convenience of preparing it in the microwave."

Make It in the Microwave Contest Winners

Apricot Chicken *(Grand Prize)*	p. 262
Garden-Style Beef Lasagna *(2nd Place)*	p. 268
Toffee-Crunch Coffee Sundaes *(3rd Place)*	p. 263
Shrimp-Stuffed Sole *(4th Place)*	p. 267
Cod Delight *(Runner-Up)*	p. 264
Chicken Enchilada Dip *(Runner-Up)*	p. 267
Buttery Garlic Potatoes *(Runner-Up)*	p. 263
Tangy Meat Sauce *(Runner-Up)*	p. 266
Caramel Apple Dip *(Runner-Up)*	p. 267
Chicken in a Hurry *(Runner-Up)*	p. 268
Asparagus with Lemon Sauce *(Runner-Up)*	p. 263
Cheese-Topped Meat Loaves *(Runner-Up)*	p. 264

Judges Selected Her Grade-A Poultry

AFTER Brenda Carpenter and husband Jerry had chicken one night at a restaurant, Brenda got to work in her kitchen. "I loved that dish so much that I just had to try to re-create it at home," she writes from Warrensburg, Missouri.

Topped with smoky bacon, sweet caramelized onion and shredded cheese, her Smothered Chicken Breasts delighted her family—and our panel of judges, too. The recipe received the Grand Prize in our "Fuss-Free Chicken" contest.

Her Speedy Salad Was the Pick of the Crop

TASTE and time are prime considerations when Leslie Lancaster prepares meals for her husband, Gabriel, and their two sons. That's why Crunchy Romaine Strawberry Salad—the top winner in our "Easy Picnic Salads" contest—is one of her favorite recipes.

"It has such a refreshing combination of flavors, and I can save time by making the dressing the day before," notes the Zachary, Louisiana cook. "Then I just toss everything together before serving."

Cook's Half-Hour Entree Is a Fast Favorite

WHEN it comes to getting a weeknight meal on the table for her family, Denise Segura doesn't sweat it. She simply whips up dishes like Chicken in Lime Butter, the Grand Prize recipe in the "30-Minute Entrees" contest.

"Three of our six children still live at home and are busy with extracurricular activities," she relates from their Draper, Utah home. "With this tasty chicken, I can give them and my husband, Harry, a fast but satisfying dinner."

Her Appetizer Makes Popular Party Fare

A MOTHER of two who runs her own business, Caren Adams still finds time to entertain friends occasionally at her Fontana, California home. And Grilled Jerk Chicken Wings are usually on the menu.

"I've been making them ever since I can remember," she says. "They're simple to fix and are always a hit with my husband, Andy, and our guests." The recipe was a winner with our panel of judges, too, who gave it top honors in the "Simple Party Starters" contest.

Chapter 1

THE NUMBER ONE MENUS in busy households across the country all have one thing in common: They deliver family-pleasing flavor fast. That's true of each exceptional meal featured in this chapter.

Shared by six on-the-go cooks just like you, these delicious dinners are top choices for even the most time-crunched days. Every rave-winning recipe can be prepared from start to finish in only 30 minutes...or less.

Enjoy a wide variety of best-loved specialties—from Alfredo Seafood Fettuccine and Tasty Onion Chicken as main dishes to Cookie Pizza a la Mode and Chocolate Peanut Butter Parfaits for dessert.

No matter which menu you choose, rest assured it will become an instant favorite!

COOK'S CHOICE. Chocolate Peanut Butter Parfaits, Almond Strawberry Salad and Alfredo Seafood Fettuccine (all recipes on p. 10).

She Serves a Finger-Lickin' Chicken Dinner

WHEN IT COMES to meal preparation, time is always at a premium in Jennifer Hoeft's rural Thorndale, Texas household.

"I run a home-based business creating and selling floral designs and gifts, and it keeps me really busy," she explains. Her husband, Daniel, works as a design project manager in Austin, about an hour from their home. Plus, the couple spends free time on church activities, square dancing and volunteer work.

But sit-down meals are important to both of them, so Jennifer puts dinner on the table at least five times a week. "We live a good 20 minutes from town," she says, "so I plan our menus for 2 weeks at a time. That way, I need to go grocery shopping only twice a month."

Jennifer relies on convenience foods, as well as her microwave and steamer, to prepare quick economical meals that are easy and delicious. The menu for four she shares here is a favorite for nights when she and Daniel have guests for dinner.

Tasty Onion Chicken is a no-fuss entree that's fast and flavorful. French-fried onions are the secret to the yummy coating that keeps the meat juicy.

Golden brown Sour Cream Pan Biscuits make a convenient meal accompaniment since they bake at the same temperature and for about as long as the chicken. "They're fluffy and tender on the inside with just a hint of sweetness," notes Jennifer.

"And I created the Spicy Garlic Green Beans recipe while trying to reproduce a dish served at my favorite Chinese restaurant," she recalls. "These come very close and use just a few handy ingredients."

Tasty Onion Chicken
Prep/Total Time: 30 min.

1/2 cup butter, melted
1 tablespoon Worcestershire sauce
1 teaspoon ground mustard
1 can (2.8 ounces) french-fried onions, crushed
4 boneless skinless chicken breast halves

In a shallow bowl, combine butter, Worcestershire sauce and mustard. Place onions in another shallow bowl. Dip chicken in butter mixture, then coat with onions. Place in a greased 11-in. x 7-in. x 2-in. baking dish; drizzle with remaining butter mixture. Bake, uncovered, at 400° for 20-25 minutes or until chicken juices run clear. **Yield:** 4 servings.

Sour Cream Pan Biscuits
Prep/Total Time: 25 min.

✓ Uses less fat, sugar or salt. Includes Nutrition Facts and Diabetic Exchanges.

2 cups biscuit/baking mix
1 teaspoon sugar
1/2 cup club soda
3 tablespoons sour cream

In a bowl, combine all ingredients; stir just until moistened. Drop into six mounds on a 9-in. round baking pan coated with nonstick cooking spray. Bake at 400° for 20 minutes or until golden. Serve warm. **Yield:** 6 servings.

Nutrition Facts: 1 biscuit (prepared with reduced-fat baking mix and reduced-fat sour cream) equals 164 calories, 3 g fat (1 g saturated fat), 3 mg cholesterol, 474 mg sodium, 29 g carbohydrate, 1 g fiber, 4 g protein. **Diabetic Exchange:** 2 starch.

Spicy Garlic Green Beans
Prep/Total Time: 15 min.

✓ Uses less fat, sugar or salt. Includes Nutrition Facts and Diabetic Exchanges.

1 pound fresh green beans, cut into 1-inch pieces
1 teaspoon minced garlic
1/4 to 1/2 teaspoon crushed red pepper flakes
1/4 teaspoon salt
1 tablespoon canola oil

In a large skillet, saute beans, garlic, red pepper flakes and salt in oil for 10-12 minutes or until beans are crisp-tender. **Yield:** 4 servings.

Nutrition Facts: 3/4 cup equals 62 calories, 4 g fat (trace saturated fat), 0 cholesterol, 154 mg sodium, 7 g carbohydrate, 3 g fiber, 2 g protein. **Diabetic Exchanges:** 1-1/2 vegetable, 1/2 fat.

Dessert in a Dash

WANT an easy idea for topping off Jennifer Hoeft's delicious dinner? Try any of the following simple dessert options:

• Cube a purchased pound cake, then layer it with chocolate pudding and whipped cream in a large bowl for a fast trifle.

• Heat apple pie filling, spice it with cinnamon and serve it over vanilla ice cream.

• Sandwich whipped cream and raspberries between two store-bought croissants and dust them with confectioners' sugar.

Her Fuss-Free Pasta Dinner Is Sure to Please

AT HER HOME in Union, Kentucky, preparing fast, simple meals is a must for Renae Rossow. "My husband, Brian, and I are real estate agents," Renae explains. "We're on call for clients who often need to see homes in the evening, so dinner has to be quick and easy, yet appealing and satisfying."

The couple has four sons, Trevor, Nick, Brett and Ben, and one daughter, Kennedy. Although not all of their older children make it home for supper each night, Renae and Brian make a point of devoting supper time to the family.

"We try to put everything aside to spend time together," Renae notes. "We ask each person at the table to tell us the high and low points of their day, so that we can share in each other's joys and sorrows."

In addition to her full-time job, Renae coaches her daughter's school cheerleading team, sings with her church and raises money for various charitable organizations. She also enjoys entertaining, playing the piano, crocheting and watching the many sports activities the children participate in.

The delicious dishes Renae shares here are perfect for the family yet special enough for company.

Renae adapted a recipe from her sister-in-law to come up with easy Alfredo Seafood Fettuccine. "Whenever I prepare this dish for guests, they say I shouldn't have worked so hard," she says. "I don't tell them what a breeze it is to assemble. The longest part of the recipe is cooking the pasta!"

As an accompaniment, Almond Strawberry Salad calls for just a few ingredients but is loaded with flavor. "Everyone loves it and says they wouldn't have thought to use fruit in a dinner salad," she relates. "It's a nice complement to a rich main course."

For dessert, Renae whips up Chocolate Peanut Butter Parfaits. The yummy parfaits require no cooking or baking, so they're ready in no time. "I've been making these for 17 years, so I do it by memory now," she notes. "Instead of sprinkling with chocolate chips, use chocolate syrup to create a gourmet design."

Alfredo Seafood Fettuccine

Prep/Total Time: 20 min.

      8 ounces uncooked fettuccine
      1 envelope Alfredo sauce mix
      1 package (8 ounces) imitation crabmeat
      6 ounces bay scallops
      6 ounces uncooked medium shrimp, peeled and deveined
      1 tablespoon plus 1-1/2 teaspoons butter
  1/8 to 1/4 teaspoon garlic powder

Cook fettuccine according to package directions. Meanwhile, prepare Alfredo sauce according to package directions.

In a large skillet, saute the crab, scallops and shrimp in butter for 2-3 minutes or until scallops are opaque and shrimp turn pink. Stir into Alfredo sauce. Season with garlic powder. Cook and stir for 5-6 minutes or until thickened. Drain fettuccine; top with seafood mixture. **Yield:** 4 servings.

Almond Strawberry Salad

Prep/Total Time: 10 min.

✓ Uses less fat, sugar or salt. Includes Nutrition Facts and Diabetic Exchanges.

      3 cups fresh baby spinach
  1/2 cup sliced fresh strawberries
  1/4 cup sliced honey-roasted almonds
      1 tablespoon cider vinegar
      1 tablespoon honey
  1-1/2 teaspoons sugar

In a large bowl, combine the spinach, strawberries and almonds. In a jar with a tight-fitting lid, combine the cider vinegar, honey and sugar; shake well. Drizzle dressing over the salad and toss to coat. Serve immediately. **Yield:** 4 servings.

Nutrition Facts: 3/4 cup equals 74 calories, 4 g fat (trace saturated fat), 0 cholesterol, 98 mg sodium, 9 g carbohydrate, 1 g fiber, 2 g protein. **Diabetic Exchanges:** 2 vegetable, 1/2 fat.

Chocolate Peanut Butter Parfaits

Prep/Total Time: 10 min.

      2 ounces cream cheese, softened
      6 tablespoons peanut butter
  3/4 cup whipped topping, *divided*
  1/2 cup plus 2 tablespoons graham cracker crumbs
      1 tablespoon sugar
  4-1/2 teaspoons butter, melted
  1-1/4 cups miniature semisweet chocolate chips

In a small mixing bowl, beat cream cheese and peanut butter until smooth. Fold in 1/2 cup whipped topping; set aside.

Combine the graham cracker crumbs and sugar. Stir in the butter until coarse crumbs form. Press 1 tablespoon of the crumb mixture onto the bottom of each of four parfait glasses. Spoon about 2 tablespoons peanut butter mixture over the crumb mixture; sprinkle with 2 tablespoons chocolate chips.

Repeat layers. Top with remaining whipped topping and chocolate chips. **Yield:** 4 servings.

Eye-Catching Meal Is Easy And Impressive

COOKING is a source of joy and special memories for Dee Drew of Aliso Viejo, California. "A favorite aunt of mine taught me a lot about cooking and seasonings," Dee recalls. "She was a wonderful cook, as were my mother and grandmothers. I miss all of them, but I'm delighted that my daughters and oldest granddaughter have also inherited the 'love-of-cooking genes.'"

These days, the mother to six adult children, grandmother to four and great-grandmother to one is often on the lookout for convenient yet simple dishes that reheat well.

"My husband, Brian, works long hours," Dee notes. "Whenever he's working late at night, I fix him light suppers."

To keep dinners quick, Dee counts on her microwave and slow cooker. She also prepares dishes ahead of time and stores them in the freezer for ready-to-heat meals later on.

When she has extra time, one of Dee's favorite pastimes is baking. In fact, she works part-time for a company that makes cookie bouquets.

"I love to share my baked creations with others," says Dee. "In today's fast-paced world, many people don't take time to bake. When I present family, friends and co-workers with homemade goodies, they're always appreciative."

Dee adds a homemade touch to the items included in this summery menu that serves six.

"Dear friends served Fruity Chicken Tossed Salad on a beautiful summer day before taking us sailing on their boat," Dee relates. "It's a cinch to put together and always looks so pretty.

"I often use the Southwestern-flavored chicken strips and heat them in a skillet just to take the chill off," she adds. "For variety, try creamy cucumber salad dressing instead of poppy seed."

To complement the main course, Dee created Sesame Breadsticks. "With just three ingredients, they couldn't be any easier to whip up!" she assures. Don't have sesame seeds in your spice rack? "Sprinkle them with garlic salt instead," Dee suggests.

For the finale, she serves irresistible Cookie Pizza a la Mode. "It's my super-fast version of a dessert we enjoyed at a restaurant in Boulder, Colorado," Dee notes. "People of all ages tell me it's delicious. For special occasions, I like to write a message with frosting on the warm cookie before serving it."

Fruity Chicken Tossed Salad

Prep/Total Time: 10 min.

✓ Uses less fat, sugar or salt. Includes Nutrition Facts and Diabetic Exchanges.

- 12 cups Italian-blend salad greens
- 3 packages (6 ounces *each*) ready-to-serve grilled chicken breast strips
- 1 can (11 ounces) mandarin oranges, drained
- 1 cup seedless red grapes, halved
- 2/3 cup poppy seed salad dressing

In a large bowl, combine the salad greens, chicken, oranges and grapes. Drizzle with dressing and toss to coat. **Yield:** 6 servings.

Nutrition Facts: 2 cups salad with 3 ounces chicken (prepared with fat-free poppy seed dressing) equals 217 calories, 3 g fat (1 g saturated fat), 60 mg cholesterol, 879 mg sodium, 24 g carbohydrate, 3 g fiber, 22 g protein. **Diabetic Exchanges:** 3 very lean meat, 1-1/2 fruit.

Sesame Breadsticks

Prep/Total Time: 20 min.

- 1 tube (11 ounces) refrigerated breadsticks
- 1 tablespoon butter, melted
- 2 tablespoons sesame seeds

Unroll and separate breadsticks; place on an ungreased baking sheet. Brush with butter and sprinkle with sesame seeds. Bake at 400° for 12-14 minutes or until golden brown. Serve warm. **Yield:** 1 dozen.

Cookie Pizza a la Mode

Prep/Total Time: 20 min.

- 1 tube (18 ounces) refrigerated chocolate chip cookie dough
- Chocolate syrup
- Vanilla ice cream
- 6 maraschino cherries, optional

Press the cookie dough onto an ungreased 12-in. pizza pan. Bake at 400° for 12-14 minutes or until golden brown. Cool on a wire rack for 5 minutes. Cut into six wedges.

Drizzle chocolate syrup over dessert plates. Top with warm cookie wedges, ice cream and additional chocolate syrup. Garnish each wedge with a cherry if desired. **Yield:** 6 servings.

Sweet Pizza Possibilities

FOR VARIETY, try different flavors to create your Cookie Pizza a la Mode. Use sugar cookie or peanut butter cookie dough and replace the chocolate topping with caramel, marshmallow or strawberry.

Garden-Fresh Goodness Gives Dinner Flair

QUICK and nutritious meals are a must for Nancee Melin of Tucson, Arizona. "My husband and I are on low-fat, high-fiber, low-cholesterol diets," Nancee explains. "We love healthy foods with full flavors."

To meet their dietary goals, Nancee makes the most of seasonal fruits and vegetables, boosting the taste of dishes with plenty of herbs and citrus juices.

A retired elementary school teacher, Nancee tutors adults and also enjoys painting, playing the piano and guitar, and walking and swimming. But she still finds time to enjoy home-cooked dinners with her husband, Dennis.

"He works from our home as an accountant, real estate agent and land developer," Nancee notes, "so it's easy to be flexible with our meals."

Nancee's no-fuss dinner solutions come in especially handy when her three stepchildren and five grandchildren pop in for a meal. The mouth-watering menu she shares here is simple to fix on a weeknight but special enough for company.

For the main course, Nancee serves Ginger Salmon Salad. "People always tell me they love this salad," she says. "After trying something similar at a restaurant, I duplicated it from taste and memory at home."

Asparagus with Sesame Vinaigrette is ready in minutes. "I toss this together when asparagus is on sale," Nancee relates. "The dressing can be made ahead."

Individual dishes of Sparkling Fresh Fruit make a yummy finale. "You can prepare it with cut-up fruit from the produce department if you're crunched for time," Nancee adds. "Sometimes I garnish it with fresh mint sprigs for an elegant touch."

Ginger Salmon Salad

Prep/Total Time: 15 min.

✓ Uses less fat, sugar or salt. Includes Nutrition Facts.

- 2/3 cup lime juice
- 1/2 cup honey
- 1/2 teaspoon minced fresh gingerroot
- 4 salmon fillets (6 ounces *each*), skin removed
- 1/4 teaspoon salt
- 1 package (5 ounces) spring mix salad greens
- 1 cup sliced peeled mango

In a small bowl, combine lime juice, honey and ginger; set aside 1/2 cup for serving.

Place fillets on a broiler pan coated with nonstick cooking spray. Spoon 1/2 cup lime juice mixture over salmon. Broil 4-6 in. from the heat for 4-5 minutes on each side or until fish flakes easily with a fork, basting occasionally with remaining lime juice mixture. Sprinkle with salt.

Divide salad greens among four plates; top with salmon and mango. Drizzle with reserved lime juice mixture. **Yield:** 4 servings.

Nutrition Facts: 1 serving equals 479 calories, 19 g fat (4 g saturated fat), 100 mg cholesterol, 278 mg sodium, 44 g carbohydrate, 3 g fiber, 36 g protein.

Asparagus with Sesame Vinaigrette

Prep/Total Time: 15 min.

✓ Uses less fat, sugar or salt. Includes Nutrition Facts and Diabetic Exchanges.

- 1 pound fresh asparagus, trimmed
- 3 tablespoons water
- 2 tablespoons reduced-sodium soy sauce
- 1 tablespoon rice wine vinegar
- 2 teaspoons sesame seeds, toasted
- 1-1/2 teaspoons olive oil
- 1-1/2 teaspoons sesame oil
- 1/2 teaspoon sugar
- 1/8 teaspoon garlic powder
- 2 tablespoons chopped sweet red pepper
- 2 tablespoons chopped tomato
- 1 teaspoon minced fresh basil

Place asparagus and water in a microwave-safe dish; cover and microwave on high for 3-4 minutes or until crisp-tender. Drain and immediately place asparagus in ice water. Drain and pat dry.

In a jar with a tight-fitting lid, combine the soy sauce, vinegar, sesame seeds, olive oil, sesame oil, sugar and garlic powder; shake well. Place the asparagus, red pepper and tomato in a serving dish. Drizzle with dressing; sprinkle with basil. **Yield:** 4 servings.

Nutrition Facts: 3/4 cup equals 62 calories, 4 g fat (1 g saturated fat), 0 cholesterol, 317 mg sodium, 5 g carbohydrate, 1 g fiber, 2 g protein. **Diabetic Exchanges:** 1 vegetable, 1 fat.

Editor's Note: This recipe was tested in a 1,100-watt microwave.

Sparkling Fresh Fruit

Prep/Total Time: 15 min.

- 1-1/2 cups sliced fresh strawberries
- 1-1/2 cups fresh blueberries
- 1 cup cubed cantaloupe
- 4 scoops raspberry sherbet *or* flavor of your choice
- 1 cup champagne *or* lemon-lime soda

Combine berries and cantaloupe; divide among four dishes. Top each with a scoop of sherbet. Drizzle with champagne or soda. Serve immediately. **Yield:** 4 servings.

She Cooks Up A Taste of the Orient...Express!

INTERNATIONAL FLAVOR is right at home in Amy Corlew-Sherlock's kitchen. This full-time, special-ed teacher in Lapeer, Michigan manages to prepare sit-down suppers for her family of four at least five times a week...and even plans menus that have around-the-world appeal.

"To keep things interesting, I try to feature a variety of dishes that reflect different cultural influences and flavors," Amy explains. "But because our household is always on the go with jobs and after-school activities, fast meals are essential to our lifestyle."

This classic Asian menu meets her family's needs on both counts and is a longtime favorite with husband Doug and children Micah and David.

"The whole meal is so easy to prepare, and the taste even beats takeout," she says. "I fix it at least once a month.

"We start with delicious Egg Drop Soup, which cooks in just minutes and requires only five simple ingredients. There are many recipe variations, but we like the addition of cornstarch to thicken the soup and give it a rich, golden color.

"I got the recipe from Grandma's old cookbook," Amy recalls. "And when my kids were slow to start eating meat, this 'souper'-quick dish provided them with easy-to-digest egg protein."

Her fast Fried Rice is a tasty and fuss-free side dish. The recipe uses leftover cooked instant rice and a packet of seasoning mix to cut the prep time, while peas and onions add nutrition.

"I often buy jasmine rice in 25-pound bags and use that if I have extra time," says Amy. "There's nothing like the aroma of sweet jasmine when you lift the lid from that steaming pot!" (She makes extra so she always has leftover rice in the fridge for the stir-fries her family enjoys.)

"But it's the main dish, Sweet-and-Sour Popcorn Chicken, that really shines," Amy notes. Frozen popcorn chicken coated in a homemade sweet-and-sour sauce is the secret to this quick entree. What a fabulous way to dress up packaged chicken nuggets!

For extra fun, purchase fortune cookies to munch on for dessert. They'll make the perfect ending for your family's Far East feast.

"This is one menu you'll find yourself returning to again and again," Amy assures. It's just the ticket for busy families seeking tasty international fare!

Egg Drop Soup
Prep/Total Time: 15 min.

3 cups chicken broth
1 tablespoon cornstarch
2 tablespoons cold water
1 egg, lightly beaten
1 green onion, sliced

In a large saucepan, bring broth to a boil over medium heat. Combine cornstarch and water until smooth; gradually stir into broth. Bring to a boil; cook and stir for 2 minutes or until thickened.

Reduce heat. Drizzle egg into broth, stirring constantly. Remove from heat; stir in onion. **Yield:** 4 servings.

Fried Rice
Prep/Total Time: 20 min.

1 envelope fried rice seasoning
2 tablespoons water
2 green onions, chopped
2 tablespoons vegetable oil
1 egg, lightly beaten
3 cups cold cooked instant rice
1/2 cup peas

In a small bowl, combine seasoning mix and water; set aside. In a large skillet or wok, stir-fry onions in oil for 2-3 minutes. Add egg; stir until scrambled.

Add rice and peas; stir-fry until heated through. Stir in seasoning mixture; stir-fry 3-4 minutes longer or until heated through. **Yield:** 4 servings.

Sweet-and-Sour Popcorn Chicken
Prep/Total Time: 25 min.

1 medium green pepper, cut into 1-inch pieces
1 small onion, thinly sliced
1 tablespoon vegetable oil
1 can (20 ounces) unsweetened pineapple chunks
3 tablespoons white vinegar
2 tablespoons soy sauce
2 tablespoons ketchup
1/3 cup packed brown sugar
2 tablespoons cornstarch
1 package (12 ounces) frozen popcorn chicken

In a large skillet or wok, stir-fry pepper and onion in oil for 3-4 minutes or until crisp-tender. Drain pineapple, reserving juice in a 2-cup measuring cup; set pineapple aside. Add enough water to juice to measure 1-1/3 cups; stir in vinegar, soy sauce and ketchup.

In a bowl, combine brown sugar and cornstarch. Stir in pineapple juice mixture until smooth. Gradually add to the skillet. Bring to a boil; cook and stir for 2 minutes or until thickened. Add pineapple. Reduce heat; simmer, uncovered, for 4-5 minutes or until heated through.

Meanwhile, microwave chicken according to package directions. Stir into pineapple mixture. Serve immediately. **Yield:** 4 servings.

Pasta Feast Earns an A+ for This Busy Cook

WITH her family's full slate of extracurricular activities, high school teacher Angie Smith finds that mouthwatering meal shortcuts really make the grade at her home in Clarksville, Tennessee.

Husband Bob works long days and often travels in his job as quality manager for a hydraulics company, while children Justin, Devon and Katie are all active with year-round, competitive sports schedules.

"We often attend two soccer practices a night, with tournaments three weekends a month," Angie notes. "That's a lot of soccer! It's tempting to go to a drive-thru restaurant after practice, but that's costly. So I cook four or five times a week and try to plan meals that are simple and quick and that can be eaten in shifts if necessary.

"I don't want a weeknight meal to take more than 45 minutes to fix," she adds. "I am also queen of the slow cooker and have several recipes for stews, roast beef and even ham with potatoes that my family loves. I pair these with a vegetable dish and bread for a meal in minutes."

The fabulous menu of Italian favorites she shares here is one her family especially likes. "And I like that it's quick and easy but special enough to serve company," Angie relates. "I enjoy cooking but don't want to be in the kitchen for hours because I want to have time to spend with my family—especially during the holidays!"

Angie's meal begins with a colorful Artichoke-Pepperoni Tossed Salad, modeled after one she and Bob first tasted at an Italian restaurant. "It's fast, fresh and goes with almost any pasta meal I make," she says. "For me, the convenience of bagged salad greens makes them worth the extra cost."

Elegant and easy, Creamy Ham Fettuccine is Angie's own creation and has earned top honors with friends and family alike. "It's my most requested main dish. I really like the thicker texture of the sauce, which is great with any hearty pasta, such as whole wheat penne."

She rounds out the meal with a buttery loaf of her crusty Italian Cheese Bread. "The aroma and flavor are wonderful," Angie points out. "We like to dip our slices in olive oil, fresh ground pepper and Parmesan cheese. And if there's any room for dessert, we top off the meal with spumoni ice cream."

Artichoke-Pepperoni Tossed Salad

Prep/Total Time: 10 min.

- 1 package (10 ounces) ready-to-serve salad greens
- 1 can (14 ounces) water-packed artichoke hearts, rinsed, drained and chopped
- 1 cup (4 ounces) shredded Italian cheese blend, optional
- 1 package (3-1/2 ounces) sliced pepperoni
- 1/4 cup chopped red onion
- 1 jar (2 ounces) sliced pimientos, drained
- 1/3 to 1/2 cup Italian salad dressing

In a large salad bowl, combine the greens, artichokes, cheese if desired, pepperoni, onion and pimientos. Drizzle with dressing and toss to coat. Serve immediately. **Yield:** 6 servings.

Creamy Ham Fettuccine

Prep/Total Time: 25 min.

- 1 package (12 ounces) fettuccine
- 3 tablespoons finely chopped onion
- 3 tablespoons butter
- 2 tablespoons plus 1 teaspoon all-purpose flour
- 3 cups heavy whipping cream
- 2 cups fresh broccoli florets
- 2 cups cubed fully cooked ham
- 1 cup shredded Parmesan cheese, *divided*
- 1/2 to 3/4 teaspoon garlic salt
- 1/4 teaspoon pepper
- 1/4 teaspoon dried oregano
- 1/4 teaspoon ground nutmeg

Cook fettuccine according to package directions. Meanwhile, in a large saucepan, saute onion in butter until tender. Stir in flour until blended. Gradually stir in cream. Bring to a boil over medium heat, stirring constantly.

Add broccoli. Reduce heat; simmer, uncovered, for 7-10 minutes or until broccoli is crisp-tender, stirring occasionally. Stir in ham, 1/2 cup cheese, garlic salt, pepper, oregano and nutmeg. Drain pasta; top with sauce. Sprinkle with remaining cheese. **Yield:** 6 servings.

Italian Cheese Bread

Prep/Total Time: 20 min.

- 1/4 cup butter, softened
- 1 loaf (1 pound) French bread, halved lengthwise
- 1 cup (4 ounces) shredded Italian cheese blend
- 1 teaspoon dried oregano
- 1/4 to 1/2 teaspoon garlic salt

Spread butter over cut sides of bread. Place on an ungreased baking sheet. Combine the cheese, oregano and garlic salt; sprinkle over bread. Bake at 350° for 12-15 minutes or until cheese is melted. Slice and serve warm. **Yield:** 6 servings.

Chapter 2

⏰ *Holiday and Seasonal Pleasers*

FESTIVE FOODS make special occasions all the more memorable. And the good news is, you don't have to spend hours and hours in the kitchen fixing these fun-filled and timely recipes for family and friends.

Surprise loved ones with a delightful Easter dinner...a tailgating spread guaranteed to score big...not-so-tricky treats for Halloween...merry Christmas candies and cookies...and much more fare-with-flair featured in this chapter.

Whether you want whimsical goodies to bring to a school party or elegant buffet dishes sure to impress guests, you'll find just the right dressed-up recipes for celebrations all year long.

SPARKLING SPREAD. Mashed Red Potatoes, Dressed-Up Beef Tips, Florets with Cheese Sauce and Stuffed Shrimp (all recipes on pp. 38 and 39).

Serve a Sweetheart of a Meal

DO YOU FEEL like there's never any time for romance on Valentine's Day? No problem! Try this menu of time-saving specialties created by our Test Kitchen home economists.

Sized just right for two, this no-fuss meal has a cozy feel that's sure to chase away midwinter blues. Best of all for busy weeknight cooks, all three recipes go together in a heartbeat!

Refrigerated pizza dough makes short work of cute Be-My-Valentine Pizza. Topped with pepperoni, three kinds of cheese, olives, onion and sauce, this yummy entree will steal the show...and the heart of your dinner partner.

Pair it with eye-catching Balsamic Asiago Salad, which can be tossed together in 10 minutes flat. Drizzle the colorful combination of greens, tomato wedges and yellow pepper with bottled dressing, add a quick sprinkle of garlic-seasoned cheese...and serve. It's that simple!

Nuts-About-You Cookie Sticks make a fancy finale that couldn't be easier to whip up. Start with purchased Pirouette cookies, which are widely available in grocery stores. Dip the cookies in a rich chocolate and peanut butter coating, then dust them with chopped peanuts for a fast finishing touch.

With only 30 minutes needed to put this on the table, you'll both have plenty of time left over to savor your evening together.

Be-My-Valentine Pizza

(Pictured at right)

Prep/Total Time: 30 min.

Making this irresistible pizza is as easy as pie! Our home economists used kitchen shears to cut a heart shape from refrigerated pizza crust. All that's left to do is add the tasty toppings, bake and enjoy.

> 1 tube (13.8 ounces) refrigerated pizza crust
> 1/4 cup shredded Italian-blend cheese
> 1/4 cup shredded part-skim mozzarella cheese
> 2 slices provolone cheese, cut in half
> 1/4 cup pizza sauce
> 18 slices pepperoni
> 1/4 cup chopped onion
> 1/4 cup sliced ripe olives

Unroll pizza dough onto a greased baking sheet; flatten dough. With kitchen scissors, cut into a 10-in. heart. (Use dough trimmings to make breadsticks if desired.) Bake at 425° for 8 minutes.

Combine the Italian and mozzarella cheeses; set aside. Arrange provolone cheese over crust to within 1/2 in. of edges. Spread with pizza sauce. Layer with the pepperoni, onion, olives and cheese mixture. Bake 8-10 min-utes longer or until crust is golden brown and cheese is melted. **Yield:** 2 servings.

Balsamic Asiago Salad

(Pictured at right)

Prep/Total Time: 10 min.

When you try this terrific toss from our Test Kitchen staff, you'll be delighted at how a simple salad can taste so special. This one requires only five ingredients.

> 2 cups torn mixed salad greens
> 1 plum tomato, cut into wedges
> 1/2 cup chopped sweet yellow pepper
> 2 tablespoons balsamic vinaigrette
> 2 tablespoons shredded mozzarella and
>   Asiago cheese with roasted garlic

In a small serving bowl, combine the salad greens, tomato and yellow pepper. Drizzle with vinaigrette and toss to coat. Sprinkle with cheese. **Yield:** 2 servings.

Nuts-About-You Cookie Sticks

(Pictured at right)

Prep/Total Time: 10 min.

Our home economists used Pirouette cookies to create these sweet-as-can-be treats. If you're a fan of chocolate-covered pretzels, use pretzel rods instead.

> 1/4 cup semisweet chocolate chips
> 3/4 teaspoon shortening
> 1-1/2 teaspoons creamy peanut butter
> 4 French vanilla Pirouette cookies
> 1/2 cup chopped peanuts

In a microwave-safe bowl, melt the chocolate chips, shortening and peanut butter; stir until smooth. Dip one end of each cookie into chocolate mixture; sprinkle with peanuts. Place on waxed paper; let stand until set. **Yield:** 2 servings.

Cut to the Quick

A pizza cutter is great for more than just pizza! It comes in really handy for cutting bread into cubes for homemade croutons and breakfast casseroles, especially if you need to remove the crusts. Our two boys also love it for cutting up their pancakes in a hurry.

And if you have a larger pizza cutter, you can use it to cube cooked chicken. I've found that it's even faster and easier than using my kitchen shears.

—*Lisa Elliot, West Plains, Missouri*

Nuts-About-You Cookie Sticks
Balsamic Asiago Salad
Be-My-Valentine Pizza

Easter Dinner Is Sure to Delight

ARE YOU HOSTING an Easter meal this year? Serving a special dinner for eight needn't require long lists of ingredients, hours in the kitchen or complicated cooking techniques.

Our Test Kitchen home economists made your job simple by selecting this holiday menu guests will love. You'll love it, too, because each impressive recipe requires only five or fewer ingredients (excluding salt, pepper and water). So you can easily assemble these tempting dishes—many of them ahead of time—without a lot of work. Happy Easter!

Chocolate Mousse Torte

(Pictured below and on the cover)

Prep: 15 min. + chilling

Our Test Kitchen developed this lovely make-ahead dessert that needs just a few minutes and a few ingredients. Rich, creamy mousse layers are surrounded by ladyfingers and topped with fresh berries for a gorgeous garnish.

   2 packages (3 ounces *each***) ladyfingers, split**
   2 cups cold milk
   3 packages (2.8 ounces *each***) chocolate mousse mix**
   3 cups whipped topping, *divided*
Fresh raspberries

Chocolate Mousse Torte

Line the bottom and sides of a lightly greased 9-in. springform pan with ladyfingers (save remaining ladyfingers for another use).

In a large mixing bowl, beat the milk and chocolate mousse mixes on medium speed for 1 minute; scrape sides of the bowl. Beat on high for 2-3 minutes or until thickened and lighter in color. Remove half of the mousse to another bowl; fold in 1/2 cup whipped topping. Spread over the ladyfinger crust.

Fold remaining whipped topping into remaining mousse; carefully spread over first layer. Refrigerate for 4 hours or overnight. Garnish with raspberries. **Yield:** 12 servings.

Editor's Note: This recipe was tested with Nestlé European Style Mousse Mix.

Ham with Ruby-Red Glaze

(Pictured at right)

Prep: 5 min. **Bake:** 2 hours + standing

I've used this recipe for more than 40 years on baked ham or ham slices. My grandchildren love to drizzle the sauce over their mashed potatoes, too. Everyone likes it, and it's quick to make with only a few ingredients.
   —Beverly Payne, El Sobrante, California

   1 boneless fully cooked ham (about 4 pounds)
   3/4 cup packed brown sugar
   3/4 cup creamy French salad dressing

Place the ham on a rack in a shallow roasting pan. Cover and bake at 325° for 1-1/2 hours.

In a small microwave-safe bowl, combine the brown sugar and salad dressing. Cover and microwave on high for 30-60 seconds or until sugar is dissolved. Pour 1/4 cup over the ham. Bake, uncovered, 30-40 minutes longer or until a meat thermometer reads 140°. Let stand for 10 minutes before slicing. Serve with remaining glaze. **Yield:** 12-16 servings.

Editor's Note: This recipe was tested in a 1,100-watt microwave.

Speedy Stuffed Potatoes

(Pictured above right)

Prep/Total Time: 30 min.

I use garlic and shredded cheddar cheese to prepare these rich, creamy potatoes cooked in the microwave. It seems that no matter when or where I serve this special side dish, it ends up being a winner with everyone who tries it.   —Marie Hattrup The Dalles, Oregon

Speedy Stuffed Potatoes
Apricot Spinach Salad
Ham with Ruby-Red Glaze

✓ Uses less fat, sugar or salt. Includes Nutrition Facts and Diabetic Exchanges.

4 large baking potatoes
3 tablespoons butter, softened
2/3 cup sour cream
1/2 teaspoon minced garlic
3/4 teaspoon salt
1/4 teaspoon pepper
1/2 cup shredded cheddar cheese

Scrub and pierce potatoes; place on a microwave-safe plate. Microwave, uncovered, on high for 10-12 minutes or until tender, turning once.

When cool enough to handle, cut potatoes in half lengthwise. Scoop out pulp, leaving a thin shell. In a large bowl, mash the pulp with butter. Stir in the sour cream, garlic, salt and pepper. Spoon into potato shells.

Place on a microwave-safe plate. Sprinkle with cheese. Microwave, uncovered, on high for 1-2 minutes or until heated through. **Yield:** 8 servings.

Nutrition Facts: 1/2 stuffed potato (prepared with reduced-fat butter, reduced-fat sour cream and reduced-fat cheese) equals 212 calories, 6 g fat (4 g saturated fat), 19 mg cholesterol, 317 mg sodium, 35 g carbohydrate, 3 g fiber, 7 g protein. **Diabetic Exchanges:** 2 starch, 1 fat.

Editor's Note: This recipe was tested in a 1,100-watt microwave.

Apricot Spinach Salad

(Pictured above)

Prep/Total Time: 10 min.

This yummy spinach salad from our home economists is tossed with store-bought raspberry vinaigrette. Canned apricots and golden raisins add sweetness and color.

1 package (10 ounces) fresh baby spinach
1 cup canned apricot halves, drained and sliced
1/2 cup golden raisins
1/2 cup raspberry vinaigrette
1 teaspoon grated lemon peel

In a large salad bowl, combine the spinach, apricots and raisins. Drizzle with vinaigrette and sprinkle with lemon peel; toss to coat. **Yield:** 8 servings.

Grads Give Party Fare Top Grades

HAVE a son or daughter graduating from high school this year? Celebrate his or her accomplishments with a casual party menu that earns top honors with guests of all ages.

Entertaining is a breeze with this simple but special spread. Sideways sub sandwiches, a colorful potluck-size salad, sparkling punch and a big batch of graduation-cap goodies will satisfy a crowd of 20—or a few slightly hungry teenagers!

You won't need to pull an all-nighter to prepare this fuss-free fare, either. The sandwich loaves, layered salad and beverage are each ready in less than half an hour...while the cute chocolate desserts can conveniently be assembled ahead of time.

Special Sandwich Loaves

(Pictured at right)

Prep/Total Time: 30 min.

These satisfying sub sandwiches from our Test Kitchen look so appetizing yet are a study in simplicity. Offering the seasoned mayonnaise and submarine sandwich dressing on the side makes it easy for guests to personalize their helpings and serve themselves.

    2 loaves (1 pound *each*) French bread
   10 slices deli smoked turkey, halved
   10 slices deli roast beef, halved
   20 small lettuce leaves
   10 slices Colby-Monterey Jack cheese, halved
   10 slices cheddar cheese, halved
    2 cups roasted sweet red peppers, drained,
        sliced and patted dry
   40 mild banana peppers, drained, sliced and
        patted dry
GARLIC-LIME MAYONNAISE:
    1 cup mayonnaise
  1/2 cup sour cream
    1 teaspoon lime juice
  1/2 teaspoon minced garlic
  1/4 teaspoon chili powder
    1 bottle (5 ounces) submarine sandwich
        dressing

Cut each loaf of French bread into 22 slices, leaving the slices attached at the bottom of the loaf (cut off and discard end pieces). Between every other slice of bread, place a piece of turkey, a piece of roast beef, a small lettuce leaf, a piece of each kind of cheese, red peppers and banana peppers.

In a small bowl, whisk the mayonnaise, sour cream, lime juice, garlic and chili powder. To serve, cut completely through the bread between the plain bread sides. Serve with mayonnaise mixture and submarine dressing. **Yield:** 20 sandwiches.

Layered Salad for a Crowd

(Pictured at right)

Prep/Total Time: 20 min.

This salad is a favorite of my three sons. When I took it to a luncheon honoring our school district's food service manager, she was very complimentary and even asked for the recipe. —Lisa Ashley, Leesburg, Georgia

    1 cup mayonnaise
  1/2 cup milk
    2 teaspoons dill weed
  1/2 teaspoon seasoning blend
    1 bunch romaine, torn
    2 medium carrots, grated
    1 cup chopped red onion
    1 medium cucumber, sliced
    1 package (10 ounces) frozen peas, thawed
1-1/2 cups (6 ounces) shredded cheddar cheese
    8 bacon strips, cooked and crumbled

For dressing, in a small bowl, whisk the mayonnaise, milk, dill and seasoning blend. In a 4-qt. clear glass serving bowl, layer the romaine, carrots, onion and cucumber (do not toss). Pour dressing over the top; sprinkle with peas, cheese and bacon. Cover and refrigerate until serving. **Yield:** 20 servings.

Editor's Note: This recipe was tested with Morton Nature's Seasons seasoning blend.

Brownie Graduation Caps

(Pictured below)

Prep: 55 min.
Bake: 25 min. per batch + cooling

You'll need just a handful of ingredients to create these cute, chocolaty caps that company will gobble up. The home economists in our Test Kitchen topped brownie cupcakes with mortarboards made from graham cookies. A licorice tassel on each cap adds the fast finishing touch.

Brownie Graduation Caps

Pretty Party Punch
Layered Salad for a Crowd
Special Sandwich Loaves

1 package fudge brownie mix (13-inch x
  9-inch pan size)
48 fudge graham cookies *or* graham cracker
  squares
1 cup chocolate frosting
48 pieces red shoestring licorice
48 Skittles bite-size candies

Prepare the fudge brownie batter according to the package directions for preparing cake-like brownies. Fill paper-lined miniature muffin cups two-thirds full. Bake at 350° for 21-24 minutes. Cool the cupcakes for 10 minutes before removing from the pans to wire racks to cool completely (remove the paper liners while the cupcakes are still warm).

Slice 1/8 in. from the top of each cupcake to level. Invert cupcakes; attach a fudge graham cookie to each with a small amount of frosting. For the tassels, place a licorice piece and a Skittles candy on top of each cookie, attaching the candy and licorice with frosting. Let stand until set. **Yield:** 4 dozen.

Pretty Party Punch

(Pictured above)

Prep/Total Time: 15 min.

This sparkling punch has been a lifesaver for many last-minute parties and get-togethers because it's quick and inexpensive. —Kelly Wilson, Bloomington, Indiana

1 cup sugar
2 envelopes unsweetened black cherry soft
  drink mix
1 cup hot water
2 liters lemon-lime soda, chilled
2 liters ginger ale, chilled

In a small bowl, stir the sugar, black cherry soft drink mix and hot water until the sugar is dissolved. Cool to room temperature.

Just before serving, combine the soft drink mixture, lemon-lime soda and ginger ale in a large punch bowl. **Yield:** 16 servings (about 4 quarts).

Throw a Fast and Fun Fiesta

LOOKING for a quick party idea to brighten spirits? Throw open the doors to your hacienda and welcome guests to a flavorful fiesta as warm and colorful as sunny Mexico itself.

Against a background of mariachi music and bright serapes, serve up sizzling shrimp or vegetable fajitas, citrusy sangria and scoops of crunchy fried ice cream for dessert. This is one fuss-free party that couldn't be much easier—or more fun—to host. Olé!

Grilled Shrimp Fajitas

(Pictured at right)

Prep/Total Time: 25 min.

For a twist on tradition, try these seafood fajitas. They're so delicious...and impressive enough to serve to guests.
—Amy Hammons, Martinez, Georgia

- 1/2 **pound sliced bacon**
- 1/2 **pound uncooked medium shrimp, peeled and deveined**
- 1 **medium green pepper, cut into 1-inch pieces**
- 1 **medium sweet red pepper, cut into 1-inch pieces**
- 1 **medium onion, cut into 1-inch pieces**
- 1/2 **cup barbecue sauce**
- 6 **flour tortillas (8 inches), warmed**
- 1 **cup shredded lettuce**
- 1 **medium tomato, diced**
- 1/2 **cup shredded cheddar cheese**

In a large skillet, cook bacon over medium heat until cooked but not crisp. Drain on paper towels. Wrap a strip of bacon around each shrimp; secure ends with toothpicks.

On six metal or soaked wooden skewers, alternately thread shrimp, peppers and onion. Grill, covered, over medium heat or broil 4 in. from the heat for 2-3 minutes on each side or until shrimp turn pink and vegetables are tender, basting frequently with barbecue sauce.

Remove shrimp and vegetables from skewers; discard toothpicks. Place on one side of tortillas. Top with lettuce, tomato and cheese; fold over. **Yield:** 6 servings.

Veggie Fajitas

(Pictured at top far right)

Prep/Total Time: 25 min.

For satisfying yet healthy fare, I fix these colorful fajitas full of vegetables. My husband prefers these to chicken or beef fajitas. *—Sarah Mercer, Wichita, Kansas*

✓ Uses less fat, sugar or salt. Includes Nutrition Facts and Diabetic Exchanges.

- 1 **small zucchini, thinly sliced**
- 1 **medium yellow summer squash, thinly sliced**
- 1/2 **pound sliced fresh mushrooms**
- 1 **small onion, halved and sliced**
- 1 **medium carrot, julienned**
- 1 **teaspoon salt**
- 1/2 **teaspoon pepper**
- 1 **tablespoon canola oil**
- 8 **flour tortillas (8 inches), warmed**
- 2 **cups (8 ounces) shredded cheddar cheese**
- 1 **cup (8 ounces) sour cream**
- 1 **cup salsa**

In a large skillet, saute the vegetables, salt and pepper in oil for 5-7 minutes or until crisp-tender. Using a slotted spoon, place 1/2 cup mixture down the center of each tortilla. Sprinkle each with 1/4 cup cheese; fold in sides. Top with sour cream and salsa. **Yield:** 8 servings.

Nutrition Facts: 1 fajita with 2 tablespoons sour cream and salsa (prepared with reduced-fat cheese and fat-free sour cream) equals 304 calories, 11 g fat (5 g saturated fat), 24 mg cholesterol, 891 mg sodium, 37 g carbohydrate, 1 g fiber, 15 g protein. **Diabetic Exchanges:** 2 starch, 1-1/2 fat, 1 lean meat, 1 vegetable.

Fried Ice Cream

(Pictured below)

Prep: 30 min. + freezing

Refrigerated pie crust sprinkled with cinnamon-sugar, then baked and crumbled, makes short work of this fun dessert from our home economists.

- 1 **sheet refrigerated pie pastry**
- 1-1/2 **teaspoons sugar**
- 1 **teaspoon ground cinnamon**

Fried Ice Cream

White Sangria
Veggie Fajitas
Grilled Shrimp Fajitas

1 quart vanilla ice cream
Oil for deep-fat frying
1/2 cup honey

Unroll pastry onto an ungreased 15-in. x 10-in. x 1-in. baking pan. Combine sugar and cinnamon; sprinkle over pastry. Prick thoroughly with a fork. Bake at 400° for 10-12 minutes or until lightly browned. Cool on a wire rack for 5 minutes.

Place pastry in a large resealable plastic bag; coarsely crush. Transfer to a shallow bowl. Using a 1/2-cup ice cream scoop, form eight scoops of ice cream. Roll in pastry crumbs. Cover and freeze for 2 hours or until firm.

In an electric skillet or deep-fat fryer, heat oil to 375°. Fry ice cream balls for 8-10 seconds or until golden. Drain on paper towels. Immediately place in chilled bowls; drizzle with honey and serve. **Yield:** 8 servings.

White Sangria

(Pictured above)

Prep: 15 min. + chilling

Fruity and sweet, this refreshing beverage from our Test Kitchen goes together in minutes. And guests will find it as welcome as a splash of sunshine.

1 cup unsweetened pineapple juice
1/4 cup lemon juice
2 medium oranges, washed and sliced
1 medium lemon, washed and sliced
1 bottle (750 ml) Riesling *or* other sweet white wine
1 medium tart apple, cut into thin slices
1/4 cup triple sec
2 cups lemon-lime soda, chilled
Ice cubes

In a large pitcher, combine juices, orange slices and lemon slices; mash gently with a wooden spoon until fruit is partially crushed. Add the wine, apple slices and triple sec. Refrigerate for 2-4 hours. Just before serving, add soda. Serve over ice. **Yield:** 7 servings.

Tortilla Tip

We eat a lot of tortillas. After heating them in the oven or skillet, we keep them soft in a warm slow cooker.　　　　　—*Stephanie and Mary Francis Wong*
Newport Beach, California

Tailgating Menu Makes Fans Cheer!

TRUE SPORTS ENTHUSIASTS know that good food and good friends only make the game more enjoyable. That's why tailgating—the practice of eating and socializing before a sporting event (often while sitting on the open tailgate of a vehicle)—is so popular.

Kick off your next tailgate party with this delicious alfresco fare that's easy to put together ahead of time and pop in the cooler. At the stadium, fire up the grill, and you're on your way to a mouth-watering meal that's sure to earn a standing ovation.

Tailgate Sausages

(Pictured at right)

Prep/Total Time: 20 min.

You'll need just a handful of ingredients to fix these tasty sandwiches from our Test Kitchen. Sausages are stuffed with cheese and a homemade relish, then wrapped in foil so they're easy to transport and grill before the game.

- 1/2 cup giardiniera
- 1/2 teaspoon sugar
- 4 cooked Italian sausage links
- 4 slices provolone cheese, cut into strips
- 4 brat buns *or* hot dog buns, split

In a small food processor, combine giardiniera and sugar; cover and process until blended. Make a lengthwise slit three-fourths of the way through each sausage to within 1/2 in. of each end. Fill with giardiniera mixture and cheese.

Place sausages in buns; wrap individually in a double thickness of heavy-duty foil (about 12 in. x 10 in.). Grill, uncovered, over medium-hot heat for 8-10 minutes or until heated through and the cheese is melted. **Yield:** 4 servings.

Editor's Note: Giardiniera, a pickled vegetable mixture, is available in mild and hot varieties and can be found in the Italian or pickle section of your grocery store.

Butter Bean Tomato Salad

(Pictured above far right)

Prep/Total Time: 20 min.

I make this simple salad often for summer barbecues because people always rave about it and ask for the recipe. I like that it can be made a day ahead and kept in the refrigerator. Plus, it's good served either cold or at room temperature.
—*Denise Neal, Castle Rock, Colorado*

 Uses less fat, sugar or salt. Includes Nutrition Facts and Diabetic Exchanges.

- 1 can (15 ounces) butter beans, rinsed and drained
- 1 pint cherry tomatoes, halved
- 1 small red onion, chopped
- 1/2 cup diced yellow summer squash
- 1/2 cup diced zucchini
- 1/4 cup minced fresh cilantro

DRESSING:
- 3 tablespoons olive oil
- 2 tablespoons lemon juice
- 1 teaspoon ground cumin
- 1/4 teaspoon salt

In a large bowl, combine the beans, tomatoes, onion, yellow squash, zucchini and cilantro. In a small bowl, whisk the dressing ingredients. Drizzle over salad; gently toss to coat. Cover and chill until serving. **Yield:** 5-6 servings.

Nutrition Facts: 1 cup equals 121 calories, 7 g fat (1 g saturated fat), 0 cholesterol, 356 mg sodium, 15 g carbohydrate, 4 g fiber, 4 g protein. **Diabetic Exchanges:** 1 starch, 1 fat.

Peanut Butter Delights

(Pictured below)

Prep/Total Time: 30 min.

I dress up refrigerated cookie dough with peanut butter and chocolate candy coating to create these yummy take-along treats. With just three ingredients, they could not be quicker or easier to make. Everyone loves them—young or old.
—*Janice Rasmussen, Atlantic, Iowa*

Peanut Butter Delights

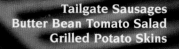

1 package (18 ounces) refrigerated
   ready-to-bake peanut butter cookies
   with candy pieces
2 tablespoons creamy peanut butter
3 ounces milk chocolate candy coating, melted

Bake cookies according to package directions. Cool on wire racks. Spread 12 cookies with 1/2 teaspoon peanut butter each; spoon melted chocolate over peanut butter. Let stand for 5 minutes or until set. Save remaining cookies for another use. **Yield:** 1 dozen.

Grilled Potato Skins

(Pictured above)

Prep/Total Time: 30 min.

The creamy topping on these terrific potato skins is one of my husband's creations and so delicious. They're an excellent summertime appetizer or side dish served with your favorite grilled meat. We have them often with barbecue ribs.
   —Stephanie Moon, Nampa, Idaho

2 medium potatoes
1-1/2 teaspoons butter, melted

2 tablespoons picante sauce
1/4 cup shredded cheddar cheese
1 tablespoon real bacon bits
1/4 cup chopped tomato
2 tablespoons chopped green onion
TOPPING:
   3 tablespoons mayonnaise
   2 tablespoons sour cream
   1 tablespoon ranch salad dressing
1-1/2 teaspoons real bacon bits
1/4 teaspoon garlic powder

Cut each potato lengthwise into four wedges. Cut away the pulp, leaving 1/4-in. shells (save the pulp for another use). Place the potato shells on a microwave-safe plate. Microwave, uncovered, on high for 8-10 minutes or until tender. Brush melted butter over the potato shells; top with the picante sauce, shredded cheddar cheese and bacon bits.

Grill potatoes, skin side down, uncovered, over medium heat for 4-6 minutes or until lightly browned. Cover and grill 2-3 minutes longer or until cheese is melted. Sprinkle with tomato and onion. In a small bowl, combine topping ingredients. Serve with potato skins. **Yield:** 4-5 servings.

Editor's Note: This recipe was tested in a 1,100-watt microwave.

Scare Up Spine-Tingling Sweets

AS THE WITCHING HOUR approaches, there are all kinds of Halloween events that call for spooky sweets and snacks—both cute and creepy. Whether you need a big batch to share at work or school or just a few festive bites for a small but spirited party of costumed characters, these to-die-for desserts are eerily easy and frightfully fast to create.

In fact, they're such a snap to assemble, even the littlest pumpkins can help out. Start an assembly line and ask kids of all ages to join the decorating fun. The eye-catching cookies, flying felines and other treats can even be prepared ahead, so you'll have plenty of time to enjoy the festivities.

Coffin Ice Cream Sandwiches

(Pictured below)

Prep/Total Time: 20 min.

Starting with ice cream sandwiches, our Test Kitchen staff made these sinister cemetery snacks shockingly simple to prepare. But kids are sure to find them hauntingly fun to decorate with jimmies or sprinkles.

1/2 cup plus 3 tablespoons vanilla frosting,
   divided
Orange and black paste food coloring
  6 ice cream sandwiches
Yellow, brown and orange jimmies *and/or*
  Halloween sprinkles

Coffin Ice Cream Sandwiches

Tint 1/2 cup frosting orange and 1 tablespoon frosting black. Cut corners off each ice cream sandwich to form coffin shapes. Dip sides of sandwiches in jimmies. Frost tops with orange frosting. Decorate with black frosting, remaining white frosting and jimmies. Freeze until serving. **Yield:** 6 servings.

Eyeball Cookies

(Pictured at right)

Prep: 25 min. + chilling

All eyes will be on these unusual cookies when you serve them. I created them for my son's kindergarten class for Halloween using vanilla wafers, chocolate and food coloring. They're so easy to make and always get grins from everyone.
   —Sherry Lee, Columbus, Ohio

  5 squares (1 ounce *each***) white baking**
    chocolate, *divided*
 20 to 25 vanilla wafers
Blue paste food coloring
  1/2 cup semisweet chocolate chips
Red paste food coloring

In a microwave-safe bowl, melt 4 squares white chocolate; stir until smooth. Dip vanilla wafers in melted chocolate. Place on a waxed paper-lined baking sheet. Chill until set.

Melt remaining white chocolate; tint blue. Spread a small amount onto the center of each cookie; place a chocolate chip in the center. For bloodshot eyes, use a toothpick dipped in red food coloring to draw lines from blue circles to outer edges of wafers. Chill until set. Store in an airtight container. **Yield:** 20-25 servings.

Flying Broomstick Cats

(Pictured above right)

Prep/Total Time: 30 min.

Perched on pretzel broomsticks, these black cats from our home economists won't bring anything but good luck—and good taste—to your party.

   5 ounces milk chocolate candy coating, *divided*
   6 pretzel dipping sticks
Yellow sprinkles
  3/4 cup potato sticks
    1 tablespoon vanilla *or* **white chips**

Trace three images of the cat pattern (on next page) onto waxed paper; place on a baking sheet. Place another sheet of waxed paper over the top and secure both to baking sheet with tape. Repeat all steps.

In a small microwave-safe bowl, melt 2 ounces of candy coating; stir until smooth. Cut a small hole in the corner of a pastry or plastic bag; insert #3 round pastry tip. Fill bag with melted chocolate. Pipe outlines of three cats and fill in centers.

Place a pretzel dipping stick at bottom of each cat for broomstick. With sprinkles, add eye and collar on each cat. Melt 2 more ounces of candy coating; repeat for remaining cats.

Melt remaining candy coating. Cut a small hole in the corner of a pastry or plastic bag; insert #3 round pastry tip. Fill bag with melted chocolate. Pipe a small amount of chocolate on one end of each pretzel stick; attach potato sticks to form broom bristles.

Melt vanilla chips; stir until smooth. Place in a pastry bag with a #3 round tip. Pipe lines where broomsticks and bristles meet. **Yield:** 6 servings.

Jack-o'-Lantern Pops

(Pictured below)

Prep/Total Time: 30 min.

Your little ghouls' and goblins' faces will light up when you surprise them with these sweet, smiling pumpkins. The crispy pops are perfect as school snacks.
—Clara Coulston, Washington Court House, Ohio

> 1 package (10-1/2 ounces) miniature marshmallows
> 3 tablespoons butter
> 1/8 teaspoon salt
> Red and yellow gel food coloring
> 6 cups crisp rice cereal
> 6 Popsicle sticks
> 3 miniature Tootsie Rolls, cut in half widthwise
> 3 miniature green apple Air Head candies, cut lengthwise into thin strips
> Black decorating gel

In a large saucepan, combine the marshmallows, butter and salt. Cook and stir over medium-low heat until melted. Remove from the heat; tint orange with red and yellow food coloring. Stir in cereal.

With buttered hands, shape mixture into six balls. Insert a Popsicle stick into each ball. Press half of a Tootsie Roll into the top of each for stem. Roll Air Head strips between hands to form vines; press vines into each pumpkin near stem. Make jack-o'-lantern faces with decorating gel. **Yield:** 6 servings.

Jack-o'-Lantern Pops

Eyeball Cookies
Flying Broomstick Cats

Cat Pattern

TO USE the pattern below to shape the cats for the Flying Broomstick Cats (recipe on p. 32), trace three images of the pattern onto one sheet of waxed paper, then trace three more onto another sheet.

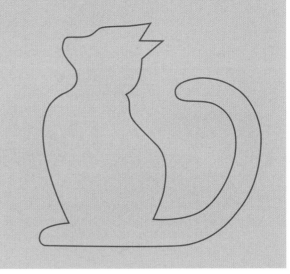

Christmas Cookie Swap Is a Snap

SHARE the work and the sweet rewards with a quick cookie exchange. Wouldn't it be great to have a fantastic variety of homemade treats to enjoy this season with minimal effort and money spent?

Here's how it works. Invite five friends to participate in a cookie exchange, and ask everyone to make six dozen of one type of Christmas cookie, brownie or other treat.

Then plan a convenient time for a get-together for swapping. Each person should bring her or his treats, copies of the recipe and a large container to fill up. Arrange all the goodies on a table, and each person picks up a fair share. That's it! You bake once and get six times the reward!

Want to make it easy on yourself? Pick one of the fuss-free recipes here. Then swap and share the yummy results with loved ones!

Waffle Cookies

(Pictured below)

Prep: 25 min. **Bake:** 10 min. + standing

I received this fun recipe when I was in high school. The unusual treats look fancy decorated with edible glitter or jimmies. People usually are surprised that these cookies are made in a waffle iron.
—Lisa Campbell-Patterson
Des Moines, Iowa

1/4 cup butter, cubed
2 squares (1 ounce *each*) unsweetened chocolate

Waffle Cookies

White Christmas Fudge

2 eggs
1 cup all-purpose flour
3/4 cup sugar
1 teaspoon vanilla extract
FROSTING:
2 tablespoons butter
1 square (1 ounce) unsweetened chocolate
1 teaspoon vanilla extract
1-1/2 cups confectioners' sugar
7-1/2 teaspoons hot water
Edible glitter and jimmies, optional

In a microwave-safe bowl, melt butter and chocolate; stir until smooth. Transfer to a mixing bowl and cool completely. Beat in eggs. Combine flour and sugar; gradually beat into egg mixture. Stir in vanilla.

Drop by tablespoonfuls 1 in. apart onto a preheated waffle iron. Bake for 1 minute or until set. Remove to a wire rack to cool completely.

For frosting, in a microwave-safe bowl, melt butter and chocolate; stir until smooth. Transfer to a mixing bowl. Beat in vanilla. Gradually add confectioners' sugar alternately with water, beating until smooth. Frost waffle cookies to within 1/4 in. of edges. Decorate with glitter and jimmies if desired. Let stand until frosting is set. **Yield:** about 2-1/2 dozen.

White Christmas Fudge

(Pictured above)

Prep: 20 min. + chilling

If you're dreaming of a white Christmas, try this sweet treat! The smooth, colorful fudge is loaded with crunchy almonds, apricots, cherries and cranberries. It's perfect for holiday gift giving—just pack some in a festive candy box or tin.
—Paula Truksa, Jewett, Texas

1 teaspoon plus 1/4 cup butter, *divided*
2-1/2 cups confectioners' sugar
2/3 cup milk
12 squares (1 ounce *each*) white baking chocolate, chopped
1/4 teaspoon almond extract
3/4 cup sliced almonds, toasted
1/4 cup chopped dried apricots
1/4 cup dried cherries
1/4 cup dried cranberries

Line a 9-in. square pan with foil and grease the foil with 1 teaspoon butter; set aside. In a heavy saucepan, combine the confectioners' sugar, milk and remaining butter. Cook and stir over medium heat until combined. Bring to a boil; boil for 5 minutes without stirring. Reduce heat to low; stir in white chocolate and extract. Cook and stir until chocolate is melted.

Remove from the heat. Fold in the almonds, apricots, cherries and cranberries. Immediately spread into prepared pan. Refrigerate for 2 hours or until set. Using foil, lift fudge out of pan. Discard foil; cut fudge into 1-in. squares. Store in the refrigerator. **Yield:** about 2 pounds.

Cherry Almond Bars

(Pictured below)

Prep: 10 min. **Bake:** 40 min. + cooling

A wonderful lady I used to work for gave me this nutty bar recipe. It's so easy, eye-catching and delicious.
—Ruth Ann Stelfox, Raymond, Alberta

2 cups all-purpose flour
1/2 cup packed brown sugar
1 cup cold butter
1 cup golden raisins
1 cup chopped red *and/or* green maraschino cherries
1 cup sliced almonds
1 can (14 ounces) sweetened condensed milk

In a bowl, combine flour and brown sugar; cut in butter until crumbly. Press into an ungreased 15-in. x 10-in.

Cherry Almond Bars

Cream Wafers

x 1-in. baking pan. Bake at 325° for 12-14 minutes or until lightly browned.

Sprinkle with raisins, cherries and almonds; drizzle with milk. Bake 25-30 minutes longer or until golden brown. Cool on a wire rack. Cut into squares. **Yield:** 4 dozen.

Cream Wafers

(Pictured above)

Prep: 25 min. + chilling
Bake: 10 min. per batch + cooling

My sons used to help me make these cookies, and now my oldest granddaughter helps. The cute little sandwiches are buttery and melt-in-your-mouth good!
—Linda Clinkenbeard, Vincennes, Indiana

1/2 cup butter, softened
1 cup all-purpose flour
3 tablespoons heavy whipping cream
Sugar
FILLING:
1/4 cup butter, softened
3/4 cup confectioners' sugar
1/2 teaspoon vanilla extract
1-1/2 to 2 teaspoons heavy whipping cream
1 drop *each* red and green food coloring

In a mixing bowl, beat the butter, flour and cream. Cover and refrigerate for 1 hour or until easy to handle.

On a lightly floured surface, roll out dough to 1/8-in. thickness. Cut dough with a floured 1-1/4-in. round cookie cutter. Place 1 in. apart on ungreased baking sheets. Sprinkle each cookie with sugar. Prick each 3-4 times with a fork. Bake at 375° for 7-9 minutes or until set. Remove to wire racks to cool.

In a small bowl, combine the butter, confectioners' sugar, vanilla and enough cream to achieve desired consistency. Remove half to another bowl; tint one portion of filling with red food coloring and the other half with green. Carefully spread filling on the bottoms of half of the cookies; top with remaining cookies. **Yield:** 2 dozen sandwich cookies.

Yule Feast Has All the Trimmings

REMEMBER when the holiday season seemed longer and less rushed? When families took time to get together, crank up the carols and deck the tree with strings of lights and favorite ornaments?

If trimming the tree has become more of a job than a joy at your house, recapture the spirit of Christmases past with a fun family party. Simply whip up the fast-fixing recipes here.

For starters, wreathe Creamy Ranch Dip with veggies and keep the Pepperoni Roll-Ups coming! Bigger appetites will enjoy the Chicken Pasta Salad.

Finish with a Santa's Coming Cookie Puzzle. Then sit back and savor the warmth of the season.

Chicken Pasta Salad

(Pictured below)

Prep: 25 min. + chilling

Santa himself might find it hard to resist this colorful chicken salad packed with veggies and pasta. Our Test Kitchen added cayenne for extra flavor.

☑ Uses less fat, sugar or salt. Includes Nutrition Facts and Diabetic Exchanges.

      1 cup uncooked spiral pasta
      1 cup cubed cooked chicken
      1 small green pepper, diced
      1 small carrot, thinly sliced
      1 celery rib, thinly sliced
  1/4 cup chopped white onion
  1/4 cup chopped red onion
  1/4 cup frozen peas, thawed
  1/4 cup sour cream
  1/4 cup mayonnaise
      1 tablespoon ranch salad dressing mix

Chicken Pasta Salad

  1/4 teaspoon garlic salt
  1/4 teaspoon paprika
  1/8 teaspoon cayenne pepper

Cook pasta according to package directions. Meanwhile, in a large bowl, combine the chicken, green pepper, carrot, celery, onions and peas.

In a small bowl, combine the sour cream, mayonnaise, ranch dressing mix, garlic salt, paprika and cayenne. Drain pasta and rinse in cold water; add to chicken mixture. Add dressing and toss to coat. Cover and refrigerate for at least 1 hour. **Yield:** 4 servings.

Nutrition Facts: 1 cup (prepared with chicken breast, reduced-fat sour cream and fat-free mayonnaise) equals 199 calories, 3 g fat (1 g saturated fat), 34 mg cholesterol, 645 mg sodium, 27 g carbohydrate, 3 g fiber, 15 g protein. **Diabetic Exchanges:** 1-1/2 starch, 1 lean meat, 1 vegetable.

Creamy Ranch Dip

(Pictured above right)

Prep/Total Time: 10 min.

This is a wonderfully thick and easy dip for fresh vegetables, crackers or chips—and it goes together with only three ingredients! I just combine cream cheese, sour cream and salad dressing mix. It's also delicious with hot wings.
—Janice Freeman, Kewanee, Illinois

      2 cups (16 ounces) sour cream
      1 package (8 ounces) cream cheese, softened
      2 envelopes ranch salad dressing mix
Fresh vegetables, crackers *or* chips

In a small mixing bowl, beat the sour cream, cream cheese and ranch dressing mix on medium speed until smooth. Transfer to a serving bowl; refrigerate until serving. Serve with vegetables, crackers or chips. **Yield:** 3 cups.

Pepperoni Roll-Ups

(Pictured above right)

Prep/Total Time: 20 min.

This fabulous finger food is sure to be a hit with busy tree trimmers of all ages. A longtime favorite, each savory bite boasts gooey, melted cheese and pizza flavor.
—Debbie Purcell, Safford, Arizona

      1 tube (8 ounces) refrigerated crescent rolls
    16 slices pepperoni, cut into quarters
      2 pieces string cheese (1 ounce *each*), cut into quarters

Creamy Ranch Dip
Pepperoni Roll-Ups

Santa's Coming Cookie Puzzle

3/4 teaspoon Italian seasoning, *divided*
1/4 teaspoon garlic salt

Unroll crescent dough; separate into eight triangles. Place eight pepperoni pieces on each. Place a piece of cheese on the long side of each triangle; sprinkle with 1/2 teaspoon Italian seasoning. Roll up each, starting with a long side; pinch seams to seal. Sprinkle with garlic salt and remaining Italian seasoning.

Place 2 in. apart on a greased baking sheet. Bake at 375° for 10-12 minutes or until golden brown. Serve warm. **Yield:** 8 appetizers.

Santa's Coming Cookie Puzzle

(Pictured above right)

Prep: 30 min. **Bake:** 20 min. + cooling

This clever confection is easy to make with store-bought cookie dough and is entirely edible to boot! Blanched almonds make it simple for little hands to grasp the puzzle pieces, which are completely removable.

   1 tube (18 ounces) refrigerated sugar cookie
      dough, softened
  1/2 cup all-purpose flour
Blanched almonds
2-1/2 cups confectioners' sugar
    4 to 5 tablespoons milk
    1 teaspoon vanilla extract
Assorted food coloring, decorating gels
  and sprinkles

In a large mixing bowl, combine cookie dough and flour. On a parchment paper-lined surface, roll dough into a 14-in. x 11-in. rectangle. With cookie cutters, cut out puzzle shapes. Slide a baking sheet under the parchment paper and dough. Chill for 5-10 minutes.

Remove shapes and place on an ungreased baking sheet. Place an almond on its side into the center of each shape for a handle. Bake puzzle shapes at 350° for 7-9 minutes or until edges are golden brown. While still warm, recut shapes with the same cookie cutters to form neat edges. (If cookies cool too quickly, return to oven until softened.) Remove to wire racks to cool.

Bake large rectangular puzzle on a parchment paper-lined baking sheet for 12-13 minutes or until edges are golden brown. Immediately recut the shapes inside the puzzle to form neat edges. Cool completely on a wire rack.

In a small bowl, combine confectioners' sugar, milk and vanilla until smooth. Tint the frosting with food coloring as desired. Frost puzzle and shapes; decorate with the decorating gel and sprinkles as desired. Place puzzle shapes inside puzzle. **Yield:** 1 cookie puzzle.

Christmas Buffet Shines Bright

WANT to turn an average party into something really special this holiday season? With the four standout recipes that follow, you can impress company and offer them a variety of buffet choices that are guaranteed to please.

Best of all, it won't take hours to put together this sensational buffet. So you can easily fit it into your busy Christmastime schedule.

To start off, lay out the effortless Stuffed Shrimp, and your party will take on an air of sophistication. Since this outstanding appetizer can be made the night before, the only thing you have to do is pull it from the refrigerator.

For the rest of the meal, set up a crowd-pleasing mashed potato bar. Instead of using the usual plates or bowls, add instant elegance to your gathering by serving delicious Mashed Red Potatoes in martini or daiquiri glasses.

Let guests help themselves to several basic stir-ins for the potatoes, such as shredded cheese, sour cream and crumbled bacon. But also offer heartier potato toppings like flavorful Florets with Cheese Sauce and Dressed-Up Beef Tips. They make a satisfying meal that's also easy on the cook.

On that note, try to do as much as you can before you turn on the stove, and everything will come together in a snap. By chopping the vegetables and herbs ahead of time, you can trim last-minute prep and spend more time socializing instead.

Stuffed Shrimp

(Pictured at right and on page 20)

Prep/Total Time: 30 min.

I love to share this delightful shrimp appetizer with my guests. The creamy three-ingredient filling has a hint of horseradish and is a breeze to whip up. If you like, place a bowl of seafood sauce alongside the shrimp as the finishing touch.
—Sandy Schneider, Naperville, Illinois

    4 ounces cream cheese, softened
4-1/2 teaspoons prepared horseradish
    1 tablespoon grated Parmesan cheese
    1 pound cooked large shrimp, peeled and deveined
Minced fresh parsley
Seafood sauce, optional

In a small bowl, combine the cream cheese, horseradish and grated Parmesan cheese until blended. Cut a small hole in the corner of a resealable plastic bag; add the cream cheese mixture. Butterfly the shrimp along their outside curves. Pipe about 1 teaspoon cream cheese mixture into each shrimp.

Arrange on a serving platter. Sprinkle with parsley. Serve with seafood sauce if desired. Refrigerate leftovers. **Yield:** about 2 dozen.

Mashed Red Potatoes

(Pictured at right and on page 20)

Prep/Total Time: 30 min.

These yummy mashed potatoes from our home economists are rich enough to stand on their own. But they're also delicious with cheese, bacon and sour cream...or one of the satisfying toppers also featured here.

4-1/2 pounds red potatoes, cut into 1-inch pieces
    6 tablespoons butter, cubed
1-1/2 teaspoons salt
   3/4 teaspoon pepper
    1 to 1-1/3 cups heavy whipping cream, warmed

Place potatoes in a large saucepan or Dutch oven and cover with water. Bring to a boil. Reduce heat; cover and cook for 15-20 minutes or until tender. Drain.

In a large mixing bowl, mash the potatoes with butter, salt, pepper and enough cream to achieve desired consistency. **Yield:** 9 cups.

Dressed-Up Beef Tips

(Pictured at right and on page 21)

Prep/Total Time: 25 min.

Our Test Kitchen staff jazzed up packaged beef tips and gravy by adding plenty of fresh vegetables and a wine-based sauce. The result was a chunky, hearty topping that pairs perfectly with Mashed Red Potatoes (above). It'll satisfy even the biggest appetites at your buffet.

    2 tablespoons cornstarch
    1 can (14-1/2 ounces) beef broth
1/4 cup dry red wine *or* additional beef broth
1/2 cup cut fresh green beans (1-inch pieces)
1/4 cup sliced fresh carrot
    1 tablespoon finely chopped onion
    1 tablespoon butter
    1 package (17 ounces) refrigerated beef tips with gravy
    1 tablespoon minced fresh parsley

In a small bowl, combine the cornstarch, broth and wine or additional broth until smooth; set aside. In a large skillet, saute the beans, carrot and onion in butter for 3-4 minutes or until tender.

Add beef tips; heat through. Stir broth mixture and add to skillet. Bring to a boil; cook and stir for 2 minutes or until thickened. Stir in parsley. **Yield:** 4 cups.

Mashed Red Potatoes
Dressed-Up Beef Tips
Florets with Cheese Sauce
Stuffed Shrimp

Florets with Cheese Sauce

(Pictured above and on page 20)

Prep/Total Time: 20 min.

Tossed in a cheese sauce, these tender cauliflower and broccoli florets from our home economists make a tasty accent for Mashed Red Potatoes (above left). The florets also can be served as a side dish for other meals.

    3 cups fresh cauliflowerets
    3 cups fresh broccoli florets
    2 tablespoons butter
    1 tablespoon all-purpose flour
1/2 teaspoon ground mustard
1/4 teaspoon salt
    1 cup milk
    1 cup (4 ounces) shredded sharp cheddar
       cheese
    4 to 5 drops hot pepper sauce

Place cauliflower and broccoli in a large steamer basket; place in a large saucepan over 1 in. of water. Bring to a boil; cover and steam for 12-15 minutes or until crisp-tender.

Meanwhile, in another large saucepan, melt butter. Stir in the flour, mustard and salt until smooth; gradually add milk. Bring to a boil; cook and stir for 2 minutes or until thickened. Reduce heat; add cheese and pepper sauce. Stir until cheese is melted. Add vegetables and toss to coat. **Yield:** 4 cups.

Keeping Your Cool

I couldn't figure out how to keep items cold at a buffet or picnic until I thought of this idea. The night before the event, I find a bowl that's slightly larger than my serving bowl. I fill it a quarter of the way with water and put it in the freezer. Just before mealtime, I put the serving bowl inside the large bowl that now has ice in it. My food stays cold the whole time.
—*Beth Van Couwenberghe, Anchorage, Alaska*

Warm Up With Wintertime Dinner

WINTER is a wonderful time for making new memories. So gather loved ones to build a snowman, go sledding or play board games in front of a fire. With the easy-to-fix menu here, you won't have to miss out on the fun...and you'll keep the chill in check with foods that'll warm you head to toe.

Before dinnertime arrives, enjoy steaming mugs of tangy cider. The hearty chili simmers in the slow cooker all afternoon, so you'll have plenty of time away from the kitchen to spend with guests.

When suppertime nears, pop the cheesy bread in the oven and toss together the fast salad. In minutes, you'll have a satisfying meal that'll keep you cozy on even the chilliest evenings.

Apple Citrus Cider

(Pictured below)

Prep/Total Time: 30 min.

With a twist of pineapple and lemon, this hot and comforting cider is perfect for the season. A mug of this tangy treat is guaranteed to warm hands of all sizes, big or small! If you like, add a cinnamon stick as a garnish.
—*Patricia Aurand*
Findlay, Ohio

2 quarts unsweetened apple juice
3/4 cup pineapple juice concentrate
3 tablespoons sugar
1 medium lemon, thinly sliced
3 cinnamon sticks (3 inches)
6 whole allspice

6 whole cloves
4 cups lemon-lime soda

In a large saucepan, combine the apple juice, pineapple juice concentrate, sugar and lemon slices. Place the cinnamon sticks, allspice and cloves on a double thickness of cheesecloth; bring up corners of cloth and tie with kitchen string to form a bag. Add to pan.

Bring to a boil over medium heat. Reduce heat; simmer, uncovered, for 10-15 minutes. Discard spice bag. Stir in soda; cook for 4-6 minutes or until heated through (do not boil). **Yield:** 12 servings (3 quarts).

Apple Citrus Cider

Chive Corn Bread

(Pictured at right)

Prep/Total Time: 30 min.

"Busy" is my middle name, so I often fix this incredibly easy, three-ingredient corn bread to simplify family meals. It helps me get back to working, volunteering and keeping my family's fast-paced schedule running smoothly.
—*Terri Keeney*
Greeley, Colorado

1 package (8-1/2 ounces) corn bread/muffin mix
1/2 cup shredded cheddar cheese
1 tablespoon minced chives

Prepare corn bread batter according to package directions. Stir in cheese and chives. Pour into a greased 8-in. square baking dish. Bake at 400° for 20-25 minutes or until lightly browned. Serve warm. **Yield:** 9 servings.

Honey Garlic Dressing

(Pictured above right)

Prep/Total Time: 15 min.

The apple and garlic flavors balance well in this sweet, honey-infused dressing. It's great on mixed greens.
—*Janet Morgan-Cavallaro, Pincourt, Quebec*

1/2 cup unsweetened apple juice
1/2 cup honey
1/2 cup white vinegar
1 teaspoon minced garlic
1/4 teaspoon ground mustard
1 cup vegetable oil
Mixed salad greens

In a blender, combine the apple juice, honey, vinegar, garlic and mustard; cover and process until blended. While processing, gradually add oil in a steady stream. Serve with salad greens. **Yield:** 2-1/2 cups.

Italian Chili

(Pictured above)

Prep: 20 min. **Cook:** 6-1/2 hours

By adding Italian seasoning and fresh vegetables, our Test Kitchen home economists put an irresistible Italian spin on slow-simmered Southwestern chili.

1 pound ground beef
1/2 pound bulk Italian sausage
1 can (28 ounces) diced tomatoes
1 can (8 ounces) tomato sauce
1 cup chopped onion
1 cup chopped sweet red pepper
1 cup water
1/2 cup chopped celery
1/4 cup beef broth
1 tablespoon chili powder
1 tablespoon Italian seasoning
1 teaspoon sugar
1 teaspoon minced garlic
1/2 teaspoon salt
1 can (16 ounces) kidney beans, rinsed and drained
1 cup sliced fresh mushrooms
1 cup diced zucchini
3 tablespoons minced fresh parsley
Shredded part-skim mozzarella cheese, optional

In a large skillet, cook beef and sausage over medium heat until no longer pink. Meanwhile, in a 3-qt. slow cooker, combine the tomatoes, tomato sauce, onion, red pepper, water, celery, broth, chili powder, Italian seasoning, sugar, garlic and salt.

Drain beef mixture; add to the slow cooker. Cover and cook on low for 6 hours or until vegetables are tender.

Add the beans, mushrooms, zucchini and parsley. Cover and cook on high for 30 minutes or until vegetables are tender. Serve with cheese if desired. **Yield:** 6 servings.

Chapter 3

⊕ *30 Minutes to Mealtime*

THINK that getting a pleasing, home-cooked, complete dinner on the table for your family in 30 minutes just isn't possible? You'll change your mind when you glance through this chock-full chapter!

It gives you several weeks' worth of meals—a total of 28, to be exact—all requiring no more than half an hour to fix from start to finish. And many of them will take you even less time than that!

Our Test Kitchen home economists paired readers' favorite recipes and their own creations to come up with these speedy yet satisfying menus. So you know that every delicious dish you choose has already been taste-tested and approved by on-the-go cooks like you.

SUPPER IN A SNAP. Sauerkraut Mashed Potatoes, Pretzels with Mustard and German Bratwurst (all recipes on p. 48).

Elegant And Effortless

CREATING a special supper for company doesn't have to take hours in the kitchen. In fact, it takes only minutes to make this mouth-watering meal that's sure to impress family and friends.

Rely on your microwave to shave cooking time from succulent Pork Chops Monterey, sent in by Robyn Herz of Overland Park, Kansas. Tender and moist pork chops are topped with onion and a sweet, tangy sauce, then served over rice.

"A college roommate shared this recipe more than 15 years ago, and I've been making it ever since," Robyn writes. "It's nice enough to serve company, and I often get requests for the recipe after guests taste it," she adds.

A main dish so delightful needs a special accompaniment, so pair the pork chops with Polly Heer's Buttery Brussels Sprouts. The Cabot, Arkansas cook gives a dressed-up touch to the simple stovetop side dish by adding a splash of white wine. But feel free to substitute chicken broth for equally tasty results.

When guests comment on the effort you put into this special meal, it can be your little secret that it took less than 30 minutes to prepare.

Pork Chops Monterey

Prep/Total Time: 25 min.

✓ Uses less fat, sugar or salt. Includes Nutrition Facts and Diabetic Exchanges.

    6 boneless pork loin chops (4 ounces *each*)
    1 medium onion, sliced
    1 cup chili sauce
2/3 cup packed brown sugar
    3 tablespoons lemon juice
    2 packages (8.8 ounces *each*) ready-to-serve long grain rice

Place pork chops in an 11-in. x 7-in. x 2-in. microwave-safe dish coated with nonstick cooking spray; top with onion. Combine the chili sauce, brown sugar and lemon juice; pour over chops. Cover and microwave on high for 15 minutes or until meat juices run clear.

Meanwhile, cook rice according to package directions. Serve with pork chops. **Yield:** 6 servings.

Editor's Note: This recipe was tested in a 1,100-watt microwave.

Nutrition Facts: 1 pork chop (calculated without rice) equals 295 calories, 6 g fat (2 g saturated fat), 55 mg cholesterol, 655 mg sodium, 37 g carbohydrate, 1 g fiber, 22 g protein. **Diabetic Exchanges:** 3 lean meat, 2-1/2 fruit.

Buttery Brussels Sprouts

Prep/Total Time: 15 min.

    1 cup chicken broth
1/3 cup white wine *or* additional chicken broth
4-1/2 teaspoons butter
1/4 teaspoon white pepper, *divided*
    2 packages (10 ounces *each*) frozen brussels sprouts
1/4 teaspoon salt

In a large saucepan, combine the broth, wine or additional broth, butter and 1/8 teaspoon white pepper; bring to a boil. Add brussels sprouts. Reduce heat; cover and simmer for 6-9 minutes or until tender. Drain and transfer to a bowl. Sprinkle with salt and remaining pepper. **Yield:** 6 servings.

Pork Chops Monterey
Buttery Brussels Sprouts

Softer Brown Sugar

If I have brown sugar that's become hard, I grate it with a cheese grater. It works like a charm and prevents waste. I store the leftover "block" of brown sugar in a resealable plastic bag for next time.
—*Lorene Brewer, Long Beach, California*

Fish Dinner In a Flash

Oriental Green Beans
Herb Fish Fillets

TRYING to prepare a quick meal that's nutritious and delicious can be challenging any time of year. And it's especially tricky during the holidays, when there are so many seasonal activities vying for precious time.

But this menu of recipes from readers fits the bill on all counts—it's healthy, tasty and ready in less than half an hour!

For the main course, fix Herb Fish Fillets from Yvonne Nemec of Stewartsville, New Jersey. Adding different herbs to the bread crumb topping gives this speedy fish fabulous flavor.

"Every Christmas season, we have a seafood dinner with lobster, shrimp, scallops and more," Yvonne relates. "And these fillets are always on the menu. They're so easy and delicious."

For a no-stress side dish, serve Oriental Green Beans from Harriet Stichter. These mildly seasoned beans will enhance most any main course.

"Since green beans are popular in our house, we're always looking for new and different ways to prepare them," explains the Milford, Indiana cook. "We have enjoyed this crunchy, fuss-free dish many times."

Herb Fish Fillets

Prep/Total Time: 20 min.

✓ Uses less fat, sugar or salt. Includes Nutrition Facts and Diabetic Exchanges.

- 1/4 cup finely chopped onion
- 2 tablespoons butter
- 1/2 teaspoon minced garlic
- 1 tablespoon lemon juice
- 2 teaspoons dried parsley flakes
- 1/4 to 1/2 teaspoon salt
- 1/4 teaspoon dried tarragon
- 1/8 teaspoon dried thyme
- 1 pound whitefish *or* sole fillets
- 1/4 cup dry bread crumbs

In a small microwave-safe dish, combine onion, butter and garlic. Microwave, uncovered, on high for 1-2 minutes or until onion is partially cooked. Stir in lemon juice, parsley, salt, tarragon and thyme.

Arrange fillets in a greased 2-qt. round microwave-safe dish. Top with half of the butter mixture. Stir bread crumbs into the remaining butter mixture; sprinkle over fillets. Cover and microwave on high for 4-6 minutes or until fish flakes easily with a fork. **Yield:** 4 servings.

Editor's Note: This recipe was tested in a 1,100-watt microwave.

Nutrition Facts: 4 ounces (prepared with reduced-fat butter and 1/4 teaspoon salt) equals 161 calories, 5 g fat (2 g saturated fat), 64 mg cholesterol, 334 mg sodium, 6 g carbohydrate, trace fiber, 23 g protein. **Diabetic Exchanges:** 3 very lean meat, 1/2 starch, 1/2 fat.

Oriental Green Beans

Prep/Total Time: 15 min.

✓ Uses less fat, sugar or salt. Includes Nutrition Facts and Diabetic Exchanges.

- 1 package (16 ounces) frozen cut green beans
- 1-1/2 teaspoons cornstarch
- 1/2 cup chicken broth
- 1 tablespoon soy sauce
- 2 tablespoons chopped onion
- 1/4 to 1/2 teaspoon ground ginger
- 1-1/2 teaspoons canola oil
- 1 jar (4-1/2 ounces) sliced mushrooms, drained
- 1/2 cup sliced water chestnuts
- 1-1/2 teaspoons sesame seeds, toasted

Cook green beans according to package directions. Meanwhile, in a small bowl, combine the cornstarch, broth and soy sauce until smooth; set aside.

In a large skillet, saute onion and ginger in oil until tender. Stir broth mixture and add to skillet. Bring to a boil; cook and stir for 1 minute or until thickened. Drain beans; add the beans, mushrooms and water chestnuts to skillet. Stir to coat. Just before serving, sprinkle with sesame seeds. **Yield:** 4 servings.

Nutrition Facts: 3/4 cup (prepared with reduced-sodium chicken broth and reduced-sodium soy sauce) equals 82 calories, 2 g fat (trace saturated fat), 0 cholesterol, 502 mg sodium, 13 g carbohydrate, 4 g fiber, 3 g protein. **Diabetic Exchange:** 3 vegetable.

Warm Chocolate Eggnog
Coconut Almond Muffins
Cream Cheese Scrambled Eggs

Cream Cheese Scrambled Eggs

Prep/Total Time: 15 min.

- 1 package (3 ounces) cream cheese, softened
- 2 tablespoons half-and-half cream
- 8 eggs
- 1/3 cup grated Parmesan cheese
- 1/2 teaspoon lemon-pepper seasoning
- 1/8 teaspoon salt
- 1/2 cup real bacon bits
- 2 tablespoons butter

In a small mixing bowl, beat cream cheese and cream until smooth. Add the eggs, Parmesan cheese, lemon-pepper and salt; mix well. Stir in bacon.

In a large skillet, melt butter; add egg mixture. Cook and stir over medium heat until eggs are completely set. **Yield:** 4 servings.

Coconut Almond Muffins

Prep/Total Time: 30 min.

- 1 cup all-purpose flour
- 1/2 cup sugar
- 1-1/4 teaspoons baking powder
- 1/4 teaspoon salt
- 1 egg
- 1/2 cup sour cream
- 1/4 cup butter, melted
- 1/4 teaspoon almond extract
- 1/2 cup flaked coconut
- 1/4 cup miniature semisweet chocolate chips
- 1/4 cup sliced almonds

Additional sugar

In a bowl, combine the flour, sugar, baking powder and salt. In another bowl, whisk the egg, sour cream, butter and almond extract. Stir into the dry ingredients just until moistened. Fold in the coconut and miniature chocolate chips.

Fill greased muffin cups two-thirds full. Sprinkle with almonds and additional sugar. Bake at 375° for 18-20 minutes or until a toothpick comes out clean. Cool for 5 minutes before removing from pan to a wire rack. **Yield:** 6 muffins.

Warm Chocolate Eggnog

Prep/Total Time: 20 min.

- 1 quart eggnog
- 1/2 cup chocolate syrup
- 1/8 to 1/4 teaspoon ground nutmeg
- 3 teaspoons vanilla extract

Whipped cream and additional ground nutmeg

In a large saucepan, combine the eggnog, chocolate syrup and nutmeg; heat through over low heat, about 15 minutes (do not boil). Remove from the heat; stir in vanilla. Pour into mugs. Top each with a dollop of whipped cream and sprinkle of nutmeg. **Yield:** 4 servings.

Editor's Note: This recipe was tested with commercially prepared eggnog.

Morning Meal For Christmas

IF THE PRESENTS under the tree aren't enough to get your family out of bed on Christmas morning, the aroma of fresh baked muffins and simmering chocolate is sure to have them scrambling to the breakfast table. And you won't have to wake up hours early to prepare this special morning meal, because it takes just 30 minutes from start to finish.

You might think almonds, coconut and chocolate chips are the start of a good cookie recipe, and you'd be right. But in this case, those ingredients dress up Coconut Almond Muffins from Sara Tatham. "These muffins have become a family favorite," writes the Plymouth, New Hampshire reader.

To complement the tender muffins and create a fantastic balance of sweet and savory, try Cream Cheese Scrambled Eggs from Jacque Hunt of Heyburn, Idaho.

"My mother-in-law introduced me to this recipe. Now it's my kids' breakfast of choice," she relates. "They always ask for the 'eggs with the bacon in it.' And we make a big batch to feed our family of six."

Tie it all together with a fun twist on a traditional treat. Warm Chocolate Eggnog from Diane Hixon of Niceville, Florida is rich, sweet and simple to stir up with store-bought eggnog. Yum!

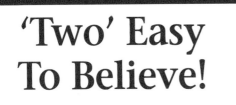
COOKING for two people is a snap when you turn to this quick, colorful menu that features crispy chicken, an eye-catching salad and a warm-from-the-oven dessert.

Corn Bread Chicken Tenders from Angela Bottger of New Canaan, Connecticut are the easiest fried chicken you've ever made. "My husband and I are proud parents of a baby girl, and life is busy," she says. "So getting dinner on the table fast is a must.

"I dreamed up this recipe using ingredients we had on hand," Angela recalls. "We both loved the taste and texture."

Angela likes to pair the chicken with Cranberry-Almond Spinach Salad. Dressed up with nutritious ingredients like crunchy almonds and chewy dried cranberries, it's a side dish you can feel good about.

For a comforting ending, dig into French Vanilla Bread Pudding, sent in by Nancy Johnson of Laverne, Oklahoma. With caramel, pecans and cinnamon, each bite is simply irresistible.

Corn Bread Chicken Tenders

Prep/Total Time: 15 min.

1/4 cup corn bread/muffin mix
3 tablespoons prepared ranch salad dressing
6 chicken tenderloins
2 teaspoons vegetable oil

Place corn bread mix and salad dressing in separate shallow bowls. Dip chicken in dressing, then roll in corn bread mix.

In a skillet, cook chicken in oil over medium heat for 3 minutes on each side or until juices run clear. **Yield:** 2 servings.

Cranberry-Almond Spinach Salad

Prep/Total Time: 10 min.

2 cups fresh baby spinach *or* mixed greens
1 large tomato, chopped, optional
2 tablespoons slivered almonds
2 tablespoons dried cranberries
2 tablespoons poppy seed salad dressing

In a small bowl, combine the spinach, tomato if desired, almonds and cranberries. Drizzle with dressing and toss to coat. Serve immediately. **Yield:** 2 servings.

French Vanilla Bread Pudding

Prep/Total Time: 25 min.

2 slices cinnamon-raisin bread, cubed
1 egg
1/2 cup refrigerated French vanilla nondairy creamer
1 caramel, cut into small pieces
1 tablespoon chopped pecans
1/4 teaspoon ground cinnamon
1 tablespoon butter

Place bread cubes in two greased 6-oz. ramekins or custard cups. In a small bowl, whisk egg and creamer; pour over bread. Sprinkle with caramel pieces, pecans and cinnamon; dot with butter.

Bake at 350° for 18-20 minutes or until bubbly and golden brown. Cool slightly before serving. **Yield:** 2 servings.

**French Vanilla Bread Pudding
Cranberry-Almond Spinach Salad
Corn Bread Chicken Tenders**

A Feast for Oktoberfest

WELCOME the fall season by serving up some genuine German hospitality with this hearty meal. Your family's sure to appreciate these tasty, traditional favorites...and you'll appreciate having a busy weeknight dinner ready in only half an hour. (And if it's the weekend and you feel like putting on some polka music and inviting the neighbors, all these recipes are easy to double for a crowd!)

Start with an entree of mouth-watering German Bratwurst from our Test Kitchen. Flavorful bacon drippings, mustard and brown sugar make these brats something special. An added bonus? You use the cooked bacon from this recipe to prepare Sauerkraut Mashed Potatoes sent in by Betsy Esley from Three Mile Bay, New York.

Even people who claim not to like sauerkraut will enjoy this side dish. "I received this recipe from a German war bride many years ago," she recalls. Handy convenience products make it as quick and simple as it is delicious. "It's also good served with ham or any pork dish," Betsy adds.

Round out this easygoing menu with our Test Kitchen's Pretzels with Mustard. The jazzed-up mustard sauce goes together in minutes and is perfect for dipping soft pretzels from the freezer section...or for slathering on the German Bratwurst.

Sauerkraut Mashed Potatoes
Pretzels with Mustard
German Bratwurst

German Bratwurst

Prep/Total Time: 30 min.

  4 bacon strips, diced
  5 uncooked bratwurst
  1 teaspoon cornstarch
1/4 cup chicken broth
  2 tablespoons Dijon mustard
  1 tablespoon brown sugar
  1 tablespoon white wine *or* additional chicken broth
  1 tablespoon cider vinegar
1/8 teaspoon celery seed

In a skillet, cook bacon over medium heat until crisp. Using a slotted spoon, remove to paper towels (save for mashed potato recipe or another use). Drain, reserving 4 tablespoons drippings. In the drippings, cook bratwurst for 10-15 minutes or until no longer pink. Remove and keep warm. Drain skillet.

In a small bowl, combine cornstarch and chicken broth until smooth; set aside. Add the mustard, brown sugar, wine or additional broth, vinegar and celery seed to skillet; cook and stir over medium heat until mixture is hot and bubbly.

Gradually add the cornstarch mixture. Bring to a boil; cook and stir until thickened. Return the bratwurst to the pan; cook and stir for 1-2 minutes or until glazed. **Yield:** 5 servings.

Sauerkraut Mashed Potatoes

Prep/Total Time: 20 min.

2-2/3 cups water
  2/3 cup milk
  1/4 cup butter, cubed
    1 teaspoon salt
2-2/3 cups mashed potato flakes
  1/3 cup chopped onion
  1/2 cup sauerkraut, rinsed and well drained
    4 bacon strips, cooked and crumbled

In a large saucepan, combine the water, milk, butter and salt; bring to a boil. Stir in potato flakes. Remove from the heat; cover and let stand for 5 minutes.

Meanwhile, in a small skillet coated with nonstick cooking spray, cook onion over medium heat until tender. Stir sauerkraut into potatoes; top with onion and bacon. **Yield:** 5 servings.

Pretzels with Mustard

Prep/Total Time: 5 min.

1/2 cup Dijon mustard
1/3 cup honey
  1 tablespoon white wine vinegar
  2 teaspoons sugar
Large soft pretzels, warmed

In a small bowl, whisk the Dijon mustard, honey, white wine vinegar and sugar until blended. Serve mustard with soft pretzels. **Yield:** 3/4 cup.

Fast Supper Italian-Style

LOOKING for a sensational yet stress-free meal you can fix in a hurry? Something everyone will love? Think Italian! There's nothing quite like it for making a crowd feel like family.

Try following your next autumn outing, football rally or neighborhood soccer game with the classic Italian menu featured here. You can have both dishes on the table in just 30 minutes...giving you plenty of time to relax and be part of the fun instead of being sidelined in the kitchen!

Start with a rich and satisfying main dish—Saucy Skillet Lasagna shared by Meghan Crihfield from Ripley, West Virginia. It makes an effortless entree thanks to no-cook lasagna noodles. And with plenty of ground beef and two kinds of cheese, it'll please even the heartiest appetites.

Pair the lasagna with crunchy slices of buttery Garlic Cheese Bread sent in by Janet Rodakowski from Wentzville, Missouri...and you've got a feast!

You might even include a fresh green salad, a bottle of Chianti (or grape juice for the kids) and spumoni ice cream for a quick dessert.

Garlic Cheese Bread
Saucy Skillet Lasagna

Saucy Skillet Lasagna

Prep/Total Time: 30 min.

1 pound ground beef
1 can (14-1/2 ounces) diced tomatoes, undrained
2 eggs, lightly beaten
1-1/2 cups ricotta cheese
4 cups Italian baking sauce
1 package (9 ounces) no-cook lasagna noodles
1 cup (4 ounces) shredded part-skim mozzarella cheese, optional

In a large skillet, cook the beef over medium heat until no longer pink; drain. Transfer to a large bowl; stir in tomatoes. In a small bowl, combine the eggs and ricotta cheese.

Return 1 cup meat mixture to the skillet; spread evenly. Layer with 1 cup ricotta mixture, 1-1/2 cups sauce and half of the noodles. Repeat layers. Top with remaining sauce.

Bring to a boil. Reduce heat; cover and simmer for 15-17 minutes or until noodles are tender. Remove from the heat. Sprinkle with mozzarella cheese if desired; let stand for 2 minutes or until cheese is melted. Serve immediately. **Yield:** 6-8 servings.

Editor's Note: This recipe was tested with Barilla Al Forno Italian Baking Sauce, found in the grocery aisle alongside the spaghetti and tomato sauces.

Garlic Cheese Bread

Prep/Total Time: 15 min.

1 cup butter, softened
1 cup (4 ounces) shredded Parmesan cheese
1/2 cup finely chopped onion
1 tablespoon garlic powder
2 teaspoons minced chives
2 teaspoons minced fresh parsley
1 loaf (1 pound) French bread, halved lengthwise
1 cup (4 ounces) shredded part-skim mozzarella cheese
1/2 cup shredded cheddar cheese

In a small bowl, combine the first six ingredients; spread over cut sides of bread. Sprinkle with mozzarella and cheddar cheeses.

Place on an ungreased baking sheet. Broil 4-6 in. from the heat for 2-3 minutes or until lightly browned. Cut into slices. **Yield:** 8 servings.

More Cheese, Please

I like to grate cheddar and mozzarella cheeses at the same time. I always grate more than I need and put the extra in a resealable bag. It really comes in handy when I need cheese for recipes later on.
—*Carol Bourgeois, Mt. Vernon, Washington*

Vegetarian Tacos
Spanish Rice

Vegetarian Tacos

Prep/Total Time: 20 min.

  8 taco shells
  3 cups shredded cabbage
  1 cup sliced onion
  1 cup julienned sweet red pepper
  2 tablespoons vegetable oil
  2 teaspoons sugar
  1 can (15 ounces) black beans, rinsed and drained
  1 cup salsa
  1 can (4 ounces) chopped green chilies
  1 teaspoon chili powder
  1 teaspoon minced garlic
  1/4 teaspoon ground cumin
  1/2 cup shredded cheddar cheese
  1 medium ripe avocado, peeled and sliced

Heat taco shells according to package directions. Meanwhile, in a large skillet, saute the cabbage, onion and red pepper in oil for 5 minutes or until crisp-tender. Sprinkle with sugar.

Stir in the black beans, salsa, chopped green chilies, chili powder, garlic and cumin. Bring to a boil. Reduce heat; cover and simmer for 5 minutes or until heated through.

Spoon the vegetable mixture into the taco shells. Garnish with the shredded cheddar cheese and sliced avocado. **Yield:** 4 servings.

Spanish Rice

Prep/Total Time: 25 min.

✓ Uses less fat, sugar or salt. Includes Nutrition Facts and Diabetic Exchanges.

  1/2 cup chopped onion
  1 tablespoon butter
  2 cups uncooked instant rice
  1 can (14-1/2 ounces) diced tomatoes with mild green chilies, undrained
  1 cup water
  3/4 cup beef broth
  1/2 teaspoon chili powder
  1/4 teaspoon salt
  1/4 teaspoon sugar
  1/4 teaspoon ground cumin
  2 tablespoons minced fresh cilantro

In a large saucepan, saute the onion in butter for 2-3 minutes or until tender. Add the rice; cook and stir for 1-2 minutes.

Stir in the diced tomatoes, water, beef broth, chili powder, salt, sugar and cumin. Bring to a boil. Reduce heat; cover and simmer for 5 minutes. Remove from the heat; let stand for 5 minutes. Sprinkle with minced cilantro. **Yield:** 4 servings.

Nutrition Facts: 1-1/8 cups (prepared with reduced-sodium broth) equals 258 calories, 3 g fat (2 g saturated fat), 9 mg cholesterol, 658 mg sodium, 51 g carbohydrate, 3 g fiber, 5 g protein. **Diabetic Exchanges:** 2-1/2 starch, 1 fat.

Southwestern Fiesta for Four

WHEN cooking time is in short supply, here is a weeknight supper that's fresh, fast and fun for the whole family. Our Test Kitchen traveled south of the border for this nutritious Mexican meal that goes together in just minutes.

They stuffed the yummy Vegetarian Tacos with a blend of sauteed cabbage, sweet red pepper and black beans that's so flavorful and filling, you won't even miss the meat!

Get the kids involved by having them garnish their own tacos. Let them choose from avocado (aguacate) or cheese (queso)—or even a dollop of sour cream (crema agria). And if they're taking Spanish classes in school, you might bring the lesson home by encouraging them to print out a Spanish label for each topping.

Serve these tasty tacos with a colorful side of good-for-you Spanish Rice sprinkled with fresh cilantro. You'll have an easy, streamlined supper your family is likely to request again and again.

All-American Favorites

FORGET about fast-food kiddie meals! Put this casual menu of short-order classics on the table, and even the gloomiest day looks a little brighter. Just watch the pickiest eaters in your household dig right into these diner favorites!

Start with hearty Grilled Ham 'n' Jack Cheese sandwiches from Jayne Ward of Eldon, Missouri, and you have the kind of comfort food that's the stuff of childhood memories. "These sandwiches are fast, filling and nice enough to serve company," Jayne says.

Complete the meal with toasty Herbed Steak Fries and thick, fudge-rippled Cola Floats from our Test Kitchen. What's not to like?

Your family is sure to be pleased with this yummy, all-American meal...and you'll be thrilled to have it all ready in less than 30 minutes!

Grilled Ham 'n' Jack Cheese

Prep/Total Time: 15 min.

4 tablespoons butter, softened
8 slices Texas toast
4 slices sharp cheddar cheese
16 thin slices deli ham
4 slices red onion, optional
4 tablespoons ranch salad dressing
4 slices pepper Jack cheese

Butter one side of each slice of Texas toast. On the unbuttered sides of four slices, layer cheddar cheese, half of the ham, onion if desired and remaining ham; spread with ranch dressing. Top with pepper Jack cheese and remaining toast, buttered side up.

On a hot griddle, cook sandwiches for 3-4 minutes or until bottoms of sandwiches are browned. Carefully turn; cook 2 minutes longer or until cheese is melted. **Yield:** 4 servings.

Herbed Steak Fries

Prep/Total Time: 25 min.

4 cups frozen steak fries
1 tablespoon olive oil
1-1/2 teaspoons dried basil
1-1/2 teaspoons dried parsley flakes
1/4 teaspoon garlic salt
1/4 teaspoon seasoned salt
1/4 cup grated Romano cheese

In a large bowl, combine the first six ingredients; toss to coat. Arrange steak fries in a single layer in a greased 15-in. x 10-in. x 1-in. baking pan. Bake at 450° for 15-

20 minutes or until lightly browned. Sprinkle with cheese. **Yield:** 4 servings.

Cola Floats

Prep/Total Time: 5 min.

4 cups cherry cola, chilled
1 teaspoon vanilla extract
8 scoops fudge ripple ice cream
Whipped cream in a can, optional
4 maraschino cherries

In a pitcher, combine the cherry cola and vanilla extract. Place two scoops of fudge ripple ice cream in each of four chilled glasses. Pour the cola over the ice cream; top each float with whipped cream if desired and a maraschino cherry. **Yield:** 4 servings.

Here's the Scoop

Think an ice cream scoop comes in handy only for scooping ice cream? Try it the next time you plan to serve cantaloupe. The scoop is great for removing the seeds. It can be used for butternut squash, too.
—*Loretta Caira, Waltham, Massachusetts*

Cola Floats
Grilled Ham 'n' Jack Cheese
Herbed Steak Fries

Home-Cooked Comfort Food

SOME FOODS just have a homey feel about them. They may bring back warm childhood memories of a delicious meal cooking on the stove...or of loved ones who prepared those wonderful dishes that made you feel so cared for and content. Guess that's why they call it "comfort food!"

Both of these fast and fabulous reader favorites—Smothered Pork Chops and Tossed Salad with Pine Nuts—fit the above description. The Smothered Pork Chops shared by Simone Greene of Winchester, Virginia can be prepared in a flash using convenient stuffing mix. But they boast a delicious from-scratch flavor and will fill your house with the mouth-watering scent of simmering apples, cinnamon and brown sugar.

"It's a dish my mom used to make when I was still living at home," Simone recalls. "The sweetness of the apple mixture makes such a nice complement to the savory stuffing and chops, and the aroma of everything cooking on the stove is wonderful."

Tossed Salad with Pine Nuts is another nostalgic winner for anyone who frequently enjoyed green salads as a side dish for meals. The salad from Alice Tremont of Rochester Hills, Michigan has lots of blue cheese flavor and a crunch from pine nuts. Topped with raspberry vinaigrette, it couldn't be much easier to toss together on a busy night.

Alice says she often serves the salad on special occasions, and it always gets compliments. Adding strips of grilled chicken turns it into a fuss-free main dish that's sure to satisfy.

The next time you need a little TLC or just want a delicious home-style dinner, try these tender pork chops and tempting tossed salad. You may find that they bring back special memories of your own.

Tossed Salad with Pine Nuts
Smothered Pork Chops

Smothered Pork Chops

Prep/Total Time: 30 min.

- 1 package (6 ounces) chicken stuffing mix
- 4 boneless pork loin chops (6 ounces *each*)
- 1 tablespoon butter
- 4 medium apples, peeled and cut into wedges
- 1/2 cup packed brown sugar
- 1/4 cup water
- 1/4 teaspoon salt
- 1/4 teaspoon ground cinnamon

Prepare the chicken stuffing mix according to the package directions. Meanwhile, in a large skillet, cook the pork chops in butter over medium heat for 2-3 minutes on each side or until lightly browned. Stir in the apple wedges, brown sugar, water and salt. Bring to a boil. Reduce heat; cover and simmer for 8-10 minutes or until apples are tender.

Top with stuffing; sprinkle with cinnamon. Cook, uncovered, over medium heat for 10-12 minutes or until a meat thermometer reads 160°. **Yield:** 4 servings.

Tossed Salad with Pine Nuts

Prep/Total Time: 10 min.

- 5 cups spring mix salad greens
- 1 small red onion, thinly sliced
- 1 cup (4 ounces) crumbled blue cheese
- 1/2 cup pine nuts, toasted
- 1/4 to 1/3 cup raspberry vinaigrette

In a large salad bowl, combine the greens and onion. Sprinkle with the blue cheese and pine nuts. Drizzle with the vinaigrette; toss to coat. Serve immediately. **Yield:** 6-7 servings.

Special Dinner Starring Steak

HAVING company over for supper? You won't have to spend hours in the kitchen when your menu includes these speedy dishes that serve six. Not only are they quick to fix, but they're sure to make guests feel like you fussed.

You'll get the event off to a sensational start with Wild Rice-Stuffed Steaks from Ardith Baker, Beaverton, Oregon. Accent them with Sauteed Garlic Mushrooms shared by Joan Schroeder of Pinedale, Wyoming and add Bacon-Swiss Tossed Salad from Heather Koetsier of Grand Rapids, Michigan.

Wild Rice-Stuffed Steaks

Prep/Total Time: 30 min.

    1 package (6.2 ounces) fast-cooking long grain
      and wild rice mix
1/4 cup chopped green onions
    6 New York strip steaks (about 12 ounces
      each)
1/2 cup teriyaki sauce, *divided*

Cook rice according to package directions for microwave; cool. Stir in onions. Cut a pocket in each steak by slicing to within 1/2 in. of bottom. Stuff each with 1/4 cup rice mixture; secure with toothpicks. Brush steaks with 2 tablespoons teriyaki sauce.

Place on a broiler pan. Broil 4-6 in. from the heat for 4-6 minutes. Turn steaks; brush with 2 tablespoons teriyaki sauce. Broil 6-8 minutes longer or until meat reaches desired doneness (for medium-rare, a meat thermometer should read 145°; medium, 160°; well-done, 170°), basting frequently with remaining sauce. Discard the toothpicks. **Yield:** 6 servings.

Sauteed Garlic Mushrooms

Prep/Total Time: 15 min.

3/4 pound sliced fresh mushrooms
    2 to 3 teaspoons minced garlic
    1 tablespoon seasoned bread crumbs
1/3 cup butter, cubed

In a large skillet, saute the mushrooms, garlic and bread crumbs in butter until mushrooms are tender. **Yield:** 6 servings.

Bacon-Swiss Tossed Salad

Prep/Total Time: 10 min.

    4 cups torn romaine
    1 cup (4 ounces) shredded Swiss cheese
3/4 cup real bacon bits
1/2 cup salted cashews
DRESSING:
    3 tablespoons brown sugar
    2 tablespoons water
    2 tablespoons red wine vinegar
    2 tablespoons olive oil
1/4 teaspoon dried minced onion
1/4 teaspoon poppy seeds
1/4 teaspoon ground mustard
Dash salt

In a large bowl, combine the romaine, cheese, bacon and cashews. In a jar with a tight-fitting lid, combine the dressing ingredients; shake well. Pour over salad and toss to coat. Serve immediately. **Yield:** 6 servings.

Wild Rice-Stuffed Steaks
Sauteed Garlic Mushrooms
Bacon-Swiss Tossed Salad

Quick Chicken Cordon Bleu
Almond Rice Pilaf

Classic But Fast Chicken

WHEN time's tight, busy cooks look for delicious recipes that can be prepared in a hurry. And the two fuss-free dishes shared here prove that easy and impressive go hand in hand.

Classic chicken cordon bleu is remade with a need for speed in this quick-to-fix microwave version from Louise Gilbert. The Quesnel, British Columbia reader relies on ham and Swiss cheese from the deli, plus an easy seasoning mix, to flavor Quick Chicken Cordon Bleu.

"If your family prefers, you can substitute cheddar cheese for the Swiss," Louise notes.

Serve it with a side of Almond Rice Pilaf from Mary Jo Nikolaus of Mansfield, Ohio. "Whenever I want to vary a menu from routine potatoes, other vegetables or noodles, I prepare this rice dish," she explains. "It goes well with grilled or broiled meats."

Round out the meal with cubes of fresh watermelon or any other favorite fruit. In no time at all, your family will be running to the table for this satisfying supper before heading off to evening activities.

Quick Chicken Cordon Bleu

Prep/Total Time: 25 min.

    4 boneless skinless chicken breast halves (6 ounces *each*)
    4 thin slices deli ham
    2 slices Swiss cheese, halved
1/4 cup butter, melted
    1 envelope seasoned coating mix

Flatten chicken to 1/4-in. thickness. Place ham and cheese down the center of each; roll up and secure with toothpicks. Place butter and coating mix in separate shallow bowls. Dip chicken in butter, then roll in coating mix.

Place in a greased 2-qt. microwave-safe dish. Cover loosely and microwave on high for 5-7 minutes. Turn chicken over; cook 5-6 minutes longer or until juices run clear. Let stand for 5 minutes. Discard toothpicks. **Yield:** 4 servings.

Editor's Note: This recipe was tested in a 1,100-watt microwave.

Almond Rice Pilaf

Prep/Total Time: 25 min.

3/4 cup chopped onion
1/2 cup slivered almonds
    1 tablespoon butter
    2 cups chicken broth
    2 cups uncooked instant rice
1/2 cup frozen peas
1/2 teaspoon salt
1/4 teaspoon pepper

In a large skillet, saute onion and almonds in butter for 5-6 minutes or until onion is tender and almonds are golden brown.

Add the chicken broth. Bring to a boil. Stir in the rice, peas, salt and pepper. Cover and remove from the heat. Let stand for 6-8 minutes or until liquid is absorbed. **Yield:** 4 servings.

Flattening Chicken Breasts

PLAN on making Quick Chicken Cordon Bleu (recipe at top) for dinner? Use the following technique to easily flatten the chicken.

Place the boneless chicken breast between two pieces of waxed paper. Starting in the center of the chicken and working out to the edges, lightly pound it with a meat mallet's flat side. Continue until you achieve an even 1/4-inch thickness.

Flavors of The Southwest

DON'T MISS OUT on the zippy flavor of this swift southwestern supper. These reader recipes are ideal for weeknights—both can be ready in 30 minutes!

Fast-cooking Basil Pork Chops are sure to make a regular appearance on your table as soon as you taste them. The glazed chops shared by Lisa Gilliland of Fort Collins, Colorado get their great flavor from a little brown sugar, chili powder and dried basil.

Pair these mild chops with Salsa Pasta 'n' Beans from Laura Perry of Exton, Pennsylvania. Her side dish is well-seasoned with cumin, cilantro and salsa.

For people who like even more spice, it's easy to change the salsa to a medium or hot variety. Or you can try using a can of black beans with jalapeno slices in place of the red beans.

Basil Pork Chops

Prep/Total Time: 25 min.

    1/4 cup packed brown sugar
1-1/2 teaspoons dried basil
    1/2 teaspoon salt
    1/2 teaspoon chili powder
      2 tablespoons vegetable oil, *divided*
      4 boneless pork loin chops (1/2 inch thick and 4 ounces *each*)

In a small bowl, combine the brown sugar, basil, salt and chili powder. Gradually stir in 1 tablespoon oil until crumbly. Rub over both sides of pork chops.

In a large skillet, cook pork in remaining oil over medium heat for 7-8 minutes on each side or until juices run clear. **Yield:** 4 servings.

Salsa Pasta 'n' Beans

Prep/Total Time: 25 min.

    8 ounces uncooked bow tie pasta
1/2 cup chopped onion
      1 medium sweet yellow pepper, chopped
      1 tablespoon olive oil
      2 teaspoons minced garlic
      1 can (16 ounces) red beans, rinsed and drained
3/4 cup vegetable broth
3/4 cup salsa
      2 teaspoons ground cumin
1/3 cup minced fresh cilantro

Cook pasta according to package directions. Meanwhile, in a large skillet, saute onion and yellow pepper in oil for 3-4 minutes or until crisp-tender. Add garlic; cook 1-2 minutes longer or until tender.

Stir in the beans, broth, salsa and cumin. Bring to a boil. Reduce heat; simmer, uncovered, for 5-6 minutes or until heated through. Drain pasta; stir into bean mixture. Sprinkle with cilantro. **Yield:** 4 servings.

Salsa Pasta 'n' Beans
Basil Pork Chops

Super Salad And Sandwich

SOMETIMES the chilliest weather can make for the warmest memories. This winter season, ask friends over for a frosty afternoon of skating, sledding, a cross-country hike in the hills or just building a snowman together. Then cap off the day with some fabulous food—the made-in-minutes menu shared here.

Come indoors to toasty Grilled Sourdough Clubs from Kristina Franklin of Clarkston, Washington. With ham, turkey and bacon, these hearty sandwiches appeal to all ages and grill up in no time.

Team them with colorful and refreshing Tuscan Bean Salad sent in by Cori Rothe from Livermore, California. It's jam-packed with wonderful flavor and the easy convenience of canned and jarred ingredients.

For a naturally sweet ending to a great-tasting meal, serve juicy wedges of fresh pear or apple with caramel sauce for dipping.

Grilled Sourdough Clubs

Prep/Total Time: 20 min.

12 slices sourdough bread
6 slices cheddar cheese
1/2 pound thinly sliced deli turkey
1/4 teaspoon garlic powder
1/2 pound thinly sliced deli ham
12 bacon strips, cooked and drained
2 tablespoons butter, softened

On six slices of bread, layer cheese and turkey; sprinkle with garlic powder. Top with ham, bacon and remaining bread. Spread butter over the top and bottom of each sandwich. Cook on an indoor grill or panini maker for 3-4 minutes or until bread is toasted and cheese is melted. **Yield:** 6 servings.

Tuscan Bean Salad

Prep/Total Time: 30 min.

2 cans (15 ounces *each*) white kidney *or* cannellini beans, rinsed and drained
1 jar (6-1/2 ounces) marinated artichoke hearts, undrained
1 cup roasted sweet red peppers, cut into 1-inch strips
3/4 cup sliced ripe olives
1/2 cup chopped red onion
1/4 cup oil-packed sun-dried tomatoes, chopped
2 tablespoons olive oil
2 tablespoons white balsamic vinegar
1/4 teaspoon salt
1/4 teaspoon pepper
1/4 cup fresh basil leaves, thinly sliced

In a large salad bowl, combine the first 10 ingredients. Refrigerate for 20 minutes or until serving. Stir in basil. Serve with a slotted spoon. **Yield:** 6 servings.

Tuscan Bean Salad
Grilled Sourdough Clubs

More Pork Chops, Please!

Hash Brown Apple Pancake
Maple-Pecan Pork Chops

TO BRING variety to dinnertime, why not introduce your family to new meal combos that just may become treasured favorites?

For a standout shortcut supper, start with this change-of-pace menu served up by our Test Kitchen and guaranteed to make any occasion special.

Begin by simmering the luscious Maple-Pecan Pork Chops in apple juice on the stovetop, then top them with sweet maple syrup and crunchy pecans.

Meanwhile, wedges of crispy Hash Brown Apple Pancake will make a fast and fabulous side dish the whole family will savor. Laced with onion, chives and Swiss cheese, they take only minutes and would go well with all kinds of entrees.

Round out the satisfying and special meal with a packaged frozen vegetable medley that's a snap to zap in the microwave...then wait for the raves!

Maple-Pecan Pork Chops

Prep/Total Time: 30 min.

- 2 tablespoons spicy brown mustard
- 1/2 teaspoon pepper
- 1/2 cup maple syrup, *divided*
- 4 bone-in pork loin chops (3/4 inch thick)
- 1 tablespoon butter
- 1/2 cup unsweetened apple juice
- 1 cup pecan halves

In a small bowl, combine the mustard, pepper and 2 teaspoons maple syrup. Brush over both sides of the pork chops. In a large nonstick skillet, brown the pork in butter over medium heat for 2-3 minutes on each side. Add the apple juice. Reduce heat; cover and simmer for 15-20 minutes or until the meat is tender. Remove pork chops and keep warm.

Add pecans and remaining syrup to the skillet; cook and stir for 1-2 minutes or until blended. Serve over the pork chops. **Yield:** 4 servings.

Hash Brown Apple Pancake

Prep/Total Time: 20 min.

- 1-1/4 cups frozen shredded hash brown potatoes, thawed
- 1/2 cup finely chopped apple
- 1/4 cup finely chopped onion
- 1 tablespoon snipped chives
- 1/4 teaspoon salt
- 1/4 teaspoon pepper
- 2 tablespoons butter, *divided*
- 2 tablespoons vegetable oil, *divided*
- 1/2 cup shredded Swiss cheese

In a small bowl, combine the hash browns, apple, onion, chives, salt and pepper. In a large nonstick skillet, melt 1 tablespoon butter with 1 tablespoon oil over medium-high heat. Spread half of the hash brown mixture in an even layer in skillet. Sprinkle with cheese; top with remaining hash browns. Press mixture gently into skillet. Cook for 5 minutes or until bottom is browned.

Invert pancake onto a plate. Heat remaining butter and oil in the skillet. Slide pancake, browned side up, into skillet. Cook 5 minutes longer or until bottom is browned and cheese is melted. Slide pancake onto a plate; cut into wedges. **Yield:** 4 servings.

Onion Ease

Whenever I chop an onion, I always chop an extra one and refrigerate it in a clean, tightly sealed jar. The odor can't escape into my refrigerator or linger on plastic containers. And the next time I need to use a chopped onion, it's ready to go without any tears.
—*Patty Reymann, Dayton, Ohio*

Herbed Beans and Carrots
Chicken a la King

of seasonings accents the fresh flavor of this crisp side dish that cooks in the microwave in a jiffy.

With its comforting taste and easy prep, this streamlined supper is sure to become a frequent addition to your weekly menu plan.

Chicken a la King

Prep/Total Time: 20 min.

✓ Uses less fat, sugar or salt. Includes Nutrition Facts and Diabetic Exchanges.

- 1/2 cup chopped celery
- 1/2 cup chopped green pepper
- 2 tablespoons butter
- 2 cans (10-3/4 ounces *each*) condensed cream of chicken soup, undiluted
- 1 cup milk
- 1/4 teaspoon pepper
- 2 cups cubed cooked chicken
- 1 jar (6 ounces) sliced mushrooms, drained
- 1/4 cup diced pimientos
- 6 slices bread, toasted and halved

In a large skillet, saute celery and green pepper in butter until crisp-tender. Stir in the soup, milk and pepper. Add the chicken, mushrooms and pimientos. Reduce heat; simmer, uncovered, for 4-6 minutes or until heated through. Serve over toast. **Yield:** 4 servings.

Nutrition Facts: 1-1/4 cups (prepared with reduced-fat butter, reduced-fat soup and reduced-calorie bread) equals 370 calories, 12 g fat (5 g saturated fat), 86 mg cholesterol, 1,069 mg sodium, 38 g carbohydrate, 5 g fiber, 30 g protein. **Diabetic Exchanges:** 3 lean meat, 2 starch, 1 vegetable.

Herbed Beans and Carrots

Prep/Total Time: 10 min.

✓ Uses less fat, sugar or salt. Includes Nutrition Facts and Diabetic Exchanges.

- 1/2 pound fresh green beans, trimmed
- 3 medium carrots, julienned
- 2 tablespoons water
- 2 tablespoons butter
- 1/2 teaspoon dried rosemary, crushed
- 1/4 teaspoon salt
- 1/4 teaspoon dried thyme
- 1/8 teaspoon lemon-pepper seasoning

Place the beans and carrots in a microwave-safe 8-in. square dish. Add water. Cover and microwave on high for 3-4 minutes or until crisp-tender; drain. Stir in the butter and seasonings. **Yield:** 4 servings.

Editor's Note: This recipe was tested in a 1,100-watt microwave.

Nutrition Facts: 3/4 cup (prepared with reduced-fat butter) equals 63 calories, 3 g fat (2 g saturated fat), 10 mg cholesterol, 216 mg sodium, 9 g carbohydrate, 3 g fiber, 2 g protein. **Diabetic Exchanges:** 1-1/2 vegetable, 1/2 fat.

Family-Pleasing Classics Fast

YOU WANT to put a hearty dinner on the table, but some nights you're so squeezed for time. Well, here's a warm and welcoming combo that's just the thing folks crave, especially when the weather is cold.

And a heartwarming bonus for busy cooks? You can have this good-tasting, good-for-you fare ready to serve your family in minutes.

Start with Jennifer Eggebraaten's swift Chicken a la King ladled over toast. "This is a quick-and-easy version of a dish that's been around a long time," writes the Hastings, Michigan cook.

Convenient canned soup creates the creamy sauce that gets color from celery, green pepper and pimientos. "It's a great recipe for using up leftover chicken or turkey and one that my family really enjoys," Jennifer adds.

To round out the meal, serve buttery Herbed Beans and Carrots from our home economists. A tasty blend

Fare with 'Far East' Flavor

WHEN you're not in the mood for a heavy, complicated dinner, turn to the delightful menu here. Asian Beef and Noodles, a sensational stir-fry from Laura Shull Stenberg of Wyoming, Minnesota, is a one-dish meal that's long on flavor but short on prep time, cost and cleanup. This colorful family favorite takes only a handful of everyday ingredients.

"It's great with a pound of ground turkey instead of beef," Laura adds.

Want a swift and tangy side dish? Serve canned pineapple slices alongside the stir-fry as shown in the photo at right.

For dessert on the double, Melissa Van Bramer's luscious Snickerdoodle Sundaes can't be beat. "I was baking sugar cookies with my two daughters when a friend brought over some cinnamon ice cream," recalls the Pickerington, Ohio reader. "The two items were a perfect match.

"When I made the dessert again, the caramel was a natural addition," Melissa notes. "It's so simple but nice enough to fix for guests."

Snickerdoodle Sundaes
Asian Beef and Noodles

Asian Beef and Noodles

Prep/Total Time: 20 min.

- 1 pound ground beef
- 2 packages (3 ounces *each*) Oriental ramen noodles, crumbled
- 2-1/2 cups water
- 2 cups frozen broccoli stir-fry vegetables
- 1/4 teaspoon ground ginger
- 2 tablespoons thinly sliced green onion

In a large skillet, cook beef over medium heat for 4-5 minutes or until no longer pink; drain. Add the contents of one ramen noodle flavoring packet; stir until dissolved. Remove beef and keep warm.

In the same skillet, combine the water, vegetables, ginger, noodles and contents of remaining flavoring packet. Bring to a boil. Reduce heat; cover and simmer for 3-4 minutes or until noodles are tender, stirring occasionally. Return beef to the pan; cook for 2-3 minutes or until heated through. Stir in onion. **Yield:** 4 servings.

Snickerdoodle Sundaes

Prep/Total Time: 30 min.

- 1 package (17-1/2 ounces) sugar cookie mix
- 2 cups cinnamon ice cream *or* ice cream of your choice
- 1/2 cup caramel ice cream topping

Prepare and bake cookies according to package directions. Set aside 8 cookies (save remaining cookies for another use). Place 2 cookies in each serving bowl. Top with 1/2 cup ice cream; drizzle with 2 tablespoons caramel topping. **Yield:** 4 servings.

Browning Ground Beef

When I'm browning ground beef in a skillet, I use a shortening cutter (also called a pastry blender) to chop up the beef. (Don't use it on nonstick pans that can be scratched by metal.) I prefer my ground beef finely chopped, and I've found that the cutter works much easier and faster than the usual spatula.
—*Marsha Marten, Lenexa, Kansas*

Mouth-Watering Mexican Spread

ON CHILLY DAYS, nothing beats the comfort and ease of a bowl of soup. And this zippy chili-like version served with homemade biscuits requires just a few minutes of preparation.

Enjoy this duo at lunch, and you'll have time for an afternoon siesta. Or turn the pair into a complete Mexican dinner by rounding out the meal with a tossed green salad.

Hearty servings of Refried Bean Soup are always welcome in Barbara Dean's Littleton, Colorado home. "My husband and I love the flavor of this yummy soup," Barbara says. "It's very quick and easy to put together, and you can add any garnishes you like."

As an accompaniment, bake a pan of Mexican Drop Biscuits. "We love these golden biscuits with big bowls of soup," Teresa Spencer notes from Wauwatosa, Wisconsin. "The green chilies and taco cheese add extra zip to everyday meals."

Refried Bean Soup

Prep/Total Time: 30 min.

    1 can (28 ounces) crushed tomatoes
1/2 cup chopped onion
1/2 teaspoon minced garlic
    1 can (31 ounces) refried beans
    1 can (14-1/2 ounces) chicken broth
    1 tablespoon minced fresh cilantro
    5 corn tortillas (6 inches), cut into 1/2-inch strips, optional
Sour cream and shredded Monterey Jack cheese, optional

In a large saucepan, bring the tomatoes, onion and garlic to a boil. Reduce heat; simmer, uncovered, for 5 minutes. Stir in the refried beans, broth and cilantro; simmer for 15 minutes.

Meanwhile, if tortilla strips are desired, place strips on a baking sheet. Bake at 350° for 12-15 minutes or until crisp. Garnish soup with tortilla strips. Serve with sour cream and Monterey Jack cheese if desired. **Yield:** 8 servings (2 quarts).

Mexican Drop Biscuits

Prep/Total Time: 20 min.

    2 cups biscuit/baking mix
    1 cup (4 ounces) shredded taco cheese
    1 can (4 ounces) chopped green chilies, undrained
1/2 cup water
    3 tablespoons butter, melted
    1 teaspoon dried parsley flakes
1/4 teaspoon garlic powder
1/4 teaspoon dried oregano
1/4 teaspoon dried thyme
1/8 teaspoon cayenne pepper

In a small bowl, combine the biscuit mix, cheese and chilies. Stir in water just until moistened. Drop into 12 mounds 2 in. apart onto a greased baking sheet. Bake at 450° for 10-15 minutes or until golden brown.

In a small bowl, combine the butter, parsley, garlic powder, oregano, thyme and cayenne pepper; brush over biscuits. Serve warm. **Yield:** 1 dozen.

Refried Bean Soup
Mexican Drop Biscuits

Impressive For Guests

Bacon-Wrapped Green Beans
Southern Pecan Catfish

DO YOU LOVE to entertain? Having friends and family over for dinner makes it all the more enjoyable. But many busy people find it tough to set aside time to prepare a fancy sit-down meal. That's why they're always on the lookout for no-fuss combinations that are quick and taste great.

Here, you'll discover not one but two outstanding dishes that each take a mere 30 minutes to prepare. Together, they make an easy weeknight meal or an elegant menu for company.

For the main course, Mary Ann Griffin's Southern Pecan Catfish is delicious and different. The Saginaw, Michigan reader coats the fish fillets with chopped pecans and tops them with a rich, lemony cream sauce your loved ones are sure to rave about. It's hard to believe that such an impressive-looking entree can be so simple!

As an accompaniment, serve Bacon-Wrapped Green Beans, shared by Julie Hewitt. Bundles of fresh green beans are wrapped in bacon and brushed with a sweet sauce.

"Every time I take these to a luncheon or family dinner, people beg me for the recipe," Julie relates from her Union Mills, Indiana home. "They're delighted when they see that these beans are dressed up with just a handful of ingredients."

Southern Pecan Catfish

Prep/Total Time: 30 min.

1 cup finely chopped pecans, *divided*
1/2 cup cornmeal
1 teaspoon salt, *divided*
1 teaspoon pepper, *divided*
4 catfish fillets (6 ounces *each*)
1/2 cup butter, *divided*
1/2 cup heavy whipping cream
2 tablespoons lemon juice
1 to 2 tablespoons minced fresh parsley

In a shallow bowl, combine 1/2 cup pecans, cornmeal, 1/2 teaspoon salt and 1/2 teaspoon pepper. Coat catfish with pecan mixture. In a large skillet, melt 1/4 cup butter over medium-high heat; fry fillets for 6-7 minutes on each side or until fish flakes easily with a fork. Remove and keep warm.

In the same skillet, melt remaining butter over medium heat. Add the remaining pecans; cook and stir for 1 minute. Add the heavy whipping cream, lemon juice and remaining salt and pepper; cook and stir for 1 minute. Stir in the parsley. Spoon the sauce over the catfish. **Yield:** 4 servings.

Bacon-Wrapped Green Beans

Prep/Total Time: 30 min.

3/4 pound fresh green beans
4 bacon strips
3 tablespoons butter, melted
1/4 cup packed brown sugar
1/4 teaspoon garlic salt
1/8 teaspoon soy sauce

Place beans in a large saucepan and cover with water. Bring to a boil. Cook, uncovered, for 8 minutes or until crisp-tender. Meanwhile, in a skillet, cook bacon over medium heat until cooked but not crisp, about 3 minutes. Remove to paper towels.

Drain beans; place about 12 beans on each bacon strip. Wrap bacon around beans and secure with toothpicks. Place on an ungreased baking sheet.

In a small bowl, combine the butter, brown sugar, garlic salt and soy sauce; brush over bundles. Bake at 400° for 10-15 minutes or until bacon is crisp. **Yield:** 4 servings.

White or Yellow Cornmeal?

THE ONLY DIFFERENCE between white and yellow cornmeal is the color of the corn used. Different regions of the United States tend to prefer one color of cornmeal to the other, but white and yellow cornmeal can be used interchangeably in recipes. Try whichever variety you like when preparing delicious Southern Pecan Catfish (recipe at left).

Asparagus-Stuffed Chicken Breasts
Parmesan Orzo

Fresh Fare For Spring

ONCE that first robin or crocus pops up outside, the kitchen is the last place many folks want to be. That's why this fast-to-fix menu sent in by readers is sure to become a mainstay at your table.

Start by using tender asparagus to turn chicken into restaurant-quality fare. You can't get much quicker than Reneé Smith's Asparagus-Stuffed Chicken Breasts, drizzled with a luscious lemon sauce and sprinkled with toasted almonds. "This easy microwave recipe has been a spring favorite for many years," she writes from Clinton Township, Michigan. "I often make it when entertaining, and everyone raves about it."

Pair the elegant entree with simple Parmesan Orzo, shared by Marian Platt of Sequim, Washington. The creamy, cheese-flavored side dish is mildly seasoned with chopped green onions and diced pimientos.

Also serve mandarin oranges as shown in the photo above for a special meal that's fast and flavorful.

Asparagus-Stuffed Chicken Breasts

Prep/Total Time: 25 min.

    2 boneless skinless chicken breast halves (6 ounces *each*)
    1 tablespoon Dijon mustard
    1 green onion, finely chopped
   10 asparagus spears, trimmed
    3 tablespoons crushed butter-flavored crackers
HOLLANDAISE SAUCE:
  1/4 cup butter, cubed
    2 egg yolks
    2 teaspoons lemon juice
    1 teaspoon water
  1/8 teaspoon salt
  1/4 cup sliced almonds, toasted

Flatten chicken to 1/4-in. thickness. Spread with mustard; sprinkle with onion. Place asparagus spears down the center of chicken; fold over and secure with toothpicks if necessary.

Place seam side down in an ungreased 8-in. square microwave-safe dish. Sprinkle with cracker crumbs. Microwave, uncovered, on high for 6-8 minutes or until chicken juices run clear. Keep warm.

For sauce, in a small microwave-safe bowl, melt butter. Gradually whisk in egg yolks, lemon juice, water and salt. Microwave, uncovered, at 30% power for 30 seconds or until mixture reaches 160° and is thickened, stirring once. Spoon over chicken. Sprinkle with almonds. Remove toothpicks. **Yield:** 2 servings.

Editor's Note: This recipe was tested in a 1,100-watt microwave.

Parmesan Orzo

Prep/Total Time: 15 min.

  2/3 cup uncooked orzo pasta
  1/3 cup chopped green onions
    2 tablespoons spreadable chive and onion cream cheese
    2 tablespoons milk
    1 tablespoon grated Parmesan cheese
  1/8 teaspoon salt
  1/8 teaspoon pepper
    2 tablespoons diced pimientos

Cook pasta according to package directions, adding onions during the last 2 minutes of cooking time. Meanwhile, in a small mixing bowl, beat the cream cheese, milk, Parmesan cheese, salt and pepper until smooth; stir in pimientos. Drain pasta; add to cream cheese mixture and toss to coat. **Yield:** 2 servings.

Flavors of
The Campfire

LOOKING FORWARD to warmer weather? Get a jump start on the summer season with quick campfire cuisine. It'll remind everyone that days are getting longer and summer fun is just around the corner! Pick a night when the whole family can take a break from the usual routine, and keep cleanup to a minimum with paper plates and napkins.

For a hearty side dish that brings real barbecue flavor to the table any time of year, serve Janet Doherty's sweet Sidesaddle Pork 'n' Beans. "My family just loves this recipe," notes the Belpre, Ohio cook.

Pair it with tasty Corn Dog Twists, sent in by Melissa Tatum of Greensboro, North Carolina. Kids will have as much fun making these cute "twists" on hot dogs as eating them! (Don't forget to offer bowls of relish, mustard and ketchup for easy dipping.)

Finally, round up Texas Two-Step Slaw. Shared by Sharon Wencel of Austin, Texas, this colorful coleslaw is jazzed up with ranch dressing. "It comes together in only 15 minutes, but I've found that chilling it awhile helps blend the flavors," she says.

Sidesaddle Pork 'n' Beans
Prep/Total Time: 20 min.

    1/2 pound bulk pork sausage
    1/3 cup chopped onion
      1 can (15-3/4 ounces) pork and beans
    1/4 cup barbecue sauce
      3 tablespoons honey
      2 tablespoons ketchup
    1/8 teaspoon salt, optional
    1/8 teaspoon dried rosemary, crushed
    1/8 teaspoon dried thyme
    1/8 teaspoon Cajun seasoning

In a large skillet, cook the sausage and onion over medium heat until meat is no longer pink; drain. Stir in the beans, barbecue sauce, honey, ketchup and seasonings. Bring to a boil. Reduce heat; simmer, uncovered, for 5-8 minutes or until slightly thickened. **Yield:** 8 servings.

Corn Dog Twists
Prep/Total Time: 20 min.

      1 tube (11-1/2 ounces) refrigerated corn
        bread twists
      8 hot dogs
      1 tablespoon butter, melted
      1 tablespoon grated Parmesan cheese

Separate corn bread twists; wrap one strip around each hot dog. Brush with butter; sprinkle with Parmesan cheese. Place on a lightly greased baking sheet. Bake at 375° for 11-13 minutes or until golden brown. **Yield:** 8 servings.

Texas Two-Step Slaw
Prep/Total Time: 15 min.

✓ Uses less fat, sugar or salt. Includes Nutrition Facts and Diabetic Exchanges.

      3 cups coleslaw mix
    1/4 cup Mexicorn, drained
      1 jalapeno pepper, seeded and chopped
      2 tablespoons chopped red onion
      1 tablespoon minced fresh cilantro
    1/2 cup shredded cheddar cheese
    1/2 cup ranch salad dressing
  1-1/2 teaspoons lime juice
    1/2 teaspoon ground cumin

In a large bowl, combine the first six ingredients. In a small bowl, combine the salad dressing, lime juice and cumin. Pour over the coleslaw and toss to coat. Refrigerate until serving. **Yield:** 8 servings.

Editor's Note: When cutting or seeding hot peppers, use rubber or plastic gloves to protect your hands. Avoid touching your face.

Nutrition Facts: 1/2 cup (prepared with reduced-fat cheese and fat-free dressing) equals 58 calories, 2 g fat (1 g saturated fat), 5 mg cholesterol, 269 mg sodium, 9 g carbohydrate, 1 g fiber, 2 g protein. **Diabetic Exchange:** 1/2 starch.

Corn Dog Twists
Texas Two-Step Slaw
Sidesaddle Pork 'n' Beans

Short List Of Ingredients

WHEN time is tight and you need to put dinner on the table right away, just count to three! Each of these recipes requires only three ingredients. And, served together, the three dishes create one mouth-watering menu. What could be better than that?

A flavorful sauce marinates the juicy lamb chops from Mitzi Sentiff, Alexandria, Virginia. Complement them with Maple Baby Carrots shared by Karen Wren of Freedom, Maine and add French Onion Drop Biscuits from Galelah Dowell of Fairland, Oklahoma.

Glazed Lamb Chops

Prep/Total Time: 25 min.

1/3 cup orange juice concentrate
1/3 cup barbecue sauce
   4 lamb loin chops (1 inch thick and about 5 ounces *each*)

In a small saucepan, combine the orange juice concentrate and barbecue sauce. Cook and stir over medium heat for 3-4 minutes or until heated through; set aside 1/3 cup for serving. Spread remaining sauce over both sides of lamb chops. Place on a broiler pan.

Broil the lamb chops 4-6 in. from the heat for 10-15 minutes on each side or until the meat reaches the desired doneness (for medium-rare, a meat thermometer should read 145°; medium, 160°; well-done, 170°). Serve with the reserved sauce. **Yield:** 4 servings.

Maple Baby Carrots

Prep/Total Time: 10 min.

   1 package (16 ounces) fresh baby carrots
1/4 cup butter, cubed
   2 tablespoons maple syrup

Place carrots and a small amount of water in a 1-1/2 -qt. microwave-safe dish. Cover and microwave on high for 4-6 minutes or until crisp-tender; drain. Add butter; microwave for 30 seconds or until melted. Drizzle with syrup and toss to coat. **Yield:** 4 servings.

Editor's Note: This recipe was tested in a 1,100-watt microwave.

French Onion Drop Biscuits

Prep/Total Time: 20 min.

✓ Uses less fat, sugar or salt. Includes Nutrition Facts and Diabetic Exchanges.

   2 cups biscuit/baking mix
   1 carton (8 ounces) French onion dip
1/4 cup milk

In a bowl, combine the baking mix and onion dip. Stir in milk just until moistened. Drop by rounded tablespoonfuls 2 in. apart onto a baking sheet coated with nonstick cooking spray. Bake at 450° for 10-14 minutes or until golden brown. Serve warm. **Yield:** 1 dozen.

Nutrition Facts: 1 biscuit (prepared with reduced-fat biscuit mix, fat-free milk and reduced-fat French onion dip) equals 99 calories, 2 g fat (1 g saturated fat), 6 mg cholesterol, 357 mg sodium, 16 g carbohydrate, trace fiber, 3 g protein. **Diabetic Exchanges:** 1 starch, 1/2 fat.

Maple Baby Carrots
Glazed Lamb Chops
French Onion Drop Biscuits

Summertime Sandwich Plate

THOSE LEGENDARY "lazy days of summer" can be anything but for busy families...especially at dinnertime. But you can serve a mouth-watering meal in less than 30 minutes with this quick and casual menu of reader-favorite recipes.

"My day starts at 5:30 a.m. and doesn't end until 10:30 p.m.," writes Tammy Ellis of Boardman, Oregon. The on-the-go mom juggles a full-time job with community and church activities plus her kids' sports schedules. So she has learned to cut time in the kitchen with easy recipes that are economical, too.

Savory Hamburger Hoagies, served with small bowls of au jus gravy for dipping, make the most of a few handy convenience items. "My family fell in love with these sandwiches the first time I made them," she says.

For a colorful and delicious side dish, add a hefty helping of Lazy Days Potato Salad. Margaret Wilson of Hemet, California cuts prep time by using canned potatoes. Slice in some crunchy veggies and diced dill pickles, then drizzle it all with a creamy dressing seasoned with garlic and mustard.

"If time allows, chill the potato salad for an hour or even overnight," Margaret adds.

Hamburger Hoagies
Lazy Days Potato Salad

Hamburger Hoagies

Prep/Total Time: 15 min.

1 pound ground beef
1 teaspoon seasoned salt
1/2 cup spreadable garden vegetable cream cheese
4 hoagie buns, split and toasted
1 jar (12 ounces) beef au jus gravy, warmed

In a bowl, combine the beef and seasoned salt. Shape into four 7-in. x 2-1/2-in. oval-shaped patties. In a large skillet, cook patties over medium-high heat for 3-4 minutes on each side or until meat is no longer pink.

Spread cream cheese over cut side of buns. Place a hamburger patty on each bun bottom; replace bun tops. Serve with au jus gravy for dipping. **Yield:** 4 servings.

Lazy Days Potato Salad

Prep/Total Time: 20 min.

✓ Uses less fat, sugar or salt. Includes Nutrition Facts and Diabetic Exchanges.

1 can (14-1/2 ounces) sliced potatoes, drained
1/4 cup thinly sliced celery
1/4 cup sliced green onions
1/4 cup shredded carrot
1 can (2-1/4 ounces) sliced ripe olives, drained
2 tablespoons chopped dill pickle
1/2 cup mayonnaise
1 to 2 tablespoons Dijon mustard
1/4 teaspoon garlic powder
1/4 teaspoon pepper

In a large bowl, combine the first six ingredients. In a small bowl, combine the mayonnaise, mustard, garlic powder and pepper. Drizzle over potato mixture and toss to coat. Cover and refrigerate until serving. **Yield:** 4 servings.

Nutrition Facts: 2/3 cup (prepared with fat-free mayonnaise) equals 93 calories, 3 g fat (trace saturated fat), 3 mg cholesterol, 780 mg sodium, 16 g carbohydrate, 3 g fiber, 1 g protein. **Diabetic Exchange:** 1 starch.

"Berry" Fast Finale

For years, a local restaurant served this simple summer dessert. They offered a large bowl of ripe strawberries with stems alongside dishes of sour cream and brown sugar. The strawberries dipped first in the sour cream and then the brown sugar are a tantalizing treat that people of all ages enjoy.
—Lillian Torres, Dover, New Hampshire

Ziti Supper
Spinach Flatbreads

Cuisine with Convenience

FOR HER FABULOUS and fuss-free Ziti Supper, Elaine Spevak of Jacksonville, Florida turns to store-bought spaghetti sauce, then dresses it up with crisp veggies, tangy olives, fresh parsley and cheese. The result? A hearty entree that's "quick to prepare and sure to please," Elaine relates. "This is my family's very favorite pasta dish."

Instead of the same old garlic bread on the side, serve up wedges of toasty Spinach Flatbreads from Kristen Westbrook of Pittsburgh, Pennsylvania.

"I always seemed to have some fresh spinach that would spoil before I could use it all," Kristen explains. "So I started making these quick, delicious flatbreads. They're lower in fat, work well with almost any vegetable I have on hand and can double as a light lunch."

To cap off this filling meal, serve individual dishes of light and refreshing lemon sorbet.

Ziti Supper

Prep/Total Time: 30 min.

1-1/4 cups uncooked ziti *or* small tube pasta
3/4 cup chopped green pepper
1/2 cup finely chopped onion
1/2 cup finely chopped celery
1/2 teaspoon minced garlic
2 tablespoons olive oil
2 tablespoons butter
1 jar (14 ounces) spaghetti sauce with meat
1/4 cup chopped pimiento-stuffed olives
1/4 cup minced fresh parsley
1/2 cup shredded cheddar cheese

Cook pasta according to package directions. Meanwhile, in a large skillet, saute green pepper, onion, celery and garlic in oil and butter for 4-5 minutes or until tender.

Stir in the spaghetti sauce, olives and parsley. Bring to a boil. Reduce heat; simmer, uncovered, for 10-12 minutes or until heated through. Drain the pasta; stir into skillet. Sprinkle with cheese. **Yield:** 4 servings.

Spinach Flatbreads

Prep/Total Time: 20 min.

✓ Uses less fat, sugar or salt. Includes Nutrition Facts and Diabetic Exchanges.

2/3 cup sliced onion
4 teaspoons olive oil, *divided*
4 whole pita flatbreads
2 cups fresh baby spinach
1-1/2 cups (6 ounces) shredded part-skim mozzarella cheese
1/4 teaspoon pepper

In a small skillet, saute onion in 2 teaspoons oil for 2-3 minutes or until tender; set aside. Place pitas on a baking sheet coated with nonstick cooking spray. Brush with the remaining oil. Layer with spinach, sauteed onion and cheese. Sprinkle with pepper. Bake at 425° for 6-8 minutes or until cheese is melted. **Yield:** 4 servings.

Nutrition Facts: 1 flatbread equals 322 calories, 12 g fat (5 g saturated fat), 24 mg cholesterol, 528 mg sodium, 37 g carbohydrate, 2 g fiber, 16 g protein. **Diabetic Exchanges:** 2 starch, 2 lean meat, 1 vegetable.

Special Seafood For Summer

EASY DOES IT when it comes to outdoor entertaining. And our Test Kitchen home economists do it just that way when it comes to planning a casual supper to serve family and friends out on the patio or deck some warm night.

In fact, they've grouped three kitchen-tested recipes that are a natural together. From fish to fettuccine to a lip-smacking lemon pie, the complete meal tastes delicious...and can be table-ready in just half an hour!

Start with Orange Roughy with Cucumber Salsa. The moist fillets are topped with a cool and colorful seven-ingredient salsa. (This summery salsa is so tempting, you just might want to mix up extra bowls for dipping tortilla chips!)

Pair the fish with a warm, buttery side dish of Basil Walnut Fettuccine, studded with toasted nuts and lightly flavored with garlic and basil. The combination of regular and spinach fettuccine is eye-catching, but you can use any flavor or shape of pasta you have on hand.

Finish off your memorable meal with the fresh-squeezed flavor of Poppy Seed Lemon Pie. Guests will love this tangy and fluffy finale to dinner...and never guess how simple it is to prepare.

Orange Roughy with Cucumber Salsa

Prep/Total Time: 20 min.

✓ Uses less fat, sugar or salt. Includes Nutrition Facts and Diabetic Exchanges.

    1 cup chopped cucumber
1/2 cup chopped yellow summer squash
    2 plum tomatoes, chopped
1/4 cup chopped red onion
    1 tablespoon lime juice
    2 teaspoons olive oil
1/4 teaspoon salt
    2 teaspoons lemon-pepper seasoning
    6 orange roughy *or* other whitefish fillets

For salsa, in a small bowl, combine the first seven ingredients; set aside. Sprinkle lemon-pepper over both sides of fillets. Place on a broiler pan coated with non-stick cooking spray. Broil 4-6 in. from the heat for 3-4 minutes on each side or until fish flakes easily with a fork. Serve with cucumber salsa. **Yield:** 6 servings.
Nutrition Facts: 1 fillet with 1/4 cup salsa equals 143 calories, 3 g fat (trace saturated fat), 34 mg cholesterol, 362 mg sodium, 3 g carbohydrate, 1 g fiber, 26 g protein. **Diabetic Exchange:** 4 very lean meat.

Basil Walnut Fettuccine

Prep/Total Time: 20 min.

    6 ounces uncooked fettuccine
    6 ounces uncooked spinach fettuccine
    1 teaspoon minced garlic
    6 tablespoons butter, *divided*
1/4 cup finely chopped walnuts, toasted
    1 tablespoon minced fresh basil *or* 1 teaspoon dried basil
1/4 teaspoon salt
1/8 teaspoon pepper

Cook both kinds of fettuccine according to package directions. In a large skillet, saute the garlic in 1 tablespoon butter for 1 minute. Add the walnuts, basil, salt, pepper and remaining butter; cook and stir for 2 minutes. Drain the fettuccine; add to skillet and toss to coat. **Yield:** 6 servings.

Poppy Seed Lemon Pie

Prep/Total Time: 10 min.

    1 can (14 ounces) sweetened condensed milk
1/3 cup lemonade concentrate
    1 carton (8 ounces) frozen whipped topping, thawed, *divided*
    1 graham cracker crust (9 inches)
    1 tablespoon poppy seeds
   10 to 12 drops yellow food coloring, optional

In a mixing bowl, beat milk and lemonade concentrate until smooth (mixture will begin to thicken). Fold in 2 cups whipped topping. Spread half into the crust.

Add poppy seeds and food coloring, if desired, to the remaining lemon mixture; stir until blended. Spoon over first layer. Spread with the remaining whipped topping. Refrigerate until serving. **Yield:** 6-8 servings.

Poppy Seed Lemon Pie
Basil Walnut Fettuccine
Orange Roughy with Cucumber Salsa

Speedy Sunrise Specialties

WHO SAYS rushed-for-time mornings have to begin with an ordinary breakfast? This nourishing meal will start the day out in a fast and delicious way. You'll need just minutes to put the delightful combination together. In fact, it's so swift and satisfying, you may decide to serve it another day for dinner!

Wake up taste buds with hearty Bacon 'n' Egg Bagels from Chris and Jenny Thackray of Corpus Christi, Texas. Better than fast-food fare, the savory sandwiches with vegetable cream cheese and zesty olives will get 'em to the table in a hurry.

"For a change of pace, prepare them with another flavor of cream cheese spread or speed things up by using cooked bacon warmed in the microwave," the couple suggests.

As a refreshing accompaniment for the bagels, serve Adell Meyer's Breakfast Parfaits. The colorful treats are layered with vanilla yogurt, crunchy almonds, chewy dates and other fruit. The Madison, Wisconsin reader whips them up in no time for breakfast or as an after-school snack.

Served with steaming mugs of coffee for the adults and cold glasses of milk for the kids, this is one morning meal the whole family will enjoy.

Bacon 'n' Egg Bagels

Prep/Total Time: 20 min.

- 4 bagels, split and toasted
- 1/2 cup garden vegetable cheese spread
- 1/2 cup sliced pimiento-stuffed olives
- 8 bacon strips, halved
- 4 eggs
- 4 slices Muenster cheese

Spread each bagel half with cheese spread. Place olives on bagel bottoms; set aside.

In a large skillet, cook bacon over medium heat until crisp. Using a slotted spoon, remove to paper towels; drain, reserving 3 tablespoons drippings. Heat drippings over medium-hot heat. Add eggs; reduce heat to low. Fry until whites are completely set and yolks begin to thicken but are not hard.

Place an egg on each bagel bottom. Layer with cheese, bacon and bagel tops. **Yield:** 4 servings.

Breakfast Parfaits

Prep/Total Time: 10 min.

- 2 cups pineapple chunks
- 1 cup fresh *or* frozen raspberries
- 1 cup (8 ounces) vanilla yogurt
- 1 cup sliced ripe banana
- 1/2 cup chopped dates *or* raisins
- 1/4 cup sliced almonds

In four parfait glasses or serving dishes, layer the pineapple, raspberries, yogurt, banana and dates. Sprinkle with almonds. Serve immediately. **Yield:** 4 servings.

Bacon 'n' Egg Bagels
Breakfast Parfaits

Cool Combo For Summer

WHEN the days heat up, do you enjoy eating light suppers that are fast to fix and have mouth-watering flavors? Is the idea of standing over the stove in an already hot kitchen less than appealing? Consider this easy menu that capitalizes on the summer season's freshest produce.

This lovely combination is not only a cinch to put together, it's absolutely delicious! The roast beef sandwiches and colorful pasta salad make a casual weeknight meal, but they're festive enough to serve at any warm-weather gathering.

Toasted Zippy Beef Sandwiches from Theresa Young of McHenry, Illinois taste just like they came from your favorite delicatessen. With sliced roast beef, two kinds of cheese, fresh veggies and a simple homemade dressing, they're comforting yet have a pleasing kick.

Since the sandwiches can even be broiled in a toaster oven, they're ideal for nights when you want to keep the kitchen cool.

To round out the meal, pair them with Colorful Pasta Salad. The bright side dish from Mary Tallman of Arbor Vitae, Wisconsin features sweet pineapple, crunchy vegetables and fresh cilantro in a tangy dressing with pasta. It requires just 15 minutes of prep, so it's perfect for a quick lunch or on-the-go dinner.

Together, these rave-winning recipes add up to a special meal you've just gotta try!

Colorful Pasta Salad
Toasted Zippy Beef Sandwiches

Toasted Zippy Beef Sandwiches
Prep/Total Time: 20 min.

1/4 cup mayonnaise
4-1/2 teaspoons Western salad dressing
   1 tablespoon prepared horseradish
   4 whole wheat sandwich buns, split
1/2 pound sliced deli roast beef
   4 slices provolone cheese
   4 slices Swiss cheese
   4 slices tomato
   4 slices onion
   1 small sweet yellow pepper, sliced
   4 large lettuce leaves

In a small bowl, combine the mayonnaise, salad dressing and horseradish; set aside. Place bun bottoms cut side up on an ungreased baking sheet; top with beef and cheeses. Broil 4 in. from the heat for 4-5 minutes or until cheese is melted.

Place bun tops cut side up on another baking sheet. Broil for 1-2 minutes or until golden brown. Meanwhile, layer the tomato, onion, yellow pepper and lettuce on sandwiches. Spread mayonnaise mixture over bun tops; place over lettuce. **Yield:** 4 sandwiches.

Colorful Pasta Salad
Prep/Total Time: 15 min.

✓ Uses less fat, sugar or salt. Includes Nutrition Facts and Diabetic Exchanges.

1-1/2 cups uncooked tricolor spiral pasta
   1 can (8 ounces) unsweetened pineapple chunks
   1 cup fresh snow peas, halved
1/2 cup thinly sliced carrot
1/2 cup sliced cucumber
   1 tablespoon minced fresh cilantro
1/4 cup Italian salad dressing

Cook pasta according to package directions. Meanwhile, drain pineapple, reserving 1/4 cup juice. In a large bowl, combine the pineapple, snow peas, carrot, cucumber and reserved pineapple juice.

Drain the pasta; rinse with cold water. Add to the pineapple mixture. Sprinkle with the cilantro. Drizzle with the salad dressing and toss to coat. Chill until serving. **Yield:** 5 servings.

Nutrition Facts: 3/4 cup (prepared with fat-free Italian dressing) equals 120 calories, 1 g fat (trace saturated fat), trace cholesterol, 153 mg sodium, 25 g carbohydrate, 2 g fiber, 4 g protein. **Diabetic Exchanges:** 2 vegetable, 1 fruit.

**Tortellini Primavera
Very Berry Peach Sauce**

prise, it was delicious on chicken and pork.

"It's also fabulous on ice cream or spooned over pound cake or angel food cake," she adds.

Tortellini Primavera

Prep/Total Time: 20 min.

✓ Uses less fat, sugar or salt. Includes Nutrition Facts and Diabetic Exchanges.

 1 package (9 ounces) refrigerated cheese tortellini
 2 medium yellow summer squash, chopped
 2 medium zucchini, chopped
 2 teaspoons olive oil
 1 pint cherry tomatoes, halved
 1/2 cup chopped green onions
 1/4 teaspoon pepper
 1/2 cup Caesar salad dressing
 1/4 cup shredded Parmesan cheese
 1/4 cup sliced almonds, toasted

Cook the cheese tortellini according to the package directions. Meanwhile, in a large skillet, saute yellow squash and zucchini in olive oil for 4-6 minutes or until crisp-tender.

Drain tortellini; place in a large bowl. Add the squash mixture, tomatoes, onions and pepper. Drizzle with salad dressing and toss to coat. Sprinkle with Parmesan cheese and almonds. **Yield:** 6 servings.

Nutrition Facts: 1 cup (prepared with fat-free salad dressing) equals 247 calories, 9 g fat (3 g saturated fat), 21 mg cholesterol, 463 mg sodium, 35 g carbohydrate, 5 g fiber, 11 g protein. **Diabetic Exchanges:** 2 starch, 1 lean meat, 1 vegetable, 1/2 fat.

Very Berry Peach Sauce

Prep/Total Time: 20 min.

 2 tablespoons sugar
 4-1/2 teaspoons cornstarch
 1/2 cup red currant jelly
 2 medium fresh peaches, peeled and sliced
 1/2 cup fresh *or* frozen blueberries
 1/2 cup fresh raspberries

In a small saucepan, combine sugar and cornstarch. Stir in jelly until smooth. Stir in the peaches, blueberries and raspberries. Cook and stir over medium heat until mixture comes to a boil. Cook 3-4 minutes longer or until thickened (some berries will remain whole). **Yield:** 6 servings.

Meatless and Memorable

IF YOU'RE HOPING to enjoy some rest and relaxation this evening instead of slaving over the stove all night, give this fast meatless dinner a try. The light and refreshing combination calls for just a few ingredients, so you're sure to be in and out of the kitchen (and on to other activities) in a dash.

Start with warm servings of delightful Tortellini Primavera. The all-in-one meal from Mary Ann Dell of Phoenixville, Pennsylvania starts with refrigerated pasta, so it's a snap to put together. Plus, it features an assortment of fresh vegetables, so you can put garden extras to delectable use.

"It's wonderful when fresh zucchini, squash and cherry tomatoes are in abundance," assures Mary Ann. "You can also chill it to serve as a salad."

Pair it with versatile Very Berry Peach Sauce from Brenda White of Hagerstown, Maryland. "The original recipe served this sauce as a side dish, so I was a bit hesitant to try it," Brenda explains. "To my sur-

Dressed for Success

NOT A FAN of Caesar salad dressing? Feel free to replace the Caesar dressing in mouth-watering Tortellini Primavera (recipe above) with Italian instead...or substitute your family's favorite vinaigrette.

Better Than Fast Food

NEED a speedy dinner on a hectic night? Instead of stopping for fast food, head home. This easy meal is ready in 30 minutes, yet it's so tasty that your family will think you've been cooking all day!

For the main course, serve Judith Wiezorek's Tender Glazed Pork Chops. Topped with a tangy apricot glaze, the moist chops are a breeze to put together. "My mother and I love this recipe," Judith notes from Gainesville, Georgia. "It's excellent with baked sweet potatoes, beets, applesauce and rolls."

Or serve the chops with a side of Teriyaki Zucchini and Onion from Cher Conley of Laurel, Montana. The crisp zucchini and onion are coated in a pleasant teriyaki sauce.

Round out this duo with dinner rolls as shown below for a delightful meal any night of the week.

Tender Glazed Pork Chops

Prep/Total Time: 30 min.

- 1/2 teaspoon onion powder
- 1/2 teaspoon garlic powder
- 1/2 teaspoon dried oregano
- 4 boneless pork loin chops (3/4 inch thick and 4 ounces *each*)
- 1 cup apricot preserves
- 1-1/2 teaspoons lemon juice
- 1-1/2 teaspoons lime juice
- 2 tablespoons olive oil

Combine the onion powder, garlic powder and oregano; sprinkle over chops. In a small saucepan, combine the preserves, lemon juice and lime juice; cook and stir over low heat for 10 minutes or until preserves are melted.

Meanwhile, in a large skillet, cook pork in oil over medium-low heat for 8-10 minutes or until lightly browned on one side. Turn chops; generously brush with apricot glaze. Cook 8-10 minutes longer or until juices run clear. Serve with remaining glaze. **Yield:** 4 servings.

Teriyaki Zucchini and Onion

Prep/Total Time: 15 min.

✓ Uses less fat, sugar or salt. Includes Nutrition Facts and Diabetic Exchanges.

- 2 medium zucchini, cut into strips
- 1 small onion, sliced and separated into rings
- 2 tablespoons butter
- 1/4 cup teriyaki sauce
- 1/8 teaspoon pepper
- 1 teaspoon sesame seeds, toasted

In a large skillet, saute zucchini and onion in butter for 7-8 minutes or until crisp-tender; drain. Stir in the teriyaki sauce and pepper. Sprinkle with sesame seeds. **Yield:** 4 servings.

Nutrition Facts: 3/4 cup (prepared with reduced-fat butter and reduced-sodium teriyaki sauce) equals 64 calories, 3 g fat (2 g saturated fat), 10 mg cholesterol, 362 mg sodium, 8 g carbohydrate, 2 g fiber, 3 g protein. **Diabetic Exchanges:** 1 vegetable, 1/2 fat.

Teriyaki Zucchini and Onion
Tender Glazed Pork Chops

Chapter 4

THESE DAYS, grocery stores stock an endless assortment of packaged mixes, canned goods, frozen foods, cooked meats and other convenience items. And that's excellent news for time-crunched cooks!

Using those handy products, you can speed up your recipes and still give loved ones all the home-style fare and flavor they crave. Just consider the rapid recipes in this chapter.

Each one takes advantage of one or more convenience products, such as jarred tomatoes, refrigerated cookie dough and prepared pesto. So you'll have built-in, time-saving shortcuts to family-pleasing foods with from-scratch taste.

Just write a quick shopping list, stop at the supermarket and you'll be well on your way!

CONVENIENT CUISINE. Orient Express Chicken Salad (p. 83).

Baked Chicken with Pasta Sauce

(Pictured below)

Prep: 10 min. **Bake:** 35 min.

This simple Italian specialty makes a family-pleasing entree. The seasoned chicken is topped with a flavorful tomato sauce. —*Gert Kaiser, Kenosha, Wisconsin*

☑ Uses less fat, sugar or salt. Includes Nutrition Facts.

- **1 egg**
- **1 cup seasoned bread crumbs**
- **4 boneless skinless chicken breast halves (6 ounces *each*)**
- **1 jar (26 ounces) garden-style pasta sauce**
- **1 cup (4 ounces) shredded part-skim mozzarella cheese**

Hot cooked pasta, optional

In a shallow bowl, beat the egg. Place the bread crumbs in another shallow bowl. Dip chicken in egg, then coat with crumbs. Place in a 13-in. x 9-in. x 2-in. baking dish coated with nonstick cooking spray.

Bake, uncovered, at 400° for 20-22 minutes or until juices run clear. Pour pasta sauce over chicken. Sprinkle with cheese. Bake 12-14 minutes longer or until sauce is bubbly and cheese is melted. Serve over pasta if desired. **Yield:** 4 servings.

Nutrition Facts: 1 serving (prepared with egg substitute; calculated without pasta) equals 499 calories, 14 g fat (5 g saturated fat), 117 mg cholesterol, 1,369 mg sodium, 42 g carbohydrate, 5 g fiber, 49 g protein.

Pesto Hamburgers

Prep/Total Time: 20 min.

Our Test Kitchen home economists came up with these deliciously different burgers smothered with prepared pesto, mozzarella and roasted red pepper strips.

- **1-1/2 pounds ground beef**
- **1/8 teaspoon salt**
- **1/8 teaspoon pepper**
- **4 slices part-skim mozzarella cheese**
- **1/2 cup prepared pesto**
- **1/3 cup roasted sweet red pepper strips**
- **4 hamburger buns, split and toasted**

Shape beef into four 3/4-in.-thick patties. Season with salt and pepper. In a large skillet over medium heat, cook patties for 5 minutes on each side or until meat is no longer pink.

Top each burger with mozzarella cheese, 2 tablespoons pesto and pepper strips. Reduce heat; cover and simmer for 2 minutes or until the cheese is melted. Serve on toasted hamburger buns. **Yield:** 4 servings.

Baked Chicken with Pasta Sauce

Cranberry Pecan Sandies

Prep: 20 min. **Bake:** 15 min. per batch

I love to share these delicate, crisp cookies featuring pecans and a hint of orange. They use a convenient cranberry bread mix. —Teresa Jarrell, Danville, West Virginia

  1 package (15.6 ounces) cranberry quick bread mix
1/2 cup butter, melted
  1 egg
  2 tablespoons orange juice
3/4 cup chopped pecans
 30 to 36 pecan halves
ORANGE GLAZE:
  1 cup confectioners' sugar
  3 to 4 teaspoons orange juice

In a large mixing bowl, combine the bread mix, butter, egg and orange juice. Stir in chopped pecans. Roll into 1-in. balls. Place 2 in. apart on ungreased baking sheets. Flatten with the bottom of a glass coated with nonstick cooking spray. Press a pecan half into center of each cookie.

Bake at 350° for 12-14 minutes or until lightly browned. Cool for 1 minute before removing to wire racks. In a small bowl, whisk glaze ingredients. Drizzle over cookies. **Yield:** 2-1/2 to 3 dozen.

Pear Pork Chops with Rice

Prep: 10 min. **Bake:** 40 min.

This recipe has become a family favorite. Thickened pan juices make a tasty gravy for the pork chops and sweet pears that are served over rice. —Sue Ware
Ortonville, Minnesota

  2 cans (15 ounces *each*) reduced-sugar pear halves
  1 cup packed brown sugar
1/4 cup butter, cubed
1/2 teaspoon ground cloves
1/2 teaspoon ground cinnamon
  6 boneless pork loin chops (3/4 inch thick and 5 ounces *each*)
  2 cups uncooked instant rice
  3 tablespoons cornstarch
1/4 cup cold water

Drain pears, reserving syrup; set pears aside. In a large microwave-safe bowl, combine the brown sugar, butter, cloves, cinnamon and reserved syrup. Microwave, uncovered, on high for 2-3 minutes, stirring every minute, or until butter is melted and sugar is dissolved.

Place pork chops in a greased 11-in. x 7-in. x 2-in. baking dish. Place a pear half over each chop; top with pear syrup mixture. Cover and bake at 350° for 40-50 minutes or until pork is tender.

Cook rice according to package directions. Remove pork and pears; keep warm. Pour pan juices into a small saucepan; bring to a boil. Combine cornstarch and cold water until smooth; gradually stir into juices. Return to a boil; cook 1-2 minutes longer or until thickened. Serve

Spinach-Stuffed Shells

with pork, pears and rice. **Yield:** 6 servings.

Editor's Note: This recipe was tested in a 1,100-watt microwave.

Spinach-Stuffed Shells

(Pictured above)

Prep: 25 min. **Bake:** 25 min.

Here's a creamy, meatless main course that's a snap to assemble but looks like you fussed. Using purchased shredded cheese and a store-bought mix for the white sauce really speeds up the preparation for this delicious dish.
—Debbie Herbert, Seymour, Indiana

 15 uncooked jumbo pasta shells
  1 envelope white sauce mix
  1 cup (8 ounces) cottage cheese
1/2 cup shredded part-skim mozzarella cheese
  1 egg white
1/2 teaspoon dried basil
1/4 teaspoon garlic powder
Dash pepper
  1 package (10 ounces) frozen chopped spinach, thawed and squeezed dry
  1 tablespoon shredded Parmesan cheese

Cook pasta according to package directions. Meanwhile, prepare sauce according to package directions; set aside.

In a bowl, combine the cottage cheese, mozzarella, egg white, basil, garlic powder, pepper and half of the spinach (save remaining spinach for another use). Pour half of the white sauce into a greased 11-in. x 7-in. x 2-in. baking dish.

Drain pasta; stuff each shell with 2 tablespoons spinach mixture. Arrange over sauce. Top with remaining white sauce. Cover and bake at 375° for 25 minutes or until heated through. Sprinkle with Parmesan cheese. **Yield:** 5 servings.

Scallop Pesto Pasta

(Pictured below)

Prep/Total Time: 25 min.

Our Test Kitchen staff topped this pasta with sea scallops, which can range from 1/2 to 1 inch thick. To cook thicker scallops more quickly, cut them in half horizontally.

    8 ounces uncooked angel hair pasta
1/2 cup all-purpose flour
1/2 teaspoon salt
1/4 teaspoon pepper
    1 pound sea scallops
    3 tablespoons butter
1/2 cup prepared pesto

Cook the angel hair pasta according to the package directions. Meanwhile, in a large resealable plastic bag, combine the flour, salt and pepper; add the sea scallops and shake to coat.

In a large skillet, cook scallops in butter for 2-1/2 to 3 minutes on each side or until opaque. Drain pasta; toss with pesto. Top with scallops. **Yield:** 4 servings.

Lime Herb Chicken

Prep: 15 min. + marinating **Grill:** 40 min.

This is a tangy recipe for grilled chicken. Lime juice and Italian salad dressing are the key ingredients in the tongue-tingling marinade.   —Jennifer Partin, Repton, Alabama

    1 cup lime juice
2/3 cup Italian salad dressing
    2 teaspoons minced garlic

    2 teaspoons dried basil
    1 teaspoon dried thyme
1/2 teaspoon salt
1/2 teaspoon pepper
    1 broiler/fryer chicken (3 to 4 pounds), cut up

In a bowl, combine the first seven ingredients; mix well. Pour 1 cup marinade into a large resealable plastic bag; add the chicken. Seal bag and turn to coat; marinate for 15 minutes. Set aside remaining marinade for basting.

Drain and discard marinade. Grill chicken, covered, over medium heat for 40-45 minutes or until juices run clear, basting occasionally with 1/2 cup reserved marinade. Brush remaining marinade over chicken just before serving. **Yield:** 6 servings.

Sausage Noodle Supper

Prep/Total Time: 25 min.

I can't recall how I came up with this main dish, but it's now a staple in our house. Because it relies on packaged coleslaw mix and noodles in a flavorful sauce, it's on the table fast. I usually serve it with cheesy garlic toast for a hearty meal.   —Mary Jo Nikolaus, Mansfield, Ohio

    1 cup thinly sliced fresh carrots
    3 tablespoons butter
1/2 pound smoked sausage, thinly sliced
3/4 cup thinly sliced green onions
    4 cups coleslaw mix
2-1/4 cups water
    1 package (4-1/2 ounces) quick-cooking noodles and sour cream and chive sauce mix

Scallop Pesto Pasta

In a large skillet, cook carrots in butter for 2 minutes. Add sausage and onions; cook for 2 minutes. Stir in the coleslaw mix; cook 1-2 minutes longer. Add water; bring to a boil.

Stir in noodles and sauce mix. Return to a boil; cook and stir for 7-9 minutes or until noodles are tender, stirring occasionally. Let stand for 2-3 minutes before serving. **Yield:** 3-4 servings.

Lasagna Pizza

(Pictured at right)

Prep: 20 min. **Bake:** 25 min.

I turn to convenience products, including a handy hot roll mix and a package of spaghetti sauce mix, when making these savory squares. They really do taste like lasagna and were a family favorite when I was growing up. —Angie Dierikx Taylor Ridge, Illinois

Lasagna Pizza

1 pound lean ground beef
1 can (8 ounces) tomato sauce
1/4 cup water
1 envelope spaghetti sauce mix, *divided*
1 package (16 ounces) hot roll mix
1 cup warm water (120° to 130°)
1 carton (12 ounces) small-curd cottage cheese
1/4 cup shredded Parmesan cheese
1 cup (4 ounces) shredded part-skim mozzarella cheese

In a large skillet, cook beef over medium heat until no longer pink; drain. Stir in the tomato sauce, water and 3 tablespoons spaghetti sauce mix; heat through.

In a large bowl, combine contents of flour and yeast packets from hot roll mix; add remaining spaghetti sauce mix. Stir in warm water until dough pulls away from sides of bowl. Turn onto a lightly floured surface; knead until smooth and elastic, about 5 minutes.

Roll into a 17-in. x 12-in. rectangle. Transfer to a greased 15-in. x 10-in. x 1-in. baking pan; build up edges slightly. Spread cottage cheese over dough. Top with meat mixture and Parmesan cheese.

Bake at 400° for 20 minutes or until bubbly. Sprinkle with mozzarella cheese. Bake 5 minutes longer or until cheese is melted. Let stand for 5 minutes before serving. **Yield:** 12-15 servings.

Chili Cheese Corn

Prep/Total Time: 15 min.

A co-worker shared this recipe with me more than 10 years ago. It's so easy and tasty that it's become a frequent side dish in our house—especially for holidays or special meals. I've had many requests for the recipe.
—Nadene Melton, San Juan Capistrano, California

1 package (8 ounces) cream cheese, cubed
2 tablespoons butter
4 cups fresh *or* frozen corn, thawed

1 can (4 ounces) chopped green chilies
1/4 cup milk
1/4 teaspoon garlic salt
1/8 teaspoon salt
1/8 teaspoon cayenne pepper

In a large saucepan, combine cream cheese and butter. Cook and stir over medium heat for 4-5 minutes or until smooth. Stir in the remaining ingredients. Cook for 5 minutes or until heated through. Serve with a slotted spoon. **Yield:** 6 servings.

Candy Cookie Cups

Prep: 15 min. **Bake:** 15 min. + cooling

These rich, three-ingredient bites take advantage of time-saving convenience products for speedy preparation.
—Sarah Vasques, Milford, New Hampshire

1/2 cup finely chopped macadamia nuts
1 package (18 ounces) individually portioned refrigerated white chip macadamia nut cookie dough
24 miniature peanut butter cups

Sprinkle macadamia nuts into 24 greased miniature muffin cups, 1 teaspoon in each. Cut each portion of cookie dough in half; place each half in a muffin cup.

Bake at 325° for 11-13 minutes or until golden brown. Immediately place a peanut butter cup in each cookie; press down gently. Cool completely before removing from pans to wire racks. **Yield:** 2 dozen.

Gnocchi with Pesto Sauce

(Pictured below)

Prep/Total Time: 20 min.

For a special, meatless main dish, try these classic Italian dumplings our Test Kitchen home economists dressed up with plenty of fresh vegetables, prepared pesto and toasted pine nuts. Don't have pine nuts handy in your kitchen? Feel free to substitute different nuts—such as pecans—or even sunflower kernels.

  1 package (17.6 ounces) potato gnocchi
  1 cup diced zucchini
1/2 cup chopped sweet yellow pepper
  2 teaspoons olive oil
1/4 cup prepared pesto
  1 cup chopped tomatoes
Toasted pine nuts, optional

Cook the potato gnocchi according to the package directions. Meanwhile, in a large skillet, saute the zucchini and sweet yellow pepper in the olive oil until crisp-tender.

   Drain gnocchi; add to skillet with the pesto. Gently stir until coated. Stir in tomatoes. Sprinkle with pine nuts if desired. **Yield:** 4 servings.

Gnocchi with Pesto Sauce

Swiss Mushroom Orzo

Prep/Total Time: 30 min.

I turn to this go-with-everything dish as a substitute for rice or potatoes when I want a change of pace. This pasta is versatile, too—if I'd like to give it a taste twist, I can toss in some roasted sweet peppers or even steamed broccoli.
   —Holly Bonds, Smyrna, Georgia

  1 cup uncooked orzo pasta
  1 cup (4 ounces) shredded Swiss cheese
  4 tablespoons cold butter, *divided*
  2 teaspoons minced garlic
1/4 teaspoon salt
1/4 teaspoon pepper
1/2 cup sliced fresh mushrooms

Cook the orzo according to package directions. Meanwhile, in a food processor, combine the Swiss cheese, 3 tablespoons butter, garlic, salt and pepper; cover and process until smooth.

   In a large saucepan, saute the sliced mushrooms in remaining butter until tender. Drain orzo and add to mushrooms. Stir in the Swiss cheese mixture until melted. **Yield:** 3 servings.

Apricot Almond Chicken

Prep: 10 min. + marinating **Cook:** 20 min.

This succulent chicken is draped with an apricot sauce and topped with almonds for a lovely look. Served over rice, the entree is impressive enough for company and a meal-in-one.   *—Sherry Keller, Lock Haven, Pennsylvania*

1/2 cup lemon juice
1/4 cup Dijon mustard
  2 teaspoons minced garlic
1/2 teaspoon white pepper
1/2 cup plus 2 tablespoons olive oil, *divided*
  6 boneless skinless chicken breast halves
    (4 ounces *each*)
  3 tablespoons cornstarch
  1 can (14-1/2 ounces) chicken broth
  1 cup apricot preserves
  2 tablespoons butter
  1 cup sliced almonds
Hot cooked rice

In a small bowl, combine the lemon juice, mustard, garlic, pepper and 1/2 cup oil. Pour 1/2 cup marinade into a large resealable plastic bag; add chicken. Seal the bag and turn to coat; refrigerate for at least 1 hour. Cover and refrigerate remaining marinade.

   Drain and discard marinade from chicken. In a large skillet over medium heat, cook chicken in remaining oil for 8-10 minutes on each side or until juices run clear.

   Meanwhile, in a small saucepan, combine cornstarch and broth until smooth. Stir in the preserves, butter and reserved marinade. Bring to a boil; cook and stir for 2 minutes or until thickened. Spoon over chicken; sprinkle with almonds. Serve with rice. **Yield:** 6 servings.

Chicken Artichoke Pasta

Chicken Artichoke Pasta

(Pictured above)

Prep/Total Time: 25 min.

Here's an entree my whole family likes, including the kids! It relies on canned artichokes, canned olives and a jar of tomatoes. —Beth Washington, Ayer, Massachusetts

    8 ounces uncooked bow tie pasta
1-1/2 pounds boneless skinless chicken breasts, cubed
  1/2 teaspoon dried oregano
  1/4 teaspoon salt
  1/4 teaspoon pepper
    3 tablespoons olive oil
    1 to 2 tablespoons minced garlic
    2 cans (14 ounces *each*) water-packed artichoke hearts, rinsed, drained and quartered
    1 jar (8-1/2 ounces) oil-packed sun-dried tomatoes, quartered
    1 can (2-1/4 ounces) sliced ripe olives, drained
Shredded Parmesan cheese

Cook pasta according to package directions. Meanwhile, sprinkle chicken with oregano, salt and pepper. In a large skillet, saute chicken in oil until no longer pink. Add the garlic; saute 1 minute longer. Stir in the artichokes, tomatoes and olives; heat through. Drain pasta; toss with chicken mixture. Sprinkle with Parmesan cheese.
Yield: 6 servings.

Feta-Stuffed Chicken

Prep: 10 min. **Bake:** 40 min.

When my husband and I were first married, I knew how to make only a few meals we'd rotate throughout the week. After some experimenting, I created this mouth-watering recipe that's still a favorite today. Drizzle the vinegar and olive oil over the chicken right when it comes out of the oven. —Lisa Herbert, Wadsworth, Ohio

    4 boneless skinless chicken breast halves (6 ounces *each*)
    1 package (4 ounces) crumbled tomato and basil feta cheese, *divided*
    1 cup seasoned bread crumbs
    4 tablespoons balsamic vinegar
    4 tablespoons olive oil
    4 plum tomatoes, sliced
Fresh basil leaves

Flatten chicken breast halves to 1/4-in. thickness. Place a tablespoon of crumbled feta cheese on each chicken breast half; roll up and secure with toothpicks. Coat with the seasoned bread crumbs. Place seam side down in a greased 13-in. x 9-in. x 2-in. baking pan. Sprinkle with the remaining feta cheese.

Bake, uncovered, at 350° for 40-45 minutes or until the chicken juices run clear. Immediately drizzle the balsamic vinegar and olive oil over chicken. Discard the toothpicks. Garnish chicken with sliced plum tomatoes and fresh basil. **Yield:** 4 servings.

Sausage Spinach Bake

(Pictured below)

Prep: 20 min. **Bake:** 35 min.

This delicious recipe using packaged stuffing mix was given to me some years ago by a friend. A salad and bread of your choice is all you'll need for a filling lunch or dinner. This casserole is so versatile, you can even serve it at brunch.
—Kathleen Grant, Swan Lake, Montana

    1 package (6 ounces) savory herb-flavored
      stuffing mix
1/2 pound bulk pork sausage
1/4 cup chopped green onions
1/2 teaspoon minced garlic
    1 package (10 ounces) frozen chopped
      spinach, thawed and squeezed dry
1-1/2 cups (6 ounces) shredded Monterey Jack
      cheese
1-1/2 cups half-and-half cream
    3 eggs
    2 tablespoons grated Parmesan cheese

Prepare stuffing according to package directions. Meanwhile, crumble sausage into a large skillet; add onions and garlic; cook over medium heat until meat is no longer pink.

In a large bowl, combine the stuffing, sausage mixture and spinach. Transfer to a greased 13-in. x 9-in. x 2-in. baking dish; sprinkle with Monterey Jack cheese. In a small bowl, combine cream and eggs; pour over sausage mixture.

Bake at 400° for 30 minutes. Sprinkle with the Parmesan cheese; bake 5 minutes longer or until a knife inserted near the center comes out clean. **Yield:** 12 servings.

Sausage Spinach Bake

Taco Casserole

Prep: 15 min. **Bake:** 30 min.

My preschool-aged child doesn't eat ground beef unless it's taco-flavored, so I came up with this casserole we all like. To make assembly easy, I prepare a big batch of taco meat and freeze it in recipe-size portions. I also cook the noodles over the weekend for supper during the week.
—Kathy Wilson, Romeoville, Illinois

    3 cups uncooked bow tie pasta
    1 pound ground beef
1/4 cup chopped onion
    2 cups (8 ounces) shredded cheddar cheese
    1 jar (16 ounces) salsa
    1 can (14-1/2 ounces) diced tomatoes,
      undrained
    1 envelope taco seasoning
    2 cups nacho tortilla chips, crushed

Cook pasta according to package directions. Meanwhile, in a large skillet, cook beef and onion over medium heat until meat is no longer pink; drain. Add the cheese, salsa, tomatoes and taco seasoning. Drain pasta; stir into the beef mixture.

Transfer to a greased 11-in. x 7-in. x 2-in. baking dish. Cover and bake at 350° for 20 minutes. Uncover; sprinkle with tortilla chips. Bake 10 minutes longer or until heated through. **Yield:** 7 servings.

Stuffed Cornish Hens

Prep: 20 min. **Bake:** 65 min.

I made this main dish at Thanksgiving one year when only a few of us gathered to celebrate. Now, these golden hens grace our table throughout the year. The wild rice stuffing has a flavor my family always enjoys.
—Jenny Holliday, Roanoke, Alabama

    1 package (6.2 ounces) fast-cooking long grain
      and wild rice mix
    2 celery ribs, chopped
    1 small onion, chopped
    2 tablespoons butter, *divided*
    1 can (10-3/4 ounces) condensed cream of
      mushroom soup, undiluted
    1 can (4 ounces) mushroom stems and pieces,
      drained
    4 Cornish game hens (24 ounces *each*)
1/4 teaspoon salt
1/4 teaspoon pepper

Cook rice according to package directions. In a small skillet, saute celery and onion in 1 tablespoon butter until tender. Stir in the soup, mushrooms and prepared rice.

Sprinkle inside and outside of hens with salt and pepper. Stuff with rice mixture. Place on a rack in a greased shallow roasting pan; cover with foil.

Bake at 350° for 40 minutes. Remove the foil. Melt the remaining butter; brush over the hens. Bake 25-35 minutes longer or until the juices run clear and a meat thermometer reads 180° for the hens and 165° for the stuffing. **Yield:** 4 servings.

Easy Shrimp Creole

Easy Shrimp Creole

(Pictured above)

Prep/Total Time: 25 min.

I found this super-quick shrimp recipe in a magazine years ago and have changed it to suit my taste. To speed things along, I cook the rice in the microwave using chicken broth instead of water. I've had only compliments whenever I've served it. —Jean Gauthier, Rives Junction, Michigan

    3/4 cup chopped onion
    3/4 cup chopped celery
    3/4 cup chopped green pepper
      2 tablespoons vegetable oil
      1 can (10-3/4 ounces) condensed tomato
        soup, undiluted
      1 cup tomato juice
    1/4 cup water
    1/4 cup salsa
      2 tablespoons lemon juice
      1 tablespoon minced fresh parsley
      2 teaspoons chili powder
  1-1/4 teaspoons garlic powder
    1/4 teaspoon pepper
      1 pound cooked medium shrimp, peeled and
        deveined
  Hot cooked rice

In a large skillet, saute the onion, celery and green pepper in oil for 6-7 minutes or until crisp-tender. Stir in the soup, tomato juice, water, salsa, lemon juice, parsley, chili powder, garlic powder and pepper. Bring to a boil. Reduce heat to medium; cover and cook for 6-8 minutes or until heated through.

Add the shrimp; cook, uncovered, for 3-4 minutes or until heated through. Serve over rice. **Yield:** 5 servings.

Pecan-Crusted Chicken

Prep: 10 min. **Bake:** 25 min.

After trying something similar when dining out, I created these impressive baked chicken breasts with a pecan coating. For special occasions, I like them with mashed sweet potatoes and a side of cooked canned cherries. —Ramona Parris, Marietta, Georgia

      3 egg whites
      1 package (4.2 ounces) seasoned coating mix
    1/2 cup chopped pecans
    1/8 teaspoon Chinese five-spice powder
      6 boneless skinless chicken breast halves (4
        ounces *each*)

In a shallow bowl, lightly beat the egg whites. In another shallow bowl, combine the coating mix, pecans and five-spice powder. Dip chicken into egg whites, then into coating mixture.

Place in a greased 15-in. x 10-in. x 1-in. baking pan. Bake, uncovered, at 400° for 25 minutes or until chicken is no longer pink. **Yield:** 6 servings.

Italian Sausage Calzone

(Pictured below)

Prep: 20 min. **Bake:** 30 min. + standing

My teenage daughter and I have been experimenting in the kitchen to re-create some old family recipes. These pizza-flavored slices with sausage and spinach are definitely a favorite. We usually double the ingredients and bake two pans at a time. —Terri Gallagher, King George, Virginia

1 tube (13.8 ounces) refrigerated pizza crust
1 can (8 ounces) pizza sauce
1 package (10 ounces) frozen chopped spinach, thawed and squeezed dry
1 pound bulk Italian sausage, cooked and drained
1 jar (4-1/2 ounces) sliced mushrooms, drained
2 cups (8 ounces) shredded part-skim mozzarella cheese

Unroll the pizza dough onto an ungreased baking sheet; pat into a 14-in. x 11-in. rectangle. Spread the pizza sauce over the long half of the dough to within 1/2 in. of the edges. Layer the spinach, sausage, mushrooms and mozzarella cheese over the sauce. Fold dough over filling; pinch seams to seal.

Bake at 400° for 30-35 minutes or until golden brown. Let stand 10-15 minutes before slicing. **Yield:** 6 servings.

Italian Sausage Calzone

Golden Sea Bass

Prep/Total Time: 25 min.

If you've ever tasted potato-crusted sea bass in a restaurant and wished you could have it at home, this version is for you. Store-bought potato flakes and a salad dressing mix combine for a great coating that's a breeze to whip up.
—Judi Markert, Mentor-on-the-Lake, Ohio

☑ Uses less fat, sugar or salt. Includes Nutrition Facts and Diabetic Exchanges.

1 cup mashed potato flakes
1 envelope Italian salad dressing mix
1/4 teaspoon pepper
1 egg
2 pounds sea bass fillets *or* halibut steaks
2 tablespoons butter, melted
Paprika

In a shallow bowl, combine the mashed potato flakes, Italian salad dressing mix and pepper. In another bowl, beat the egg. Dip the fillets into egg, then coat with potato flake mixture.

Place fillets in a single layer in a 15-in. x 10-in. x 1-in. baking pan coated with nonstick cooking spray. Drizzle with butter; sprinkle with paprika. Bake, uncovered, at 450° for 10-14 minutes or until fish flakes easily with a fork. **Yield:** 8 servings.

Nutrition Facts: 4 ounces cooked fish equals 180 calories, 6 g fat (3 g saturated fat), 81 mg cholesterol, 451 mg sodium, 8 g carbohydrate, trace fiber, 22 g protein. **Diabetic Exchanges:** 3 very lean meat, 1 fat, 1/2 starch.

Tex-Mex Turkey Burgers

Prep/Total Time: 25 min.

Flavored with taco seasoning and cilantro, these Southwestern turkey burgers are so good. I top them with a mixture of salsa and sour cream instead of ketchup. Round out the menu with roasted corn on the cob and deep-fried pita wedges sprinkled with cinnamon. —Nancy Bourget Round Rock, Texas

1-1/4 pounds ground turkey
1 envelope reduced-sodium taco seasoning
1 tablespoon dried cilantro flakes
1 cup (4 ounces) shredded Mexican cheese blend
1/2 cup sour cream
1/2 cup salsa
4 hamburger buns, split
4 lettuce leaves

In a large bowl, combine the turkey, taco seasoning and cilantro; shape into four patties. Grill, covered, over medium heat or broil 4-6 in. from the heat for 5 minutes on each side.

Sprinkle the shredded cheese over the burgers; grill 2-3 minutes longer or until a meat thermometer reads 165° and cheese is melted. Combine sour cream and salsa. Serve burgers on buns with sour cream mixture and lettuce. **Yield:** 4 servings.

Stuffed Pepper Soup

Prep/Total Time: 30 min.

This is an excellent example of how convenience foods can be combined for a tasty entree. Ready in minutes, this soup is part of a balanced meal with a salad, rolls and fruit.
—*Tracy Thompson, Cranesville, Pennsylvania*

1 pouch (8.8 ounces) ready-to-serve long grain and wild rice
1 pound ground beef
2 cups frozen chopped green peppers, thawed
1 cup chopped onion
1 jar (26 ounces) chunky tomato pasta sauce
1 can (14-1/2 ounces) Italian diced tomatoes, undrained
1 can (14 ounces) beef broth

Prepare the rice according to the package directions. Meanwhile, in a large saucepan, cook the ground beef, green peppers and onion until the meat is no longer pink; drain. Stir in the tomato pasta sauce, diced tomatoes, beef broth and prepared rice; heat through. **Yield:** 6-8 servings (about 2 quarts).

Turkey Biscuit Potpie

Prep/Total Time: 30 min.

For a comforting weeknight meal, try this easy version of a turkey potpie. Refrigerated biscuits create the golden crust that covers creamy ground turkey and vegetables.
—*Vicki Herron, Portland, Maine*

1 pound ground turkey
3 tablespoons all-purpose flour
2 cups milk
2-1/2 cups frozen peas and carrots, thawed
1/4 to 1/2 teaspoon salt
1/4 teaspoon pepper
1 tube (12 ounces) refrigerated buttermilk biscuits, separated into 10 biscuits

In a large skillet coated with nonstick cooking spray, cook turkey until no longer pink; drain.

Meanwhile, in a large saucepan, combine flour and milk until smooth. Bring to a boil; cook and stir for 2 minutes or until thickened. Stir in vegetables, salt, pepper and turkey; keep warm.

Place biscuits 2 in. apart on an ungreased baking sheet. Bake at 400° for 5 minutes. Transfer turkey mixture to a greased 8-in. square baking dish. Place nine biscuits over mixture. Bake potpie and extra biscuit for 5-7 minutes or until biscuits are golden brown. **Yield:** 5 servings.

Orient Express Chicken Salad

(Pictured above right and on page 72)

Prep: 25 min. + marinating **Cook:** 10 min.

This always-popular medley makes good use of convenience items but is still wholesome and nutritious. I created it for Mother's Day one year and got rave reviews.
—*Sara Dziadosz, Olathe, Kansas*

Orient Express Chicken Salad

4 boneless skinless chicken breast halves (4 ounces *each*)
1 cup sesame ginger marinade
1/2 cup balsamic vinaigrette
2 tablespoons brown sugar
1 tablespoon reduced-sodium soy sauce
1/2 teaspoon ground ginger
1/4 teaspoon crushed red pepper flakes, optional
1 package (5 ounces) spring mix salad greens
1 cup chow mein noodles
1/2 cup sliced green onions
1/2 cup shredded Parmesan cheese
1/3 cup dried cranberries
1 tablespoon sesame seeds
1 can (11 ounces) mandarin oranges, drained
1/4 cup slivered almonds, toasted

Place chicken and marinade in a plastic bag. Seal bag; refrigerate for 30 minutes. In a small bowl, whisk the next five ingredients for dressing. Refrigerate.

Discard marinade. Broil chicken 4 in. from the heat for 10-12 minutes or until juices run clear. Slice and set aside.

In a bowl, toss the next six ingredients. Divide among plates. Top with oranges, almonds and chicken. Serve with dressing. **Yield:** 4 servings.

Chapter 5

⟨⟩ *Give Me 5 or Fewer*

PUT THE RECIPES here on your "short list" of favorites. They'll keep your shopping list nice and short when you're off to the supermarket!

Every uncomplicated dish in this chapter calls for only five ingredients (not including the basic staples of water, salt and pepper)...so you won't have to gather together a grocery bag full of food items before you can even start cooking.

You'll be amazed at the sensational yet secretly simple delights you'll find, from Pepper Jack Pepperoni Rolls and Firecracker Shrimp to Cinnamon-Apple Crumb Pie.

Because these recipes don't use unusual items, you likely have most—if not all—of the necessary ingredients in your kitchen cupboard right now!

TAKE FIVE. Cucumber Onion Dip (p. 90).

Sunny Fruit Salad

Prep/Total Time: 15 min.

I created this refreshing medley when I wanted a salad that featured mandarin oranges. My guests just ate it up! Canned fruits make it convenient and perfect any time of year. —Jennifer Van Delinder, Milton, Florida

- 1 can (11 ounces) mandarin oranges
- 1 package (3.4 ounces) instant vanilla pudding mix
- 1 can (14 ounces) unsweetened pineapple tidbits, drained
- 1-1/2 cups miniature marshmallows
- 1 cup whipped topping

Drain oranges, reserving juice; set the oranges aside. In a large bowl, whisk pudding mix and reserved juice until smooth (mixture will be thick). Stir in the pineapple, marshmallows and oranges. Fold in whipped topping. Refrigerate until serving. **Yield:** 8 servings.

Ham 'n' Cheddar Corn Bread

(Pictured below)

Prep/Total Time: 25 min.

This layered corn bread "sandwich" baked in the oven is a great accompaniment for steaming soup and a salad. —Christa Habegger, Greenville, South Carolina

- 2 packages (8-1/2 ounces *each*) corn bread/muffin mix
- 2/3 cup milk
- 2 eggs
- 1/4 pound thinly sliced deli ham
- 6 slices cheddar cheese

In a bowl, combine bread mixes, milk and eggs. Pour half of batter into an 11-in. x 7-in. x 2-in. baking dish coated with nonstick cooking spray. Layer with ham and cheese; carefully spread remaining batter over top.

Bake at 400° for 20-25 minutes or until a toothpick inserted near the center comes out clean. Serve warm. **Yield:** 10 servings.

Fabulous Feta Salad

Prep/Total Time: 25 min.

On hectic days, I turn to this simple and pretty pasta when I need a fast, flavorful side dish. It's especially good with Italian entrees. —Amy Adams, Ogden, Utah

✓ Uses less fat, sugar or salt. Includes Nutrition Facts and Diabetic Exchanges.

- 2-1/2 cups uncooked bow tie pasta
- 4 cups torn romaine
- 1 cup cubed cooked chicken
- 1/2 cup crumbled feta cheese
- 1/2 cup Italian salad dressing

Cook pasta according to package directions; drain and rinse in cold water. In a large bowl, combine pasta, romaine, chicken and feta cheese. Drizzle with the dressing and toss to coat. **Yield:** 9 servings.

Nutrition Facts: 3/4 cup (prepared with fat-free Italian dressing) equals 95 calories, 3 g fat (1 g saturated fat),

Ham 'n' Cheddar Corn Bread

Sausage Wonton Cups
Brie Phyllo Cups

18 mg cholesterol, 267 mg sodium, 10 g carbohydrate, 1 g fiber, 8 g protein. **Diabetic Exchanges:** 1 lean meat, 1/2 starch.

Brie Phyllo Cups

(Pictured above)

Prep/Total Time: 20 min.

Mini phyllo shells from the freezer section hurry along these elegant cups. They look fancy and taste delicious but are a snap to put togther for a special occasion.
—*Brenda Little, Boise, Idaho*

- **15 frozen miniature phyllo tart shells**
- **3 tablespoons crushed gingersnaps**
- **6 ounces Brie, rind removed and cubed**
- **1/4 cup spreadable fruit of your choice**

Place the tart shells on an ungreased baking sheet. Sprinkle about 1/2 teaspoon gingersnap crumbs into each shell; top with Brie and spreadable fruit. Bake at 325° for 5 minutes or until cheese is melted. **Yield:** 15 appetizers.

Sausage Wonton Cups

(Pictured above)

Prep/Total Time: 30 min.

I get repeated requests for this easy-to-prepare appetizer. It's one of the first to disappear from the table.
—*Sheila Styles, Travelers Rest, South Carolina*

- **1/2 pound bulk Italian sausage**
- **3 green onions, chopped**
- **16 wonton wrappers**
- **1 tablespoon olive oil**
- **1 cup (4 ounces) shredded pepper Jack cheese**

In a small skillet, cook sausage over medium heat until no longer pink; drain. Stir in onions; set aside.

Press wonton wrappers into greased miniature muffin cups; lightly brush with oil. Bake at 350° for 6-7 minutes or until golden brown.

Spoon 1 rounded tablespoon of sausage mixture into each wonton cup; top with 1 tablespoon of cheese. Bake 3-4 minutes longer or until cheese is melted. Serve immediately. **Yield:** 16 appetizers.

Broccoli Cranberry Slaw

(Pictured below)

Prep/Total Time: 10 min.

I need just four items to toss together this crunchy coleslaw that gets a sweet twist from dried cranberries. It's lightly coated with convenient prepared salad dressing. After cutting the green onions and combining the ingredients, I'm done!
—Marie Siciliano, Westerly, Rhode Island

    1 package (12 ounces) broccoli coleslaw mix
    1 package (3 ounces) dried cranberries
    6 green onions, cut into 1/2-inch pieces
  1/4 cup coleslaw salad dressing

In a large bowl, combine the coleslaw mix, cranberries and onions. Add dressing and toss to coat. Refrigerate until serving. **Yield:** 8 servings.

Ranch Chicken Wings

Prep/Total Time: 30 min.

My family loved a local restaurant's chicken wings, but when we tried to make them at home, we couldn't figure out how to get their ranch flavor right. When I found a dried ranch dressing mix, I knew it would be perfect.
—Jennifer Bender, Venice, Florida

    1 pound chicken wings
    1 cup all-purpose flour

    Oil for deep-fat frying
    1 envelope ranch salad dressing mix
    1 teaspoon minced garlic
  1/2 teaspoon salt
  1/2 teaspoon pepper

Cut chicken wings into three sections; discard wing tips. Place flour in a large resealable plastic bag; add chicken wings, a few at a time, and shake to coat.

In an electric skillet or deep-fat fryer, heat oil to 375°. Fry chicken wings, a few at a time, for 8 minutes or until golden brown and crispy and juices run clear, turning occasionally. Drain on paper towels.

In a large resealable plastic bag, combine the dressing mix, garlic, salt and pepper; add chicken wings, a few at a time, and shake to coat. Place chicken in a greased 15-in. x 10-in. x 1-in. baking pan. Sprinkle with remaining salad dressing mixture. Bake, uncovered, at 350° for 8-10 minutes or until coating is set. **Yield:** 1 dozen.

Chicken Crescent Appetizer

Prep/Total Time: 30 min.

This savory sandwich ring takes advantage of convenience products, including refrigerated crescent rolls, french-fried onions and a spinach souffle from the freezer section. The appetizer is quick and easy...but doesn't look that way!
—Debbie Todd, Arrington, Tennessee

    1 package (12 ounces) frozen spinach souffle
    2 cups cubed cooked chicken

Broccoli Cranberry Slaw

Broccoli Saute

1 can (2.8 ounces) french-fried onions
1/2 cup shredded Parmesan cheese
1 tube (8 ounces) refrigerated crescent rolls

Heat spinach souffle according to package directions. Meanwhile, in a small bowl, combine the chicken, onions and Parmesan cheese; set aside.

Unroll crescent dough; separate into eight triangles. Arrange on an ungreased 12-in. round baking pan or pizza pan, forming a ring with pointed ends facing the outer edge of pan and wide ends overlapping.

Stir souffle into chicken mixture; spoon over wide ends of rolls. Fold points over filling and tuck under wide ends (filling will be visible). Bake at 375° for 11-13 minutes or until golden brown. **Yield:** 8 servings.

Broccoli Saute

(Pictured above)

Prep/Total Time: 15 min.

I invented this recipe while looking for a different treatment for broccoli that was lower in sodium. Quick and tasty, it's a colorful accompaniment to a seasonal dinner and makes an eye-catching side dish when you have company.
—*Jim MacNeal, Waterloo, New York*

1/2 cup chopped onion
1/2 cup julienned sweet red pepper
2 tablespoons olive oil
6 cups fresh broccoli florets
2/3 cup water
1-1/2 teaspoons minced garlic
1/4 teaspoon salt
1/4 teaspoon pepper

In a large skillet, saute onion and red pepper in oil for 2-3 minutes or until crisp-tender. Stir in the broccoli, water, garlic, salt and pepper. Cover and cook over medium heat for 5-6 minutes or until broccoli is crisp-tender. **Yield:** 5 servings.

Mushroom Green Bean Medley

Prep/Total Time: 15 min.

This is a 40-year-old family favorite. My kids are grown and gone now, but they still treasure this tangy veggie dish from their younger days. —*Dorothy Harris*
Indianapolis, Indiana

4 bacon strips, diced
1/2 cup chopped onion
1 package (16 ounces) frozen French-style green beans
1 jar (4-1/2 ounces) sliced mushrooms, drained
1/3 cup chili sauce

In a large skillet, cook bacon and onion over medium heat until bacon is crisp. Using a slotted spoon, remove to paper towels; drain, reserving 1-2 tablespoons drippings. In the drippings, saute green beans and mushrooms until beans are tender and heated through. Stir in chili sauce and bacon mixture. **Yield:** 4 servings.

Cucumber Onion Dip

(Pictured below and on page 84)

Prep/Total Time: 15 min.

My family members request this fast and flavorful dip often. I'm always happy to oblige! Surrounded by a plate of crackers or rye chips, this rich and creamy cheese-based snack is a mouth-watering way to ease your hunger before dinnertime.
—*Judith Priglmeier, Aitkin, Minnesota*

✓ Uses less fat, sugar or salt. Includes Nutrition Facts and Diabetic Exchanges.

    1 package (8 ounces) cream cheese, softened
 1/2 cup finely chopped seeded peeled cucumber
 1/4 cup finely chopped onion
    2 tablespoons mayonnaise
 1/8 teaspoon salt
 1/8 teaspoon pepper
Rye chips *or* crackers

In a small mixing bowl, combine the cream cheese, cucumber, onion, mayonnaise, salt and pepper; beat until blended. Refrigerate until serving. Serve with rye chips or crackers. **Yield:** 1-1/2 cups.

   Nutrition Facts: 2 tablespoons dip (prepared with reduced-fat cream cheese and fat-free mayonnaise; calculated without crackers) equals 50 calories, 4 g fat (3 g saturated fat), 14 mg cholesterol, 125 mg sodium, 1 g carbohydrate, trace fiber, 2 g protein. **Diabetic Exchange:** 1 fat.

Pepper Jack Pepperoni Rolls

Prep: 20 min. **Bake:** 20 min.

Need a speedy after-school snack, quick lunch or movie-night appetizer? Try these kid-friendly, three-ingredient pizza bites. Packed with cheese and chopped pepperoni, they're delicious and a snap to make using frozen rolls.
—*Judy Pinnow, Akron, Ohio*

    1 package (3 pounds) frozen white dinner rolls, thawed
 1/2 pound pepper Jack cheese, shredded
    4 ounces pepperoni, finely chopped

Flatten dinner rolls into 3-1/2-in. circles. Top each with about 1 tablespoon of shredded pepper Jack cheese and 1 rounded teaspoon of pepperoni. Bring up edges and pinch to seal. Place seam side down 2 in. apart on greased baking sheets.

   Bake at 350° for 20-25 minutes or until golden brown. Serve warm. Refrigerate leftovers. **Yield:** 3 dozen.

Cucumber Onion Dip

Cranberry-Apple Sweet Potatoes

Prep/Total Time: 30 min.

For this quick casserole, I cover canned sweet potatoes and apple pie filling with a sweet-and-tangy fruit glaze.
—Nella Parker, Hersey, Michigan

1 can (21 ounces) apple pie filling
1 can (2 pounds 8 ounces) cut sweet potatoes, drained and sliced
3/4 cup whole-berry cranberry sauce
2 tablespoons apricot preserves
2 tablespoons orange marmalade

Spread pie filling into a greased 8-in. square baking dish. Top with sweet potatoes. In a small bowl, combine cranberry sauce, preserves and marmalade; spread over potatoes. Cover and bake at 350° for 20-25 minutes or until heated through. **Yield:** 6-8 servings.

Firecracker Shrimp

(Pictured at right)

Prep/Total Time: 20 min.

These delightful grilled shrimp are coated in a spiced-up sauce that comes together in mere moments.
—Mary Tallman, Arbor Vitae, Wisconsin

✓ Uses less fat, sugar or salt. Includes Nutrition Facts and Diabetic Exchanges.

1/2 cup apricot preserves
1 teaspoon canola oil
1 teaspoon soy sauce
1/2 teaspoon crushed red pepper flakes
1 pound uncooked large shrimp, peeled and deveined

In a small bowl, combine the first four ingredients. Thread shrimp onto metal or soaked wooden skewers.

Grill, uncovered, over medium heat or broil 4 in. from the heat for 2-3 minutes on each side or until shrimp turn pink, basting frequently with apricot mixture. **Yield:** 10-12 servings.

Nutrition Facts: 2 shrimp equals 65 calories, 1 g fat (trace saturated fat), 56 mg cholesterol, 95 mg sodium, 9 g carbohydrate, trace fiber, 6 g protein. **Diabetic Exchanges:** 1 very lean meat, 1/2 starch.

Great Grilling Hints

- **Be prepared.** Have everything you need, including the food, extra charcoal or gas, gloves and tools, grillside before you start.
- **Keep it clean.** Food cooks best on a clean grill, so make sure to clean the grill before you begin and after you've finished grilling.
- **Have the right tools.** To prevent natural cooking juices from escaping, use tongs or a spatula to turn meats instead of a fork.

Firecracker Shrimp

Garlic Oregano Zucchini

(Pictured below)

Prep/Total Time: 15 min.

I've found that this flavorful side dish complements almost any main course, from chicken to fish. If you like, use half yellow summer squash for a colorful variation.
—*Teresa Kraus, Cortez, Colorado*

☑ Uses less fat, sugar or salt. Includes Nutrition Facts and Diabetic Exchanges.

- **1 teaspoon minced garlic**
- **2 tablespoons canola oil**
- **4 medium zucchini, sliced**
- **1 teaspoon dried oregano**
- **1/2 teaspoon salt**
- **1/8 teaspoon pepper**

In a large skillet, cook and stir the garlic in oil over medium heat for 1 minute. Add the zucchini, oregano, salt and pepper. Cook and stir for 4-6 minutes or until the zucchini is crisp-tender. **Yield:** 4 servings.

Nutrition Facts: 1 cup equals 90 calories, 7 g fat (1 g saturated fat), 0 cholesterol, 301 mg sodium, 6 g carbohydrate, 3 g fiber, 2 g protein. **Diabetic Exchanges:** 1-1/2 fat, 1 vegetable.

Family-Favorite Poke Cake

Prep: 10 min. **Bake:** 35 min. + cooling

I need a yellow cake mix and only four other ingredients for this yummy version of popular poke cake. It's so simple to prepare, kids may want to whip it up themselves!
—*Kristine Sims, St. Joseph, Michigan*

- **1 package (18-1/4 ounces) yellow cake mix**
- **10 fun-size Milky Way candy bars, *divided***
- **1 can (14 ounces) sweetened condensed milk**
- **1 jar (12 ounces) Milky Way ice cream topping**
- **1 carton (12 ounces) frozen whipped topping, thawed**

Prepare and bake cake according to package directions, using a greased 13-in. x 9-in. x 2-in. baking pan. Chop six candy bars. Remove cake from the oven; immediately sprinkle with chopped candy bars. Cool on a wire rack for 10 minutes.

Using the end of a wooden spoon handle, poke 20 holes in warm cake. Pour milk over cake; cool for 10 minutes. Pour the ice cream topping over cake; cool completely.

Spread whipped topping over cake. Chop remaining candy bars; sprinkle over cake. Cover and store in the refrigerator. **Yield:** 12-15 servings.

Angel Peach Melba

Prep/Total Time: 15 min.

Store-bought angel food cake, canned peaches, frozen yogurt and raspberries combine to make a sweet, summery dessert in just minutes. But this easy recipe is a keeper all year round!
—*Janice Prytz, Murrieta, California*

- **1 package (12 ounces) frozen unsweetened raspberries, thawed**
- **2 tablespoons sugar**
- **1 loaf (8 ounces) angel food cake, cut into 10 slices**
- **1 can (16 ounces) peach halves, drained**
- **2-1/2 cups vanilla frozen yogurt**

Garlic Oregano Zucchini

In a small bowl, combine raspberries and sugar; set aside. Place cake slices on an ungreased baking sheet. Broil 4 in. from the heat for 1-2 minutes on each side or until lightly toasted. Using a 2-1/2-in. biscuit cutter, cut a hole in the center of each slice. Remove cutouts and set aside.

Place each cake slice in an individual bowl; place a peach half, cut side up, in each hole. Top each with a scoop of frozen yogurt and a reserved cake cutout. Drizzle with raspberry mixture. Serve immediately. **Yield: 10 servings.**

Blueberry Corn Muffins

(Pictured above)

Prep/Total Time: 25 min.

I dress up a box of corn bread mix with blueberries to make these moist, tender muffins. This is a simple recipe, but a tasty one. —Diane Hixon, Niceville, Florida

✓ Uses less fat, sugar or salt. Includes Nutrition Facts and Diabetic Exchanges.

1 package (8-1/2 ounces) corn bread/muffin mix
1 tablespoon brown sugar
1 egg, beaten
1/3 cup milk
1/2 cup fresh *or* frozen blueberries

In a large bowl, combine the corn bread/muffin mix and brown sugar. Combine the beaten egg and milk; stir into the dry ingredients just until moistened. Fold in the blueberries.

Coat muffin cups with nonstick cooking spray or use paper liners. Fill half full with batter. Bake at 400° for 12-15 minutes or until a toothpick comes out clean. Cool for 5 minutes before removing from pan to a wire rack. Serve warm. **Yield: 8 muffins.**

Editor's Note: If using frozen blueberries, do not thaw before adding to batter.

Nutrition Facts: 1 muffin equals 146 calories, 4 g fat (1 g saturated fat), 33 mg cholesterol, 264 mg sodium, 25 g carbohydrate, 1 g fiber, 3 g protein. **Diabetic Exchanges:** 1-1/2 starch, 1/2 fat.

Fried Ravioli

Prep/Total Time: 30 min.

This recipe conveniently starts with packages of cheese ravioli. I add a handful of seasonings after frying them until crispy, and sometimes I garnish them with extra parsley. Blue cheese dressing is the perfect finishing touch. —Lee Server, Catonsville, Maryland

2 packages (9 ounces *each*) refrigerated cheese ravioli
3 tablespoons olive oil
1 teaspoon minced garlic
1/2 teaspoon salt
1/4 teaspoon pepper
2 tablespoons minced fresh parsley
1/4 cup blue cheese salad dressing

Cook ravioli according to package directions just until pasta is very firm; drain well. In a large skillet over medium heat, brown ravioli in oil in batches until crispy, turning often. Sprinkle with garlic, salt and pepper while ravioli is frying. Drain on paper towels. Sprinkle with parsley. Serve with blue cheese dressing. **Yield: about 3 dozen.**

Crusty Cheese Bread

Prep/Total Time: 15 min.

Your family will love the melt-in-your-mouth goodness of these toasted bread slices, which get a kick from cayenne pepper. —Tanya Brady, Montague, Michigan

- 3 tablespoons butter, softened
- 1/2 teaspoon garlic powder
- 1/8 teaspoon cayenne pepper
- 1/2 loaf French bread (8 ounces), halved lengthwise
- 3/4 to 1 cup shredded part-skim mozzarella cheese

In a small bowl, combine the butter, garlic powder and cayenne. Spread over cut sides of bread; sprinkle with cheese. Place on a baking sheet. Bake at 350° for 9-11 minutes or until cheese is melted. Cut into slices. **Yield:** 4-6 servings.

Creamy Fruit Salad

(Pictured below)

Prep/Total Time: 20 min.

I'm on a low-fat diet, so I created this light, refreshing salad using my favorite fruits. When I take it to church quiltings for lunch, everyone loves it. The mango is a little different, and the chopped walnuts add a pleasant crunch.
—Gerldean Cade, Brookhaven, Mississippi

☑ Uses less fat, sugar or salt. Includes Nutrition Facts and Diabetic Exchanges.

- 2 medium apples, cut into 1-inch pieces
- 2 cups chopped peeled mango
- 2 cups halved seedless red grapes
- 3 tablespoons sour cream
- 3 tablespoons chopped walnuts, toasted

In a large bowl, combine apples, mango, grapes and sour cream. Refrigerate until serving. Just before serving, stir in walnuts. **Yield:** 8 servings.

Nutrition Facts: 3/4 cup (prepared with reduced-fat sour cream) equals 101 calories, 3 g fat (1 g saturated fat), 2 mg cholesterol, 5 mg sodium, 20 g carbohydrate, 2 g fiber, 2 g protein. **Diabetic Exchange:** 1-1/2 fruit.

Butter Garlic Beans

Prep/Total Time: 20 min.

These frozen green beans taste almost fresh-picked when cooked with a little butter, garlic and onion.
—Laura McNeill, Dothan, Alabama

- 2 tablespoons finely chopped onion
- 1-1/2 teaspoons minced garlic
- 2 tablespoons butter
- 3 cups frozen cut green beans, thawed and drained
- 1/2 cup chicken broth
- 1/8 teaspoon salt
- 1/8 teaspoon pepper

In a large skillet, saute onion and garlic in butter for 2-3 minutes or until onion is crisp-tender. Add the beans, broth, salt and pepper. Bring to a boil. Reduce heat; simmer, uncovered, for 8-10 minutes or until beans are crisp-tender. **Yield:** 4 servings.

Creamy Fruit Salad

Creamy Mushroom Bow Ties

Creamy Mushroom Bow Ties

(Pictured above)

Prep/Total Time: 20 min.

This pasta side dish has become one of our favorites. It is so easy! But it tastes like it took much longer in the kitchen than it does.
—Dodi Walker
Peachtree City, Georgia

      6 cups uncooked bow tie pasta
      1 pound sliced fresh mushrooms
      1/2 teaspoon salt
      1/4 teaspoon pepper
      2 tablespoons butter
      1 (4.4 ounces) garlic-herb cheese spread
      1/4 cup chicken broth

Cook pasta according to package directions. Meanwhile, in a large skillet, saute the mushrooms, salt and pepper in butter until tender. Add cheese spread and broth; cook and stir until blended. Drain pasta; add to skillet and toss to coat. **Yield:** 9 servings.

Old-Fashioned Lemonade

Prep: 15 min. + chilling

Memorial Day and Fourth of July picnics just wouldn't be the same without the fresh flavor of homemade lemonade. Try this version from our home economists.

      2 to 2-1/2 cups sugar
      5 cups water, *divided*
      1 tablespoon grated lemon peel
1-3/4 cups lemon juice (about 6 lemons), *divided*

In a large saucepan, combine sugar, 1 cup water and lemon peel. Cook and stir over medium heat until sugar is dissolved, about 4 minutes.

Remove from the heat. Stir in lemon juice and remaining water. Pour into a pitcher and refrigerate until chilled. Serve over ice. **Yield:** 2 quarts.

Raspberry Iced Tea

Prep: 10 min. + chilling

Frozen raspberries lend summertime flavor and lovely color to this iced tea. Our Test Kitchen staff created it using just a few common ingredients.

✓ Uses less fat, sugar or salt. Includes Nutrition Facts.

      4 quarts water
1-1/2 cups sugar
      1 package (12 ounces) frozen unsweetened
         raspberries
      10 individual tea bags
      1/4 cup lemon juice

In a large kettle or Dutch oven, bring water and sugar to a boil. Remove from the heat; stir until sugar is dissolved. Add the raspberries, tea bags and lemon juice. Cover and steep for 3 minutes. Strain; discard berries and tea bags.

Transfer tea to a large container or pitcher. Refrigerate until chilled. Serve over ice. **Yield:** 16 servings (4 quarts).

Nutrition Facts: 1 cup equals 83 calories, trace fat (0 saturated fat), 0 cholesterol, 1 mg sodium, 21 g carbohydrate, 1 g fiber, trace protein.

Buttermilk Salad Dressing

(Pictured below)

Prep/Total Time: 5 min.

Buttermilk gives a tangy twist to this mild and creamy salad dressing from our home economists. You'll love drizzling it on your favorite fresh greens and vegetables.

- 1 cup mayonnaise
- 1 cup buttermilk
- 1/2 teaspoon onion salt
- 1/4 teaspoon paprika
- 1/8 teaspoon pepper
- Mixed salad greens

In a small bowl, whisk the mayonnaise, buttermilk, onion salt, paprika and pepper. Serve with salad greens. Refrigerate leftovers. **Yield:** 2 cups.

Pea 'n' Mushroom Medley

Prep/Total Time: 25 min.

This side dish is a snap to throw together. Fresh mushrooms and bacon jazz up the frozen peas with ease. It's pretty and impressive enough for company, so I make it often. —Laurie LaClair, North Richland Hills, Texas

- 3 bacon strips, diced
- 3 cups sliced fresh mushrooms
- 3/4 cup finely chopped onion
- 3/4 cup chopped sweet red pepper

Buttermilk Salad Dressing

- 4 cups frozen peas, thawed
- 3/4 teaspoon pepper
- 1/4 to 1/2 teaspoon salt

In a large skillet, cook bacon over medium heat until crisp. Stir in the mushrooms, onion and red pepper. Saute for 6-8 minutes or until vegetables are crisp-tender.

Stir in the peas, pepper and salt. Reduce heat; cover and simmer for 3-4 minutes or until heated through. **Yield:** 6 servings.

Sausage Pasta Skillet

Prep/Total Time: 25 min.

I made this up one night when I came home from work with no plan for supper. My kids really liked it, and we've had it many times since. It's almost hard to believe that just four ingredients can create such a family-pleasing main dish. —Patricia Weller, Emmitsburg, Maryland

✓ Uses less fat, sugar or salt. Includes Nutrition Facts and Diabetic Exchanges.

- 5 cups uncooked penne *or* medium tube pasta
- 5 Italian turkey sausage links
- 2 cans (10 ounces *each*) diced tomatoes and green chilies
- 1/2 cup grated Parmesan cheese

Cook pasta according to package directions. Meanwhile, remove and discard casings from sausage; cut sausage into 1/2-in. slices. In a large skillet, brown the sausage; drain. Drain the pasta. Add pasta and tomatoes to the skillet; heat through. Sprinkle with Parmesan cheese. **Yield:** 8 servings.

Nutrition Facts: 1 cup equals 313 calories, 9 g fat (3 g saturated fat), 42 mg cholesterol, 818 mg sodium, 37 g carbohydrate, 2 g fiber, 20 g protein. **Diabetic Exchanges:** 2-1/2 starch, 2-1/2 lean meat, 1 fat.

Artichoke Blue Cheese Fettuccine

Prep/Total Time: 20 min.

Store-bought Alfredo sauce speeds along this flavorful, meatless entree. I use dry pasta, but you can use refrigerated fettuccine to make this recipe even faster. —Jolanthe Erb, Harrisonburg, Virginia

- 1 package (12 ounces) fettuccine
- 1 can (14 ounces) water-packed artichoke hearts, rinsed, drained and chopped
- 1 cup sliced fresh mushrooms
- 1-1/2 cups Alfredo sauce
- 1/4 cup crumbled blue cheese

Cook fettuccine according to package directions. Meanwhile, in a large nonstick skillet coated with nonstick cooking spray, saute artichokes and mushrooms until tender. Stir in Alfredo sauce; heat through.

Drain fettuccine; toss with artichoke mixture. Sprinkle with blue cheese. **Yield:** 4 servings.

Ravioli with Sausage

Ravioli with Sausage

(Pictured above)

Prep/Total Time: 20 min.

My family loves this dish—it's on our menu at least once a month. It's easy to double for large crowds...just keep it warm in a slow cooker. I usually serve the ravioli with green beans amandine and garlic bread.   —Krendi Ford
Belleville, Michigan

✓ Uses less fat, sugar or salt. Includes Nutrition Facts.

- **4 cups frozen cheese ravioli (about 12 ounces)**
- **1/2 pound smoked sausage, sliced**
- **1 cup chopped green pepper**
- **1 jar (26 ounces) meatless spaghetti sauce**
- **1/4 cup shredded Parmesan cheese**

Cook the ravioli according to the package directions. In a large skillet, saute the sausage and green pepper for 2-3 minutes or until the green pepper is tender. Stir in the spaghetti sauce; heat through. Drain the ravioli; toss with the sausage mixture. Sprinkle with Parmesan cheese. **Yield:** 5 servings.

Nutrition Facts: 1 cup (prepared with smoked turkey sausage) equals 361 calories, 13 g fat (5 g saturated fat), 49 mg cholesterol, 1,304 mg sodium, 43 g carbohydrate, 5 g fiber, 19 g protein.

Carrot Parsnip Puree

Prep/Total Time: 30 min.

Our home economists came up with this good-tasting, good-for-you side dish that's a nice change from mashed potatoes. The natural sweetness of the parsnips and carrots is complemented by a hint of ground nutmeg.

✓ Uses less fat, sugar or salt. Includes Nutrition Facts and Diabetic Exchanges.

- **3 cups sliced fresh carrots**
- **2 cups sliced peeled parsnips**
- **1/4 cup butter, softened**
- **1/4 teaspoon ground nutmeg**
- **1/4 teaspoon salt**
- **1/8 teaspoon pepper**

Place 2 in. of water in a large saucepan; add carrots. Bring to a boil. Reduce heat; cover and simmer for 5 minutes. Add parsnips; cover and simmer for 15-20 minutes or until vegetables are tender. Drain.

Place the vegetables in a food processor; add butter, nutmeg, salt and pepper. Cover and process until smooth. Transfer to a serving bowl. **Yield:** 6 servings.

Nutrition Facts: 1/2 cup (prepared with reduced-fat butter) equals 93 calories, 4 g fat (3 g saturated fat), 13 mg cholesterol, 171 mg sodium, 14 g carbohydrate, 4 g fiber, 2 g protein. **Diabetic Exchanges:** 2 vegetable, 1 fat.

Dolloped Sweet Potatoes

(Pictured below)

Prep/Total Time: 15 min.

Our Test Kitchen used the microwave to turn sweet potatoes into a speedy and special side dish. Pie spice and brown sugar flavor the cream cheese topping.

✓ Uses less fat, sugar or salt. Includes Nutrition Facts and Diabetic Exchanges.

4 small sweet potatoes
1 package (3 ounces) cream cheese, softened
1 tablespoon butter, softened
2 tablespoons brown sugar
1/4 teaspoon pumpkin pie spice

Scrub and pierce sweet potatoes; place on a microwave-safe plate. Microwave, uncovered, on high for 10-13 minutes or until tender, turning twice.

Meanwhile, in a small mixing bowl, beat cream cheese, butter, brown sugar and pie spice. Make a slice in the top of each potato; fluff pulp with a fork. Dollop with cream cheese mixture. **Yield:** 4 servings.

Editor's Note: This recipe was tested in a 1,100-watt microwave.

Nutrition Facts: 1 sweet potato with 2 tablespoons topping (prepared with reduced-fat cream cheese) equals 166 calories, 7 g fat (5 g saturated fat), 23 mg cholesterol, 128 mg sodium, 22 g carbohydrate, 2 g fiber, 3 g protein. **Diabetic Exchanges:** 1-1/2 starch, 1-1/2 fat.

Dolloped Sweet Potatoes

Pesto Chicken Pasta

Prep/Total Time: 20 min.

Prepared pesto accents this warm pasta toss that calls for convenient rotisserie chicken. Our home economists prepared this recipe with cellentani pasta. If you can't find it, use 16 ounces of spiral pasta instead.

1 package (16 ounces) cellentani *or* spiral pasta
2 cups cubed cooked rotisserie chicken
1 cup chopped fresh tomatoes
1 container (7 ounces) prepared pesto
1/4 cup pine nuts, toasted

Cook pasta according to package directions. Meanwhile, in a nonstick skillet, saute chicken and tomatoes for 2 minutes. Stir in pesto; heat through. Drain pasta; toss with chicken mixture. Sprinkle with pine nuts. **Yield:** 6 servings.

Caramel-Pecan Apple Slices

Prep/Total Time: 15 min.

To jazz up a pork entree or any festive spread, I rely on these glazed apple wedges that please my family and friends. —Carol Gillespie, Chambersburg, Pennsylvania

1/3 cup packed brown sugar
2 tablespoons butter
2 large apples
1/4 cup chopped pecans, toasted

In a large skillet, cook and stir the brown sugar and butter over medium heat until sugar is dissolved and butter is melted.

Cut each apple into 16 slices; add to brown sugar mixture. Cook, uncovered, over medium heat for 5-7 minutes or until tender, stirring occasionally. Stir in pecans. Transfer to a serving bowl. Serve warm. **Yield:** 6 servings.

Glazed Carrots

Prep/Total Time: 20 min.

This tempting treatment for baby carrots is dressy enough for any holiday meal. Everyone likes the peach-orange flavor. —Nella Parker, Hersey, Michigan

✓ Uses less fat, sugar or salt. Includes Nutrition Facts and Diabetic Exchanges.

1 package (16 ounces) fresh baby carrots
1/4 cup water

3 tablespoons peach jam *or* preserves
1 teaspoon grated orange peel
1 teaspoon Dijon mustard
1/4 teaspoon dried thyme

In a saucepan, bring carrots and water to a boil. Reduce heat; cover and simmer for 10-15 minutes or until tender. Drain. Stir in the jam, orange peel, mustard and thyme; cook and stir until glazed and heated through. **Yield:** 4 servings.

Nutrition Facts: 1 cup equals 80 calories, trace fat (trace saturated fat), 0 cholesterol, 120 mg sodium, 19 g carbohydrate, 2 g fiber, 1 g protein. **Diabetic Exchanges:** 2 vegetable, 1/2 fruit.

Cinnamon Apple Crumb Pie

(Pictured above)

Prep: 15 min. **Bake:** 50 min. + cooling

Here's a dessert any busy hostess could love! It goes together in mere minutes, tastes like you spent hours in the kitchen and is easily doubled to feed any size gathering.
—*Carolyn Ruch, New London, Wisconsin*

1 can (21 ounces) apple pie filling
1 unbaked pastry shell (9 inches)
1/2 teaspoon ground cinnamon
4 tablespoons butter, *divided*
1-1/2 to 2 cups crushed pecan shortbread cookies

Pour pie filling into pastry shell. Sprinkle with cinnamon and dot with 1 tablespoon butter. Melt remaining butter. Place cookie crumbs in a small bowl; stir in butter until coarse crumbs form. Sprinkle over filling. Cover edges of pastry loosely with foil.

Bake at 450° for 10 minutes. Reduce heat to 350°; remove foil and bake for 40-45 minutes or until crust is golden brown and filling is bubbly. Cool on a wire rack for at least 2 hours. **Yield:** 6-8 servings.

Cranberry Mallow Dessert

(Pictured above)

Prep/Total Time: 5 min.

A holiday tradition, this fluffy salad-like dessert seems lighter than air. It can make a great alternative to plain cranberry sauce and an easy potluck dish for seasonal get-togethers. —*Cristie Hunt, Rossville, Georgia*

1 can (16 ounces) whole-berry cranberry sauce
2 cups miniature marshmallows
1 can (8 ounces) crushed pineapple, drained
1 teaspoon lemon juice
2 cups whipped topping

In a large bowl, combine the cranberry sauce, marshmallows, pineapple and lemon juice. Fold in whipped topping. Transfer to a serving dish. Cover and refrigerate until serving. **Yield:** 6-8 servings.

Chapter 6

☉ *10 Minutes to the Table*

FEELING a little flustered because you're running late and have a hungry family to feed? Don't race to a fast food drive-thru. Just take a deep breath…count to 10…and look here!

From start to finish, preparing each recipe in this chapter will take you no more than 10 minutes. That's practically the same amount of time it would require to get takeout!

Plus, every family-approved dish you'll discover gives you home-cooked, wholesome fare you just can't get at a fast food restaurant. Try Pineapple Ham Pizzas, Cheddar Bean Quesadillas…even Frosty Tiramisu for a quick-as-can-be dessert.

Simply keep the ingredients on hand, and you'll have 10-minute fare any time you like.

DONE IN A DASH. Parmesan Party Mix and Cheddar Bean Quesadillas (recipes on p. 108).

Holiday Snack Mix

Prep/Total Time: 10 min.

This Christmas season, whether you're traveling cross-country on vacation or just across town, be sure to have a bag of this crunchy snack on hand. It combines sweet and salty flavors for a mix everyone is sure to love.
—Jessie Sarrazin
Livingston, Montana

    3 cups miniature pretzels
    2 cups chocolate-covered peanuts *or* bridge
      mix
    2 cups mixed nuts
    1 package (7 ounces) dried fruit bits
    6 low-fat chewy granola bars, cut into 1-inch
      pieces

In a large bowl, combine all of the ingredients. Store in an airtight container. **Yield:** about 9 cups.

Garlic Toast Pizzas

(Pictured below)

Prep/Total Time: 10 min.

With working full-time, going to school and raising three children, finding time-saving recipes for my family is one of my biggest challenges. These pizzas are fast to fix.
—Amy Grim, Chillicothe, Ohio

    1 package (11-1/4 ounces) frozen garlic bread,
      thawed
  1/2 cup pizza sauce
    1 package (3-1/2 ounces) sliced pepperoni
    2 cups (8 ounces) shredded part-skim
      mozzarella cheese

Garlic Toast Pizzas

Place the garlic bread in a foil-lined 15-in. x 10-in. x 1-in. baking pan. Spread with pizza sauce; top with pepperoni and cheese. Broil 3-4 in. from the heat for 4-6 minutes or until cheese is melted. **Yield:** 8 slices.

Toffee Coffee Ice Cream

Prep/Total Time: 10 min.

Need an afternoon pick-me-up...or a cool dessert? Try this grown-up blend of coffee ice cream from our Test Kitchen staff. They jazzed it up with chocolaty almonds, toffee bits and miniature marshmallows.

    1 pint coffee ice cream, softened
  1/4 cup miniature marshmallows
  1/4 cup milk chocolate-covered almonds, halved
    1 English toffee candy bar, chopped

In a bowl, combine the ice cream, marshmallows, almonds and chopped candy bar until blended. Serve immediately. **Yield:** 5 servings.

Cranberry Quencher

Prep/Total Time: 5 min.

You need just three items to prepare this rosy fruit punch. Our home economists suggest floating fresh cranberries on top or garnishing each glass with a pineapple wedge.

    1 bottle (1 gallon) cranberry-apple juice,
      chilled
    1 can (46 ounces) pineapple juice, chilled
    1 can (6 ounces) frozen lemonade *or* orange
      juice concentrate, thawed

In a large container or punch bowl, combine the juices. Stir in lemonade concentrate. Serve immediately. **Yield:** 6 quarts.

Tortilla Soup

(Pictured at right)

Prep/Total Time: 10 min.

Tasty toppings perk up this no-fuss soup that has Mexican flavor. The recipe was given to me by a friend, and I make it regularly for guests. They like to garnish their bowls with crushed tortilla chips, sour cream and shredded cheddar.
—Michelle Larson, Greentown, Indiana

    1 can (10-1/2 ounces) condensed chicken with
      rice soup, undiluted
1-1/3 cups water
    1 cup salsa
    1 cup canned pinto beans, rinsed and drained
    1 cup canned black beans, rinsed and drained
    1 cup frozen corn
    1 cup frozen diced cooked chicken
    1 teaspoon ground cumin
Crushed tortilla chips, shredded cheddar cheese
  and sour cream

In a large saucepan, combine the first eight ingredients. Cook over medium-high heat for 5-7 minutes or until heated through. Serve with tortilla chips, cheese and sour cream. **Yield:** 5 servings.

Zesty Potato Cheese Soup

(Pictured at right)

Prep/Total Time: 10 min.

I really like to make potato cheese soup from scratch. But one night, we were in a hurry, so I added a few ingredients to canned potato soup instead. It was so good that now I always keep a few cans on hand...it's so quick and easy!
—Karen Pigmon, Corning, California

    3 cans (10-3/4 ounces *each*) condensed cream
      of potato soup, undiluted
    2 cans (12 ounces *each*) evaporated milk
  3/4 cup shredded cheddar cheese
  3/4 cup shredded pepper Jack cheese
    6 slices ready-to-serve fully cooked bacon,
      crumbled

In a large saucepan, combine the potato soup and milk. Cook over medium heat for 5-7 minutes or until heated through. Ladle into serving bowls. Sprinkle with cheeses and bacon. **Yield:** 6 servings.

Beef Soup in a Hurry

(Pictured at right)

Prep/Total Time: 10 min.

I need just five pantry goods to stir up this comforting microwave mixture. I call this "throw-together" soup. Serve it with a green salad and hot bread or rolls.
—Loellen Holley, Topock, Arizona

    1 can (24 ounces) beef stew
    1 can (14-1/2 ounces) stewed tomatoes, cut up
    1 can (10-3/4 ounces) condensed vegetable
      beef soup, undiluted
    1 can (8-3/4 ounces) whole kernel corn, drained
  1/8 teaspoon hot pepper sauce

Combine all ingredients in a microwave-safe bowl. Cover and microwave on high for 2-3 minutes or until heated through, stirring once. **Yield:** 6 servings.

Editor's Note: This recipe was tested in a 1,100-watt microwave.

Swift Soup Starter

Don't throw leftover vegetables away. Instead, use them to help jump-start a batch of soup.

I place the extra veggies in a freezer bag and label each bag with the date and contents. Then, when I make soup or stew, I check the bags in the freezer and choose which vegetables I'll add. I save time by not cutting up veggies, and the results are always delicious. —Bridget Guerra, Waterford, Michigan

Tortilla Soup
Beef Soup in a Hurry
Zesty Potato Cheese Soup

Pizza-Style Tossed Salad

(Pictured below)

Prep/Total Time: 10 min.

If you love pizza, you'll love this salad that tastes like pizza in a bowl. Almost every ingredient is packaged, so there's little measuring—just open and toss.
—Pat Habiger, Spearville, Kansas

- 1 package (10 ounces) Italian blend salad greens
- 1 cup (4 ounces) shredded part-skim mozzarella cheese
- 1 package (3-1/2 ounces) sliced pepperoni
- 1 can (2-1/4 ounces) sliced ripe olives, drained
- 1/2 cup Italian salad dressing
- 1 cup onion and garlic seasoned salad croutons

In a large salad bowl, combine the greens, mozzarella cheese, pepperoni and olives. Drizzle with dressing and toss to coat. Sprinkle with croutons. Serve immediately. **Yield:** 8 servings.

Cashew Pea Salad

Prep/Total Time: 10 min.

No one will guess this eye-catching salad comes together so quickly. The ginger-spiced dressing gives it fast flavor.
—Amy Balenzano, Spokane, Washington

☑ Uses less fat, sugar or salt. Includes Nutrition Facts and Diabetic Exchanges.

- 1 package (16 ounces) frozen peas, thawed
- 1 can (8 ounces) sliced water chestnuts, drained
- 1/2 to 1 cup whole cashews
- 6 green onions, chopped
- 1/2 cup mayonnaise
- 1 teaspoon soy sauce
- 1/2 teaspoon ground ginger

Dash garlic powder

In a large salad bowl, combine all of the ingredients. Serve immediately. **Yield:** 5 servings.

Nutrition Facts: 3/4 cup (prepared with 1/2 cup un-

Pizza-Style Tossed Salad

Hot Turkey Sandwiches
Tuna Cheese Sandwiches

salted cashews and fat-free mayonnaise) equals 196 calories, 7 g fat (1 g saturated fat), 3 mg cholesterol, 364 mg sodium, 27 g carbohydrate, 7 g fiber, 8 g protein. **Diabetic Exchanges:** 1-1/2 starch, 1 vegetable,1 fat.

Tuna Cheese Sandwiches

(Pictured above)

Prep/Total Time: 10 min.

I whip up a double batch of these when lots of family and friends are over. I prepare the tuna mixture in advance and gently stir in the lettuce just before assembling the sandwiches. This gives me more time to visit with my company.
—Barbara Billeter, Clovis, California

 1 can (6 ounces) tuna, drained and flaked
 1 cup (4 ounces) shredded cheddar cheese
1/2 cup chopped walnuts
1/2 cup mayonnaise
 1 tablespoon milk
 1 teaspoon lemon juice
1/2 teaspoon Worcestershire sauce
1/4 teaspoon onion salt
1/8 teaspoon pepper
 10 slices whole wheat bread
2-1/2 cups finely shredded lettuce

In a small bowl, combine the first nine ingredients. On five bread slices, layer 1/2 cup lettuce and 1/4 cup tuna mixture; top with remaining bread. **Yield:** 5 servings.

Hot Turkey Sandwiches

(Pictured above)

Prep/Total Time: 10 min.

I like to team these tasty open-faced sandwiches with cranberry sauce and green beans for a pretty meal that's really filling. I often turn to this convenient recipe as a way to use up our leftovers from a Thanksgiving or Christmas meal.
—Margery Bryan, Moses Lake, Washington

1 package (6 ounces) chicken stuffing mix
4 slices white bread, toasted
1 pound thinly sliced deli turkey
1 cup turkey gravy

Prepare stuffing mix according to package directions. Place the toast on a large microwave-safe plate; top each with turkey, stuffing and gravy. Microwave, uncovered, on high for 30-40 seconds or until heated through. **Yield:** 4 servings.

 Editor's Note: This recipe was tested in a 1,100-watt microwave.

Frosty Tiramisu

(Pictured below)

Prep/Total Time: 10 min.

Tiramisu is a family favorite but time-consuming to make, so I created an easy version to enjoy during the week. This rich, creamy treat can be whipped up in minutes. Top off each serving with chocolate curls for an elegant finishing touch.
—*Margee Berry, Trout Lake, Washington*

 3 tablespoons brewed coffee
 6 ladyfingers
 1 quart vanilla ice cream, softened
 1 container (8 ounces) Mascarpone cheese
 1 cup chocolate milk
 2 tablespoons baking cocoa
Whipped cream and chocolate curls

Brush coffee over ladyfingers; set aside. In a large mixing bowl, beat ice cream, cheese and milk until smooth. Divide among six parfait glasses. Sprinkle with cocoa. Place a ladyfinger in each glass. Top with whipped cream and chocolate curls. **Yield:** 6 servings.

Frosty Tiramisu

Seven-Fruit Salad

Prep/Total Time: 10 min.

This makes a great-tasting fruit medley that's speedy and pretty enough for holidays or any special occasion. With bananas, strawberries, peaches and four other kinds of fruit, the salad has beautiful color. Best of all, there's little cutting to do.
—*Nancy Zimmerman*
Cape May Court House, New Jersey

✓ Uses less fat, sugar or salt. Includes Nutrition Facts.

 1 can (29 ounces) sliced peaches, drained
 2 medium firm bananas, sliced
 1 can (11 ounces) mandarin oranges, drained
 1 cup sliced fresh strawberries
 1 cup fresh *or* frozen blueberries
 1 cup seedless grapes
 1 jar (16 ounces) maraschino cherries, drained
 1/3 cup corn syrup

In a large bowl, combine all of the ingredients. Serve with a slotted spoon. **Yield:** 10-12 servings.
 Nutrition Facts: 3/4 cup equals 149 calories, trace fat (trace saturated fat), 0 cholesterol, 18 mg sodium, 40 g carbohydrate, 2 g fiber, 1 g protein.

Tomato Cheese Pizzas

Prep/Total Time: 10 min.

My mom prepared these topped English muffins in the toaster oven for me when I was little. Today, these yummy pizzas are still a part of my menus. They're quick, healthy and delicious!
—*Michelle Wise*
Cookeville, Tennessee

✓ Uses less fat, sugar or salt. Includes Nutrition Facts and Diabetic Exchanges.

 2 English muffins, split and toasted
 4 slices (1 ounce *each*) process American cheese
 4 slices tomato
 1/2 teaspoon dried oregano

Place the English muffins cut side up on a broiler pan. Top each English muffin with a slice of cheese and a tomato slice; sprinkle with oregano. Broil the pizzas 4-6 in. from the heat for 2-3 minutes or until the cheese is melted. **Yield:** 4 pizzas.
 Nutrition Facts: 1 pizza (prepared with reduced-fat cheese) equals 125 calories, 2 g fat (1 g saturated fat), 7 mg cholesterol, 403 mg sodium, 17 g carbohydrate, 1 g fiber, 9 g protein. **Diabetic Exchanges:** 1 starch, 1 lean meat.

Mint Chip Deluxe

Prep/Total Time: 10 min.

You'll need just three ingredients to create this dressed-up treat from our Test Kitchen home economists. The brownie and candies make the mint chocolate chip ice cream taste decadent, but it comes together in a dash.

1 pint mint chocolate chip ice cream, softened
1 prepared brownie, chopped
6 mint Andes candies, chopped

In a bowl, combine the ice cream, brownie and chopped candies. Serve immediately. **Yield:** 4 servings.

Tossed Chicken Salad

(Pictured above)

Prep/Total Time: 10 min.

My husband can be picky about salads, but he loves this tasty combination of fruit, meat and cheese.
—*Vanetta Servoss, Southaven, Mississippi*

✓ Uses less fat, sugar or salt. Includes Nutrition Facts and Diabetic Exchanges.

1 package (10 ounces) hearts of romaine salad mix
1 package (6 ounces) fresh baby spinach
4 green onions, thinly sliced
8 slices ready-to-serve fully cooked bacon strips, warmed and crumbled
2 cans (15 ounces *each*) mandarin oranges
1 package (9 ounces) frozen diced cooked chicken, thawed
1 cup (4 ounces) shredded part-skim mozzarella cheese
1/2 to 1 cup slivered almonds
2/3 cup ranch salad dressing
1/4 cup shredded Parmesan cheese, optional

In a large salad bowl, combine the romaine, spinach and onions. Add the bacon, oranges, chicken, mozzarella cheese and almonds; toss gently. Drizzle with dressing; sprinkle with Parmesan cheese if desired. **Yield:** 8 servings.

Nutrition Facts: 1-3/4 cups (prepared with fat-free dressing and 1/2 cup almonds; calculated without Parmesan cheese) equals 220 calories, 9 g fat (3 g saturated fat), 30 mg cholesterol, 406 mg sodium, 20 g carbohydrate, 2 g fiber, 14 g protein. **Diabetic Exchanges:** 1-1/2 lean meat, 1 vegetable, 1 fruit, 1 fat.

Strawberry Shortcake Ice Cream

Prep/Total Time: 10 min.

Our home economists combined strawberries, pound cake and marshmallow creme for this scrumptious spin on a traditional summer dessert. Serve it as a weekend treat or make it your next meal's happy ending.

1 pint strawberry ice cream, softened
1/2 cup sliced fresh strawberries
1/4 cup marshmallow creme
2 slices frozen pound cake (3/4 inch thick), cubed

In a bowl, combine the ice cream, strawberries and marshmallow creme until blended. Very gently fold in cake cubes. Serve immediately. **Yield:** 5 servings.

Cheddar Bean Quesadillas

(Pictured below and on page 100)

Prep/Total Time: 10 min.

These quesadillas are so tasty. With refried beans, cheese and an assortment of toppings, they're hearty enough to satisfy teenagers yet easy enough for them to whip up themselves. —Grace Sandvigen, Rochester, New York

    4 flour tortillas (8 inches)
  2/3 cup refried beans
1-1/2 cups (6 ounces) shredded cheddar cheese
  1/4 cup canned chopped green chilies
  1/3 cup sliced green onions
  1/3 cup sliced ripe olives
Salsa

On two tortillas, spread refried beans to within 1 in. of edges. Sprinkle each with 1/2 cup cheese; top with chilies, onions, olives, remaining cheese and remaining tortillas.

  On a lightly greased griddle, cook quesadillas over medium heat for 2-4 minutes on each side or until browned and cheese is melted. Cut into wedges. Serve with salsa. **Yield:** 2 servings.

Parmesan Party Mix

(Pictured below and on page 101)

Prep/Total Time: 10 min.

This is our snack mix of choice, whether we're entertaining, giving a hostess gift or just relaxing in front of the TV. The combination of savory seasonings creates just the right flavor, and the mix doesn't require any baking time. —Karen Smith, Thornton, Colorado

    7 cups Crispix
    2 cups cheese-flavored snack crackers
    1 cup pretzel sticks
    3 tablespoons olive oil
    1 teaspoon Italian seasoning
  1/4 teaspoon fennel seed, crushed
  1/8 teaspoon hot pepper sauce
  1/2 cup grated Parmesan *or* Romano cheese

In a 2-gal. resealable plastic bag, combine the cereal, crackers and pretzels. In a small bowl, combine the oil, Italian seasoning, fennel seed and hot pepper sauce. Pour over the cereal mixture; seal the bag and toss to

Parmesan Party Mix
Cheddar Bean Quesadillas

coat. Add Parmesan cheese; seal bag and toss to coat. Store in an airtight container. **Yield:** 8 cups.

Strawberry Cream Graham Crackers

Prep/Total Time: 10 min.

Our Test Kitchen created these yummy graham cracker snacks. Banana slices and a creamy strawberry topping provide a pleasant sweetness.

- 1/4 cup chopped fresh strawberries
- 1/4 cup sour cream
- 1 tablespoon chopped walnuts
- 1 teaspoon brown sugar
- 3 graham crackers, halved
- 1 small banana, sliced

In a small bowl, combine the strawberries, sour cream, walnuts and brown sugar; spread over graham cracker squares. Top with banana slices. Serve immediately. **Yield:** 3 servings.

Guacamole Chicken Wraps

Prep/Total Time: 10 min.

Convenience items, including seasoned chicken strips, prepared guacamole and jarred salsa, add great Southwest flavor to these roll-ups from our home economists.

- 1/2 cup prepared guacamole
- 4 spinach tortillas (8 inches)
- 1/2 cup salsa
- 1 cup (4 ounces) shredded Mexican cheese blend
- 12 ounces ready-to-use Southwestern chicken strips
- 4 lettuce leaves

Spread guacamole over half of each tortilla. Layer with salsa, cheese, chicken and lettuce to within 2 in. of edges. Roll up tightly. **Yield:** 4 servings.

Berry Cashew Ice Cream

Prep/Total Time: 10 min.

Two kinds of fresh berries, crunchy nuts, pieces of a graham cracker tart shell and other extras make this Test Kitchen treat a pure delight.

- 2 cups French vanilla ice cream, softened
- 1/4 cup salted cashews
- 1/4 cup fresh raspberries
- 1/4 cup fresh blueberries
- 1 tablespoon miniature semisweet chocolate chips
- 1 tablespoon caramel ice cream topping
- 1 individual graham cracker tart shell, broken into large pieces

In a bowl, combine the ice cream, cashews, berries, chocolate chips and caramel ice cream topping until

Pineapple Ham Pizzas

blended. Gently fold in graham cracker pieces. Serve immediately. **Yield:** 5 servings.

Pineapple Ham Pizzas

(Pictured above)

Prep/Total Time: 10 min.

I like to make these barbecue Hawaiian pizzas as a swift after-school snack. Prepared on toasted English muffins, the cheesy bites easily come together with a snack cup of pineapple bits, deli ham and three other ingredients.
—Vicky Priestley, Alum Creek, West Virginia

✓ Uses less fat, sugar or salt. Includes Nutrition Facts and Diabetic Exchanges.

- 2 English muffins, split and toasted
- 2 tablespoons barbecue sauce
- 2 ounces sliced deli ham, cut into strips
- 1 snack-size cup (4 ounces) pineapple tidbits, well drained
- 2 slices (1 ounce *each*) Swiss cheese, quartered

Place English muffins cut side up on a broiler pan. Spread with barbecue sauce; top with ham, pineapple and cheese. Broil 4-6 in. from the heat for 2-3 minutes or until cheese is melted. **Yield:** 4 pizzas.

Nutrition Facts: 1 pizza (prepared with reduced-fat cheese) equals 112 calories, 2 g fat (1 g saturated fat), 7 mg cholesterol, 324 mg sodium, 18 g carbohydrate, 1 g fiber, 6 g protein. **Diabetic Exchanges:** 1 starch, 1 lean meat.

Chapter 7

WOULDN'T it be nice to have a whole workweek's worth of family dinners all planned out for you? Now you have exactly that—in this handy chapter!

Our home economists took some of their best Test Kitchen recipes and created 6 weeks of Monday-through-Friday suppers. Then, they put together a complete shopping list for each week...so you can get everything you need in just one trip.

You'll savor a wide variety of dishes every week while using many of the same ingredients to prepare them—cutting down on waste and leftovers.

Just glance at the recipes in Week 1, and you'll see specialties ranging from Apricot Beef Stir-Fry to Parmesan Chicken Pasta. We've done all the planning, so just relax and enjoy!

WEEKDAY DELIGHTS. Dressed-Up Steaks and Two-Cheese Baked Potatoes (recipes on p. 123).

Week 1

Crab Salad Croissants

Shopping List

Check for these staples:

- canola oil
- butter
- milk
- soy sauce
- cider vinegar
- lemon juice
- mustard
- mayonnaise
- favorite salad dressing
- cornstarch
- brown sugar
- crushed red pepper flakes
- dill weed
- dried basil
- minced garlic
- salt
- pepper

Shop for these items:

1	head leaf lettuce
1	bunch celery
1-1/4	pounds fresh green beans
1	package (8 ounces) sliced fresh mushrooms
2	medium tomatoes
1	medium onion
1	pound boneless beef sirloin steak
7	boneless skinless chicken breast halves (6 ounces *each*)
1	package (8 ounces) imitation crabmeat
1	package (16 ounces) hot dogs
1	carton (15 ounces) fat-free vegetarian chili
1	bottle (18 ounces) barbecue sauce
1	jar (12 ounces) apricot preserves
1	package (14 ounces) instant rice
2	packages (4.3 ounces *each*) Parmesan cheese pasta sauce mix
4	croissants
4	slices pepper Jack cheese
1	package (8 ounces) shredded cheddar cheese
1	package (16 ounces) frozen asparagus stir-fry vegetable blend
1	package (32 ounces) frozen french-fried potatoes

Time-Saving Tips

- When fixing Monday's crab salad, get a head start on your Wednesday menu by tearing the remainder of the leaf lettuce and by chopping extra onion and celery.
- On Tuesday, trim and cut the green beans that aren't used in the Barbecue Jack Chicken. You'll hurry along Thursday night's Parmesan Chicken Pasta.

Monday

Crab Salad Croissants

(Pictured above)

Prep/Total Time: 15 min.

Celery and onion add crunch to this dill-seasoned crab salad that's tucked into buttery croissants from your grocer's bakery.

- 1 package (8 ounces) imitation crabmeat, chopped
- 1/2 cup mayonnaise
- 1/4 cup chopped celery
- 2 tablespoons shredded cheddar cheese
- 1 tablespoon finely chopped onion
- 1 teaspoon prepared mustard
- 1/4 teaspoon dill weed
- 1/8 teaspoon salt
- 1/8 teaspoon pepper
- 4 lettuce leaves
- 4 croissants, split

In a small bowl, combine the first nine ingredients. Serve on lettuce-lined croissants. **Yield:** 4 servings.

Tuesday

Barbecue Jack Chicken

(Pictured at right)

Prep/Total Time: 25 min.

Pepper Jack cheese and bottled barbecue sauce are all you need to dress up these grilled chicken breasts. Your family will never guess how simple they are!

**4 boneless skinless chicken breast halves
(6 ounces *each*)
4 slices pepper Jack cheese
1 cup barbecue sauce**

Carefully cut a pocket in each chicken breast half. Fill with cheese; secure with metal or soaked wooden skewers. Grill chicken, covered, over medium heat or broil 4 in. from the heat for 6-8 minutes on each side or until juices run clear, basting frequently with barbecue sauce. Remove skewers before serving. **Yield:** 4 servings.

Seasoned Green Beans

(Pictured below)

Prep/Total Time: 20 min.

The mild flavor of the crisp-tender green beans and mushrooms in this side dish is sure to appeal to everyone at the dinner table.

**1 tablespoon canola oil
1 tablespoon lemon juice
1 tablespoon cider vinegar
2 teaspoons dried basil
3/4 teaspoon brown sugar
1/4 teaspoon salt
1/8 teaspoon pepper
1 pound fresh green beans, trimmed
1 cup sliced fresh mushrooms
2 tablespoons butter**

In a small bowl, combine the first seven ingredients; set aside. In a large skillet, saute green beans and mushrooms in butter until almost tender.

Add lemon juice mixture; bring to a boil. Reduce heat; cover and simmer for 5 minutes or until vegetables are tender. **Yield:** 4 servings.

**Seasoned Green Beans
Barbecue Jack Chicken**

**Chili Dog Fries
Simple Side Salad**

Wednesday

Chili Dog Fries

(Pictured above)

Prep/Total Time: 30 min.

Who needs hot dog buns when you serve these saucy chili dogs over french fries from the freezer section? Folks of all ages will enjoy this hearty combo.

**4 cups frozen french-fried potatoes
1 carton (15 ounces) fat-free vegetarian chili
5 hot dogs, halved lengthwise and sliced
1/2 cup chopped onion
1 cup (4 ounces) shredded cheddar cheese**

Prepare fries according to package directions. Meanwhile, in a microwave-safe dish, combine the chili, hot dogs and onion. Cover and microwave on high for 5-6 minutes or until heated through, stirring once. Serve over fries; sprinkle with cheese. **Yield:** 4 servings.

Editor's Note: This recipe was tested in a 1,100-watt microwave.

Simple Side Salad

(Pictured above)

Prep/Total Time: 5 min.

Toss together the remaining lettuce and celery from Monday's croissants for this speedy salad. For a fast finishing touch, top it off with tomato and your favorite dressing.

**2 cups torn leaf lettuce
1 medium tomato, chopped
1/2 cup chopped celery
Salad dressing of your choice**

Divide the lettuce, tomato and celery among four salad plates. Drizzle with dressing. Serve immediately. **Yield:** 4 servings.

Parmesan Chicken Pasta

Apricot Beef Stir-Fry

(Pictured below)

Prep/Total Time: 25 min.

Apricot preserves lend sweetness to this tasty beef stir-fry while red pepper flakes provide a bit of kick. A frozen vegetable medley shaves minutes off prep time...no chopping necessary!

✓ Uses less fat, sugar or salt. Includes Nutrition Facts.

  1 teaspoon cornstarch
  1/4 cup cold water
  1/2 cup apricot preserves
  2 tablespoons soy sauce
  1/2 teaspoon minced garlic
  1/4 teaspoon salt
  1/4 teaspoon crushed red pepper flakes
  1 pound boneless beef sirloin steak, thinly sliced
  1 tablespoon canola oil
  1 package (16 ounces) frozen asparagus stir-fry vegetable blend
Hot cooked rice

In a small bowl, whisk cornstarch and cold water until smooth. Stir in the apricot preserves, soy sauce, garlic, salt and pepper flakes; set aside.

In a large skillet or wok, stir-fry beef in oil until no longer pink; remove and keep warm. In the same pan, stir-fry the vegetable blend according to package directions. Return beef to the pan. Stir apricot mixture and add to beef mixture. Cook and stir until slightly thickened. Serve with rice. **Yield:** 4 servings.

Nutrition Facts: 1 cup (prepared with reduced-sodium soy sauce; calculated without rice) equals 309 calories, 10 g fat (3 g saturated fat), 63 mg cholesterol, 531 mg sodium, 34 g carbohydrate, 3 g fiber, 23 g protein.

Apricot Beef Stir-Fry

Parmesan Chicken Pasta

(Pictured above)

Prep/Total Time: 25 min.

Pasta mixes simplify assembly of this skillet supper that's loaded with tender chicken. Keep in mind that you'll need water, milk and butter to prepare the mixes.

  2 packages (4.3 ounces *each*) Parmesan cheese pasta sauce mix
  3 boneless skinless chicken breasts (about 1 pound), cut into strips
  1 cup sliced fresh mushrooms
  1 cup fresh green beans, cut into 1-inch pieces
  2 tablespoons canola oil
  1 medium tomato, chopped

Prepare pasta mixes according to package directions. Meanwhile, in a large skillet, cook chicken, mushrooms and beans in oil over medium heat for 10-15 minutes or until chicken juices run clear and vegetables are tender; drain. Add to pasta and sauce. Stir in tomato. **Yield:** 4 servings.

Editor's Note: This recipe was tested with Lipton Pasta Sides fettuccine and spinach pasta in a Parmesan cheese sauce mix.

Week 2

Shopping List

Check for these staples:

- all-purpose flour
- butter
- minced garlic
- lemon juice
- 1 egg
- white wine
- balsamic vinegar
- olive oil
- cornstarch
- chicken bouillon granules
- dried rosemary
- rubbed sage
- dried thyme
- ground ginger
- salt
- pepper

Shop for these items:

1-1/2	pounds fresh asparagus
1-1/2	pounds fresh broccoli
2	medium tomatoes
2-1/2	pounds boneless skinless chicken breasts
1	pound medium shrimp, peeled and deveined
4	bone-in pork loin chops (7 ounces *each*, 1-3/4 pounds total)
2	packages (17 ounces *each*) refrigerated beef tips with gravy
1	package (24 ounces) refrigerated mashed potatoes
2	packages (15 ounces *each*) refrigerated pie pastry
1	package (8 ounces) shredded cheddar cheese
1	package (12.7 to 14.8 ounces) sun-dried tomato tortillas
1	bottle (1 pint) orange juice
1	pound prepared deli coleslaw
1	package (8 ounces) Caribbean rice mix
1	can (20 ounces) pineapple tidbits

Time-Saving Tips

- You need only half a pound of asparagus for Monday's meal. Store the rest, unwashed, in the refrigerator to use in Thursday's side dish.
- Clean all of the broccoli on Tuesday and refrigerate what you don't need for Wednesday's side dish.
- Keep the extra pineapple from Thursday's pork chops for Friday's Chicken Coleslaw Wraps.
- If Friday's going to be an extra-busy night, trim time from meal prep by buying grilled chicken strips rather than cooking fresh chicken yourself.

Monday

Caribbean Rice 'n' Shrimp

(Pictured above)

Prep/Total Time: 25 min.

A flavorful rice mix gives a jump start to this skillet supper that's hearty with fresh shrimp, asparagus and tomato. It's not too spicy, so it will please the whole family.

- 1 package (8 ounces) Caribbean rice mix
- 6 cups water
- 1/2 pound fresh asparagus, trimmed and cut into 1-inch pieces
- 1 pound uncooked medium shrimp, peeled and deveined
- 1 medium tomato, chopped

Prepare rice mix according to package directions, omitting chicken. Meanwhile, in a large saucepan, bring water to a boil. Add asparagus; cover and cook for 2 minutes. Stir in shrimp; cook for 2-3 minutes or until shrimp turn pink. Drain. Add asparagus, shrimp and tomato to rice; toss gently. **Yield:** 4 servings.

Tuesday

Beef Tips on Potatoes

(Pictured on page 116)

Prep/Total Time: 15 min.

Dressing up store-bought convenience items makes this satisfying supper a snap to put on the table. It's hot, hearty and ready to eat in minutes.

- 2 packages (17 ounces *each*) refrigerated beef tips with gravy
- 1 package (24 ounces) refrigerated mashed potatoes
- 3/4 cup fresh broccoli florets, finely chopped

1 tablespoon water
3/4 cup shredded cheddar cheese, *divided*

Prepare the beef tips and mashed potatoes according to package directions. Place broccoli and water in a microwave-safe dish; cover and microwave on high for 3 minutes or until crisp-tender.

Stir the broccoli and 1/2 cup cheese into potatoes. Serve beef tips over potatoes; sprinkle with remaining cheese. **Yield:** 4 servings.

Editor's Note: This recipe was tested in a 1,100-watt microwave.

Wednesday

Chicken Wellington

(Pictured below)

Prep: 30 min. **Bake:** 20 min. + standing

Celebrating a special occasion during the week? For an elegant entree, serve this tender chicken tucked inside a golden pie crust and topped with wine sauce.

- **4 boneless skinless chicken breast halves (6 ounces *each*)**
- **1 tablespoon olive oil**
- **2 tablespoons butter, softened, *divided***
- **1 teaspoon dried rosemary, crushed**
- **1/2 teaspoon rubbed sage**
- **1/4 teaspoon salt**
- **1/4 teaspoon pepper**
- **2 packages (15 ounces *each*) refrigerated pie pastry**
- **1 egg, lightly beaten**

SAUCE:
- **1-1/4 teaspoons chicken bouillon granules**
- **1-1/4 cups hot water**
- **2 tablespoons butter**
- **3 tablespoons all-purpose flour**
- **2 tablespoons white wine *or* chicken broth**

Beef Tips on Potatoes

Flatten chicken to an even thickness. In a large skillet, cook chicken in oil and 1 tablespoon butter for 4-5 minutes on each side or until browned.

Meanwhile, in a small bowl, combine rosemary, sage, salt, pepper and remaining butter. Unroll pastry sheets; cut each into a 9-in. square (discard scraps). Place a chicken breast half on each; spread chicken with butter mixture. Fold pastry over chicken. Trim off excess pastry; pinch seams to seal. Place on a greased baking sheet; brush with egg. Bake at 450° for 18-20 minutes or until a meat thermometer reads 170°. Let stand for 10 minutes before serving.

Meanwhile, for sauce, dissolve bouillon in hot water. In a small saucepan, melt butter; stir in flour until smooth. Gradually stir in bouillon and wine or broth. Bring to a boil; cook and stir for 2 minutes or until thickened. Serve with chicken. **Yield:** 4 servings.

Short Thyme Broccoli

(Pictured at left)

Prep/Total Time: 15 min.

Bottled lemon juice adds a splash of citrus to this simple treatment for fresh broccoli. Keep this recipe handy—the versatile side dish will complement many main courses.

✓ Uses less fat, sugar or salt. Includes Nutrition Facts and Diabetic Exchanges.

- **1/2 pound fresh broccoli florets**
- **1 tablespoon olive oil**
- **3/4 teaspoon lemon juice**
- **1/8 teaspoon salt**
- **1/8 teaspoon dried thyme**

Place the broccoli and 1 in. of water in a saucepan; bring to a boil. Reduce heat; cover and simmer for 5-8 minutes or until crisp-tender. Meanwhile, in a small bowl, combine the oil, lemon juice, salt and thyme. Drain broccoli; toss with oil mixture. **Yield:** 4 servings.

Nutrition Facts: 3/4 cup equals 45 calories, 4 g fat (trace saturated fat), 0 cholesterol, 88 mg sodium, 3 g carbohydrate, 2 g fiber, 2 g protein. **Diabetic Exchanges:** 1 vegetable, 1/2 fat.

Short Thyme Broccoli
Chicken Wellington

Thursday

Pineapple Ginger Chops
(Pictured below)

Prep/Total Time: 30 min.

Here, pork chops pick up sweet flavor when simmered on the stovetop in a ginger-seasoned pineapple mixture.

- 1 can (20 ounces) unsweetened pineapple tidbits
- 1 teaspoon pepper
- 1/2 teaspoon ground ginger
- 4 bone-in pork loin chops (7 ounces *each*)
- 1 tablespoon butter
- 1/2 cup orange juice
- 1 tablespoon cornstarch
- 1/8 teaspoon salt
- 1/4 cup water

Drain pineapple, reserving 1/4 cup juice; set aside. Combine pepper and ginger; rub over both sides of pork chops. In a skillet, brown chops in butter for 2-3 minutes on each side. Add orange juice, 1 cup pineapple and reserved pineapple juice. (Refrigerate remaining pineapple for another use.)

Bring to a boil. Reduce heat; cover and simmer for 15-20 minutes or until meat is tender. Remove pork chops and keep warm. In a small bowl, combine the cornstarch, salt and water until smooth; stir into pan juices. Bring to a boil; cook and stir for 2 minutes or until thickened. Serve with pork. **Yield:** 4 servings.

Balsamic Asparagus
(Pictured below)

Prep/Total Time: 15 min.

These pretty green spears of crisp-tender asparagus are drizzled with a balsamic vinegar mixture for a sensational side dish that's ready in no time.

Balsamic Asparagus
Pineapple Ginger Chops

Chicken Coleslaw Wraps

- 1 cup water
- 1 pound fresh asparagus, trimmed
- 2 tablespoons balsamic vinegar
- 1 tablespoon butter, melted
- 1 teaspoon minced garlic
- 1/4 teaspoon salt
- 1/4 teaspoon pepper

In a large skillet, bring water to a boil. Add asparagus; cover and cook for 2-4 minutes or until crisp-tender. In a small bowl, combine the vinegar, butter, garlic, salt and pepper. Drain asparagus; drizzle with balsamic mixture. **Yield:** 4 servings.

Friday

Chicken Coleslaw Wraps
(Pictured above)

Prep/Total Time: 20 min.

Leftover pineapple bits are stirred into deli coleslaw to add refreshing flair to these tasty chicken sandwiches rolled in tortillas.

- 1 pound boneless skinless chicken breasts, cut into 1-inch strips
- 1/4 teaspoon salt
- 1/8 teaspoon pepper
- 1 tablespoon olive oil
- 1-1/2 cups deli coleslaw
- 1/2 cup pineapple tidbits
- 4 sun-dried tomato tortillas (10 inches), warmed
- 1 medium tomato, sliced
- 1 cup (4 ounces) shredded cheddar cheese

Sprinkle chicken with salt and pepper. In a skillet, cook chicken in oil over medium heat for 10-15 minutes or until juices run clear. Combine coleslaw and pineapple; spread evenly over each tortilla. Layer with tomato, cheese and chicken; roll up tightly. **Yield:** 4 servings.

Week 3

Asian Pork Tenderloin Salad

Shopping List

Check for these staples:

- butter
- olive oil
- canola oil
- brown sugar
- minced garlic
- ketchup
- cider vinegar
- soy sauce
- Worcestershire sauce
- hot pepper sauce
- sugar
- maple syrup
- honey
- grated Parmesan cheese
- Italian seasoning
- salt
- pepper
- ground ginger
- ground mustard
- paprika

Shop for these items:

2 packages (9-3/4 ounces *each*) Asian crunch salad mix
1 package (6 ounces) fresh baby spinach
1 pint fresh strawberries
1 onion
1 pork tenderloin (1 pound)
1 beef flank steak (1 pound)
1 pound smoked sausage
1 pound thinly sliced deli turkey
1 pound deli pasta salad
4 slices provolone cheese
2 packages (5.8 ounces *each*) roasted garlic and olive oil couscous
1 can (15 ounces) apricot halves
1 jar (7 ounces) roasted sweet red peppers
1 bottle (8 ounces) Italian salad dressing
1 tube (11 ounces) refrigerated breadsticks
2 packages (7.6 ounces *each*) frozen Cajun blackened grilled fish fillets
1 package (19 ounces) frozen garden vegetable medley
1 loaf (10 ounces) frozen garlic bread

Time-Saving Tips

- Look for Asian crunch salad mix (for Monday's meal) in the produce section near other bagged salad blends. If you can't find it, pick up mixed greens, snow peas, shredded carrot, chow mein noodles and a bottle of sesame ginger or Asian-style salad dressing.
- Tuesday's sandwiches call for part of a jar of roasted red peppers. Save the rest to use on Wednesday.

Monday

Asian Pork Tenderloin Salad

(Pictured above)

Prep: 10 min. + marinating **Cook:** 5 min.

A homemade marinade adds delicious flavor to the stir-fried pork in this main-dish salad. The fast, fresh meal is easy to toss together with canned apricots and convenient salad kits.

✓ Uses less fat, sugar or salt. Includes Nutrition Facts and Diabetic Exchanges.

1 can (15 ounces) apricot halves
1/4 cup soy sauce
1 tablespoon brown sugar
1 tablespoon canola oil
1/2 teaspoon ground ginger
1/2 teaspoon minced garlic
1/4 teaspoon ground mustard
1 pork tenderloin (1 pound), thinly sliced
2 packages (9-3/4 ounces *each*) Asian crunch salad mix

Drain apricots, reserving 1/2 cup juice; set apricots aside. In a large resealable plastic bag, combine the soy sauce, brown sugar, oil, ginger, garlic, mustard and reserved apricot juice; add pork. Seal bag and turn to coat; refrigerate for at least 1 hour.

Drain and discard marinade. In a large skillet or wok, stir-fry pork for 4-5 minutes or until juices run clear. Prepare salad mixes according to package directions; top with apricots and pork. **Yield:** 4 servings.

 Nutrition Facts: 1-1/2 cups salad with 3 ounces cooked meat (prepared with reduced-sodium soy sauce) equals 361 calories, 15 g fat (3 g saturated fat), 63 mg cholesterol, 580 mg sodium, 24 g carbohydrate, 4 g fiber, 26 g protein. **Diabetic Exchanges:** 3 lean meat, 2 vegetable, 2 fat, 1 fruit.

Tuesday

Provolone Turkey Sandwiches

(Pictured below)

Prep/Total Time: 20 min.

These warm open-faced sandwiches make a quick and filling entree before evening activities. Starting with garlic bread from your supermarket's frozen food section hurries along the preparation.

 1 loaf (10 ounces) frozen garlic bread, thawed
 1 pound thinly sliced deli turkey
 1 cup fresh baby spinach
 1/2 cup roasted sweet red peppers, drained and patted dry
 4 slices provolone cheese

Bake garlic bread according to package directions. Layer with turkey, spinach, red peppers and cheese. Bake 3-4 minutes longer or until cheese is melted. Cut into serving-size pieces. **Yield:** 4 servings.

Flank Steak with Couscous

Wednesday

Flank Steak with Couscous

(Pictured above)

Prep/Total Time: 25 min.

It takes just minutes to broil this nicely seasoned flank steak that's served with made-in-minutes couscous. Slicing the meat on an angle across the grain produces the most tender results.

 1 teaspoon olive oil
 1 teaspoon minced garlic
 1/2 teaspoon Italian seasoning
 1/4 teaspoon pepper
 1/8 teaspoon salt
 1 beef flank steak (1 pound)
 2 packages (5.8 ounces *each*) roasted garlic and olive oil couscous
 3/4 cup diced roasted sweet red peppers, drained
 1/2 cup Italian salad dressing

In a small bowl, combine the first five ingredients; rub over flank steak. Place on a broiler pan. Broil 4 in. from the heat for 7-8 minutes on each side or until meat reaches desired doneness (for medium-rare, a meat thermometer should read 145°; medium, 160°; well-done, 170°).

 Meanwhile, cook couscous according to package directions. Stir in roasted peppers. Thinly slice steak across the grain; drizzle with Italian dressing. Serve with couscous. **Yield:** 4 servings.

Provolone Turkey Sandwiches

Strawberry Breadstick Rolls
Blackened Fish Salad

ar and remaining sugar; sprinkle over dough. Reroll, starting with a short end. Cut along seam lines.

Place rolls cut side down on a greased baking sheet. Bake at 375° for 11-13 minutes or until golden brown. Brush with syrup. Serve with reserved strawberry mixture. **Yield:** 6 servings.

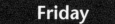
Friday

Smoked Sausage with Vegetables

(Pictured below)

Prep/Total Time: 30 min.

Hearty appetites are sure to be satisfied with this great combo of zippy smoked sausage and colorful vegetables. Using a frozen vegetable medley makes it easy to fix.

- 1 package (19 ounces) frozen garden vegetable medley
- 1/3 cup chopped onion
- 1 tablespoon canola oil
- 1/2 cup water
- 1/2 cup ketchup
- 1/4 cup cider vinegar
- 1 tablespoon Worcestershire sauce
- 1 tablespoon honey
- 1 teaspoon ground mustard
- 1 teaspoon paprika
- 1/4 teaspoon salt
- 1/4 teaspoon sugar
- 1/8 teaspoon pepper
- 1/8 teaspoon hot pepper sauce
- 1 pound smoked sausage, sliced

Cook vegetables according to package directions. Meanwhile, in a large skillet, saute onion in oil until tender. Stir in the water, ketchup, vinegar, Worcestershire sauce, honey, mustard, paprika, salt, sugar, pepper and hot pepper sauce. Add sausage.

Bring to a boil. Reduce heat; simmer, uncovered, for 10-12 minutes or until sauce is slightly thickened and sausage is heated through, stirring occasionally and turning sausage once. Serve with the vegetable medley. **Yield:** 4 servings.

Thursday

Blackened Fish Salad

(Pictured above)

Prep/Total Time: 25 min.

A handful of convenience items, including pasta salad from the deli and Cajun-style fish fillets from the freezer section, makes it a snap to fix this fast main dish.

- 2 packages (7.6 ounces *each*) frozen Cajun blackened grilled fish fillets
- 1 pound deli pasta salad
- 1 cup fresh baby spinach
- 2 tablespoons grated Parmesan cheese

Bake fish fillets according to package directions. Meanwhile, in a large bowl, toss the pasta salad and spinach. Divide among four plates. Cut fish into slices; arrange over salad. Sprinkle with cheese. **Yield:** 4 servings.

Strawberry Breadstick Rolls

(Pictured above)

Prep/Total Time: 30 min.

For a simple dessert, bake these sweet fruit-topped rolls that call for just six ingredients. They're so yummy, your family may request them for breakfast, too.

- 2 cups sliced fresh strawberries
- 5 teaspoons sugar, *divided*
- 1 tube (11 ounces) refrigerated breadsticks
- 2 tablespoons butter, melted
- 2 tablespoons brown sugar
- 2 tablespoons maple syrup

In a small bowl, combine the strawberries and 2 teaspoons sugar; set aside. On a lightly floured surface, unroll breadstick dough (do not separate). Seal perforations; brush dough with butter. Combine brown sug-

Smoked Sausage with Vegetables

Week 4

Black Bean Taco Salad

Shopping List

Check for these staples:

- butter
- olive oil
- minced garlic
- lemon juice
- mayonnaise
- eggs
- dried oregano
- dried parsley flakes
- salt
- pepper

Shop for these items:

- 1 head green leaf lettuce
- 4 large tomatoes
- 4 large baking potatoes
- 2 packages (.75 ounce *each*) fresh basil
- 2 pounds boneless skinless chicken breasts
- 1 pound ground beef
- 4 salmon fillets (6 ounces *each*, 1-1/2 pounds total)
- 4 boneless beef sirloin steaks (6 ounces *each*, 1-1/2 pounds total)
- 1 package (16 ounces) shredded part-skim mozzarella cheese
- 1 package (10 ounces) shredded Parmesan cheese
- 1 package (12 ounces) pita breads
- 1 Italian bread shell crust (14 ounces)
- 1 package (25 ounces) nacho cheese tortilla chips
- 1 jar (16 ounces) Catalina dressing
- 1 can (15 ounces) black beans

Time-Saving Tips

- On Monday, clean the entire head of lettuce to ease dinner prep later in the week. Set aside eight leaves for Friday night's Nacho Chicken Pitas and tear up the rest of the lettuce, placing 2 cups in a plastic bag for Tuesday's salad.
- Save the extra pesto from Tuesday's fish to prepare the Chicken Pizza on Wednesday.
- Is Wednesday going to be an extra-busy night? Hurry along the Chicken Pizza recipe by using rotisserie chicken from your supermarket's deli instead of cooking chicken breast strips yourself.
- If the weather forecast for Thursday looks good for grilling, cook the Dressed-Up Steaks on the grill to give them even more flavor.

Monday

Black Bean Taco Salad
(Pictured above)

Prep/Total Time: 20 min.

After assembling this mild main-dish salad, be sure to set aside the remaining canned black beans to use in Wednesday's meal.

- 1 pound ground beef
- 4 cups torn leaf lettuce
- 1 large tomato, chopped
- 1 cup canned black beans, rinsed and drained
- 1/2 cup Catalina salad dressing
- 4 cups nacho cheese tortilla chips

In a large skillet, cook beef over medium heat until no longer pink; drain. In a large bowl, combine the lettuce, tomato, beans and beef. Drizzle with dressing and toss to coat. Arrange tortilla chips on a serving plate; top with beef mixture. **Yield:** 4 servings.

No-Fuss Salads

My family loves to eat salad, so I buy a lot of salad mixes in bags. But the lettuce pieces are often too big. To solve the problem, I put the mix into a bowl and use kitchen scissors to cut the lettuce into bite-size pieces before adding the other ingredients.
—*Mary-Dawn Selby, Ashland, Kentucky*

Basil Salmon
Catalina Parmesan Salad

2 cups torn leaf lettuce
2/3 cup chopped fresh tomato
1/4 cup shredded Parmesan cheese
1/4 cup Catalina salad dressing

Divide the lettuce and tomato among four small salad plates. Sprinkle with Parmesan cheese and drizzle with dressing. **Yield:** 4 servings.

Wednesday

Chicken Pizza

(Pictured below)

Prep/Total Time: 30 min.

Your family will never guess that this fun twist on typical pizza uses up leftover pesto. Loaded with chicken and black beans, hearty slices will fill them up fast.

1 pound boneless skinless chicken breasts, cut into 1-inch strips
1 tablespoon olive oil
1 prebaked Italian bread shell crust (14 ounces)
1/4 cup prepared pesto
1 large tomato, chopped
1/2 cup canned black beans, rinsed and drained
1 cup (4 ounces) shredded part-skim mozzarella cheese
1/2 cup shredded Parmesan cheese

In a large skillet, cook chicken in oil over medium heat for 10-15 minutes or until juices run clear. Place the crust on a lightly greased 12-in. pizza pan. Spread with pesto; top with the chicken, tomato, beans and cheeses. Bake at 400° for 10-12 minutes or until cheese is melted. **Yield:** 6 servings.

Chicken Pizza

Tuesday

Basil Salmon

(Pictured above)

Prep: 15 min. **Bake:** 25 min.

Homemade pesto adds instant flair to these tasty salmon fillets. While they bake in the oven, you can assemble the simple green salad.

1-1/2 cups fresh basil leaves
3 tablespoons plus 2 teaspoons olive oil
1-1/2 teaspoons minced garlic
3/4 teaspoon pepper
1/2 teaspoon lemon juice
1/4 teaspoon salt
1 tablespoon plus 4 teaspoons shredded Parmesan cheese, *divided*
4 salmon fillets (6 ounces *each*)

For pesto, combine basil, oil, garlic, pepper, lemon juice, salt and 1 tablespoon Parmesan cheese in a food processor; cover and process until finely chopped. Place the salmon in a greased 13-in. x 9-in. x 2-in. baking dish. Spread 2 tablespoons pesto over fillets. (Cover and refrigerate remaining pesto for tomorrow's Chicken Pizza or another use.)

Bake, uncovered, at 400° for 20-22 minutes or until fish flakes easily with a fork. Sprinkle with remaining cheese. Bake 2-3 minutes longer or until cheese is melted. **Yield:** 4 servings.

Catalina Parmesan Salad

(Pictured above)

Prep/Total Time: 10 min.

Served with the salmon, this salad is a terrific way to make the most of the ingredients from your shopping trip. Toss in any additional salad fixings you have on hand.

Dressed-Up Steaks
Two-Cheese Baked Potatoes

Thursday

Dressed-Up Steaks

(Pictured above and on page 110)

Prep/Total Time: 20 min.

Just five pantry ingredients nicely season these special-looking broiled steaks that are accented with extra Catalina salad dressing.

    1 tablespoon olive oil
1-1/2 teaspoons minced garlic
    1 teaspoon dried oregano
    1 teaspoon pepper
    4 boneless beef sirloin steaks (6 ounces *each*)
 3/4 cup Catalina salad dressing, *divided*

In a small bowl, combine the oil, garlic, oregano and pepper. Rub over both sides of steaks. Brush with 1/4 cup salad dressing. Place on a broiler pan.

  Broil 4 in. from the heat for 5-6 minutes on each side or until meat reaches desired doneness (for medium-rare, a meat thermometer should read 145°; medium, 160°; well-done, 170°). Serve with the remaining dressing. **Yield:** 4 servings.

Two-Cheese Baked Potatoes

(Pictured above and on page 110)

Prep/Total Time: 25 min.

What's a steak without a baked potato? Here's an easy way to top tender baked potatoes that are cooked in the microwave in minutes.

    4 large baking potatoes
 1/4 cup shredded Parmesan cheese
 1/4 cup shredded part-skim mozzarella cheese
 1/4 teaspoon salt
 1/4 teaspoon pepper

    4 teaspoons butter
 1/2 teaspoon dried parsley flakes

Scrub and pierce potatoes; place on a microwave-safe plate. Microwave, uncovered, on high for 13-15 minutes or until tender, turning once. Meanwhile, combine the cheeses, salt and pepper in a small bowl.

  Cut an X in the top of each potato; fluff pulp with a fork. Top with butter and cheese mixture; sprinkle with parsley. **Yield:** 4 servings.

  Editor's Note: This recipe was tested in a 1,100-watt microwave.

Friday

Nacho Chicken Pitas

(Pictured below)

Prep: 20 min. **Bake:** 20 min.

Crushed nacho tortilla chips left over from the taco salad made earlier in the week coat these tender chicken strips. This is a great sandwich recipe for families.

    1 egg
    1 cup crushed nacho cheese tortilla chips
    1 pound boneless skinless chicken breasts, cut
      into 1-inch strips
 1/2 cup mayonnaise
    4 pita breads (6 inches), halved
    8 lettuce leaves
    1 large tomato, sliced
 1/2 cup shredded part-skim mozzarella cheese

In a shallow bowl, beat the egg. Place crushed chips in another shallow bowl. Dip chicken in egg, then coat with chips. Place in a single layer in a greased 11-in. x 7-in. x 2-in. baking dish. Bake at 400° for 20-25 minutes or until juices run clear.

  Spread mayonnaise inside pita halves; line with lettuce. Fill with chicken and tomato; sprinkle with cheese. **Yield:** 4 servings.

Nacho Chicken Pitas

Week 5

Check for these staples:

- olive oil
- butter
- red wine vinegar
- mayonnaise
- milk
- all-purpose flour
- sugar
- dried basil
- dried parsley flakes
- dried thyme
- dried oregano
- pepper
- rubbed sage
- salt

Shop for these items:

2	bunches green leaf lettuce
3	medium tomatoes
1/2	pound fresh sugar snap peas
1-1/4	pounds sliced deli roast beef
1	pound cubed fully cooked ham
1	package (2.1 ounces) fully cooked bacon
6	boneless skinless chicken breast halves (6 ounces *each*)
1	pouch (3.6 ounces) roasted garlic instant mashed potatoes
1	jar (12 ounces) honey mustard
1	jar (4 ounces) prepared horseradish
1	loaf (12 ounces) focaccia bread
1	package (2-count) hard-cooked eggs
6	ounces deli Swiss cheese
1	container (8 ounces) sour cream
1	package (16 ounces) frozen corn
1	package (24 ounces) frozen pasta, broccoli and Alfredo sauce

Time-Saving Tips

- Use some of the deli roast beef for Monday's Roast Beef BLT sandwiches and cut the remainder into strips for the Swiss Cobb Salad on Tuesday.
- For Tuesday night's main-dish salad, you'll need two chopped, hard-cooked eggs. But you can easily cook them the night before...and even cook a few extras for a high-protein snack.
- You can flatten Thursday's chicken breasts to shave minutes off cooking time, but you'll need a very large skillet to cook all four at once.
- On Friday, you should have lettuce left over from Tuesday's salad in the refrigerator. Use that lettuce to toss together a green salad drizzled with your favorite dressing to round out Friday's meal.

Roast Beef BLT

Monday

Roast Beef BLT

(Pictured above)

Prep/Total Time: 15 min.

A creamy horseradish spread adds zip to each satisfying wedge of this stacked sandwich. It tastes special, yet is incredibly simple to prepare. Use any bread you like or change the sandwich fillings to suit your tastes.

- 1 loaf (12 ounces) focaccia bread
- 1/2 cup mayonnaise
- 1 teaspoon prepared horseradish
- 3 lettuce leaves
- 3/4 pound sliced deli roast beef
- 6 bacon strips, cooked
- 8 slices tomato

Cut focaccia bread in half horizontally. Combine mayonnaise and horseradish; spread over cut sides of bread. Layer the lettuce, roast beef, bacon and tomato over bread bottom; replace bread top. Cut into wedges. **Yield:** 4 servings.

Tuesday

Swiss Cobb Salad

(Pictured at right)

Prep/Total Time: 20 min.

Topped with ham, roast beef, bacon and other fixings, this hearty salad has an excellent blend of flavors. A from-scratch vinaigrette adds the refreshing final touch.

- 8 cups torn leaf lettuce
- 1/2 pound sliced deli roast beef, cut into strips

1/4 pound cubed fully cooked ham
1 medium tomato, chopped
2 hard-cooked eggs, chopped
4 bacon strips, cooked and crumbled
1/2 cup shredded Swiss cheese
DRESSING:
1/2 cup olive oil
3 tablespoons red wine vinegar
2 tablespoons honey mustard
2 teaspoons sugar
3/4 teaspoon dried oregano
1/8 teaspoon pepper

In a serving bowl, layer the lettuce, roast beef, ham, tomato, eggs, bacon and cheese. In a jar with a tight-fitting lid, combine the dressing ingredients; shake well. Serve with the salad. **Yield:** 4 servings.

Chicken Shepherd's Pie

Wednesday

Chicken Shepherd's Pie

(Pictured above right)

Prep: 25 min. **Bake:** 25 min.

Warm up your family with this easy mashed-potato-topped casserole featuring tender chicken, sugar snap peas and sweet corn in a homemade cheese sauce.

✓ Uses less fat, sugar or salt. Includes Nutrition Facts and Diabetic Exchanges.

2 boneless skinless chicken breast halves (6 ounces *each*), cubed
4 tablespoons butter, *divided*
1 pouch (3.6 ounces) roasted garlic mashed potatoes
3 tablespoons all-purpose flour
2-1/4 cups milk
1 teaspoon rubbed sage
1 teaspoon dried thyme

Swiss Cobb Salad

1/2 teaspoon salt
1/2 teaspoon pepper
1 cup (4 ounces) shredded Swiss cheese, *divided*
1 cup fresh sugar snap peas, trimmed and chopped
1/2 cup frozen corn

In a small skillet, cook chicken in 1 tablespoon butter until no longer pink; set aside and keep warm. Prepare mashed potatoes according to package directions.

Meanwhile, in a large saucepan, melt remaining butter over medium heat. Whisk in flour until smooth. Gradually add milk; stir in seasonings. Bring to a boil. Reduce heat; cook and stir for 1-2 minutes or thickened.

Remove from the heat. Stir in 3/4 cup Swiss cheese until melted. Add peas, corn and chicken. Transfer to a 2-qt. baking dish coated with nonstick cooking spray. Top with mashed potatoes; sprinkle with remaining cheese.

Bake, uncovered, at 350° for 25-30 minutes or until heated through. Let stand for 5 minutes before serving. **Yield:** 6 servings.

Nutrition Facts: 1 serving (prepared with reduced-fat butter, fat-free milk and reduced-fat Swiss cheese) equals 316 calories, 13 g fat (7 g saturated fat), 68 mg cholesterol, 660 mg sodium, 27 g carbohydrate, 2 g fiber, 26 g protein. **Diabetic Exchanges:** 2 starch, 2 lean meat, 1 fat.

Thursday

Chicken with Mustard Gravy

(Pictured on page 126)

Prep/Total Time: 25 min.

A rich gravy made with honey mustard and sour cream drapes nicely over these golden brown chicken breasts. They're cooked on the stove in minutes and are guaranteed to please the whole family.

4 boneless skinless chicken breast halves
  (6 ounces *each***)**
1/2 teaspoon salt, *divided*
1/4 teaspoon pepper, *divided*
2 tablespoons butter
4 teaspoons honey mustard
1 tablespoon milk
1/2 teaspoon dried basil
1/2 teaspoon dried parsley flakes
1/2 cup sour cream

Rub chicken with 1/4 teaspoon salt and 1/8 teaspoon pepper. In a large skillet over medium heat, cook chicken in butter for 6-8 minutes on each side or until no longer pink. Remove and keep warm.

In the same skillet, combine the mustard, milk, basil, parsley, and remaining salt and pepper. Cook and stir over low heat until heated through. Remove from the heat; stir in the sour cream. Serve with the chicken. **Yield:** 4 servings.

Nutrition Facts: 1 chicken breast half with 2 tablespoons gravy (prepared with reduced-fat butter and reduced-fat sour cream) equals 262 calories, 10 g fat (5 g saturated fat), 115 mg cholesterol, 476 mg sodium, 5 g carbohydrate, trace fiber, 37 g protein. **Diabetic Exchanges:** 4 very lean meat, 2-1/2 fat.

Flavorful Corn

(Pictured below)

Prep/Total Time: 15 min.

A pinch of sage and thyme season this quick-and-easy treatment for frozen corn. The speedy side dish is versatile enough to serve with most any entree.

2-1/2 cups frozen corn
1/4 cup water

Chicken with Mustard Gravy
Flavorful Corn

Snap Peas 'n' Ham Alfredo

1 tablespoon butter
1/4 teaspoon rubbed sage
1/8 teaspoon dried thyme
1/8 teaspoon pepper

In a large saucepan, bring the corn and water to a boil. Reduce heat; cover and simmer for 4-6 minutes or until corn is tender. Drain; add the butter and seasonings. Stir until butter is melted. **Yield:** 4 servings.

Friday

Snap Peas 'n' Ham Alfredo

(Pictured above)

Prep/Total Time: 20 min.

This fast-to-fix entree comes together in a jiffy with help from a frozen pasta and veggie combo. Adding ham and fresh sugar snap peas really jazzes it up. Stir some red pepper flakes into the creamy mixture for an extra kick.

1 package (24 ounces) frozen pasta, broccoli
  and Alfredo sauce
2 cups fresh sugar snap peas
1/4 cup water
2 cups cubed fully cooked ham
1/2 teaspoon dried oregano
1/8 teaspoon pepper

Prepare pasta and sauce according to package directions. Meanwhile, place peas and water in a microwave-safe dish. Cover and microwave on high for 2-3 minutes or until crisp-tender; drain.

Stir the peas, ham, oregano and pepper into pasta mixture; cook and stir for 3-4 minutes or until heated through. **Yield:** 4 servings.

Editor's Note: This recipe was tested in a 1,100-watt microwave.

Week 6

Shopping List

Check for these staples:

- milk
- olive oil
- butter
- brown sugar
- honey
- flour
- eggs
- lemon juice
- minced garlic
- grated Parmesan cheese
- cayenne pepper
- dill weed
- dried parsley
- ground cinnamon
- ground nutmeg
- Italian seasoning
- lemon-pepper seasoning
- pepper
- salt

Shop for these items:

- 2 medium acorn squash
- 2 medium zucchini
- 1 sweet orange pepper
- 2 medium onions
- 1 package (6 ounces) fresh baby spinach
- 1 package (5 ounces) spring mix salad greens
- 1 package (6 ounces) baby portobello mushrooms
- 1 pound boneless beef sirloin steak
- 1 pound boneless skinless chicken breasts
- 4 tilapia fillets (6 ounces *each*)
- 1 pound bulk spicy pork sausage
- 1/2 pound sliced bacon
- 1 package (16 ounces) linguine
- 1 package (9.3 ounces) minestrone soup mix
- 1 bottle (16 ounces) balsamic vinaigrette
- 1 package (6 ounces) dried cranberries
- 1 package (4 ounces) pine nuts
- 1 package (8 ounces) cream cheese
- 1 package (4 ounces) blue cheese
- 1 loaf (1 pound) French bread

Time-Saving Tips

- Tear extra bread from Monday into chunks. Process them in a blender or food processor in batches to get the soft bread crumbs needed for Tuesday.
- To grind the pine nuts for Thursday's Pine Nut-Crusted Tilapia, pulse them in a food processor just until ground. Be careful not to overprocess, or the nuts will turn into a paste. In a pinch, use walnuts, hazelnuts or pecans instead of pine nuts.

Monday

Chicken Minestrone
(Pictured above)
Prep/Total Time: 30 min.

A packaged minestrone soup mix is perked up with cubed chicken, sliced zucchini, portobello mushrooms and crunchy croutons for this mouth-watering main course. It's easy to prepare, yet seems like you fussed.

- 1 package (9.3 ounces) minestrone soup mix
- 1 medium zucchini, quartered lengthwise and sliced
- 1 cup chopped baby portobello mushrooms
- 1 pound boneless skinless chicken breasts, cubed
- 1 tablespoon olive oil
- 1/4 cup butter, melted
- 1 teaspoon dried parsley flakes
- 6 slices day-old French bread (1 inch thick), cubed
- 2 tablespoons grated Parmesan cheese

Prepare soup mix according to package directions, adding zucchini and mushrooms. Meanwhile, in a large skillet, cook chicken in oil for 10-12 minutes or until juices run clear. Stir into soup.

For croutons, in a large bowl, combine butter and parsley. Add bread cubes and toss to coat. Arrange in a single layer on an ungreased baking sheet. Sprinkle with Parmesan cheese. Bake at 400° for 7-8 minutes or until golden brown, stirring occasionally. Serve with soup. **Yield:** 5 servings.

Sausage-Stuffed Acorn Squash

On a chilly evening, this creamy pasta toss is sure to please. It's rich and flavorful with smoky bacon, fresh spinach and toasted pine nuts.

    12 ounces uncooked linguine
    1/2 pound sliced bacon, diced
    5 cups fresh baby spinach
    1/2 cup chopped onion
    1/2 teaspoon minced garlic
    1-1/4 cups milk
    1 package (8 ounces) cream cheese, cubed
    2 tablespoons butter
    1/2 teaspoon salt
    1/4 teaspoon ground nutmeg
    1/4 teaspoon pepper
    1/2 cup pine nuts, toasted

Cook linguine according to package directions. Meanwhile, in a large skillet, cook bacon over medium heat until crisp. Using a slotted spoon, remove to paper towels; drain, reserving 1 tablespoon drippings.

In the drippings, saute spinach, onion and garlic until tender. Add milk, cream cheese, butter, salt, nutmeg and pepper; stir until smooth. Stir in nuts and bacon; heat through. Drain pasta; toss with sauce. **Yield:** 4-6 servings.

Tuesday

Sausage-Stuffed Acorn Squash

(Pictured above)

Prep/Total Time: 25 min.

This acorn squash gets dressed up in a sweet-and-savory way with a stuffing of sausage, spinach and cranberries. Using the microwave speeds up the preparation.

    2 medium acorn squash
    1 pound bulk spicy pork sausage
    1/2 cup chopped onion
    1 egg
    2 tablespoons milk
    1 cup fresh baby spinach, finely chopped
    1-1/2 cups soft bread crumbs
    1/2 cup dried cranberries

Cut squash in half; remove and discard seeds. Put squash cut side down in a microwave-safe dish. Cover and microwave on high for 10-12 minutes or until tender.

Meanwhile, crumble sausage into a large skillet; add onion. Cook over medium heat until meat is no longer pink; drain. In a large bowl, beat egg and milk; stir in spinach, bread crumbs, berries and sausage mixture.

Turn squash cut side up. Stuff with sausage mixture. Cover and microwave on high for 2-3 minutes or until heated through. **Yield:** 4 servings.

Editor's Note: This recipe was tested in a 1,100-watt microwave.

Wednesday

Linguine with Garlic Sauce

(Pictured at right)

Prep/Total Time: 30 min.

Thursday

Pine Nut-Crusted Tilapia

(Pictured above right)

Prep/Total Time: 25 min.

This golden brown fish has a tender texture, nutty coating and hint of honey. It's fast to fix and can be served for a special family meal or when you want to impress guests.

    1/2 cup pine nuts, ground
    1/4 cup all-purpose flour
    1/4 teaspoon dill weed
    1/4 teaspoon lemon-pepper seasoning
    1 egg
    3 tablespoons lemon juice

Linguine with Garlic Sauce

Pine Nut-Crusted Tilapia
Roasted Italian Vegetables

1 teaspoon honey
4 tilapia fillets (6 ounces *each*)
2 tablespoons butter
Additional honey, optional

In a shallow bowl, combine nuts, flour, dill and lemon-pepper. In another shallow bowl, combine egg, juice and honey. Dip fillets in egg mixture; coat with nut mixture.

In a large nonstick skillet, cook fillets in butter over medium heat for 4-5 minutes on each side or until fish flakes easily with a fork. Drizzle with additional honey if desired. **Yield:** 4 servings.

Roasted Italian Vegetables

(Pictured above)

Prep/Total Time: 25 min.

This buttery medley of oven-baked vegetables is ideal with fish or most any meat. Zucchini and sweet orange pepper make it colorful.

 Uses less fat, sugar or salt. Includes Nutrition Facts and Diabetic Exchanges.

1 medium zucchini, cut into 1/4-inch slices
1-1/2 cups sliced baby portobello mushrooms
1 medium sweet orange pepper, julienned
1 tablespoon olive oil
1 tablespoon butter, melted
1 teaspoon Italian seasoning
1/2 teaspoon salt
1/8 teaspoon pepper

In a large bowl, combine zucchini, mushrooms and orange pepper. Add remaining ingredients; toss to coat.

Arrange vegetables in a single layer in a 15-in. x 10-in. x 1-in. baking pan coated with nonstick cooking spray. Bake, uncovered, at 450° for 15-20 minutes or until tender, stirring occasionally. **Yield:** 4 servings.

Nutrition Facts: 1/2 cup (prepared with reduced-fat butter) equals 68 calories, 5 g fat (1 g saturated fat), 5 mg cholesterol, 316 mg sodium, 5 g carbohydrate, 2 g fiber, 2 g protein. **Diabetic Exchanges:** 1 vegetable, 1 fat.

Savory Steak Salad

(Pictured below)

Prep/Total Time: 30 min.

Caramelized onion and sirloin steak seasoned with a cinnamon rub make this main-dish salad different from typical versions. It's easy to toss together with packaged greens, crumbled blue cheese, dried cranberries and store-bought vinaigrette.

2 tablespoons brown sugar, *divided*
1 teaspoon salt
3/4 teaspoon ground cinnamon
1/4 teaspoon cayenne pepper
1/4 teaspoon pepper
1 boneless beef sirloin steak (1 inch thick and 1 pound)
3/4 cup balsamic vinaigrette, *divided*
1 medium onion, sliced
2 tablespoons butter
1 package (5 ounces) spring mix salad greens
1/2 cup dried cranberries
1/4 cup crumbled blue cheese

In a small bowl, combine 1 tablespoon brown sugar, salt, cinnamon, cayenne and pepper. Rub over both sides of steak. Brush with 1/4 cup vinaigrette.

Place steak on a broiler pan. Broil 4 in. from the heat for 5-6 minutes on each side or until meat reaches desired doneness (for medium-rare, a meat thermometer should read 145°; medium, 160°; well-done, 170°).

Meanwhile, in a large skillet, saute onion in butter for 10 minutes or until tender. Add remaining brown sugar; cook and stir over medium heat for 5-10 minutes or until onion is browned.

Cut steak across the grain into thin slices. In a large bowl, combine the greens, cranberries, blue cheese, onion and beef. Drizzle with remaining vinaigrette; toss to coat. **Yield:** 4 servings.

Savory Steak Salad

Chapter 8

⏱ *Look Ahead for Lively Leftovers*

IT CAN BE your little secret... these taste-tempting, satisfying recipes rely on yesterday's leftovers. Your family will enjoy them so much, they'll probably never even notice!

From main dishes and appetizers to sandwiches and soups, this creative fare takes advantage of cooked chicken, rice, day-old bread and other common extras. You'll avoid waste and get a head start on dinner using ready-made ingredients.

Plus, at the end of this chapter, we've included two main courses designed to *create* leftovers. Those recipes are followed by deliciously different dishes you can fix later in the week to use up the extras. You get two meals out of one!

EXTRA, EXTRA! Herbed Pork and Potatoes (p. 139).

**Philly Beef 'n' Pepper Strata
Garden Chicken Salad**

ate for 8 hours or overnight.

Remove from the refrigerator 30 minutes before baking. Bake, covered, at 325° for 1 hour. Uncover; bake 15-20 minutes longer or until a knife inserted near the center comes out clean. Let stand for 10 minutes before serving. **Yield:** 12 servings.

Garden Chicken Salad

(Pictured at left)

Prep/Total Time: 25 min.

Extra chicken is the key to this refreshing salad. The first time I served it, my father-in-law teased me about being a gourmet cook. —Polly Thayer, Sunbury, Pennsylvania

    1 package (10 ounces) fresh baby spinach
2-1/2 cups cubed cooked chicken
    2 cups fresh broccoli florets
    2 medium tomatoes, cut into thin wedges
    1 cup chopped seeded peeled cucumber
    1 cup fresh snow peas
  1/3 cup chopped red onion
DRESSING:
  1/3 cup mayonnaise
  1/4 cup plain yogurt
    2 teaspoons dill weed
  1/4 teaspoon salt

In a large salad bowl, combine spinach, chicken, broccoli, tomatoes, cucumber, snow peas and onion. In a small bowl, combine dressing ingredients. Drizzle over salad and toss to coat. **Yield:** 8 servings.

Philly Beef 'n' Pepper Strata

(Pictured above)

Prep: 15 min. + chilling **Bake:** 1-1/4 hours + standing

This beefy bake is a mouth-watering entree for brunch, lunch or dinner and is quick to assemble. The recipe combines several convenient ingredients and left-overs to yield a crowd-size casserole that pleases everyone. —Betty Claycomb Alverton, Pennsylvania

    7 cups cubed Italian bread
    1 package (16 ounces) frozen pepper and onion stir-fry blend
  3/4 pound cooked roast beef, cut into thin strips
    2 cups (8 ounces) shredded Monterey Jack cheese
    8 eggs
2-1/4 cups milk
    2 tablespoons Dijon mustard
  1/2 teaspoon *each* salt and pepper

Place a third of the bread cubes in a greased 13-in. x 9-in. x 2-in. baking dish. Layer with a third of the pepper/onion mix, roast beef and cheese. Repeat layers twice. In a large bowl, whisk the eggs, milk, mustard, salt and pepper; pour over the top. Cover and refriger-

Sausage Egg Bake

Prep: 25 min. **Bake:** 25 min.

Here's a busy-day breakfast dish that's fast, flavorful and fun to make. The added bonus? It uses any hard-cooked eggs you may have left over from Easter.
—Erika Anderson, Wausau, Wisconsin

  1/2 pound bulk pork sausage
    3 tablespoons butter, melted, *divided*
    2 tablespoons all-purpose flour
  1/4 teaspoon salt
  1/4 teaspoon pepper
1-1/4 cups milk
    2 cups frozen shredded hash brown potatoes
    4 hard-cooked eggs, sliced
  1/2 cup crushed cornflakes
  1/4 cup sliced green onions

In a large skillet, cook sausage over medium heat until no longer pink; drain. Stir in 2 tablespoons butter, flour, salt and pepper until blended. Gradually add milk. Bring to a boil; cook and stir for 2 minutes or until thickened. Stir in the hash browns and eggs. Transfer to a greased 1-qt. baking dish.

Toss cornflakes and remaining butter; sprinkle over sausage mixture. Bake, uncovered, at 350° for 25-30 minutes or until heated through. Sprinkle with onions. **Yield:** 3 servings.

Easy Chicken Enchiladas

(Pictured below)

Prep: 20 min. **Bake:** 25 min.

This southwestern dish is so easy to prepare, and I always receive a ton of compliments on it. Whenever I share the recipe with friends, the hearty enchiladas instantly become favorites in their households as well. —Kristi Black
Harrison Township, Michigan

1 can (10 ounces) enchilada sauce, *divided*
4 ounces cream cheese, cubed
1-1/2 cups salsa
2 cups cubed cooked chicken
1 can (15-1/2 ounces) pinto beans, rinsed and drained
1 can (4 ounces) chopped green chilies
10 flour tortillas (6 inches)
1 cup (4 ounces) shredded Mexican cheese blend
Shredded lettuce, chopped tomato, sour cream and sliced ripe olives, optional

Spoon 1/2 cup enchilada sauce into a greased 13-in. x 9-in. x 2-in. baking dish. In a large saucepan, cook and stir the cream cheese and salsa over medium heat for 2-3 minutes or until blended. Stir in the chicken, beans and chilies.

Place about 6 tablespoons of chicken mixture down the center of each tortilla. Roll up and place seam side down over sauce. Top with remaining enchilada sauce; sprinkle with cheese.

Cover and bake at 350° for 25-30 minutes or until heated through. Serve with lettuce, tomato, sour cream and olives if desired. **Yield:** 5 servings.

Easy Chicken Enchiladas

Supper Sandwiches

Supper Sandwiches

(Pictured above)

Prep/Total Time: 20 min.

All main dishes should be as effortless as these hefty and flavorful sandwiches! I especially like them in the summertime, when I'm busy with lots of activities and don't want to be held up in the kitchen with dinner. —Esther Danielson
Lake Arrowhead, California

1/2 pound fully cooked kielbasa *or* Polish sausage
1/2 medium sweet red pepper, julienned
1 small onion, halved and thinly sliced
1-1/2 teaspoons butter
1/2 cup chopped tomato, optional
1 to 2 tablespoons mustard *or* mayonnaise
2 hoagie buns, split and toasted

Cut sausage in half widthwise; cut each piece lengthwise to within 1/4 in. of opposite side. Place cut side down in a large skillet; add red pepper, onion and butter. Cook over medium-high heat until vegetables are tender.

Add tomato if desired; heat through. Spread mustard over cut sides of buns; fill with sausage and vegetables. **Yield:** 2 servings.

Chicken Choices

WHEN recipes in this book call for cooked chicken, it usually doesn't matter how the chicken was prepared—whether baked, roasted, poached or grilled. Don't have leftovers? Packages of cooked chicken strips or cubes are available in the meat case. Rotisserie chicken from the deli is another good option.

Turkey Wild Rice Salad

(Pictured below)

Prep/Total Time: 25 min.

Serve up a medley of textures and tastes with this colorful luncheon idea from our Test Kitchen home economists. Crunchy celery, red pepper and pecans combine with juicy grapes, dried cherries, wild rice and leftover turkey in this standout salad.

✓ Uses less fat, sugar or salt. Includes Nutrition Facts and Diabetic Exchanges.

    2 cups cubed cooked turkey breast
    2 cups cooked wild rice
    1 cup seedless red grapes, halved
  1/2 cup diced sweet red pepper
  1/2 cup chopped celery
  1/2 cup dried cherries
  1/2 cup coarsely chopped pecans, toasted
    4 green onions, sliced
  1/3 cup raspberry vinaigrette

In a large bowl, combine the first eight ingredients. Drizzle with vinaigrette and toss to coat. Refrigerate until serving. **Yield:** 7 servings.

Nutrition Facts: 1 cup (prepared with fat-free vinaigrette) equals 228 calories, 7 g fat (1 g saturated fat), 34 mg cholesterol, 83 mg sodium, 28 g carbohydrate, 3 g fiber, 15 g protein. **Diabetic Exchanges:** 1 starch, 1 very lean meat, 1 fruit, 1 fat.

Turkey Wild Rice Salad

Cauliflower Ham Chowder

Prep/Total Time: 25 min.

Even if you aren't crazy about cauliflower, you'll like this thick, comforting soup. My two daughters, who are now grown, always enjoyed it...and my husband and I do, too. It's a great way to use up leftover ham from a holiday meal.
—Carla Garloff, Burney, California

    2 cups sliced fresh cauliflower
    1 can (14-1/2 ounces) chicken broth
    1 can (10-3/4 ounces) condensed cream of
      chicken soup, undiluted
    1 cup half-and-half cream
  1/8 teaspoon white pepper
    2 tablespoons cornstarch
  1/4 cup cold water
    2 cups cubed fully cooked ham
Sliced green onion

In a large saucepan, cook cauliflower in broth for 4 minutes or until crisp-tender. Stir in the soup, cream and pepper.

Combine the cornstarch and water until smooth; gradually stir into cauliflower mixture. Bring to a boil; cook and stir for 2 minutes or until thickened. Reduce heat. Add ham; cook and stir for 2 minutes or until heated through. Garnish with onion. **Yield:** 6 servings.

Italian Beef with Spaghetti

Prep/Total Time: 15 min.

Savory and stir-fry fast, this easy entree adds colorful zucchini and tomatoes, plus a splash of Italian dressing, to last night's steak. Fabulous!
—Dette Rainwater
Baker, Louisiana

      1 small zucchini, cut into 1/4-inch slices
      1 teaspoon minced garlic
      1 tablespoon olive oil
1-1/2 cups thinly sliced cooked beef sirloin steak
    3/4 cup halved cherry tomatoes
    1/4 cup prepared Italian salad dressing
Hot cooked spaghetti
      1 tablespoon grated Parmesan cheese

In a large skillet, saute zucchini and garlic in oil until zucchini is crisp-tender. Add the beef, tomatoes and salad dressing; cook and stir until heated through. Serve with spaghetti. Sprinkle with Parmesan cheese. **Yield:** 2 servings.

Pretzel-Crusted Drumsticks

Prep: 10 min. **Bake:** 50 min.

The first time I fixed this effortless main dish for guests, I received plenty of recipe requests. With their pretzel and pecan coating, these well-seasoned drumsticks satisfy everyone's appetites. I serve them most often with rice, buttered broccoli spears and oven-fresh dinner rolls.
—Joann Frazier Hensley, McGaheysville, Virginia

Ham 'n' Cheese Lasagna

1 cup grated Parmesan cheese
9 no-cook lasagna noodles

In a large skillet, saute the mushrooms, celery, carrots and onion in oil for 4-5 minutes or until crisp-tender. Add ham and garlic; cook 1-2 minutes longer or until garlic is tender. In a small bowl, combine the flour and cream; stir into ham mixture. Add tomatoes and pepper.

Bring to a boil; cook and stir for 2 minutes. Reduce heat; simmer, uncovered, for 8-10 minutes or until heated through (sauce will be thin).

In a small bowl, combine cheeses. Place three noodles in a greased 13-in. x 9-in. x 2-in. baking dish; top with a third of the ham mixture and a third of the cheese mixture. Repeat layers twice.

Cover and bake at 350° for 30 minutes. Uncover; bake 15-20 minutes longer or until bubbly and cheese is melted. Let stand for 20 minutes before cutting. **Yield:** 8-10 servings.

Chicken Creole Deviled Eggs

(Pictured below)

Prep/Total Time: 15 min.

Scrambling for a quick-and-easy recipe to use up some of those Easter eggs? Just add a little diced chicken, and these zippy deviled-egg snacks from our Test Kitchen are almost lunch in themselves!

  6 hard-cooked eggs
1/2 cup diced cooked chicken
  5 tablespoons mayonnaise
  1 tablespoon finely chopped onion
  1 teaspoon honey mustard
1/2 teaspoon ground mustard
1/2 teaspoon Creole seasoning
1/8 teaspoon hot pepper sauce
  1 tablespoon minced fresh parsley

Cut eggs in half lengthwise. Remove yolks; set whites aside. In a small bowl, mash the yolks. Stir in the chicken, mayonnaise, onion, honey mustard, ground mustard, Creole seasoning and hot pepper sauce. Pipe or spoon into egg whites. Sprinkle with parsley. Refrigerate until serving. **Yield:** 1 dozen.

1/2 cup butter, melted
  1 teaspoon cayenne pepper
1/8 teaspoon garlic powder
  1 cup finely crushed pretzels
1/4 cup chopped pecans
1/2 teaspoon pepper
1-1/2 to 2 pounds chicken drumsticks

In a shallow bowl, combine the butter, cayenne and garlic powder. In another shallow bowl, combine the pretzels, pecans and pepper. Dip chicken in butter mixture, then roll in pretzel mixture.

Place in a greased 13-in. x 9-in. x 2-in. baking dish. Bake, uncovered, at 350° for 50-55 minutes or until the chicken juices run clear, turning once. **Yield:** 5 servings.

Ham 'n' Cheese Lasagna

(Pictured above)

Prep: 30 min. **Bake:** 45 min. + standing

This recipe came from a friend who's a wonderful cook. No-cook noodles make it a breeze to put this cheesy main dish on the table. —Carla Specht, Annawan, Illinois

  3 cups sliced fresh mushrooms
  2 cups thinly sliced celery
  2 cups chopped carrots
  1 cup chopped onion
  1 tablespoon olive oil
  2 cups cubed fully cooked ham
  1 teaspoon minced garlic
  1 tablespoon all-purpose flour
  2 cups heavy whipping cream
  1 can (14-1/2 ounces) diced tomatoes with basil, oregano and garlic, undrained
1/4 teaspoon pepper
  2 cups (8 ounces) shredded part-skim mozzarella cheese
  1 package (5 ounces) shredded Swiss cheese

Chicken Creole Deviled Eggs

Bacon-Chili Stuffed Squash

con. Bake 5-10 minutes longer or until cheese is melted. **Yield:** 6 servings.

Asparagus Ham Salad

Prep/Total Time: 25 min.

I toss leftover Easter ham with shredded Swiss cheese, spring asparagus and fresh mushrooms to make this deliciously different main-dish salad. We love it!
—Jean Graf-Joyce, Albany, Oregon

  3 cups water
  1 pound fresh asparagus, trimmed and cut
     into 1-inch pieces
  2 cups cubed fully cooked ham
  1 package (5 ounces) shredded Swiss cheese
1/2 cup sliced fresh mushrooms
1/3 cup chopped onion
  1 tablespoon sesame seeds, toasted
1/2 cup Italian salad dressing
  5 large lettuce leaves
  1 large tomato, cut into thin wedges

In a large saucepan, bring water to a boil. Add asparagus; cover and boil for 3 minutes. Drain and immediately place asparagus in ice water. Drain and pat dry.

In a large bowl, combine the ham, cheese, mushrooms, onion and sesame seeds. Add asparagus. Drizzle with dressing and toss to coat. Spoon onto lettuce-lined serving plates; top with tomato wedges. **Yield:** 5 servings.

Cheddar Ham Soup

Prep/Total Time: 30 min.

I knew this hearty soup was a keeper when my mother-in-law asked for the recipe! Chock-full of cooked ham, veggies and cheese, it's creamy and comforting. Plus, it will feed several post-holiday guests. —Marty Matthews
Clarksville, Tennessee

✓ Uses less fat, sugar or salt. Includes Nutrition Facts and Diabetic Exchanges.

  2 cups diced peeled potatoes
  2 cups water
1/2 cup sliced carrot
1/4 cup chopped onion
1/4 cup butter, cubed
1/4 cup all-purpose flour
  2 cups milk
1/4 to 1/2 teaspoon salt
1/4 teaspoon pepper
  2 cups (8 ounces) shredded cheddar cheese
1-1/2 cups cubed fully cooked ham
  1 cup frozen peas, thawed

In a large saucepan, combine the potatoes, water, carrot and onion. Bring to a boil. Reduce heat; cover and cook for 10-15 minutes or until tender.

Meanwhile, in another saucepan, melt butter. Stir in flour until smooth. Gradually add the milk, salt and pepper. Bring to a boil; cook and stir for 2 minutes or until thickened. Stir in cheese until melted. Stir into

Bacon-Chili Stuffed Squash

(Pictured above)

Prep: 30 min. **Bake:** 25 min.

This is such an excellent recipe and one of my very best side dishes. It looks special and is much easier to fix than it might sound. —Karen Grant, Tulare, California

  4 quarts water
  2 teaspoons salt, *divided*
  6 medium yellow summer squash
  2 tablespoons finely chopped onion
  3 tablespoons butter, *divided*
  2 tablespoons all-purpose flour
1/2 cup milk
  1 can (4 ounces) chopped green chilies,
     drained
  1 cup (4 ounces) shredded cheddar cheese,
     divided
  6 tablespoons crumbled cooked bacon, *divided*
1/8 teaspoon pepper
1/3 cup dry bread crumbs

In a Dutch oven, bring water and 1 teaspoon salt to a boil. Add squash; cover and cook for 8-10 minutes or until crisp-tender. Drain. When cool enough to handle, cut squash in half lengthwise; scoop out and reserve pulp, leaving a 3/8-in. shell. Invert shells on paper towel.

In a saucepan, saute onion in 2 tablespoons butter. Stir in flour until blended; gradually add milk. Bring to a boil; cook and stir for 2 minutes or until thickened. Add the chilies, 1/2 cup cheese, 3 tablespoons bacon, pepper and remaining salt. Drain reserved squash pulp and stir into bacon mixture. Spoon into shells.

Place in two lightly greased 11-in. x 7-in. x 2-in. baking dishes. Melt remaining butter; toss with bread crumbs. Sprinkle over squash. Bake, uncovered, at 375° for 20 minutes. Sprinkle with remaining cheese and ba-

undrained potato mixture. Add ham and peas; heat through. **Yield:** 7 servings.

Nutrition Facts: 1 cup (prepared with fat-free milk, 1/4 teaspoon salt, reduced-fat cheese and lean ham) equals 281 calories, 15 g fat (9 g saturated fat), 53 mg cholesterol, 798 mg sodium, 20 g carbohydrate, 2 g fiber, 19 g protein. **Diabetic Exchanges:** 2 lean meat, 1-1/2 fat, 1 starch, 1 vegetable.

Rice Stir-Fry

(Pictured below)

Prep/Total Time: 30 min.

This colorful stir-fry comes together in no time with left-over rice. It's one of our family favorites because it's easy and makes a terrific dinner.
—*Gloria Warczak*
Cedarburg, Wisconsin

☑ Uses less fat, sugar or salt. Includes Nutrition Facts and Diabetic Exchanges.

    4 ounces pork tenderloin, cut into 1/2-inch cubes
4-1/2 teaspoons canola oil, *divided*
    1/2 cup sliced fresh mushrooms
    1/2 cup fresh sugar snap peas
    1/2 cup sliced water chestnuts
    2 tablespoons chopped green pepper
    2 tablespoons chopped sweet red pepper
    1 tablespoon chopped green onion
    1/4 teaspoon minced garlic
    1 tablespoon soy sauce
    1/4 teaspoon sugar
1-1/2 cups cooked long grain rice

In a large skillet or wok, saute the pork in 2 teaspoons oil for 3-5 minutes or until no longer pink. Remove and keep warm. In the same pan, heat remaining oil. Add the mushrooms, peas, water chestnuts, peppers, onion and garlic; stir-fry until vegetables are crisp-tender.

Combine the soy sauce and sugar; stir into vegetable

Rice Stir-Fry

Turkey Cordon Bleu Pasta

mixture. Cook for 1-2 minutes. Return pork to the pan. Stir in rice; cook for 3-5 minutes or until heated through, stirring occasionally. **Yield:** 4 servings.

Nutrition Facts: 3/4 cup (prepared with reduced-sodium soy sauce) equals 181 calories, 6 g fat (1 g saturated fat), 16 mg cholesterol, 166 mg sodium, 22 g carbohydrate, 2 g fiber, 9 g protein. **Diabetic Exchanges:** 1 starch, 1 lean meat, 1 vegetable, 1/2 fat.

Turkey Cordon Bleu Pasta

(Pictured above)

Prep/Total Time: 30 min.

This creamy pasta is a great use for extra turkey and ham. The recipe has undergone a few changes over the years, but it remains popular in our household when a lot of other dishes have fallen by the wayside. To make a pretty garnish, I like to sprinkle chopped fresh parsley on top.
—*Sandra Netherton, Marietta, Georgia*

    2 cups sliced fresh mushrooms
    1/2 cup sliced green onions
    1/4 cup chopped green pepper
    2 tablespoons butter
    2 cups cubed cooked turkey
    1 cup cubed fully cooked ham
    1 can (10-3/4 ounces) condensed cream of mushroom soup, undiluted
    1/2 cup water
    1/4 cup sherry *or* chicken broth
Hot cooked linguine
    1/4 cup shredded Swiss cheese

In a large skillet, saute the mushrooms, onions and green pepper in butter for 4-5 minutes or until crisp-tender.

In a large bowl, combine the turkey, ham, soup, water and sherry or broth. Stir into vegetables. Bring to a boil. Reduce heat to medium; cook, uncovered, for 3-4 minutes or until heated through. Serve over linguine. Sprinkle with Swiss cheese. **Yield:** 4 servings.

Cooking Up Extra Servings

Italian Meat Loaf Sandwiches

OUR KITCHEN CREW knows that fixing a little more one night can streamline supper prep another night. That's because tonight's leftovers can make a quick meal tomorrow without looking or tasting the same.

While combing our recipe files, our staff found two delicious entrees—Sun-Dried Tomato Meat Loaf and Herbed Pork and Potatoes—that make enough for two meals. Enjoy these main dishes as is, then use the leftovers in the other two recipes later in the week.

Sun-Dried Tomato Meat Loaf

(Pictured below)

Prep: 25 min. **Bake:** 55 min. + standing

Our kitchen staff gave Italian flair to this lighter meat loaf. The recipe yields a large loaf, so extra slices can be used to fix the tasty sandwiches that follow.

☑ Uses less fat, sugar or salt. Includes Nutrition Facts and Diabetic Exchanges.

1-1/4 cups sun-dried tomatoes (not packed in oil)
   3 cups boiling water
  1/2 cup chopped onion
  1/2 cup chopped green pepper
   2 teaspoons canola oil
  1/2 cup milk
   1 egg, beaten
   1 cup soft bread crumbs
   2 teaspoons dried basil
   1 teaspoon dried oregano
   1 teaspoon salt
   1 teaspoon pepper
  1/2 teaspoon dried thyme
1-1/2 pounds ground beef
  1/4 cup ketchup

In a large bowl, combine tomatoes and water; let stand for 15 minutes or until softened. Meanwhile, in a small skillet, saute onion and green pepper in oil for 3 minutes or until tender. In a large bowl, combine the milk, egg and bread crumbs.

Drain and chop the tomatoes; set aside 1/4 cup for topping. Add onion mixture, basil, oregano, salt, pepper, thyme and remaining tomatoes to the crumb mixture. Crumble beef over mixture and mix well. Shape into a loaf in an ungreased 13-in. x 9-in. x 2-in. baking dish.

In a small bowl, combine ketchup and reserved tomatoes. Spread over loaf. Bake, uncovered, at 350° for 55-60 minutes or until a meat thermometer reads 160°. Drain; let stand for 10 minutes before slicing. **Yield:** 10 servings.

Nutrition Facts: 1 slice (prepared with lean ground beef) equals 169 calories, 8 g fat (3 g saturated fat), 65 mg cholesterol, 515 mg sodium, 10 g carbohydrate, 2 g fiber, 16 g protein. **Diabetic Exchanges:** 2 lean meat, 2 vegetable.

Italian Meat Loaf Sandwiches

(Pictured above)

Prep/Total Time: 30 min.

You'll need leftover meat loaf and only five other ingredients for these yummy sandwiches our home economists prepared on a griddle.

1/4 cup butter, softened
 12 slices Italian bread (3/4 inch thick)
  6 slices provolone cheese
1/3 cup pizza sauce

Sun-Dried Tomato Meat Loaf

1/2 cup giardiniera
6 slices cooked meat loaf, warmed

Butter one side of each slice of bread. Place six slices on a griddle, buttered side down. Top with cheese, pizza sauce, giardiniera, meat loaf and remaining bread, buttered side up. Cook over medium heat until golden brown, turning once. **Yield:** 6 servings.

Editor's Note: Giardiniera, a pickled vegetable mixture, is available in mild and hot varieties and can be found in the Italian or pickle section of grocery stores.

Herbed Pork and Potatoes

(Pictured below and on page 130)

Prep: 10 min. **Bake:** 40 min.

By making two rosemary-seasoned pork tenderloins, you can serve one with the potatoes for dinner, then save the leftover pork for the fuss-free recipe that follows.
—Denise Dowd, St. Louis, Missouri

1/2 cup olive oil
3 teaspoons minced fresh thyme *or* 1
   teaspoon dried thyme
2 teaspoons minced garlic
2 teaspoons dried minced onion
2 teaspoons minced fresh rosemary *or* 1/2
   teaspoon dried rosemary, crushed
1 teaspoon seasoned salt
1 teaspoon coarsely ground pepper
1 teaspoon ground mustard
2 pork tenderloins (1 pound *each*)
1 pound small red potatoes, quartered

In a small bowl, combine the first eight ingredients. Place the pork in a large shallow baking pan. Drizzle with three-fourths of the herb mixture. Toss potatoes with remaining herb mixture; place around pork.

Bake, uncovered, at 375° for 40-45 minutes or until a meat thermometer reads 160° and potatoes are tender. Let pork stand for 5 minutes before slicing. **Yield:** 3-4 servings with potatoes plus 1 pound leftover pork.

Herbed Pork and Potatoes

Snow Pea Pork Medley

Snow Pea Pork Medley

(Pictured above)

Prep/Total Time: 15 min.

Last night's leftover pork tenderloin stars in this easy microwave dish that pleases the whole family. We love Chinese food, and this is a favorite in our home.
—Gloria Bisek, Deerwood, Minnesota

2 tablespoons cornstarch
3 tablespoons soy sauce
1 teaspoon chicken bouillon granules
1/2 cup water
1/4 teaspoon ground ginger, optional
1 can (8 ounces) sliced water chestnuts,
   drained
1 can (8 ounces) bamboo shoots, drained
1 package (6 ounces) frozen snow peas,
   thawed
1/2 cup sliced white onion
1/2 cup sliced green onions
2 cups sliced cooked pork tenderloin
   (1/2 inch thick and about 1 pound)
Hot cooked rice

In a large microwave-safe bowl, combine the cornstarch, soy sauce, bouillon, water and ginger if desired; stir until smooth. Cover and microwave on high for 2 minutes, stirring once.

Add the water chestnuts, bamboo shoots, peas and onions. Cover and cook on high for 4-5 minutes or until vegetables are crisp-tender, stirring occasionally. Stir in the pork; cook 2-3 minutes longer or until heated through. Serve over rice. **Yield:** 4 servings.

Editor's Note: This recipe was tested in a 1,100-watt microwave.

Chapter 9

Breads in a Jiffy

DREAMING of golden brown braids, moist muffins, yummy coffee cakes and other fresh-baked breads? They don't have to be a dream! It's easy to whip up warm-from-the-oven treats with the recipes here.

Just page through this chapter, and you'll see how quickly you can give your family irresistible goodies such as Maple-Glazed Long Johns, Zucchini Chip Loaves, Rosemary Focaccia, Chocolate Toffee Biscuits and Pesto Breadsticks.

In fact, some of the delights you'll find will be on the table in less than half an hour! So go ahead—plan on baking for dinner tonight...breakfast tomorrow morning...weekend parties or any time you like.

FAST AND FRESH. Pistachio Pumpkin Bread (p. 142).

Spinach Spirals

Pistachio Pumpkin Bread

(Pictured on page 140)

Prep: 15 min. **Bake:** 30 min. + cooling

These cute little loaves blend pumpkin, pistachio, rum and raisin flavors with festive results. A few years ago, during the Christmas season, a friend shared this delightful recipe with me. Since then, I've made it for every holiday.
—Kathy Kittell, Lenexa, Kansas

> 1 package (14 ounces) pumpkin quick bread/muffin mix
> 2 eggs
> 1 cup water
> 3 tablespoons vegetable oil
> 1/4 to 1/2 teaspoon rum extract
> 1/2 cup raisins
> 1/2 cup chopped pistachios
> GLAZE:
> 1/4 cup sugar
> 2 tablespoons water
> 1 tablespoon butter
> 1/4 teaspoon rum extract

In a large bowl, combine the bread mix, eggs, water, oil and extract just until blended. Stir in raisins and pistachios. Transfer to three greased 5-3/4-in. x 3-in. x 2-in. loaf pans. Bake at 375° for 30-35 minutes or until a toothpick inserted near the center comes out clean. Cool for 5 minutes.

Meanwhile, in a small saucepan, combine the sugar, water and butter. Bring to a boil; cook and stir for 3 minutes or until sugar is dissolved. Remove from the heat; stir in extract.

Remove loaves from pans to wire racks. With a toothpick, poke holes in the top of each loaf; brush with glaze. Cool completely. **Yield:** 3 mini loaves.

Spinach Spirals

(Pictured above)

Prep: 15 min. **Bake:** 25 min.

This is a delicious and easy roll for a side dish or just by itself. I bring printed copies of the recipe whenever I take it to a potluck because someone always asks for it.
—Isabel Mancini, Youngstown, Ohio

✓ Uses less fat, sugar or salt. Includes Nutrition Facts.

> 1 package (10 ounces) frozen chopped spinach, thawed and squeezed dry
> 1 cup (4 ounces) shredded Monterey Jack cheese
> 1 egg, beaten
> 2 tablespoons dried minced onion
> 1 tube (13.8 ounces) refrigerated pizza crust
> 1 tablespoon butter, melted
> 2 tablespoons grated Parmesan cheese

In a small bowl, combine the spinach, Monterey Jack cheese, egg and onion. On a baking sheet coated with nonstick cooking spray, roll pizza dough into a 14-in. x 10-in. rectangle; seal any holes. Spread spinach mixture to within 1/2 in. of edges.

Roll up jelly-roll style, starting with a long side; seal ends and place seam side down. Brush with butter; sprinkle with Parmesan cheese. Bake at 400° for 25-27 minutes or until golden brown. Slice and serve warm. **Yield:** 14 slices.

Nutrition Facts: 2 slices (prepared with reduced-fat Monterey Jack cheese, egg substitute and reduced-fat butter) equals 224 calories, 7 g fat (3 g saturated fat), 15 mg cholesterol, 594 mg sodium, 30 g carbohydrate, 2 g fiber, 12 g protein.

Rosemary Focaccia

(Pictured at right)

Prep/Total Time: 25 min.

With rosemary and lots of cheese, these Italian bread squares make an everyday dinner seem special. My husband and I sometimes add anchovy fillets to the dough.
—Shelley Ross, Bow, Washington

✓ Uses less fat, sugar or salt. Includes Nutrition Facts and Diabetic Exchanges.

> 1 loaf (1 pound) frozen bread dough, thawed
> 2 tablespoons olive oil
> 1/4 cup thinly sliced onion
> 1-1/2 teaspoons minced garlic
> 1 cup (4 ounces) shredded part-skim mozzarella cheese
> 2 tablespoons minced fresh rosemary

Roll the dough into an ungreased 15-in. x 10-in. x 1-in. baking pan; build up edges slightly. Brush with oil; top with onion, garlic, cheese and rosemary. Bake at 400° for

15-20 minutes or until cheese is melted and golden brown. Let stand for 5 minutes before slicing. **Yield:** 15 servings.

Nutrition Facts: 1 piece equals 123 calories, 5 g fat (1 g saturated fat), 6 mg cholesterol, 197 mg sodium, 16 g carbohydrate, 1 g fiber, 5 g protein. **Diabetic Exchanges:** 1 starch, 1 fat.

Pesto Breadsticks

(Pictured below)

Prep/Total Time: 20 min.

Our Test Kitchen dressed up refrigerated dough to fix these savory breadsticks flavored with garlic pepper and pesto. The easy twists add fun to any menu, whether paired with soup, salad or a pasta entree.

   1 tube (11 ounces) refrigerated breadsticks
   2 tablespoons prepared pesto
1/4 teaspoon garlic pepper blend
   1 tablespoon butter, melted
   2 tablespoons shredded Parmesan cheese

Unroll and separate breadsticks; place on an ungreased baking sheet. Combine pesto and garlic pepper; brush over breadsticks. Twist each breadstick three times. Brush with butter; sprinkle with Parmesan cheese. Bake at 375° for 10-13 minutes or until golden brown. Serve warm. **Yield:** 1 dozen.

Golden Wheat Bread

Pesto Breadsticks
Rosemary Focaccia

Golden Wheat Bread

(Pictured above)

Prep: 10 min. **Bake:** 4 hours

The bread machine makes it simple to bake a loaf of this beautiful bread. With a crispy crust, it's great alone or alongside a bowl of bean soup. I think slices are also wonderful for making ham or chicken sandwiches.
—Cindy Reams
Philipsburg, Pennsylvania

   1 cup plus 2 tablespoons water (70° to 80°)
1/4 cup vegetable oil
   2 tablespoons prepared mustard
   2 tablespoons honey
   1 teaspoon salt
2-1/2 cups bread flour
   1 cup whole wheat flour
2-1/4 teaspoons active dry yeast

In bread machine pan, place all ingredients in order suggested by manufacturer. Select basic bread setting. Choose crust color and loaf size if available. Bake according to bread machine directions (check dough after 5 minutes of mixing; add 1-2 tablespoons of water or flour if needed). **Yield:** 1 loaf (1-1/2 pounds).

Measuring Made Easy

Before unwrapping stick butter or margarine, I make a slight indentation in the stick at the tablespoon measure marks on the wrapper. That way, I can easily measure out a tablespoon (or more) without any guesswork.
—*Pat DeRyke, Wellborn, Florida*

Maple-Glazed Long Johns

(Pictured below)

Prep: 30 min. **Cook:** 5 min. per batch

This is a very old recipe from my aunt that I revamped for my bread machine. The pastries are deep-fried, then glazed with a simple maple frosting. When it comes to breakfast treats, you can't do much better than these!
—Peggy Burdick, Burlington, Michigan

   1 cup water (70° to 80°)
1/2 cup sugar
1/4 cup shortening
   1 egg, lightly beaten
1/2 teaspoon salt
1/2 teaspoon vanilla extract
   3 cups bread flour
2-1/4 teaspoons active dry yeast
Oil for deep-fat frying
GLAZE:
   2 cups confectioners' sugar
1/4 cup half-and-half cream
   1 tablespoon maple flavoring

In bread machine pan, place the first eight ingredients in order suggested by manufacturer. Select dough setting (check dough after 5 minutes of mixing; add 1 to 2 tablespoons of water or flour if needed).

When cycle is completed, turn dough onto a lightly floured surface. Divide into four portions. Roll each into a 12-in. x 5-in. rectangle. Cut each rectangle widthwise into 1-1/2-in. strips.

In an electric skillet or deep-fat fryer, heat oil to 375°. Drop dough strips, a few at a time, into hot oil. Turn with a slotted spoon and fry for 1 minute on each side or un-

Lemon Poppy Seed Muffins

til golden brown. Drain on paper towels.

In a small bowl, combine the glaze ingredients. Place the long johns on a wire rack; drizzle with glaze. **Yield:** about 2-1/2 dozen.

Editor's Note: If your bread machine has a time-delay feature, we recommend you do not use it for this recipe.

Maple-Glazed Long Johns

Lemon Poppy Seed Muffins

(Pictured above)

Prep/Total Time: 30 min.

Made with lemon juice and peel—as well as instant lemon pudding—these heart-warming goodies are simply bursting with citrusy flavor. They're wonderful with coffee or tea, and it takes just 30 minutes to bake up a fresh batch. —Donna Gonda
North Canton, Ohio

   2 cups biscuit/baking mix
   1 package (3.4 ounces) instant lemon pudding mix
1/4 cup poppy seeds
1/4 teaspoon grated lemon peel
   2 eggs
   1 cup milk
1/4 cup vegetable oil
3/4 cup confectioners' sugar
   1 tablespoon lemon juice

In a large bowl, combine the baking mix, pudding mix, poppy seeds and lemon peel. In another bowl, combine the eggs, milk and oil; stir into dry ingredients just until moistened. Fill paper-lined muffin cups two-thirds full.

Bake at 375° for 20-25 minutes or until a toothpick comes out clean. Cool for 5 minutes before removing from pan to a wire rack. In a small bowl, combine sugar and lemon juice; drizzle over muffins. **Yield:** 1 dozen.

Raspberry Swirl Coffee Cake

Prep: 15 min. **Bake:** 40 min. + cooling

This recipe was a "Best of Show" bread winner at our local fair…and it's sure to be a winner at your house, too.
—Jeanette Redman, Newark, Ohio

   2 cups all-purpose flour
3/4 cup sugar
   2 teaspoons baking powder
1/2 teaspoon salt
   1 egg
   1 cup (8 ounces) raspberry yogurt
1/2 cup butter, melted
   1 teaspoon vanilla extract
1/2 cup chopped almonds, toasted
1/2 cup seedless raspberry preserves, *divided*
   2 tablespoons sliced almonds, toasted

In a large bowl, combine the flour, sugar, baking powder and salt. In another bowl, whisk the egg, yogurt, butter and vanilla until blended; stir into dry ingredients just until moistened. Stir in the chopped almonds.

Pour into a greased 9-in. springform pan. Drop 1/3 cup preserves by tablespoonfuls over batter; cut through with a knife to swirl. Sprinkle with sliced almonds. Bake at 350° for 40-45 minutes or until a toothpick inserted near the center comes out clean. Cool on a wire rack for 10 minutes; remove sides of pan.

In a small saucepan, heat remaining preserves until melted; drizzle over serving plates. Top each with a piece of coffee cake. **Yield:** 10-12 servings.

Onion French Bread

(Pictured below right)

Prep: 25 min. + rising **Bake:** 20 min.

I often bake my own French bread to go with soup. I added dried minced onion to my usual recipe for these two tasty loaves. —Ruth Fueller, Barmstedt, Germany

   1 cup water (70° to 80°)
1/2 cup dried minced onion
   1 tablespoon sugar
   2 teaspoons salt
   3 cups bread flour
2-1/4 teaspoons active dry yeast
   1 tablespoon cornmeal
   1 egg yolk, beaten

In bread machine pan, place the first six ingredients in order suggested by manufacturer. Select dough setting (check dough after 5 minutes of mixing; add 1 to 2 tablespoons of water or flour if needed).

When cycle is completed, turn dough onto a lightly floured surface. Cover; let rest for 15 minutes. Divide dough in half. Roll each half into a 15-in. x 10-in. rectangle. Roll up jelly-roll style, starting with a long side; pinch seams to seal. Pinch ends to seal and tuck under.

Sprinkle the cornmeal onto a greased baking sheet. Place loaves on pan. Cover and let rise in a warm place until doubled, about 30 minutes.

Brush with egg yolk. Make 1/4-in.-deep cuts 2 in. apart in each loaf. Bake at 375° for 20-25 minutes or until golden brown. Remove from pan to a wire rack. **Yield:** 2 loaves (about 3/4 pound each).

Peppy Cheese Bread

(Pictured below)

Prep: 10 min. **Bake:** 4 hours

As a stay-at-home mother of two little girls, I pack a lot of activity into my days. The bread machine makes it a snap for me to turn out this zippy loaf. We love the flavor it gets from cayenne pepper and Mexican cheese. —Dusti Christensen Goodridge, Minnesota

   1 cup water (70° to 80°)
   1 tablespoon butter
   2 tablespoons sugar
   2 teaspoons ground mustard
1/2 teaspoon salt
1/2 teaspoon cayenne pepper
1/4 teaspoon garlic powder
   3 cups bread flour
2-1/4 teaspoons active dry yeast
1-1/2 cups (6 ounces) shredded Mexican cheese blend
   1 cup chopped pepperoni

In bread machine pan, place the first nine ingredients in order suggested by manufacturer. Select basic bread setting. Choose crust color and loaf size if available. Bake according to bread machine directions (check dough after 5 minutes of mixing; add 1 to 2 tablespoons of water or flour if needed).

Just before the final kneading (your machine may audibly signal this), add the cheese and pepperoni. **Yield:** 1 loaf (about 1-1/2 pounds).

Editor's Note: If your bread machine has a time-delay feature, we recommend you do not use it for this recipe.

Onion French Bread
Peppy Cheese Bread

Banana Berry Muffins
Zucchini Chip Loaves

til a toothpick comes out clean. Cool for 5 minutes before removing from pans to wire racks. **Yield:** 1-1/2 dozen.
   Editor's Note: If using frozen blueberries, do not thaw before adding to batter.

Zucchini Chip Loaves

(Pictured at left)

Prep: 20 min. **Bake:** 1 hour + cooling

This recipe yields two nicely spiced loaves—one to eat and one to share. I like to make it for family and friends.
   —Chantelle Ross, Forest Grove, British Columbia

   3 cups all-purpose flour
   2 cups sugar
   3 teaspoons ground cinnamon
   1 teaspoon baking soda
   1/2 teaspoon salt
   1/2 teaspoon baking powder
   1/2 teaspoon ground allspice
   3 eggs
   2 cups grated zucchini
   1 cup vegetable oil
   3 teaspoons vanilla extract
   1 cup (6 ounces) semisweet chocolate chips
   1 cup raisins, optional

In a large bowl, combine the first seven ingredients. In a small bowl, beat the eggs, zucchini, oil and vanilla. Stir into dry ingredients just until moistened. Fold in the chocolate chips and raisins if desired.
   Pour into two greased 8-in. x 4-in. x 2-in. loaf pans. Bake at 325° for 60-65 minutes or until a toothpick inserted near the center comes out clean. Cool for 10 minutes before removing from pans to wire racks. **Yield:** 2 loaves.

Banana Berry Muffins

(Pictured above)

Prep: 20 min. **Bake:** 20 min. per batch

I love these moist muffins that have a sweet nut topping. The original recipe called for bran cereal with raisins. But I was out of that cereal one day, so I used plain bran flakes and added blueberries. Now I always make it this way.
   —Alyce Wyman, Pembina, North Dakota

   4 cups bran flakes
   1/2 cup buttermilk
   1/2 cup butter, softened
   1 cup sugar
   2 eggs
1-1/2 cups mashed ripe bananas (about 3 medium)
   1 teaspoon vanilla extract
1-1/2 cups all-purpose flour
1-1/2 teaspoons baking powder
   1/2 teaspoon salt
   1/4 teaspoon baking soda
   1 cup fresh *or* frozen blueberries
   1/3 cup finely chopped pecans
   1/3 cup packed brown sugar
   3/4 teaspoon ground cinnamon

In a bowl, combine bran flakes and buttermilk; set aside. In a large mixing bowl, cream butter and sugar. Beat in eggs, one at a time. Add the bananas and vanilla; mix well (mixture will appear curdled).
   Combine the flour, baking powder, salt and baking soda; stir into creamed mixture just until moistened. Stir in bran mixture. Fold in blueberries. Fill greased or paper-lined muffin cups three-fourths full.
   Combine the pecans, brown sugar and cinnamon; sprinkle over batter. Bake at 350° for 20-25 minutes or un-

Pecan Sunrise Coffee Cake

Prep: 20 min. **Bake:** 25 min. + cooling

I remember my mom making this breakfast treat when I was growing up. The crunchy topping with its hint of orange flavor is unforgettable. Now, I often bake this family favorite myself to enjoy with loved ones.
   —Cathy Murray
   Acushnet, Massachusetts

   1/3 cup shortening
   3/4 cup sugar
   2 eggs
1-1/2 cups all-purpose flour
   1/2 cup quick-cooking oats
   2 teaspoons baking powder
   1/2 teaspoon salt
   3/4 cup milk
   1/4 cup pecan halves
TOPPING:
   1/3 cup sugar
   1 tablespoon grated orange peel
   2 tablespoons cold butter

In a mixing bowl, cream shortening and sugar. Add eggs, one at a time, beating well after each addition. Combine the flour, oats, baking powder and salt; add to creamed mixture alternately with milk. Pour into a greased 9-in. square baking pan. Arrange pecans over batter.

For topping, combine sugar and orange peel. Cut in butter until mixture resembles coarse crumbs; sprinkle over batter. Bake at 375° for 25-30 minutes or until a toothpick inserted near the center comes out clean. Cool on a wire rack. **Yield:** 10 servings.

Coconut Banana Bread

Prep: 20 min. **Bake:** 50 min. + cooling

I served this quick bread to a group of ladies I had over for lunch, and every one of them wanted the recipe! Studded with cherries and nuts, the loaf is pretty and also easily doubled. —Carole Lanthier, Courtice, Ontario

  1-1/2 cups all-purpose flour
      1 cup sugar
  1-1/2 teaspoons baking powder
    1/2 teaspoon baking soda
    1/2 teaspoon salt
      2 eggs
      1 cup mashed ripe bananas (2 medium)
    1/2 cup butter, melted
    1/2 cup flaked coconut
    1/2 teaspoon almond extract
    1/2 cup chopped walnuts
    1/2 cup chopped maraschino cherries

In a large bowl, combine the flour, sugar, baking powder, baking soda and salt. In a small bowl, beat the eggs, bananas, butter, coconut and extract. Stir into the dry ingredients just until moistened. Fold in the walnuts and maraschino cherries.

Transfer to a greased 9-in. x 5-in. x 3-in. loaf pan. Bake at 350° for 50-55 minutes or until a toothpick inserted near the center comes out clean. Cool for 10 minutes before removing from pan to a wire rack. **Yield:** 1 loaf.

Little Texas Corn Bread

Prep: 10 min. **Bake:** 30 min.

I love to serve squares of this cheesy corn bread alongside a bowl of heartwarming chili. The green chilies add a nice little kick. —Sarah Thompson, Greendale, Wisconsin

      1 cup cornmeal
      1 cup (4 ounces) shredded cheddar cheese
      1 tablespoon baking powder
      2 eggs
      1 can (8-1/2 ounces) cream-style corn
      1 cup (8 ounces) sour cream
    1/2 cup vegetable oil
      1 can (4 ounces) chopped green chilies, drained

In a large bowl, combine the cornmeal, cheese and baking powder. In another bowl, combine the eggs, corn, sour cream, oil and chilies. Stir into dry ingredients just until moistened.

Pour into a greased 8-in. square baking pan. Bake at 400° for 30-35 minutes or until a toothpick comes out clean. Serve warm. Refrigerate leftovers. **Yield:** 8 servings.
Editor's Note: This recipe does not use flour.

Banana Wheat Bread

(Pictured below)

Prep: 15 min. **Bake:** 4 hours

The subtle banana flavor is terrific in this moist, whole wheat loaf. I like my slice warm and spread with butter.
—Louise Myers, Pomeroy, Ohio

    3/4 cup water (70° to 80°)
    1/4 cup honey
      1 egg, lightly beaten
  4-1/2 teaspoons vegetable oil
      1 medium ripe banana, sliced
      2 teaspoons poppy seeds
      1 teaspoon salt
    1/2 teaspoon vanilla extract
  1-3/4 cups bread flour
  1-1/2 cups whole wheat flour
  2-1/4 teaspoons active dry yeast

In bread machine pan, place all ingredients in order suggested by manufacturer. Select basic bread setting. Choose crust color and loaf size if available. Bake according to bread machine directions (check dough after 5 minutes of mixing; add 1 to 2 tablespoons of water or flour if needed). **Yield:** 1 loaf (1-1/2 pounds).

Editor's Note: If your bread machine has a time-delay feature, we recommend you do not use it for this recipe.

Banana Wheat Bread

Chocolate Toffee Biscuits

(Pictured below)

Prep/Total Time: 25 min.

If you love chocolate, these sweet and crunchy bites will be perfect with your morning cup of coffee. You'll also appreciate how quick these are to make—the fresh-from-the-oven biscuits are on the table in under half an hour.
—*Wendy Weatherall, Cargill, Ontario*

>   2 cups all-purpose flour
>   1/4 cup sugar
>   3 teaspoons baking powder
>   1/4 teaspoon baking soda
>   1/2 cup cold butter
>   3/4 cup milk
>   1/4 cup semisweet chocolate chips
>   1/4 cup English toffee bits *or* almond brickle chips

TOPPING:

>   1 teaspoon butter, melted
>   1 teaspoon sugar

In a large bowl, combine the flour, sugar, baking powder and baking soda. Cut in butter until mixture resembles coarse crumbs. Stir in milk just until moistened. Fold in chocolate chips and toffee bits.

Drop by 2 tablespoonfuls 2 in. apart onto ungreased baking sheets. Brush with melted butter; sprinkle with sugar. Bake at 425° for 13-15 minutes or until golden brown. Serve warm. **Yield:** 1 dozen.

Squash Corn Muffins

(Pictured below)

Prep/Total Time: 25 min.

I like to serve these savory muffins at brunch or with soup. Using frozen squash makes them a snap to stir up, but leftover cooked buttercup, acorn or butternut squash works well, too. —*Colette Maher, Livonia, Michigan*

☑ Uses less fat, sugar or salt. Includes Nutrition Facts and Diabetic Exchanges.

>   1 cup all-purpose flour
>   1 cup cornmeal
>   1 tablespoon minced fresh parsley *or* 1 teaspoon dried parsley flakes
> 1-1/2 teaspoons baking powder
>   1 teaspoon baking soda
>   1 teaspoon dried oregano
>   1/2 teaspoon salt
>   2 eggs
>   1 cup frozen winter squash, thawed
>   3/4 cup plain yogurt
>   1/4 cup olive oil
>   1 cup frozen corn
>   2 green onions, chopped

In a large bowl, combine the first seven ingredients. In another bowl, combine the eggs, squash, yogurt and oil; stir into dry ingredients just until moistened. Stir in corn and onions.

Coat muffin cups with nonstick cooking spray; fill three-fourths full. Bake at 425° for 12-16 minutes or un-

Chocolate Toffee Biscuits
Squash Corn Muffins

til a toothpick comes out clean. Cool for 5 minutes before removing from pan to a wire rack. Serve warm. **Yield:** 1 dozen.

Nutrition Facts: 1 muffin (prepared with fat-free yogurt) equals 160 calories, 6 g fat (1 g saturated fat), 36 mg cholesterol, 274 mg sodium, 23 g carbohydrate, 2 g fiber, 4 g protein. **Diabetic Exchanges:** 1-1/2 starch, 1 fat.

Honey-Glazed Drop Biscuits

Prep/Total Time: 20 min.

A handful of ingredients is all you'll need for these moist biscuits. I whip up these easy bites for my church and by special request. I made 350 the last time!
—*Diane Patton, Toledo, Ohio*

    3-1/4 cups self-rising flour
        1 cup milk
      1/2 cup mayonnaise
      1/2 cup honey
      1/2 cup butter, melted

In a large bowl, combine the flour, milk and mayonnaise just until moistened. Turn onto a lightly floured surface; knead 8-10 times. Drop by tablespoonfuls 2 in. apart onto a greased baking sheet.

Bake at 425° for 10-14 minutes or until golden brown. Combine honey and butter; brush 1/2 cup over hot biscuits. Serve warm with remaining honey butter. **Yield:** 16 biscuits.

Editor's Note: As a substitute for each cup of self-rising flour, place 1-1/2 teaspoons baking powder and 1/2 teaspoon salt in a 1-cup measuring cup. Add all-purpose flour to measure 1 cup. As a substitute for 1/4 cup of self-rising flour, place 3/8 teaspoon baking powder and 1/8 teaspoon salt in a 1/4-cup measuring cup. Add all-purpose flour to measure 1/4 cup.

Cinnamon Almond Braid

(Pictured above right)

Prep: 20 min. **Bake:** 10 min. + cooling

Refrigerated dough makes this pretty braid both flaky and fuss-free, while cinnamon and almonds make it simply delicious. —*Nancy Gunn, Orem, Utah*

✓ Uses less fat, sugar or salt. Includes Nutrition Facts and Diabetic Exchanges.

        1 tube (8 ounces) refrigerated crescent rolls
        2 tablespoons plus 1/4 cup sugar, *divided*
        1 teaspoon ground cinnamon
      1/2 cup finely chopped slivered almonds
        1 tablespoon butter, melted
      1/4 teaspoon almond extract
    ICING:
      1/2 cup confectioners' sugar
      1/4 teaspoon almond extract
    1-1/2 to 2 teaspoons milk
      1/4 teaspoon ground cinnamon

Line a 15-in. x 10-in. x 1-in. baking pan with parchment paper. Unroll crescent dough into prepared pan;

Cinnamon Almond Braid
Cran-Apple Cups

seal seams and perforations. Combine 2 tablespoons sugar and cinnamon; sprinkle over dough.

Combine the almonds, butter, extract and remaining sugar; spread lengthwise down the center of dough. On each long side, cut 1-in.-wide strips about 2-1/2 in. into center. Starting at one end, fold alternating strips at an angle across filling. Pinch ends to seal.

Bake at 375° for 10-15 minutes or until golden brown. Cool for 10 minutes; remove to a wire rack. For icing, in a bowl, combine confectioners' sugar, extract and enough milk to achieve desired consistency. Drizzle over braid; sprinkle with cinnamon. Serve warm. **Yield:** 1 loaf (10 slices).

Nutrition Facts: 1 slice (prepared with reduced-fat crescent rolls) equals 177 calories, 8 g fat (2 g saturated fat), 3 mg cholesterol, 199 mg sodium, 25 g carbohydrate, 1 g fiber, 3 g protein. **Diabetic Exchanges:** 1-1/2 starch, 1 fat.

Cran-Apple Cups

(Pictured above)

Prep/Total Time: 25 min.

These scrumptious rolls are perfect for a holiday breakfast. And with only four ingredients, they couldn't be easier to prepare! —*Barbara Brittain, Santee, California*

        1 tube (12.4 ounces) refrigerated cinnamon
          roll dough
        1 cup apple pie filling
      1/3 cup dried cranberries
      1/4 teaspoon ground cinnamon

Set aside icing packet from cinnamon rolls. Place rolls in ungreased muffin cups. Bake at 400° for 8 minutes.

Meanwhile, in a small bowl, combine the pie filling, cranberries and cinnamon. With the back of a teaspoon, make an indentation in the center of each roll; fill with apple mixture. Bake 4-5 minutes longer or until golden brown. Cool on a wire rack for 5 minutes. Drizzle with icing. Serve warm. **Yield:** 8 servings.

Chapter 10

⊕ Slow-Cooked Sensations

SLOW DOWN and ease your dinnertime rush after a hectic day of work or errands. It's as simple as switching on a slow cooker, thanks to the fuss-free dishes in this chapter!

Just fill your slow cooker in the morning, turn this convenient appliance on and let it do the work for you. By the time your family is hungry for supper, you'll have a homemade, delicious dinner ready to enjoy.

Try meal-in-one specialties such as Apple Cider Beef Stew and Pork Burritos...or whip up some pasta or rice to go with pleasers like Mom's Spaghetti Sauce or Three Beans and Sausage. You'll find 31 tempting, easy recipes to choose from—enough for an entire month!

SWITCH AND GO. Chuck Roast Dinner (p. 152).

Mushroom Pepper Steak

Mushroom Pepper Steak

(Pictured above)

Prep: 15 min. **Cook:** 6-1/4 hours

This is a hearty meat-and-potatoes meal. Round steak is slow-simmered until tender and smothered with a gravy that's packed with colorful peppers. No one will leave the dinner table hungry when this home-style supper is on the menu.
—Katie Goble, Valparaiso, Indiana

2 pounds boneless beef top round steak
2 cups *each* sliced green, sweet red and yellow peppers (1/2-inch strips)
1 can (7 ounces) mushroom stems and pieces, drained
2 medium onions, quartered and sliced
1/2 cup water
1 teaspoon salt
1/2 teaspoon pepper
1 can (15 ounces) tomato sauce
1/4 cup cornstarch
1/4 cup cold water
Hot mashed potatoes

Cut steak into serving-size pieces. Place in a 5-qt. slow cooker. Add the peppers, mushrooms, onions, water, salt and pepper. Pour tomato sauce over the top. Cover and cook on low for 6 to 6-1/2 hours or until the meat is tender.

Using a slotted spoon, remove beef and vegetables; keep warm. In a small bowl, combine cornstarch and cold water until smooth. Gradually stir into cooking juices; cover and cook on high for 15 minutes or until thickened. Serve with beef, vegetables and mashed potatoes. **Yield:** 8 servings.

Chuck Roast Dinner

(Pictured on page 150)

Prep: 10 min. **Cook:** 6 hours

A tasty tomato sauce nicely coats this comforting combination of beef, potatoes and carrots. My father gave me the recipe, which takes just minutes to throw together. It was one of our favorites when we would go hiking all day.
—Cindy Miller, Estes Park, Colorado

1 boneless beef chuck roast (3 pounds), cut into serving-size pieces
3 medium potatoes, peeled and cut into chunks
4 medium carrots, cut into chunks
2 cans (11-1/2 ounces *each*) tomato juice
1/4 cup Worcestershire sauce
3 tablespoons quick-cooking tapioca

In a 5-qt. slow cooker, combine all ingredients. Cover and cook on high for 6-8 hours or until meat is tender. **Yield:** 8-10 servings.

Italian Beef Sandwiches

Prep: 25 min. **Cook:** 6 hours + standing

If you're looking for a great dish for a casual fall get-together or half-time fare for a football party, try these simple hot sandwiches. They're also terrific alongside your favorite salad and steaming bowls of soup for a complete lunch or dinner.
—LaDonna Reed, Ponca City, Oklahoma

1 boneless beef rump roast (3 pounds)
3 large green peppers, diced

1 cup white wine *or* beef broth
1 tablespoon Worcestershire sauce
1/2 teaspoon salt
1/2 teaspoon garlic salt
1/2 teaspoon dried oregano
8 kaiser rolls, split

Cut roast in half. Place in a 5-qt. slow cooker. Add the green peppers, wine or broth, Worcestershire sauce, salt, garlic salt and oregano. Cover and cook on low for 6-7 hours or until meat is tender.

Remove beef and let stand for 10-15 minutes; cut across the grain into 1/8-in. slices. Serve on rolls; top with green peppers. Strain cooking juices to serve with sandwiches. **Yield:** 8 servings.

Soft Chicken Tacos

Prep: 30 min. **Cook:** 5 hours

My family really loves these mildly seasoned tacos. The chicken simmers in the slow cooker, so it's convenient to put together before work. At the end of the day, I just shred the chicken and roll it up in tortillas with the remaining ingredients. Dinner's ready in mere minutes!
—*Cheryl Newendorp, Pella, Iowa*

1 broiler/fryer chicken (3-1/2 pounds),
  cut up and skin removed
1 can (8 ounces) tomato sauce
1 can (4 ounces) chopped green chilies
1/3 cup chopped onion
2 tablespoons chili powder
2 tablespoons Worcestershire sauce
1/4 teaspoon garlic powder
10 flour tortillas (8 inches), warmed
1-1/4 cups shredded cheddar cheese
1-1/4 cups salsa
1-1/4 cups shredded lettuce
1 large tomato, chopped
3/4 cup sour cream, optional

Place the chicken in a 3-qt. slow cooker. In a small bowl, combine the tomato sauce, chilies, onion, chili powder, Worcestershire sauce and garlic powder; pour over chicken. Cover and cook on low for 5-6 hours or until chicken is tender and juices run clear.

Remove the chicken. Shred meat with two forks and return to the slow cooker; heat through. Spoon 1/2 cup chicken mixture down the center of each tortilla. Top with cheese, salsa, lettuce, tomato and sour cream if desired; roll up. **Yield:** 5 servings.

Switch and Go Ribs

Prep: 10 min. **Cook:** 6 hours

A slightly sweet sauce provides mild teriyaki flavor when drizzled over these tender, delicious ribs. Using boneless ribs adds to the five-ingredient ease of this recipe.
—*Lil Neuls, Caballo, New Mexico*

1-1/2 pounds boneless country-style pork ribs
1 tablespoon vegetable oil
1/3 cup orange marmalade

1/3 cup teriyaki sauce
1 teaspoon minced garlic

In a large skillet, brown ribs in oil on both sides. In a small bowl, combine the marmalade, teriyaki sauce and garlic. Pour half of the sauce into a 3-qt. slow cooker; top with ribs. Drizzle with remaining sauce. Cover and cook on low for 6-8 hours or until the meat is tender. **Yield:** 4 servings.

Saucy Chicken Thighs

(Pictured below)

Prep: 20 min. **Cook:** 4 hours

Everyone raves about the sauce for these slow-cooked chicken thighs. It's simple to make by jazzing up prepared barbecue sauce with honey and a few other ingredients. While the chicken simmers, you can take care of other things. —*Kim Puckett, Reagan, Tennessee*

9 chicken thighs (6 ounces *each*)
1/2 teaspoon salt
1/4 teaspoon pepper
1-1/2 cups barbecue sauce
1/2 cup honey
2 teaspoons prepared mustard
2 teaspoons Worcestershire sauce
1/8 to 1/2 teaspoon hot pepper sauce

Sprinkle chicken with salt and pepper. Place on a broiler pan. Broil 4-5 in. from the heat for 6-8 minutes on each side or until juices run clear. Transfer to a 5-qt. slow cooker.

In a small bowl, combine the barbecue sauce, honey, mustard, Worcestershire sauce and hot pepper sauce. Pour over chicken; stir to coat. Cover and cook on low for 4-5 hours or until heated through. **Yield:** 9 servings.

Saucy Chicken Thighs

Ham Barbecue

(Pictured below)

Prep: 10 min. **Cook:** 4 hours

We have used this recipe countless times for our family gatherings and birthday parties. The sandwiches are so easy to prepare, and they taste terrific. Try them with a side of your favorite baked beans or potato salad.
—Jennifer Middlekauff
New Holland, Pennsylvania

- 2 pounds thinly sliced deli ham
- 1 cup water
- 1 cup ketchup
- 1/4 cup packed brown sugar
- 1/4 cup Worcestershire sauce
- 2 tablespoons white vinegar
- 2 teaspoons prepared mustard
- 12 hamburger buns, split and toasted

Place the ham in a greased 3-qt. slow cooker. In a bowl, combine the water, ketchup, brown sugar, Worcestershire sauce, vinegar and mustard; pour over ham and stir well. Cover and cook on low for 4-5 hours or until heated through. Serve on buns. **Yield:** 12 servings.

Ranch Beans

(Pictured below)

Prep: 10 min. **Cook:** 3 hours

A friend sent me this recipe, which is nice to serve at picnics. The sweet and tangy side dish takes advantage of lots of store-bought convenience items, including four kinds of canned beans, so it's a snap to make. I just toss everything in the slow cooker and switch it on.
—Barbara Gordon, Roswell, Georgia

- 1 can (16 ounces) kidney beans, rinsed and drained
- 1 can (15-3/4 ounces) pork and beans, undrained
- 1 can (15 ounces) lima beans, rinsed and drained
- 1 can (14-1/2 ounces) cut green beans, drained
- 1 bottle (12 ounces) chili sauce
- 3/4 cup packed brown sugar
- 1 small onion, chopped

In a 3-qt. slow cooker, combine all ingredients. Cover and cook on high for 3-4 hours or until heated through. **Yield:** 8-10 servings.

Ranch Beans
Ham Barbecue

Beer-Braised Beef

Prep: 20 min. **Cook:** 6 hours

I modified the ingredients in this main dish to suit my family. It's quick to put together in the morning, and at the end of the day, all we need to do is cook the noodles and eat! Everyone enjoys this delicious, home-style dinner.
—Geri Faustich, Appleton, Wisconsin

  3 bacon strips, diced
  2 pounds beef stew meat, cut into 1-inch cubes
1/2 teaspoon pepper
1/4 teaspoon salt
  1 teaspoon vegetable oil
  1 medium onion, cut into wedges
  1 teaspoon minced garlic
  1 bay leaf
  1 can (12 ounces) beer *or* nonalcoholic beer
  1 tablespoon soy sauce
  1 tablespoon Worcestershire sauce
  1 teaspoon dried thyme
  2 tablespoons all-purpose flour
1/4 cup water
Hot cooked noodles

In a large skillet, cook the diced bacon over medium heat until crisp. Remove to paper towels; drain, discarding the drippings. Sprinkle the beef cubes with pepper and salt. In the same skillet, brown the beef in oil. Transfer to a 5-qt. slow cooker.

Add the bacon, onion, garlic and bay leaf. In a small bowl, combine the beer, soy sauce, Worcestershire sauce and thyme. Pour over the beef mixture. Cover and cook on low for 5-1/2 to 6 hours or until the meat is tender.

In a small bowl, combine flour and water until smooth. Gradually stir into slow cooker. Cover and cook on high for 30 minutes or until thickened. Discard bay leaf. Serve beef over noodles. **Yield:** 8 servings.

Mini Hot Dogs 'n' Meatballs

Prep: 5 min. **Cook:** 3 hours

Hot appetizers don't come much easier than this recipe. It vanishes in minutes whenever I serve it. In fact, it's so popular I usually double the recipe and use an extra-large slow cooker. Serve these bites with colorful party picks. —Andrea Chamberlain, Macedon, New York

 36 frozen cooked Italian meatballs (1/2 ounce *each*)
  1 package (16 ounces) miniature hot dogs *or* smoked sausages
  1 package (3-1/2 ounces) sliced pepperoni
  1 jar (26 ounces) meatless spaghetti sauce
  1 bottle (18 ounces) barbecue sauce
  1 bottle (12 ounces) chili sauce

In a 5-qt. slow cooker, combine all ingredients. Cover and cook on low for 3 hours or until heated through. **Yield:** 8 cups.

Squash 'n' Chicken Stew

Squash 'n' Chicken Stew

(Pictured above)

Prep: 15 min. **Cook:** 6 hours

Our Test Kitchen staff slowly simmered chicken thighs with stewed tomatoes, butternut squash, green peppers and onion for meal-in-one convenience.

  2 pounds boneless skinless chicken thighs, cut into 1/2-inch pieces
  1 can (28 ounces) stewed tomatoes, cut up
  3 cups cubed butternut squash
  2 medium green peppers, cut into 1/2-inch pieces
  1 small onion, sliced and separated into rings
  1 cup water
  1 teaspoon salt
  1 teaspoon ground cumin
1/2 teaspoon ground coriander
1/2 teaspoon pepper
  2 tablespoons minced fresh parsley
Hot cooked couscous, optional

In a 5-qt. slow cooker, combine the first 10 ingredients. Cover and cook on low for 6-7 hours or until chicken juices run clear. Sprinkle with parsley. Serve with couscous if desired. **Yield:** 5 servings.

Miniature Meatballs

My husband likes small meatballs (marble-size) in spaghetti and other sauces. Instead of rolling them out by hand, I press the meat mixture into a 13- x 9-inch pan and bake until cooked through. When it has cooled, I transfer the meat to a cookie sheet and cut it into little squares with a pizza cutter.
—Lori DeThomas, Westland, Pennsylvania

Tender Pork Chops

Sauerkraut Sausage Soup

Prep: 20 min. **Cook:** 5 hours

My husband and I make our own sauer-kraut and grow many of the vegetables that go in this easy slow cooker soup. It cooks all day and smells delicious when we come home from work. Pair it with your favorite bread or rolls.
—Yvonne Kett, Appleton, Wisconsin

  4 cups chicken broth
  1 pound smoked Polish sausage, cut into 1/2-inch slices
  1 can (16 ounces) sauerkraut, rinsed and well drained
  2 cups sliced fresh mushrooms
1-1/2 cups cubed peeled potatoes
  1 can (10-3/4 ounces) condensed cream of mushroom soup, undiluted
1-1/4 cups chopped onions
  2 large carrots, chopped
  2 celery ribs, chopped
  2 tablespoons white vinegar
  2 teaspoons dill weed
  1 teaspoon sugar
1/4 teaspoon pepper

In a 5-qt. slow cooker, combine all ingredients. Cover and cook on low for 5-6 hours or until vegetables are tender. **Yield:** 10 servings.

Tender Pork Chops

(Pictured above)

Prep: 15 min. **Cook:** 5-1/2 hours

Not only is it easy to make these chops in my slow cooker, but the results are fabulous—always so tender and juicy. The meat gets great flavor from the thick tomato sauce. —Bonnie Marlow, Ottoville, Ohio

✓ Uses less fat, sugar or salt. Includes Nutrition Facts and Diabetic Exchanges.

  6 boneless pork loin chops (1/2 inch thick and 6 ounces *each*)
  1 tablespoon canola oil
  1 medium green pepper, diced
  1 can (6 ounces) tomato paste
  1 jar (4-1/2 ounces) sliced mushrooms, drained
1/2 cup water
  1 envelope spaghetti sauce mix
1/2 to 1 teaspoon hot pepper sauce

In a large skillet, brown the pork chops in oil over medium heat for 3-4 minutes on each side; drain. In a 5-qt. slow cooker, combine the remaining ingredients. Top with the pork chops. Cover and cook on low for 5-1/2 to 6 hours or until a meat thermometer reads 160°. **Yield:** 6 servings.

Nutrition Facts: 1 pork chop with 2 tablespoons sauce equals 303 calories, 12 g fat (4 g saturated fat), 82 mg cholesterol, 763 mg sodium, 13 g carbohydrate, 3 g fiber, 34 g protein. **Diabetic Exchanges:** 4 lean meat, 1 starch.

Hungarian Goulash

Prep: 15 min. **Cook:** 8 hours

This simple treatment for beef features a creamy tomato sauce that's certain to satisfy goulash lovers. I enjoy sharing recipes with friends and family, and this one's great for potluck suppers, too. Garnish it with minced parsley for flavor and color.
—Jackie Kohn, Duluth, Minnesota

  2 pounds round steak, cut into 1-inch cubes
  1 cup chopped onion
  2 tablespoons all-purpose flour
1-1/2 teaspoons paprika
  1 teaspoon garlic salt
1/2 teaspoon pepper
  1 bay leaf
  1 can (14-1/2 ounces) diced tomatoes, undrained
  1 cup (8 ounces) sour cream
Hot cooked noodles

Place the beef and onion in a 3-qt. slow cooker. Combine the flour, paprika, garlic salt and pepper; sprinkle over beef mixture and stir to coat. Add bay leaf and tomatoes; mix well. Cover and cook on low for 8-10 hours or until meat is tender.

Discard bay leaf. Just before serving, stir in sour cream; heat through. Serve over noodles. **Yield:** 6-8 servings.

Mom's Spaghetti Sauce

(Pictured below)

Prep: 20 min. **Cook:** 4 hours

My mother used to make this when we were kids, and it was always my first choice for birthday dinners. Now I do the prep work in the morning and just let the sauce simmer all day. When I get home, all I have to do is boil the spaghetti, brown some garlic bread and serve.
—Kristy Hawkes, South Ogden, Utah

    1 pound ground beef
    1 medium onion, chopped
    1 medium green pepper, chopped
    8 to 10 fresh mushrooms, sliced
    3 celery ribs, chopped
1-1/2 teaspoons minced garlic
    2 cans (14-1/2 ounces *each*) Italian stewed
      tomatoes
    1 jar (26 ounces) spaghetti sauce
  1/2 cup ketchup
    2 teaspoons brown sugar
    1 teaspoon sugar
    1 teaspoon salt
    1 teaspoon dried oregano
    1 teaspoon chili powder
    1 teaspoon prepared mustard
Hot cooked spaghetti

In a large skillet, cook the beef, onion, green pepper, mushrooms, celery and garlic over medium heat until meat is no longer pink; drain.

In a 3-qt. slow cooker, combine the tomatoes, spaghetti sauce, ketchup, sugars, salt, oregano, chili powder and mustard. Stir in the beef mixture. Cover and cook on low for 4-5 hours or until heated through. Serve over spaghetti. **Yield:** 10-12 servings.

Mom's Spaghetti Sauce

Chunky Chicken Soup

Chunky Chicken Soup

(Pictured above)

Prep: 15 min. **Cook:** 4-1/2 hours

I am a stay-at-home mom who relies on my slow cooker for fast, nutritious meals with minimal cleanup and prep time. I knew this recipe was a hit when I didn't have any leftovers and my husband asked me to make it again!
—Nancy Clow, Mallorytown, Ontario

1-1/2 pounds boneless skinless chicken breasts, cut
      into 2-inch strips
    2 teaspoons vegetable oil
  2/3 cup finely chopped onion
    2 medium carrots, chopped
    2 celery ribs, chopped
    1 cup frozen corn
    2 cans (10-3/4 ounces *each*) condensed cream
      of potato soup, undiluted
1-1/2 cups chicken broth
    1 teaspoon dill weed
    1 cup frozen peas
  1/2 cup half-and-half cream

In a large skillet over medium-high heat, brown chicken in oil. With a slotted spoon, transfer to a 5-qt. slow cooker. Add the onion, carrots, celery and corn. In a small bowl, whisk the soup, broth and dill until blended; stir into slow cooker.

Cover and cook on low for 4 hours or until vegetables are tender. Stir in peas and cream. Cover and cook 30 minutes longer or until heated through. **Yield:** 7 servings.

Lime Chicken Tacos

(Pictured above)

Prep: 10 min. **Cook:** 5-1/2 hours

Lime juice adds zest to this good-for-you filling for tortillas. It's a fun recipe that makes a great casual dinner for my family and friends. I like that the chicken mixture also can double as a topping for a plate of nachos or a taco salad.
—Tracy Gunter, Boise, Idaho

✓ Uses less fat, sugar or salt. Includes Nutrition Facts and Diabetic Exchanges.

1-1/2 **pounds boneless skinless chicken breasts**
   3 **tablespoons lime juice**
   1 **tablespoon chili powder**
   1 **cup frozen corn**
   1 **cup chunky salsa**
  12 **flour tortillas (6 inches), warmed**
Sour cream, shredded cheddar cheese and
  shredded lettuce, optional

Place the chicken in a 3-qt. slow cooker. Combine lime juice and chili powder; pour over chicken. Cover and cook on low for 5-6 hours or until chicken is tender.

Remove chicken; cool slightly. Shred and return to the slow cooker. Stir in corn and salsa. Cover and cook on low for 30 minutes or until heated through. Serve in tortillas with sour cream, cheese and lettuce if desired. **Yield:** 12 tacos.

Nutrition Facts: 1 taco (prepared with fat-free tortillas; calculated without sour cream and cheese) equals 148 calories, 2 g fat (trace saturated fat), 31 mg cholesterol, 338 mg sodium, 20 g carbohydrate, 2 g fiber, 15 g protein. **Diabetic Exchanges:** 2 very lean meat, 1 starch.

Herbed Chicken and Tomatoes

Prep: 5 min. **Cook:** 5 hours

I put a tangy spin on chicken by adding just a few pantry ingredients. Recipes like this are such a plus when you work a full-time job but still want to put a healthy, satisfying meal on the table. —Rebecca Popke, Largo, Florida

   1 **pound boneless skinless chicken breasts, cut**
     into 1-1/2-inch pieces
   2 **cans (14-1/2 ounces *each*) Italian diced**
     tomatoes
   1 **envelope savory herb with garlic soup mix**
1/4 **teaspoon sugar**
Hot cooked pasta
Shredded Parmesan cheese

In a 3-qt. slow cooker, combine the chicken, tomatoes, soup mix and sugar. Cover and cook on low for 5-6 hours or until chicken juices run clear. Serve with pasta; sprinkle with Parmesan cheese. **Yield:** 4 servings.

Sirloin Roast with Gravy

(Pictured below)

Prep: 15 min. **Cook:** 5-1/2 hours

This recipe is always a winner with my husband, who is a meat-and-potatoes kind of guy. The peppery, fork-tender roast and rich gravy create a tasty centerpiece for any meal. —Rita Clark, Monument, Colorado

✓ Uses less fat, sugar or salt. Includes Nutrition Facts and Diabetic Exchanges.

- 1 boneless beef sirloin tip roast (about 3 pounds)
- 1 to 2 tablespoons coarsely ground pepper
- 1-1/2 teaspoons minced garlic
- 1/4 cup reduced-sodium soy sauce
- 3 tablespoons balsamic vinegar
- 1 tablespoon Worcestershire sauce
- 2 teaspoons ground mustard
- 2 tablespoons cornstarch
- 1/4 cup cold water

Rub roast with pepper and garlic; cut in half and place in a 3-qt. slow cooker. Combine the soy sauce, vinegar, Worcestershire sauce and mustard; pour over beef. Cover and cook on low for 5-1/2 to 6 hours or until the meat is tender.

Remove roast and keep warm. Strain cooking juices into a saucepan; skim fat. Combine cornstarch and water until smooth; gradually stir into cooking juices. Bring to a boil; cook and stir 2 minutes or until thickened. Serve with beef. **Yield:** 10 servings.

Nutrition Facts: 4 ounces cooked meat with 3 tablespoons gravy equals 185 calories, 6 g fat (2 g saturated fat), 72 mg cholesterol, 318 mg sodium, 4 g carbohydrate, trace fiber, 26 g protein. **Diabetic Exchanges:** 3 lean meat, 1/2 fat.

Apple-Dijon Pork Roast

Prep: 15 min. **Cook:** 4 hours

This is one of my family's favorites for cold-weather comfort. The recipe takes less than 5 minutes to assemble, and we all agree it's absolutely delicious. I like to serve the roast with rice, then use the tangy sauce as a gravy for both. —Cindy Steffen, Cedarburg, Wisconsin

✓ Uses less fat, sugar or salt. Includes Nutrition Facts and Diabetic Exchanges.

- 1 boneless whole pork loin roast (2 to 3 pounds)
- 1 can (14-1/2 ounces) chicken broth
- 1 cup unsweetened apple juice
- 1/2 cup Dijon mustard
- 6 tablespoons cornstarch
- 6 tablespoons cold water

Cut roast in half; place in a 5-qt. slow cooker. Combine the broth, apple juice and mustard; pour over roast. Cover and cook on low for 4 to 4-1/2 hours or until a meat thermometer reads 160°.

Remove the roast and keep warm. For gravy, strain the cooking juices and skim the fat. Pour the juices into a saucepan. Combine the cornstarch and water until smooth; gradually stir into the juices. Bring to a boil; cook and stir for 2 minutes or until thickened. Serve with pork. **Yield:** 8 servings.

Nutrition Facts: 4 ounces cooked pork with about 1/3 cup gravy (prepared with reduced-sodium chicken broth) equals 197 calories, 7 g fat (2 g saturated fat), 56 mg cholesterol, 413 mg sodium, 11 g carbohydrate, trace fiber, 23 g protein. **Diabetic Exchanges:** 3 lean meat, 1/2 starch.

Sirloin Roast with Gravy

Honey Pineapple Chicken

(Pictured below)

Prep: 15 min. **Cook:** 3 hours

Crushed pineapple, honey and soy sauce season this irresistible chicken entree. I adapted this recipe to use my slow cooker. It makes it so much easier to do the preparation in advance, then let it simmer all day.
—Carol Gillespie
Chambersburg, Pennsylvania

- 3 pounds boneless skinless chicken breast halves
- 2 tablespoons vegetable oil
- 1 can (8 ounces) unsweetened crushed pineapple, undrained
- 1 cup packed brown sugar
- 1/2 cup honey
- 1/3 cup lemon juice
- 1/4 cup butter, melted
- 2 tablespoons prepared mustard
- 2 teaspoons soy sauce

In a skillet, brown the chicken breast halves in oil in batches on both sides; transfer to a 5-qt. slow cooker. Combine the remaining ingredients; pour over the chicken. Cover and cook on low for 3-4 hours or until the chicken is no longer pink. Strain the pan juices, reserving the crushed pineapple. Serve the pineapple over the chicken. **Yield:** 12 servings.

Honey Pineapple Chicken

Sweet 'n' Tangy Chicken

Prep: 15 min. **Cook:** 4-1/2 hours

My slow cooker is a real lifesaver during the haying and harvest seasons. We're so busy that if supper isn't prepared before I serve lunch, it doesn't seem to get done on time. This recipe is perfect—it's delicious, hearty and fuss-free.
—Joan Airey, Rivers, Manitoba

- 1 medium onion, chopped
- 1-1/2 teaspoons minced garlic
- 1 broiler/fryer chicken (3 pounds), cut up and skin removed
- 2/3 cup ketchup
- 1/3 cup packed brown sugar
- 1 tablespoon lemon juice
- 1 tablespoon chili powder
- 1 teaspoon dried basil
- 1/2 teaspoon salt
- 1/4 teaspoon pepper
- 1/8 teaspoon hot pepper sauce
- 2 tablespoons cornstarch
- 3 tablespoons cold water

In a 3-qt. slow cooker, combine onion and garlic; top with chicken. In a small bowl, combine the ketchup, brown sugar, lemon juice, chili powder, basil, salt, pepper and pepper sauce; pour over chicken.

Cover and cook on low for 4-1/2 to 5 hours or until chicken juices run clear. Remove chicken and keep warm.

Transfer cooking juices to a saucepan. Combine cornstarch and water until smooth; stir into juices. Bring to a boil; cook and stir for 2 minutes or until thickened. Serve over chicken. **Yield:** 4 servings.

Sloppy Joe Supper

Prep: 15 min. **Cook:** 4 hours

The original recipe calls for this dish to be baked in the oven, but I switched it to use the slow cooker...and we like the results even better. I get it ready in the morning and have time to spend with my family the rest of the day.
—Karla Wiederholt, Cuba City, Wisconsin

- 1 package (32 ounces) frozen shredded hash brown potatoes, thawed
- 1 can (10-3/4 ounces) condensed cheddar cheese soup, undiluted
- 1/4 cup egg substitute
- 1 teaspoon salt
- 1/2 teaspoon pepper
- 2 pounds ground beef
- 2 tablespoons finely chopped onion
- 1 can (15-1/2 ounces) sloppy joe sauce

In a large bowl, combine the potatoes, soup, egg substitute, salt and pepper. Spread into a lightly greased 5-qt. slow cooker. In a large skillet, cook beef and onion over medium heat until meat is no longer pink; drain. Stir in sloppy joe sauce. Spoon over potato mixture. Cover and cook on low for 4 to 4-1/2 hours or until heated through. **Yield:** 8 servings.

Braised Beef Short Ribs

Prep: 15 min. **Cook:** 6 hours

The slow cooker was designed for recipes like this one! My mom used to make these ribs when I was a teenager, and now I prepare them myself. I work long shifts, and when I get home at 6 p.m., dinner is ready to serve. —Cheryl Martinetto
Grand Rapids, Minnesota

    4 pounds bone-in beef short ribs
    2 tablespoons vegetable oil
2-1/2 cups sliced onions
1-1/2 cups beef broth
1-1/2 cups chili sauce
  2/3 cup cider vinegar
    1 tablespoon brown sugar
    2 teaspoons paprika
1-1/2 teaspoons curry powder
    1 teaspoon minced garlic
    1 teaspoon salt
  1/2 teaspoon ground mustard
  1/2 teaspoon pepper

In a large skillet, brown the ribs in oil in batches. Transfer to a 5-qt. slow cooker; add the onions. Combine the remaining ingredients; pour over the ribs. Cover and cook on low for 6-7 hours or until the meat is tender. **Yield:** 8 servings.

Cranberry-Mustard Pork Loin

Prep: 15 min. **Cook:** 4 hours

This dressed-up pork recipe is so easy that you have to spend only a few minutes in the morning preparing it. It's become a family favorite because it's so tasty, and a favorite of mine because it's so simple! —Laura Cook
Wildwood, Missouri

    1 boneless whole pork loin roast (2 pounds)
    1 can (16 ounces) whole-berry cranberry sauce
1/4 cup Dijon mustard
    3 tablespoons brown sugar
    3 tablespoons lemon juice
    1 tablespoon cornstarch
1/4 cup cold water

Place roast in a 3-qt. slow cooker. Combine the cranberry sauce, mustard, brown sugar and lemon juice; pour over roast. Cover and cook on low for 4 to 4-1/2 hours or until a meat thermometer reads 160°.

Remove roast and keep warm. Strain cooking juices into a 2-cup measuring cup; add enough water to measure 2 cups. In a small saucepan, combine cornstarch and cold water until smooth; stir in cooking juices. Bring to a boil; cook and stir for 2 minutes or until thickened. Serve with pork. **Yield:** 8 servings.

Three Beans and Sausage

Three Beans and Sausage

(Pictured above)

Prep: 15 min. **Cook:** 4 hours

For a stick-to-your ribs meal, try this hearty combination of beans and sausage. Because it calls for several canned items, it's quick to prepare and pop in the slow cooker. —Judy Sumner, Holladay, Utah

1-1/2 pounds smoked sausage, cut into 1-inch
      pieces
    1 can (16 ounces) kidney beans, rinsed and
      drained
    1 can (15-1/2 ounces) great northern beans,
      rinsed and drained
    1 can (15 ounces) black beans, rinsed and
      drained
    1 cup chopped onion
    1 cup water
    1 can (8 ounces) tomato sauce
  2/3 cup chopped celery
    1 teaspoon chicken bouillon granules
    1 teaspoon minced garlic
    1 bay leaf
  1/2 teaspoon pepper
  1/4 teaspoon dried oregano, optional
  1/4 teaspoon dried thyme, optional
Hot cooked rice

In a 5-qt. slow cooker, combine the first 12 ingredients. Sprinkle with oregano and thyme if desired. Cover and cook on low for 4 to 4-1/2 hours or until heated through. Discard the bay leaf. Serve with rice. **Yield:** 8 servings.

Apple Cider Beef Stew

(Pictured below)

Prep: 20 min. **Cook:** 6-1/4 hours

I created this slow cooker recipe using store-bought convenience products to save time chopping vegetables and browning beef. Apple cider and cinnamon are the unique additions that give down-home flavor to this oh-so-easy stew. —Margaret Wilson, Hemet, California

    4 cups frozen vegetables for stew (about 24 ounces), thawed
    1 can (8 ounces) sliced water chestnuts, drained
    1 can (4-1/2 ounces) sliced mushrooms, drained
    1 tablespoon dried minced onion
    2 envelopes brown gravy mix
    2 tablespoons onion soup mix
    2 teaspoons steak seasoning
    1/8 teaspoon ground cinnamon
    2 pounds beef stew meat, cut into 1-inch cubes
    1 can (14-1/2 ounces) beef broth
1-1/4 cups apple cider *or* unsweetened apple juice
    1 can (8 ounces) tomato sauce
    1 bay leaf
    3 tablespoons cornstarch
    1/3 cup cold water

Place the vegetables, water chestnuts, mushrooms and onion in a 5-qt. slow cooker. In a large resealable plastic bag, combine the gravy mix, soup mix, steak seasoning and cinnamon; add beef, a few pieces at a time, and shake to coat. Add to slow cooker.

Combine the broth, cider and tomato sauce; pour over beef. Add bay leaf. Cover and cook on low for 6-7 hours or until meat is tender.

Combine cornstarch and water until smooth; stir into stew. Cover and cook on high for 15 minutes or until

thickened. Discard bay leaf. **Yield:** 12 servings.

Editor's Note: This recipe was tested with McCormick's Montreal Steak Seasoning.

Prosciutto Chicken Cacciatore

Prep: 30 min. **Cook:** 4 hours

I tailored my mother's recipe to take advantage of my slow cooker's convenience. The hearty chicken entree is wonderful to sit down to after a hectic day. Just add linguine and Parmesan cheese for a fantastic meal-in-one. —Sandra Putnam, Gallatin Gateway, Montana

    1/2 cup all-purpose flour
    1 teaspoon salt
    1/4 teaspoon pepper
    8 boneless skinless chicken thighs (3 ounces *each*)
1-1/2 pounds boneless skinless chicken breast halves
    3 tablespoons olive oil
    1 can (14-1/2 ounces) chicken broth
    1 can (14-1/2 ounces) diced tomatoes, undrained
    1 cup sliced fresh mushrooms
    1 medium onion, chopped
    1 package (3 ounces) thinly sliced prosciutto *or* deli ham
    1 tablespoon diced pimientos
    1 teaspoon minced garlic
    1/2 teaspoon Italian seasoning
Hot cooked linguine
Grated Parmesan cheese

In a large resealable plastic bag, combine the flour, salt and pepper. Add chicken, a few pieces at a time, and shake to coat. In a large skillet, brown chicken in oil in batches. Transfer to a 5-qt. slow cooker.

Stir in the broth, tomatoes, mushrooms, onion, prosciutto, pimientos, garlic and Italian seasoning. Cover and cook on low for 4 to 4-1/2 hours or until chicken is no longer pink. Serve with a slotted spoon over linguine; sprinkle with Parmesan cheese. **Yield:** 6-8 servings.

Glazed Kielbasa

Prep: 5 min. **Cook:** 4 hours

You'll need only three items to prepare this pleasantly sweet treatment for sausage. Serve it as a main dish...or with toothpicks for a hearty appetizer. —Jody Sands Taylor, Richmond, Virginia

    3 pounds fully cooked kielbasa *or* Polish sausage, cut into 1-inch chunks
    1/2 cup packed brown sugar
1-1/2 cups ginger ale

Place the sausage in a 3-qt. slow cooker; sprinkle with brown sugar. Pour ginger ale over the top. Cover and cook on low for 4-5 hours or until heated through. Serve with a slotted spoon. **Yield:** 12-16 servings.

Apple Cider Beef Stew

Pork Burritos
Zippy Steak Chili

Zippy Steak Chili

(Pictured above)

Prep: 15 min. **Cook:** 6 hours

Looking for a thick and chunky chili with a little extra-special kick for Super Bowl Sunday? Try this recipe! It was given to me by a co-worker originally from Texas.
—Denise Habib, Poolesville, Maryland

✓ Uses less fat, sugar or salt. Includes Nutrition Facts and Diabetic Exchanges.

   1 pound boneless beef sirloin steak, cut into 1/2-inch cubes
1/2 cup chopped onion
   2 tablespoons canola oil
   2 tablespoons chili powder
   1 teaspoon garlic powder
   1 teaspoon ground cumin
   1 teaspoon dried oregano
   1 teaspoon pepper
   2 cans (10 ounces *each*) diced tomatoes and green chilies, undrained
   1 can (15-1/2 ounces) chili starter
Shredded cheddar cheese, chopped onion and sour cream, optional

In a large skillet, cook steak and onion in oil over medium heat until meat is no longer pink. Sprinkle with seasonings.

In a 5-qt. slow cooker, combine the tomatoes and chili starter. Stir in beef mixture. Cover and cook on low for 6-8 hours or until meat is tender. Serve with cheese, onion and sour cream if desired. **Yield:** 5 servings.

Editor's Note: This recipe was tested with Bush's Traditional Chili Starter.

Nutrition Facts: 1 cup (calculated without optional toppings) equals 275 calories, 11 g fat (3 g saturated fat), 50 mg cholesterol, 1,127 mg sodium, 21 g carbohydrate, 6 g fiber, 22 g protein. **Diabetic Exchanges:** 3 lean meat, 1 starch, 1 vegetable.

Pork Burritos

(Pictured above)

Prep: 25 min. **Cook:** 8 hours

As a working mother, I depend on my slow cooker to help feed my family. We love the spicy, slightly sweet flavor of these burritos. —Kelly Gengler, Theresa, Wisconsin

   1 boneless pork shoulder roast (3 to 4 pounds)
   1 can (14-1/2 ounces) diced tomatoes with mild green chilies, undrained
1/4 cup chili powder
   3 tablespoons minced garlic
   2 tablespoons lime juice
   2 tablespoons honey
   1 tablespoon chopped seeded jalapeno pepper
   1 teaspoon salt
 10 flour tortillas (8 inches), warmed
Sliced avocado and sour cream, optional

Cut roast in half; place in a 5-qt. slow cooker. In a blender, combine the tomatoes, chili powder, garlic, lime juice, honey, jalapeno and salt; cover and process until smooth. Pour over pork. Cover and cook on low for 8-10 hours or until meat is tender.

Shred the pork with two forks. Using a slotted spoon, place about 1/2 cup pork mixture down the center of each tortilla; top with sliced avocado and sour cream if desired. Fold the sides and ends over the filling and roll up. **Yield:** 10 burritos.

Editor's Note: When cutting or seeding hot peppers, use rubber or plastic gloves to protect your hands. Avoid touching your face.

Chapter 11

164

⏱ *Breakfast & Brunch Favorites*

WHY START off the day with takeout from a fast food restaurant...or worse, only a cup of coffee? With rapid recipes for homemade egg bakes, fruity French toast, waffles and more, you don't have to!

Every daybreak dish here is so quick to fix, you and your family will be able to enjoy it any day of the week. Most of these foods can be either made in under 30 minutes or assembled the night before to hurry things along in the morning.

Yet these speedy recipes are so taste-tempting and impressive, they're perfect for your Sunday brunch with guests or for holidays when you want to treat your loved ones to breakfast fare that's extra special.

SUNNY SENSATIONS. Jazzed-Up French Toast Sticks and Fruity Peanut Butter Pitas (recipes on p. 176).

Fajita Frittata

(Pictured below)

Prep/Total Time: 25 min.

This is a super-flavorful and quick entree that takes me just a few minutes to prepare. It's not only fantastic for breakfast and brunch but also a satisfying main dish for dinner. In fact, whenever I ask my family what they want for supper, this is their most popular request.
—Mary Ann Gomez, Lombard, Illinois

✓ Uses less fat, sugar or salt. Includes Nutrition Facts and Diabetic Exchanges.

1/2 pound boneless skinless chicken breast, cut into strips
1 small onion, cut into thin strips
1/2 medium green pepper, cut into thin strips
1 teaspoon lime juice
1/2 teaspoon salt
1/2 teaspoon ground cumin
1/2 teaspoon chili powder
2 tablespoons canola oil
8 eggs, beaten
1 cup (4 ounces) shredded Colby-Monterey Jack cheese
Salsa and sour cream, optional

In a large ovenproof skillet, saute the chicken, onion, green pepper, lime juice, salt, cumin and chili powder in oil until chicken juices run clear.

Pour eggs over chicken mixture. Cover and cook over medium-low heat for 8-10 minutes or until eggs are nearly set. Uncover; broil 6 in. from the heat for 2-3 minutes or until eggs are completely set. Sprinkle with cheese. Cover and let stand for 1 minute or until cheese is melted. Serve with salsa and sour cream if desired. **Yield:** 8 servings.

Nutrition Facts: 1 serving (prepared with egg substitute and reduced-fat cheese; calculated without salsa and sour cream) equals 137 calories, 7 g fat (2 g saturated fat), 23 mg cholesterol, 393 mg sodium, 3 g carbohydrate, trace fiber, 15 g protein. **Diabetic Exchanges:** 2 lean meat, 1 fat.

Biscuit Egg Bake

Prep: 20 min. **Bake:** 40 min.

Determined to come up with a brunch dish that didn't keep me in the kitchen all morning, I created this fast egg casserole packed with tomatoes, onions, chilies, bacon and cheddar cheese. Your family and friends will be thrilled with it.
—Jenny Flake, Gilbert, Arizona

1 tube (16.3 ounces) large refrigerated buttermilk biscuits
12 eggs
1 cup milk
1 cup chopped fresh tomatoes

Fajita Frittata

Light 'n' Crispy Waffles

1/2 cup chopped green onions
1 can (4 ounces) chopped green chilies
1 teaspoon salt
1/2 teaspoon pepper
1/2 teaspoon salt-free garlic seasoning blend
1 package (2.1 ounces) ready-to-serve fully cooked bacon, diced
2 cups (8 ounces) shredded cheddar cheese

Separate biscuits. Cut each biscuit into fourths; arrange in a greased 13-in. x 9-in. x 2-in. baking dish. Whisk eggs, milk, tomatoes, onions, chilies, salt, pepper and seasoning blend. Pour over biscuits. Sprinkle with bacon and cheese. Bake, uncovered, at 350° for 40-45 minutes or until golden brown. **Yield:** 10-12 servings.

Blueberry Syrup

Prep/Total Time: 15 min.

Blueberries and blueberry preserves make this syrup from our Test Kitchen burst with flavor. Try it over your favorite pancakes, French toast or waffles.

1 cup sugar
1 cup packed brown sugar
1/2 cup fresh or frozen blueberries
1/2 cup water
1/2 cup blueberry preserves
1 teaspoon maple flavoring

In a small saucepan, combine the sugars, blueberries and water. Bring to a boil; cook and stir for 2 minutes. Remove from the heat; stir in the preserves and maple flavoring. Refrigerate leftovers. **Yield:** about 2 cups.

Light 'n' Crispy Waffles

(Pictured above)

Prep/Total Time: 20 min.

Club soda gives these crisp waffles from our home economists a fluffy texture. With only four ingredients, homemade waffles don't get much easier than this!

2 cups biscuit/baking mix
2 eggs, lightly beaten
1/2 cup vegetable oil
1 cup club soda

In a small bowl, combine the biscuit mix, eggs and oil. Add club soda and stir until smooth. Bake in a preheated waffle iron according to manufacturer's directions until golden brown. **Yield:** 12 waffles.

Homemade Maple Syrup

Prep/Total Time: 10 min.

Our Test Kitchen staff made traditional maple syrup a snap to prepare on the stovetop. You'll need just 10 minutes to serve your family this morning treat.

1 cup sugar
1 cup packed brown sugar
1 cup water
1 teaspoon maple flavoring

In a small saucepan, combine the sugars and water. Bring to a boil; cook and stir for 2 minutes. Remove from the heat; stir in maple flavoring. Refrigerate leftovers. **Yield:** 2 cups.

Creamy Hazelnut Dip

(Pictured below)

Prep/Total Time: 15 min.

Created by our Test Kitchen, this rich chocolate dip is a sweet way to begin your morning. With crunchy hazelnuts stirred into the mousse-like mixture, it's wonderful with fresh fruit or cookies.

> 2 packages (3 ounces *each*) cream cheese, softened
> 1/2 cup chocolate hazelnut spread
> 1 teaspoon vanilla extract
> 1/2 cup confectioners' sugar
> 1 cup heavy whipping cream, whipped
> 1/2 cup chopped hazelnuts
> **Fresh strawberries, biscotti and Milano cookies**

In a small mixing bowl, combine the cream cheese, chocolate hazelnut spread and vanilla. Beat in confectioners' sugar until smooth. Fold in whipped cream and hazelnuts. Serve with strawberries, biscotti and cookies. **Yield:** about 3 cups.

Strawberry Banana Omelet

(Pictured at right)

Prep/Total Time: 20 min.

What's odd about omelets for breakfast? Nothing, but you may be surprised by the sweet, fruity filling our home economists whipped up for this unusual version of the classic morning mainstay.

Creamy Hazelnut Dip

> 3 tablespoons butter, *divided*
> 2 tablespoons brown sugar
> 1/8 teaspoon ground cinnamon
> 2 medium firm bananas, sliced
> 1/4 teaspoon vanilla extract
> 1-1/2 cups sliced fresh strawberries
> 6 eggs
> 2 tablespoons water
> 1/2 teaspoon salt
> **Confectioners' sugar**

In a small saucepan, heat 1 tablespoon butter, brown sugar and cinnamon over medium heat until sugar is dissolved. Add bananas and vanilla; toss to coat. Remove from the heat; stir in strawberries. Set aside.

In a large bowl, beat the eggs, water and salt. Heat remaining butter in a 10-in. nonstick skillet over medium heat; add egg mixture. As eggs set, lift edges, letting uncooked portion flow underneath.

When eggs are almost set, spread two-thirds of fruit mixture over one side; fold omelet over filling. Cover and cook for 1-2 minutes or until heated through. Slide onto a serving plate; top with remaining fruit mixture and dust with confectioners' sugar. **Yield:** 2-3 servings.

Bacon Blueberry Scones

(Pictured at right)

Prep/Total Time: 30 min.

Blueberry scones are a nice alternative to muffins in the morning. And the bacon in these scones adds a savory twist, making them a great addition to any brunch or a hunger-easing snack later in the day. I think they're best served warm.
—Patricia Harmon, Baden, Pennsylvania

> 2 cups all-purpose flour
> 2 tablespoons sugar
> 2 teaspoons baking powder
> 1/2 teaspoon baking soda
> 1/2 teaspoon salt
> 1/2 teaspoon ground cinnamon
> 1/3 cup cold butter
> 3/4 cup buttermilk
> 1 tablespoon vegetable oil
> 1 cup fresh *or* frozen blueberries
> 4 bacon strips, cooked and crumbled
> 1 egg
> 1 tablespoon milk

In a large bowl, combine the first six ingredients. Cut in butter until mixture resembles coarse crumbs. In a small bowl, whisk buttermilk and oil; add to crumb mixture. Stir in blueberries and bacon.

Turn onto a floured surface; knead 10 times. Pat into an 8-in. circle. Cut into eight wedges. Separate wedges and place on a greased baking sheet.

In a small bowl, beat egg and milk; brush over scones. Bake at 425° for 12-15 minutes or until golden brown. Serve warm. **Yield:** 8 servings.

Editor's Note: If using frozen blueberries, do not thaw before adding to batter.

**Strawberry Banana Omelet
Bacon Blueberry Scones**

Overnight Egg Casserole
Tomato Asparagus Frittata

Overnight Egg Casserole

(Pictured above)

Prep: 10 min. + chilling **Bake:** 1 hour + standing

I appreciate how easy this casserole is to assemble. Putting it together the night before really frees up your time for doing other things in the morning. And no one is ever disappointed with the taste of this cheesy, ham-filled bake.
—Jennifer Howell, Fort Collins, Colorado

  4 cups frozen shredded hash brown potatoes, thawed
  1 cup cubed fully cooked ham
  1 can (4 ounces) chopped green chilies
1/2 cup shredded Monterey Jack cheese
1/2 cup shredded cheddar cheese
  6 eggs
  1 can (12 ounces) evaporated milk
1/4 teaspoon pepper
Salsa, optional

In a greased 8-in. square baking dish, layer the hash browns, ham, chilies and cheeses. In a large bowl, whisk the eggs, milk and pepper; pour over the cheese. Cover and refrigerate overnight.

Remove the casserole from the refrigerator 30 minutes before baking. Bake, uncovered, at 350° for 1 hour or until a knife inserted near the center comes out clean. Let casserole stand for 5-10 minutes. Serve with salsa if desired. **Yield:** 9 servings.

Tomato Asparagus Frittata

(Pictured above)

Prep/Total Time: 25 min.

With sliced tomatoes and fresh asparagus spears on top, this hearty garden frittata is ready to eat in no time.
—Barbara Nowakowski, North Tonawanda, New York

1/4 pound fresh asparagus, trimmed and cut in half
  6 eggs
  8 bacon strips, cooked and crumbled
  1 cup sliced fresh mushrooms
1/3 cup chopped onion
1/4 cup butter
  1 medium tomato, sliced
  1 cup (4 ounces) shredded cheddar cheese

Place asparagus in a steamer basket; place in a saucepan over 1 in. of water. Bring to a boil; cover and steam for 4-5 minutes or until crisp-tender. Drain and set aside.

In a bowl, whisk eggs until frothy; stir in bacon. In a large skillet, saute mushrooms and onion in butter until tender. Add egg mixture. As eggs begin to set, lift edges, letting uncooked portion flow underneath until eggs are soft-set.

Arrange asparagus over eggs to resemble spokes of a wheel. Top with tomato. Cover and cook over medium-low heat until eggs are set. Sprinkle with cheese. Remove from heat. Cover; let stand for 3-4 minutes or until cheese is slightly melted. **Yield:** 6-8 servings.

Raspberry-Cinnamon French Toast

(Pictured below)

Prep: 10 min. + chilling **Bake:** 35 min.

Our Test Kitchen staff came up with this moist French toast bake that's a snap to assemble the night before and bake in the morning. While it's pleasantly sweet as is, raspberry syrup makes an extra-special finishing touch.

    12 slices cinnamon bread, cubed
     5 eggs, beaten
1-3/4 cups milk
     1 cup packed brown sugar, *divided*
   1/4 teaspoon ground cinnamon
   1/4 teaspoon ground nutmeg
   1/2 cup slivered almonds
   1/4 cup butter, melted
     2 cups fresh raspberries

Place bread cubes in a greased 13-in. x 9-in. x 2-in. baking dish. In a bowl, combine the eggs, milk, 3/4 cup brown sugar, cinnamon and nutmeg; pour over bread. Cover and refrigerate for 8 hours or overnight.

Remove from the refrigerator 30 minutes before baking. Sprinkle almonds over egg mixture. Combine butter and remaining brown sugar; drizzle over the top.

Bake, uncovered, at 400° for 25 minutes. Sprinkle with raspberries. Bake 10 minutes longer or until a knife inserted near the center comes out clean. **Yield:** 6-8 servings.

Lemon Poppy Seed Waffles

Prep/Total Time: 20 min.

Lemon comes through nicely in these poppy seed-dotted waffles from our home economists. They used a convenient biscuit mix to speed up prep.

     2 cups biscuit/baking mix
     2 eggs, lightly beaten
   1/2 cup vegetable oil
     1 cup club soda
     1 tablespoon lemon juice
     1 teaspoon vanilla extract
     2 teaspoons poppy seeds

In a small bowl, combine the biscuit mix, eggs and oil. Add club soda, lemon juice and vanilla; stir until smooth. Gently fold in poppy seeds. Bake in a preheated waffle iron according to manufacturer's directions until golden brown. **Yield:** 12 waffles.

Raspberry-Cinnamon French Toast

Toffee-Flavored Coffee

(Pictured above)

Prep/Total Time: 15 min.

With its distinctive flavor, this Test Kitchen java drink makes mornings pleasantly perk along. Or treat yourself to a cup in the afternoon as a quick pick-me-up. Sweet tooths especially will love the chocolate and toffee flavor...as well as the dollop of whipped cream and drizzle of butterscotch ice cream sauce on top. Yum!

- 1/2 cup heavy whipping cream
- 1 tablespoon confectioners' sugar
- 1/2 cup milk chocolate toffee bits
- 5 cups hot brewed coffee
- 2 tablespoons butterscotch ice cream topping

In a small mixing bowl, beat whipping cream until it begins to thicken. Add confectioners' sugar; beat until stiff peaks form. Stir chocolate toffee bits into coffee; let stand for 30 seconds.

Strain and discard any undissolved chocolate toffee bits. Pour coffee into mugs; top with the whipped cream and drizzle with the butterscotch ice cream topping. **Yield:** 5 servings.

Citrus Spiced Coffee

(Pictured above)

Prep/Total Time: 15 min.

You'll rouse sleepyheads with this anything-but-average cup of joe from our home economists. Brewed with lemon peel, this coffee adds zest to sunrise schedules.

- 3/4 cup ground coffee
- 1 teaspoon grated lemon peel
- 1 cup water
- 3/4 cup packed brown sugar
- 3 cinnamon sticks (3 inches)
- 2 fresh orange slices
- 2 tablespoons unsweetened pineapple juice
- 1/2 teaspoon vanilla extract

Place the coffee grounds in a filter or basket of a coffeemaker; add lemon peel. Prepare nine cups brewed coffee according to manufacturer's directions.

In a small saucepan, combine water, brown sugar, cinnamon sticks, orange slices, pineapple juice and vanilla. Cook and stir over medium heat until sugar is dissolved. Strain; discard cinnamon and oranges. Pour sugar mixture into mugs; add coffee. Stir. **Yield:** 9 servings.

Caramel-Drizzled Spoons

(Pictured at right)

Prep: 20 min. + standing

Sweet on coffee drinks? Then you'll love these pretty stirrers created by our home economists. Coated with white chocolate and a dressy caramel drizzle, they're great for coffee and even tea or hot cocoa.

    4 squares (1 ounce *each*) white baking
        chocolate, *divided*
    12 metal *or* plastic spoons
    8 caramels
    2 teaspoons heavy whipping cream

In a microwave-safe bowl, melt two squares of white chocolate; stir until smooth. Dip six spoons into chocolate; tap spoon handles on edge of bowl to remove excess chocolate. Place on waxed paper; let stand until set. Repeat with remaining chocolate and spoons.

In a microwave-safe bowl, melt caramels and cream; stir until smooth. Drizzle over spoons. Let stand until set. **Yield:** 1 dozen.

Caramel-Drizzled Spoons
Chocolate-Dipped Spoons

Chocolate-Dipped Spoons

(Pictured above right and at left)

Prep: 20 min. + standing

Coffee goes down in the most delightful way when stirred with these chocolaty, sugar-coated spoons. Our Test Kitchen staff gave them a hint of raspberry flavor that's sure to perk up your favorite warm drinks.

    1/2 cup raspberry chocolate chips
    2 teaspoons shortening, *divided*
    12 metal *or* plastic spoons
    2 squares (1 ounce *each*) semisweet chocolate
    4 teaspoons coarse sugar

In a microwave-safe bowl, melt chocolate chips and 1 teaspoon shortening; stir until smooth. Dip each spoon into chocolate; tap spoon handles on edge of bowl to remove excess chocolate. Place on waxed paper; let stand until set.

In a microwave-safe bowl, melt semisweet chocolate and remaining shortening; stir until smooth. Dip coated spoons into chocolate mixture; tap spoon handles on edge of bowl to remove excess chocolate. Place on waxed paper; sprinkle with coarse sugar. Let stand until set. **Yield:** 1 dozen.

Cheddar Broccoli Quiche

Cheddar Broccoli Quiche

(Pictured at left)

Prep: 10 min. **Bake:** 35 min.

This savory quiche is a snap to create with a prepared pastry crust and a can of broccoli and cheese soup. Pair it with fresh fruit for a complete breakfast or lunch.
    —Barbara Cusimano, Manchester, Connecticut

    1 pastry shell (9 inches), baked
    1 cup (4 ounces) shredded cheddar cheese,
        divided
    6 eggs
    1 can (10-3/4 ounces) condensed cream of
        broccoli and cheese soup, undiluted
    2/3 cup milk

Sprinkle pastry shell with 1/2 cup cheese. In a bowl, combine the eggs, soup and milk. Pour into crust. Cover edges loosely with foil. Bake at 350° for 30 minutes. Sprinkle with remaining cheese; bake 5-10 minutes longer or until a knife inserted near the center comes out clean. Let stand for 5 minutes before cutting. **Yield:** 6-8 servings.

Bunny Pineapple Smoothies

(Pictured below)

Prep/Total Time: 15 min.

After trying these bunny-topped smoothies from our Test Kitchen, you'll want to hop back to the buffet for more! Flavored with orange juice, pineapple sherbet and piña colada yogurt, they give breakfast a tropical taste.

2 cups orange juice
2 pints pineapple sherbet
4 cartons (8 ounces *each*) piña colada yogurt
4 medium bananas, quartered
1 cup milk
1 teaspoon vanilla extract
2 cups whipped topping, *divided*
1 drop red food coloring

In a blender, combine half of the orange juice, sherbet, yogurt, bananas, milk and vanilla; cover and process until smooth. Pour into chilled glasses. Repeat.

Place 1-1/2 cups whipped topping in a pastry or plastic bag; cut a medium hole in a corner of the bag. Pipe a bunny face on each smoothie.

Tint remaining whipped topping with food coloring; place in another bag. Cut a small hole in a corner of the bag. Pipe the eyes, nose and inside of the ears on each bunny face. Beginning from the nose, gently pull a toothpick through the whipped topping toward the edge of the glass to form the whiskers. Serve immediately. **Yield:** 10 servings.

Bunny Pineapple Smoothies

Nutty Apple Syrup

Prep/Total Time: 15 min.

Our home economists used pecans and apple jelly to dress up this delightfully different syrup. Try serving it with Canadian Bacon Waffles (recipe at bottom).

1 cup sugar
1 cup packed brown sugar
1/2 cup water
1/4 cup apple jelly
1/4 cup chopped pecans, toasted
1 teaspoon maple flavoring

In a small saucepan, combine the sugars and water. Bring to a boil; cook and stir for 2 minutes. Remove from the heat; stir in the jelly, pecans and maple flavoring. Refrigerate leftovers. **Yield:** 1-1/2 cups.

Orange Pineapple Syrup

Prep/Total Time: 15 min.

Crushed pineapple and orange marmalade add citrusy flair to this Test Kitchen syrup. It'll make plain pancakes, waffles or French toast extra special.

1 cup sugar
1 cup packed brown sugar
1/2 cup water
1/4 cup crushed pineapple
2 tablespoons orange marmalade
1 teaspoon maple flavoring

In a small saucepan, combine the sugars and water. Bring to a boil; cook and stir for 2 minutes. Remove from the heat; stir in the pineapple, marmalade and maple flavoring. Refrigerate leftovers. **Yield:** 1-3/4 cups.

Canadian Bacon Waffles

Prep/Total Time: 20 min.

With Canadian bacon and cheese, these waffles from our home economists have a savory flavor. Even the heartiest appetites will be satisfied with this breakfast fare.

2 cups biscuit/baking mix
2 eggs, lightly beaten
1/2 cup vegetable oil
1 cup club soda
1/2 cup chopped Canadian bacon
1/2 cup shredded cheddar cheese
1 teaspoon snipped chives

In a small bowl, combine the biscuit mix, eggs and oil. Add club soda and stir until smooth. Gently fold in Canadian bacon, cheese and chives. Bake in a preheated waffle iron according to manufacturer's directions until golden brown. **Yield:** 12 waffles.

Peachy Rolls

(Pictured above)

Prep: 10 min. **Bake:** 35 min. + cooling

I adapted a recipe for peach sauce, then paired it with frozen cinnamon rolls to make this quick breakfast. Feel free to use your favorite prepared cinnamon rolls. Whatever kind you choose, you'll need just 10 minutes to get them in the oven.
—Renae Jacobson, Elm Creek, Nebraska

2 cups frozen unsweetened sliced peaches,
  thawed and chopped
1/2 cup packed brown sugar
1/2 cup orange juice
1 teaspoon ground cinnamon
1 teaspoon vanilla extract
2 packages (19 ounces *each*) freezer-to-oven
  cinnamon rolls

In a small saucepan, combine the first five ingredients. Bring to a boil; cook and stir for 2 minutes. Pour into a greased 13-in. x 9-in. x 2-in. baking dish; top with cinnamon rolls.

Bake at 350° for 35-40 minutes or until golden brown. Cool for 10 minutes before inverting onto a serving plate. If desired, drizzle with the contents of the frosting packets from the packaged cinnamon rolls. Serve warm. **Yield:** 1 dozen.

Editor's Note: This recipe was tested with Rhodes Any Time Cinnamon Rolls, which are available in foil pans in the freezer section.

Bacon Crescent Rolls

(Pictured above)

Prep/Total Time: 25 min.

The mouth-watering aroma of warm bacon from these three-ingredient rolls will draw your guests to the table. These are fun for children to assemble and easy to prepare with ready-cooked bacon.
—Jane Nearing
Indianapolis, Indiana

1 tube (8 ounces) refrigerated crescent rolls
6 bacon strips, cooked and crumbled
1 teaspoon onion powder

Separate crescent dough into eight triangles. Set aside 1 tablespoon of bacon. Sprinkle onion powder and remaining bacon over triangles; roll up and place point side down on an ungreased baking sheet. Sprinkle with reserved bacon.

Bake at 375° for 10-15 minutes or until golden brown. Serve warm. **Yield:** 8 servings.

Coconut Pecan Waffles

Prep/Total Time: 20 min.

Toasted coconut and pecans add a nutty taste to these delicious waffles from our Test Kitchen. Give them a try the next time you're warming up the waffle iron.

- 2 cups biscuit/baking mix
- 2 eggs, lightly beaten
- 1/2 cup vegetable oil
- 1 cup club soda
- 1/4 to 1/2 teaspoon coconut extract
- 1/2 cup flaked coconut, toasted
- 1/2 cup chopped pecans, toasted

In a small bowl, combine the biscuit mix, eggs and oil. Add club soda and coconut extract; stir until smooth. Gently fold in the coconut and pecans. Bake in a preheated waffle iron according to manufacturer's directions until golden brown. **Yield:** 12 waffles.

Hole-in-One Eggs

Prep/Total Time: 30 min.

An egg fills the center of each savory serving of this fried bread, and shredded Wheat gives each slice a crispy texture. Enjoy it plain or with syrup. —Terri Prudhomme Moorhead, Minnesota

- 8 slices bread
- 12 eggs
- 1/2 cup milk
- 2 tablespoons butter
- 1-1/2 cups crushed Shredded Wheat
- Salt and pepper to taste

With a 3-in. round cookie cutter, cut out a circle in the center of each slice of bread; set the circles aside. In a bowl, beat four eggs and the milk. On a hot griddle, melt butter. Carefully dip both sides of the bread slices in the egg mixture, then coat with the crushed cereal; place on griddle.

Break one egg into the center of each slice of bread. Cook for 3-4 minutes over medium heat until bread is lightly browned. Turn and cook until egg is completely set. Season with salt and pepper. Fry reserved bread circles if desired. **Yield:** 8 servings.

Fruity Peanut Butter Pitas

(Pictured at right and on page 165)

Prep/Total Time: 5 min.

My children often request these yummy sandwiches. They taste so good, the kids never notice that these pitas are chock-full of nutrition. —Kim Holmes Emerald Park, Saskatchewan

✓ Uses less fat, sugar or salt. Includes Nutrition Facts and Diabetic Exchanges.

- 1/4 cup peanut butter
- 1/8 teaspoon *each* ground allspice, cinnamon and nutmeg
- 1 whole wheat pita bread, cut in half
- 1/2 medium apple, thinly sliced
- 1/2 medium firm banana, sliced

In a small bowl, blend the peanut butter, allspice, cinnamon and nutmeg. Spread the peanut butter inside the pita bread halves; fill with the apple and banana slices. **Yield:** 2 servings.

Nutrition Facts: 1 filled pita half equals 324 calories, 17 g fat (4 g saturated fat), 0 cholesterol, 320 mg sodium, 36 g carbohydrate, 6 g fiber, 12 g protein. **Diabetic Exchanges:** 3 fat, 1 starch, 1 lean meat, 1 fruit.

Jazzed-Up French Toast Sticks

(Pictured at right and on page 164)

Prep/Total Time: 25 min.

These store-bought sticks of toast are spread with strawberry cream cheese to create special breakfast fare. I serve the "stuffed" French toast with a citrusy fruit puree, and this dish always goes over big with young and old alike.
—Anna Free, Bradner, Ohio

- 4 ounces spreadable strawberry cream cheese
- 12 French toast sticks
- 1 snack-size cup (4 ounces) mixed fruit
- 1 tablespoon orange juice
- Sliced fresh strawberries, optional

Spread the strawberry cream cheese over six French toast sticks, about 1 tablespoon on each; top with the remaining French toast sticks. Place in a greased 9-in. square baking pan. Bake at 400° for 15-17 minutes or until golden brown.

Meanwhile, in a blender, combine mixed fruit and orange juice; cover and process until smooth. Serve with French toast sticks. Garnish with strawberries if desired. **Yield:** 3 servings.

Spicy Maple Sausages

Prep/Total Time: 15 min.

The next time you have overnight guests or company for brunch, wake up their taste buds with this easy treatment for breakfast sausages from our home economists. Just five ingredients are needed for the glaze. You may never want plain sausage again!

- 2 packages (7 ounces *each*) brown-and-serve sausage links
- 1/4 cup maple syrup
- 1/4 cup honey
- 2 teaspoons Dijon mustard
- 1/2 teaspoon ground cinnamon
- 1/2 teaspoon cayenne pepper

In a large skillet, cook the sausage links until browned; drain. Combine the syrup, honey, mustard, cinnamon and cayenne pepper; stir into the skillet. Bring to a boil; cook and stir for 2-3 minutes or until the sausages are glazed. **Yield:** 6-8 servings.

Jazzed-Up French Toast Sticks
Fruity Peanut Butter Pitas

Chapter 12

Snappy Soups, Salads & Sandwiches

WHETHER you're looking for a lickety-split lunch or speedy meal for supper, you can't go wrong serving up a steaming bowl of soup, satisfying salad or hearty sandwich...or a combination of all three!

These family-favorite classics always please and go together in a snap. Just try any of the best-loved recipes featured in this chapter.

Simmer up a pot of cheesy Winter Chowder to warm you when the weather's cool. Toss together Antipasto Picnic Salad for a summer gathering, or assemble Ham and Mango Wraps for your next on-the-go lunch.

You'll soon see it's true—this terrific fare fits right into the meal plans of busy cooks.

FRESH FAVORITE. Strawberry Chicken Salad (p. 180).

Strawberry Chicken Salad

(Pictured below and on page 178)

Prep/Total Time: 15 min.

This salad is similar to one I loved at a local restaurant. When we moved away, I created my own version. It goes together in minutes and is perfect for picnics. But it makes a sensational main-dish salad anytime.

—Michelle Hallock, Warwick, Rhode Island

✓ Uses less fat, sugar or salt. Includes Nutrition Facts and Diabetic Exchanges.

> 1 package (5 ounces) spring mix salad greens
> 1 small red onion, thinly sliced and separated into rings
> 1/2 cup cubed fresh pineapple
> 2 packages (6 ounces *each*) ready-to-serve grilled chicken breast strips
> 2 medium tomatoes, seeded and chopped
> 1 medium cucumber, chopped
> 1 pint fresh strawberries, sliced
> 3/4 cup crumbled blue cheese
> 3/4 cup raspberry vinaigrette

Place salad greens in a large shallow bowl. In rows, arrange the onion, pineapple, chicken, tomatoes, cucumber and strawberries. Sprinkle with blue cheese. Drizzle with vinaigrette. **Yield:** 10 servings.

Nutrition Facts: 1-1/2 cups (prepared with fat-free vinaigrette) equals 130 calories, 4 g fat (2 g saturated fat), 30 mg cholesterol, 538 mg sodium, 13 g carbohydrate, 2 g fiber, 11 g protein. **Diabetic Exchanges:** 1 lean meat, 1 vegetable, 1/2 starch.

Strawberry Chicken Salad

Veggie Tortellini Salad

Prep/Total Time: 30 min.

My family always asks for and enjoys this nicely dressed pasta salad when we have special gatherings. It also works wonderfully for potlucks since it not only feeds a crowd, but is quick and easy to prepare. —Patricia Mallon
Yakima, Washington

> 2 packages (9 ounces *each*) refrigerated cheese tortellini
> 2 cups fresh broccoli florets
> 1-1/2 cups thinly sliced celery
> 1-1/2 cups thinly sliced carrots
> 1 large sweet red pepper, cut into 2-inch strips
> 1 medium red onion, halved and thinly sliced
> 1 can (14 ounces) water-packed artichoke hearts, drained and quartered
> 1 can (2-1/4 ounces) sliced ripe olives, drained

DRESSING:
> 1/2 cup red wine vinegar
> 1 envelope Italian salad dressing mix
> 2 tablespoons grated Parmesan cheese
> 1 tablespoon sugar
> 1 tablespoon dried parsley flakes
> 2 teaspoons dried basil
> 1/4 teaspoon salt
> 1/4 teaspoon pepper
> 3/4 cup olive oil

Cook the tortellini according to package directions; drain and rinse in cold water. In a large bowl, combine the tortellini, broccoli, celery, carrots, red pepper, onion, artichokes and olives.

In a blender, combine the first eight dressing ingredients; cover and process until smooth. While processing, gradually add oil in a steady stream. Drizzle over salad and toss to coat. Cover and chill until serving. **Yield:** 15-20 servings.

Speedy Seafood Gumbo

Prep/Total Time: 15 min.

I needed a fast dinner one blustery night when my husband was coming home late with the kids. So I threw together this simple gumbo with ingredients I had handy, and my family really liked it. The leftovers are great the next day.

—Lori Costo, The Woodlands, Texas

✓ Uses less fat, sugar or salt. Includes Nutrition Facts and Diabetic Exchanges.

> 3 cups water, *divided*
> 1 tablespoon butter
> 1/4 teaspoon salt
> 1 cup uncooked instant rice
> 4 cans (10-3/4 ounces *each*) condensed chicken gumbo soup, undiluted
> 1 pound frozen cooked shrimp, peeled and deveined
> 1 package (10 ounces) frozen cut okra

1 package (8 ounces) imitation crabmeat,
  flaked
1 tablespoon dried minced onion
1 teaspoon Cajun seasoning
1/2 teaspoon garlic powder

In a small saucepan, bring 1 cup of water, butter and salt
to a boil. Stir in rice; cover and remove from the heat.
Let stand for 5 minutes.

Meanwhile, in a Dutch oven or soup kettle, combine
the soup, shrimp, okra, crab, onion, Cajun seasoning,
garlic powder and remaining water. Bring to a boil. Reduce heat; cover and cook over medium heat until heated through. Stir in the cooked rice. **Yield:** 12 servings
(3 quarts).

Nutrition Facts: 1 cup equals 155 calories, 3 g fat
(1 g saturated fat), 94 mg cholesterol, 1,010 mg sodium, 18 g carbohydrate, 2 g fiber, 13 g protein. **Diabetic Exchanges:** 2 very lean meat, 1 starch.

Layered Salad Reuben-Style

Prep/Total Time: 30 min.

*Here's a tasty twist on the traditional seven-layer salad. It
combines lettuce and tomato with Reuben sandwich fixings. If you like, substitute leftover corned beef for the pastrami.* —Amy Smith, Avon, Connecticut

4-1/2 teaspoons butter, melted
1/8 teaspoon salt
1/8 teaspoon pepper
  2 cups cubed rye bread
  1 package (16 ounces) ready-to-serve salad
    greens
  2 cups chopped pastrami
  1 large tomato, diced
1/2 cup sauerkraut, rinsed and well drained
1/4 cup thinly sliced green onions
  1 bottle (8 ounces) Thousand Island salad
    dressing
3/4 cup shredded Swiss cheese

In a bowl, combine the butter, salt and pepper. Add
bread cubes and toss to coat. Arrange in a single layer in
an ungreased 15-in. x 10-in. x 1-in. baking pan. Bake
at 400° for 8-10 minutes or until golden brown, stirring occasionally. Cool.

In a large salad bowl, layer half of the salad greens,
pastrami, tomato, sauerkraut, onions and dressing; repeat layers. Sprinkle with croutons and Swiss cheese.
Yield: 12 servings.

Tuna Schooners

(Pictured above right)

Prep/Total Time: 15 min.

*These whimsical ships made with English muffins will
spark kids' imaginations and make lunchtime extra fun.*
—Judy Archuleta, Escalon, California

  1 can (6 ounces) tuna, drained and flaked
1/2 cup chopped apple

Tuna Schooners

1/4 cup mayonnaise
1/4 teaspoon salt
  4 lettuce leaves
  2 English muffins, split and toasted
  8 tortilla chips

In a bowl, combine tuna, apple, mayonnaise and salt.
Place lettuce on muffin halves; top with the tuna mix-
ture. Place tortilla chips in tuna mixture to resemble sails.
Yield: 2-4 servings.

Spinach Turkey Burgers

Prep/Total Time: 20 min.

*If you're looking for a change-of-pace burger, try these easy
but scrumptious sandwiches. Instead of beef, the patties
are made with ground turkey, spinach and stuffing mix for
deliciously different grilled fare.* —C.A. Hedges
Clarence Center, New York

  1 cup stuffing mix, finely crushed
1/3 cup chicken broth
1/2 teaspoon Italian seasoning
1/4 teaspoon salt
1/4 teaspoon pepper
  1 package (10 ounces) frozen chopped
    spinach, thawed and squeezed dry
  1 pound ground turkey
  4 sandwich buns, split
Cheese slices, lettuce leaves and tomato slices,
  optional

In a large bowl, combine the stuffing mix, broth, Italian
seasoning, salt, pepper and half of the spinach (save remaining spinach for another use). Crumble turkey over
mixture and mix well. Shape into four 3/4-in.-thick
patties.

Grill, uncovered, over medium-hot heat or broil 3-4
in. from the heat for 3-4 minutes on each side or until
juices run clear. Serve on buns with cheese, lettuce and
tomato if desired. **Yield:** 4 servings.

Hacienda Hot Dogs

Veggie Bean Soup

Prep/Total Time: 25 min.

As chairman of the kitchen at my church, I needed a meat-less soup for a Lenten lunch. I came up with this colorful blend of vegetables, and it received rave reviews. When you want a more substantial soup, simply stir in chunks of leftover roast beef and heat through. —Lois Dean Williamson, West Virginia

☑ Uses less fat, sugar or salt. Includes Nutrition Facts and Diabetic Exchanges.

  1/2 cup chopped onion
  1/2 cup sliced celery
  1/2 cup sliced fresh carrots
  1/2 teaspoon minced garlic
    1 tablespoon olive oil
    2 cups water
    1 can (15-1/2 ounces) great northern beans, rinsed and drained
  3/4 cup chicken broth
  3/4 cup Italian stewed tomatoes
  1/2 cup cubed peeled potato
  1/2 cup frozen cut green beans
    1 bay leaf
  1/2 teaspoon salt, optional
  1/4 teaspoon pepper

In a large saucepan, saute onion, celery, carrots and garlic in oil until tender. Stir in remaining ingredients. Bring to a boil. Reduce heat; simmer, uncovered, for 15 minutes or until heated through. Discard bay leaf. **Yield:** 4 servings.

Nutrition Facts: 1 cup (prepared with reduced-sodium chicken broth; calculated without salt) equals 171 calories, 4 g fat (trace saturated fat), 0 cholesterol, 567 mg sodium, 28 g carbohydrate, 8 g fiber, 7 g protein. **Diabetic Exchanges:** 2 vegetable, 1 starch, 1 lean meat.

Hacienda Hot Dogs

(Pictured above)

Prep/Total Time: 30 min.

This concoction with cheese, taco sauce and refried beans makes even inexpensive hot dogs taste great. I sometimes wrap each hot dog with a strip of bacon before baking. Then, just add a side of fries for a winning meal kids will ask for again. —Kelly Williams, La Porte, Indiana

    8 Chicago-style beef hot dogs (4 ounces *each*)
    1 cup (4 ounces) shredded Colby-Monterey Jack cheese
    1 bottle (8 ounces) taco sauce
    8 hot dog buns, split
    1 cup refried beans
Shredded lettuce
    1 large tomato, diced
  24 pickled pepper rings
Minced fresh cilantro

Cut a lengthwise slit three-quarters of the way through each hot dog and to within 1/2 in. of each end. Fill each pocket with 2 tablespoons cheese. Place in an ungreased 13-in. x 9-in. x 2-in. baking dish. Pour taco sauce over hot dogs. Bake, uncovered, at 350° for 15-17 minutes or until cheese is melted.

Spread the inside of each bun with 2 tablespoons refried beans. Top with lettuce, a hot dog, tomato, pepper rings and cilantro. **Yield:** 8 servings.

Cantonese Chicken Burgers

Prep/Total Time: 30 min.

Ground chicken is perked up with sesame oil, soy sauce, sliced green onion and chopped peanuts to make these delectably different burgers. They may take a bit of extra effort to prepare, but the taste is definitely worth it! —Betty Carr, Huntsville, Ohio

    1 egg
    1 teaspoon sesame oil
    1 teaspoon soy sauce
  1/3 cup dry bread crumbs
  1/4 cup chopped salted peanuts
    2 tablespoons sliced green onion
    2 tablespoons shredded carrot
  1/8 teaspoon garlic powder
    1 pound ground chicken
    4 hamburger buns, split and toasted
  1/2 cup plum sauce
    8 spinach leaves, chopped

In a large bowl, whisk the egg, oil and soy sauce. Stir in the bread crumbs, peanuts, onion, carrot and garlic powder. Crumble chicken over mixture and mix well. Shape into four patties.

Grill, uncovered, over medium-hot heat or broil 3-4 in. from the heat for 8-10 minutes on each side or until juices run clear. Serve on buns, topped with plum sauce and spinach. **Yield:** 4 servings.

Balsamic Chicken Salad

Prep/Total Time: 20 min.

Here's an easy, elegant and delicious alternative to TV dinners. My husband fell in love with this main-dish salad the first time I served it, and now he regularly requests it when we want a fabulous meal in a hurry.
—Rebecca Lindamood, Le Roy, New York

✓ Uses less fat, sugar or salt. Includes Nutrition Facts and Diabetic Exchanges.

6 boneless skinless chicken breast halves (4 ounces *each*), cut into 3-inch strips
1/2 teaspoon minced garlic
4 tablespoons olive oil, *divided*
1/4 cup balsamic vinegar
1-1/2 cups halved cherry tomatoes
1 tablespoon minced fresh basil *or* 1 teaspoon dried basil
1/4 teaspoon salt
1/8 teaspoon pepper
6 cups torn mixed salad greens

In a large skillet, saute chicken and garlic in 1 tablespoon oil until chicken juices run clear; remove from pan.

In the same skillet, bring vinegar to a boil. Add chicken, tomatoes, basil, salt, pepper and remaining oil; cook and stir until heated through. Divide salad greens among six plates; top with chicken mixture. **Yield:** 6 servings.

Nutrition Facts: 1 cup salad with 1 chicken breast half equals 226 calories, 12 g fat (2 g saturated fat), 63 mg cholesterol, 173 mg sodium, 5 g carbohydrate, 2 g fiber, 24 g protein. **Diabetic Exchanges:** 3 lean meat, 1 vegetable, 1 fat.

Pea 'n' Peanut Salad

Prep/Total Time: 15 min.

Even people who don't care for peas—including my own children—like this crunchy combo. I also like the fact that it's so easy to fix and makes a refreshing alternative to more traditional salads. A friend gave me the recipe years ago, and I've been making it ever since.
—Laurinda Nelson, Phoenix, Arizona

1 package (10 ounces) frozen peas, thawed
1 cup dry roasted peanuts
1 cup chopped celery
6 bacon strips, cooked and crumbled
1/4 cup chopped red onion
1/2 cup mayonnaise
1/4 cup prepared zesty Italian salad dressing

In a large bowl, combine the peas, peanuts, celery, bacon and onion. In a small bowl, combine the mayon-naise and Italian dressing. Pour over salad and toss to coat. Chill until serving. **Yield:** 5 servings.

Sweet-and-Sour Squash Salad

(Pictured below)

Prep/Total Time: 20 min.

This is a cherished family recipe I received from my mother. It's a good way to get kids to eat squash and goes over well with folks of all ages. Let it sit overnight for the best flavor.
—Anita West, Levelland, Texas

2 medium yellow summer squash, thinly sliced
2 medium zucchini, thinly sliced
1 cup chopped celery
1 cup chopped red onion
1/2 cup *each* chopped green and sweet red pepper
DRESSING:
3/4 cup sugar
1/2 cup cider vinegar
1/4 cup olive oil
2 tablespoons ranch salad dressing mix
1/4 to 1/2 teaspoon pepper
1/8 teaspoon salt

In a large salad bowl, combine the yellow squash, zucchini, celery, onion and peppers. In a jar with a tight-fitting lid, combine dressing ingredients; shake well. Drizzle over vegetables; toss to coat. Chill until serving. Serve with a slotted spoon. **Yield:** 7 servings.

Sweet-and-Sour Squash Salad

Deli Sandwich Party Platter

(Pictured above)

Prep/Total Time: 30 min.

With four kinds of meat, two spreads and an array of breads, this Test Kitchen platter adds up to dozens of delicious sandwiches guests can assemble themselves.

- 1 bunch green leaf lettuce
- 2 pounds sliced deli turkey
- 2 pounds sliced deli roast beef
- 1 pound sliced deli ham
- 1 pound thinly sliced hard salami
- 2 cartons (7 ounces *each*) roasted red pepper hummus
- 2 cartons (6-1/2 ounces *each*) garden vegetable cheese spread

Assorted breads and mini bagels

Arrange lettuce leaves on a serving platter; top with deli meats, rolled up if desired. Serve with hummus, cheese spread, breads and bagels. **Yield:** 24 servings.

Buffalo Chicken Lettuce Wraps

Prep/Total Time: 25 min.

These homemade buffalo chicken wraps are super. Honey and lime juice give the hot wing sauce a refreshing zip. —Priscilla Gilbert, Indian Harbour Beach, Florida

- 1/3 cup crumbled blue cheese
- 1/4 cup mayonnaise
- 2 tablespoons milk
- 4-1/2 teaspoons lemon juice
- 1 tablespoon minced fresh parsley
- 1 teaspoon Worcestershire sauce
- 1 pound boneless skinless chicken breasts, cubed
- 1 teaspoon salt
- 1 tablespoon vegetable oil
- 1/4 cup lime juice
- 1/4 cup Louisiana-style hot sauce
- 1/4 cup honey
- 1 small cucumber, halved lengthwise, seeded and thinly sliced
- 3/4 cup julienned carrots
- 1 celery rib, thinly sliced
- 8 Bibb *or* Boston lettuce leaves

For dressing, in a small bowl, combine the first six ingredients. Cover and refrigerate until serving.

Sprinkle chicken with salt. In a skillet, cook chicken in oil for 3-4 minutes or until no longer pink. Combine lime juice, hot sauce and honey; pour over chicken. Bring to a boil. Reduce heat; simmer, uncovered, for 2-3 minutes or until heated through. Remove from heat; stir in cucumber, carrots and celery.

Spoon 1/2 cup chicken mixture onto each lettuce leaf; fold sides over filling and secure with a toothpick. Serve with dressing. **Yield:** 8 servings.

Watermelon Tomato Salad

Prep/Total Time: 25 min.

Watermelon and tomatoes may seem an unlikely pairing, but they team up to make a winning combination in this eye-catching salad dressed with parsley, basil and lime juice. Slice up any leftover watermelon for juicy snacks. —Matthew Denton, Seattle, Washington

☑ Uses less fat, sugar or salt. Includes Nutrition Facts and Diabetic Exchanges.

  10 cups cubed seedless watermelon
   2 pints yellow grape *or* pear tomatoes
   1 medium red onion, chopped
 1/2 cup minced fresh parsley
 1/2 cup minced fresh basil
 1/4 cup lime juice

In a large bowl, combine the watermelon, tomatoes and onion. In a small bowl, combine the parsley, basil and lime juice. Pour over watermelon mixture and toss to coat. Refrigerate until serving. Yield: 16-18 servings.

Nutrition Facts: 3/4 cup equals 33 calories, trace fat (trace saturated fat), 0 cholesterol, 7 mg sodium, 10 g carbohydrate, 1 g fiber, 1 g protein. **Diabetic Exchange:** 1/2 fruit.

Cheddar-Almond Lettuce Salad

Prep/Total Time: 30 min.

Sugared almonds and a homemade honey-mustard dressing make this salad a real standout for picnics, potlucks and other get-togethers. In fact, I keep slivered almonds in my freezer so I can whip it up on the spur of the moment when I need something fast. For a bit of extra nutrition and color, I sometimes toss in broccoli and tomatoes. —Julia Musser, Lebanon, Pennsylvania

 1/2 cup slivered almonds
   3 tablespoons sugar
   9 cups torn romaine
   2 hard-cooked eggs, sliced
   1 cup (4 ounces) shredded cheddar cheese
HONEY-MUSTARD DRESSING:
 1/4 cup sugar
   2 tablespoons white vinegar
   2 tablespoons honey
   1 tablespoon lemon juice
 1/2 teaspoon onion powder
 1/2 teaspoon celery seed
 1/2 teaspoon ground mustard
 1/2 teaspoon paprika
 1/4 teaspoon salt
 1/2 cup vegetable oil

In a small heavy skillet, combine almonds and sugar. Cook and stir over medium heat for 5-6 minutes or until nuts are coated and golden. Spread onto foil to cool.

Divide romaine among salad plates; top with eggs and cheese.

In a blender, combine the sugar, vinegar, honey, lemon juice, onion powder, celery seed, mustard, paprika and salt. While processing, gradually add oil in a steady stream. Drizzle over salads; sprinkle with almonds. Serve immediately. **Yield:** 9 servings.

Onion Soup with Sausage

(Pictured below)

Prep/Total Time: 20 min.

With broiled mozzarella cheese bread on top, bowls of this hearty soup make an impressive lunch or supper. It's ready in no time and is excellent in both taste and presentation. I keep the recipe handy for weeknights and special occasions alike. —Sundra Hauck, Bogalusa, Louisiana

 1/2 pound pork sausage links, cut into 1/2-inch pieces
   1 pound sliced fresh mushrooms
   1 cup sliced onion
   2 cans (14-1/2 ounces *each*) beef broth
   4 slices Italian bread
 1/2 cup shredded part-skim mozzarella cheese

In a large saucepan, cook sausage over medium heat until no longer pink; drain. Add mushrooms and onion; cook for 4-6 minutes or until tender. Stir in the broth. Bring to a boil. Reduce heat; simmer, uncovered, for 4-6 minutes or until heated through.

Ladle the soup into four 2-cup ovenproof bowls. Top each bowl with a slice of bread; sprinkle with the shredded mozzarella cheese. Broil until cheese is melted. **Yield:** 4 servings.

Onion Soup with Sausage

Baked Potato Soup

(Pictured below)

Prep: 1 hour 20 min. **Cook:** 15 min.

This soup has a rich, creamy texture, and the green onions, cheese and bacon add great flavor and color. It's a wonderful way to use up leftover baked potatoes, but I'm always happy to bake some especially for this soup!
—Amy Welk-Thieding, Milwaukee, Wisconsin

      4 large baking potatoes (about 2-3/4 pounds)
  2/3 cup butter
  2/3 cup all-purpose flour
  3/4 teaspoon salt
  1/4 teaspoon white pepper
      6 cups milk
      1 cup (8 ounces) sour cream
  1/4 cup thinly sliced green onions
    10 bacon strips, cooked and crumbled
      1 cup (4 ounces) shredded cheddar cheese

Bake potatoes at 350° for 65-75 minutes or until tender; cool completely. Peel and cube potatoes.

In a large saucepan, melt butter; stir in flour, salt and pepper until smooth. Gradually add milk. Bring to a boil; cook and stir for 2 minutes or until thickened. Remove from the heat; whisk in sour cream. Add potatoes and green onions. Garnish with bacon and cheese. **Yield:** 10 servings.

Winter Chowder

Prep/Total Time: 30 min.

As a mother of three, I often have no idea what's on the menu as dinnertime nears. So I must rely on my imagination to come up with something that's nutritious, delicious and quick. I whipped up this chowder one night, and my 7-year-old son said it was "awesome!"
—Brenda Turner, Schererville, Indiana

Baked Potato Soup

      3 medium potatoes, peeled and cut into 1/4-inch pieces
  1/2 cup chopped onion
      1 cup water
  3/4 teaspoon onion salt *or* onion powder
  1/2 teaspoon pepper
  1/8 teaspoon salt
      2 drops Louisiana-style hot sauce
  1/2 cup cubed fully cooked ham (1/4-inch pieces)
      1 cup fresh *or* frozen brussels sprouts, quartered
1-1/2 cups milk
  3/4 cup shredded Colby-Monterey Jack cheese, *divided*

In a large saucepan, bring potatoes, onion and water to a boil. Reduce heat; cover and cook for 10-12 minutes or until tender. Do not drain. Mash potatoes (mixture will not be smooth). Stir in onion salt, pepper, salt and hot sauce; set aside.

In a large nonstick skillet coated with nonstick cooking spray, saute ham and brussels sprouts for 5-6 minutes or until sprouts are tender. Stir into the potato mixture. Add milk. Bring to a boil. Reduce heat; simmer, uncovered, for 5-6 minutes or until heated through, stirring occasionally.

Gradually stir in 1/2 cup cheese; cook for 2-3 minutes or until cheese is melted. Garnish with remaining cheese. **Yield:** 5 servings.

Nutrition Facts: 1 cup (prepared with onion powder, fat-free milk and reduced-fat cheese) equals 403 calories, 7 g fat (3 g saturated fat), 21 mg cholesterol, 457 mg sodium, 66 g carbohydrate, 23 g fiber, 33 g protein.

Cashew-Chicken Rotini Salad

Prep: 30 min. + chilling

I've tried many different chicken salad recipes over the years, but this one is still my all-time favorite. It's fruity and refreshing, and the cashews add wonderful crunch. Whenever I bring it to a potluck or other gathering, I get rave reviews...and always come home with an empty bowl!
—Kara Cook, Elk Ridge, Utah

      1 package (16 ounces) rotini *or* spiral pasta
      4 cups cubed cooked chicken
      1 can (20 ounces) pineapple tidbits, drained
1-1/2 cups sliced celery
  3/4 cup thinly sliced green onions
      1 cup seedless green grapes
      1 cup seedless red grapes
      1 package (6 ounces) dried cranberries
      1 cup ranch salad dressing
  3/4 cup mayonnaise
      2 cups salted cashews

Cook the pasta according to package directions. Meanwhile, in a large bowl, combine the chicken, pineapple, celery, onions, grapes and cranberries. Drain pasta and rinse in cold water; stir into chicken mixture.

In a small bowl, whisk the ranch dressing and mayonnaise. Pour over salad and toss to coat. Cover and refrigerate for at least 1 hour. Just before serving, stir in cashews. **Yield:** 12 servings.

Spicy Cheeseburgers

(Pictured below)

Prep/Total Time: 30 min.

We think these are the best burgers in the world! To give them an extra kick, we added cayenne to the beef, then topped the patties with pepper Jack cheese. Summer just wouldn't be the same without these fantastic sandwiches.
—*Jonna Tuchscherer, Bellevue, Washington*

  1 small onion, finely chopped
  2 teaspoons minced garlic
  2 teaspoons Worcestershire sauce
  2 teaspoons Liquid Smoke, optional
  1 teaspoon lemon-pepper seasoning
  1 teaspoon pepper
1/2 teaspoon salt
1/2 teaspoon ground mustard
1/2 teaspoon cayenne pepper
1/2 teaspoon lemon juice
  3 pounds ground beef
  9 slices pepper Jack cheese
  9 hamburger buns, split
Lettuce leaves and tomato slices, optional

In a large bowl, combine the first 10 ingredients. Crumble beef over mixture and mix well. Shape into nine patties.

Grill, uncovered, over medium heat for 7-8 minutes on each side or until no longer pink. Top with cheese. Grill 3-5 minutes longer or until cheese is melted. Serve on buns with lettuce and tomato if desired. **Yield:** 9 servings.

Spicy Cheeseburgers

Ham and Mango Wraps

Ham and Mango Wraps

(Pictured above)

Prep/Total Time: 25 min.

The unusual pairing of savory ham and sweet, juicy mangoes in these tasty wraps makes a cool luncheon treat.
—*Bonnie Austin, Grenada, Mississippi*

1/3 cup sour cream
1/3 cup mayonnaise
  2 tablespoons minced fresh basil
  2 tablespoons minced chives
  1 tablespoon lemon juice
1/8 teaspoon salt
1/8 teaspoon pepper
  3 cups cubed fully cooked ham (about 1 pound)
  2 to 3 medium mangoes, peeled, chopped and patted dry (about 2 cups)
  6 flour tortillas (10 inches), warmed

In a large bowl, combine the first seven ingredients. Stir in the ham and mangoes. Spoon about 2/3 cup down the center of each tortilla; roll up tightly. **Yield:** 6 servings.

That's a Wrap

To use up steak left over from restaurant meals, I slice the meat and combine it with mashed, ranch-style pinto beans. I add fajita seasoning and spread the mixture on a tortilla. Then I sprinkle on cheese, roll it up and heat it in the microwave.
—*Mariana Neff Pankratz, Chandler, Texas*

Stromboli Ladder Loaf

to center. Starting at one end, fold alternating strips at an angle across filling. Pinch ends to seal.

Beat the egg white and water; brush over the dough. Bake at 425° for 20-25 minutes or until golden brown. Let stand for 10 minutes before cutting. **Yield:** 1 loaf (2 pounds).

Editor's Note: If your bread machine has a time-delay feature, we recommend you do not use it for this recipe.

Stromboli Ladder Loaf

(Pictured above)

Prep: 25 min. + rising **Bake:** 20 min.

I whip up homemade dough in my bread maker to make this tasty sandwich loaf. For variation, try adding vegetables instead of pepperoni to the pizza-flavored filling. Or give it a completely different taste by substituting a Reuben filling of corned beef, sauerkraut, Swiss cheese and Thousand Island dressing. —Chrystie Wear
Greensboro, North Carolina

1-1/2 cups water (70° to 80°)
   2 tablespoons canola oil
   1 teaspoon lemon juice
   2 tablespoons nonfat dry milk powder
   2 tablespoons sugar
   1 teaspoon salt
   4 cups bread flour
   3 teaspoons active dry yeast
FILLING:
  3/4 cup pizza sauce
   1 package (3-1/2 ounces) sliced pepperoni
   2 cups (8 ounces) shredded part-skim mozzarella cheese
  1/2 cup grated Parmesan cheese
   1 egg white
   1 tablespoon water

In bread machine pan, place the first eight ingredients in order suggested by manufacturer. Select the dough setting (check dough after 5 minutes of mixing; add 1-2 tablespoons of water or flour if needed). When cycle is completed, turn dough onto a lightly floured surface. Roll into a 15-in. x 12-in. rectangle. Place on a greased baking sheet.

Spread pizza sauce in a 3-in. strip lengthwise down the center of dough to within 2 in. of short ends. Arrange pepperoni over sauce; sprinkle with cheeses. On each long side, cut 1-in.-wide strips about 2-1/2 in. in-

Colorful Corn 'n' Bean Salad

Prep/Total Time: 15 min.

This recipe couldn't be easier...the liquid from the jar of corn relish serves as the fuss-free dressing! Because there's no mayonnaise, it's perfect to bring to outdoor events on hot days. —TerryAnn Moore, Oaklyn, New Jersey

☑ Uses less fat, sugar or salt. Includes Nutrition Facts and Diabetic Exchanges.

   1 can (15 ounces) black beans, rinsed and drained
   1 jar (13 ounces) corn relish
  1/2 cup canned kidney beans, rinsed and drained
  1/2 cup quartered cherry tomatoes
  1/2 cup chopped celery
  1/4 cup chopped sweet orange pepper
  1/4 cup sliced pimiento-stuffed olives
   2 teaspoons minced fresh parsley

In a large bowl, combine all ingredients. Cover and refrigerate until serving. **Yield:** 12 servings.

Nutrition Facts: 1/2 cup equals 80 calories, 1 g fat (trace saturated fat), 0 cholesterol, 217 mg sodium, 16 g carbohydrate, 2 g fiber, 2 g protein. **Diabetic Exchange:** 1 starch.

Crispy Crouton Salad

Prep/Total Time: 20 min.

Nothing says "summer" at our house like this unique salad! It's also a great way to use up basil and tomatoes from the garden. I've brought it to many women's luncheons at church because it's a much-requested favorite. —LaNae Sanchez, Canyon Country, California

   3 cups cubed Italian bread
   3 medium tomatoes, chopped
   6 ounces part-skim mozzarella cheese, cubed
   1 medium sweet yellow pepper, cut into 1-inch pieces
  1/3 cup minced fresh basil
   6 tablespoons olive oil
   3 tablespoons white *or* brown balsamic vinegar
1-1/2 teaspoons minced garlic
  1/8 teaspoon salt
  1/8 teaspoon pepper

Place bread cubes in a single layer in an ungreased 15-in. x 10-in. x 1-in. baking pan. Bake at 450° for 6-8 minutes or until golden brown, stirring twice. Cool.

In a large bowl, combine the tomatoes, mozzarella, yellow pepper and basil. In a jar with a tight-fitting lid, combine the oil, vinegar, garlic, salt and pepper; shake well. Drizzle over salad and toss to coat. Sprinkle with croutons. **Yield:** 8 servings.

Spicy Warm Chicken Salad

Prep/Total Time: 30 min.

Packed with well-seasoned chicken, pinto beans, peppers and lots more, this dish will satisfy even man-sized appetites. —*Iola Egle, Bella Vista, Arkansas*

    1 envelope onion soup mix
    4 boneless skinless chicken breast halves
      (4 ounces *each*)
    2 tablespoons olive oil
    1 can (15 ounces) pinto beans, rinsed and
      drained
    1 cup frozen corn
  1/2 cup picante sauce
    1 can (4 ounces) chopped green chilies
  1/4 cup chopped green onions
  1/2 cup sour cream
  1/2 cup jalapeno pepper jelly
    1 tablespoon lemon juice
    2 cups chopped iceberg lettuce
    2 cups torn romaine
    1 small sweet red pepper, thinly sliced
  1/4 cup minced fresh cilantro
    2 jalapeno peppers, seeded and chopped,
      optional

Rub soup mix over both sides of chicken. In a large skillet, cook chicken in oil over medium heat for 8-10 minutes on each side or until juices run clear. Remove and keep warm.

In the same skillet, combine the beans, corn and picante sauce. Cook and stir over medium heat for 2-3 minutes or until heated through. Stir in chilies and onions; set aside. In a small bowl, combine the sour cream, pepper jelly and lemon juice; set aside. Toss iceberg lettuce and romaine; divide among four salad plates.

Slice chicken; arrange on greens. Place red pepper slices and bean mixture around chicken. Drizzle with sour cream mixture; sprinkle with cilantro. Serve with jalapenos if desired. **Yield:** 4 servings.

Editor's Note: When cutting or seeding hot peppers, use rubber or plastic gloves to protect your hands. Avoid touching your face.

Antipasto Picnic Salad

(Pictured at right)

Prep: 30 min. Cook: 15 min.

Everybody just loves this tempting blend of meats, vegetables and pasta. It goes together in no time, serves a crowd and tastes as delicious at room temperature as it does chilled. Also, it's chunky enough for the kids to pick out any individual ingredient they might not like.
—*Michele Larson, Baden, Pennsylvania*

    1 package (16 ounces) medium pasta shells
    2 jars (16 ounces *each*) giardiniera
    1 pound fresh broccoli florets
  1/2 pound part-skim mozzarella cheese, cubed
  1/2 pound hard salami, cubed
  1/2 pound deli ham, cubed
    2 packages (3-1/2 ounces *each*) sliced
      pepperoni, halved
    1 large green pepper, cut into chunks
    1 can (6 ounces) pitted ripe olives, drained
DRESSING:
  1/2 cup olive oil
  1/4 cup red wine vinegar
    2 tablespoons lemon juice
    1 teaspoon Italian seasoning
    1 teaspoon coarsely ground pepper
  1/2 teaspoon salt

Cook the pasta according to package directions. Meanwhile, drain giardiniera, reserving 3/4 cup liquid. In a large bowl, combine giardiniera, broccoli, mozzarella, salami, ham, pepperoni, green pepper and olives.

Drain pasta and rinse in cold water; stir into meat mixture. For dressing, in a small bowl, whisk oil, vinegar, lemon juice, Italian seasoning, pepper, salt and reserved giardiniera liquid. Pour over salad and toss to coat. Chill until serving. **Yield:** 25 servings.

Editor's Note: Giardiniera, a pickled vegetable mixture, is available in mild and hot varieties and can be found in the Italian or pickle section of grocery stores.

Antipasto Picnic Salad

Lemon-Linguine Shrimp Salad

(Pictured below)

Prep/Total Time: 30 min.

I love this summery medley of spicy shrimp, fresh asparagus and pasta. With a subtle splash of lemon, it gives a touch of elegance to outdoor gatherings and luncheons. If you make it ahead, add the basil just before serving.
—Laureen Pittman, Riverside, California

- 1/4 cup olive oil
- 2 tablespoons white wine vinegar
- 2 tablespoons minced fresh parsley
- 1/2 to 1 teaspoon cayenne pepper
- 1/2 teaspoon dried oregano
- 1/4 teaspoon salt
- 1 pound cooked small shrimp, peeled and deveined
- 1 package (16 ounces) linguine
- 1/2 pound fresh asparagus, trimmed and cut into 1-inch pieces

LEMON DRESSING:
- 2/3 cup olive oil
- 2/3 cup shredded Parmesan cheese
- 1/2 cup lemon juice
- 1 tablespoon grated lemon peel
- 1/3 cup minced fresh basil

In a large resealable plastic bag, combine the oil, vinegar, parsley, cayenne, oregano and salt; add shrimp. Seal bag and turn to coat; set aside.

Cook linguine according to package directions, adding asparagus during the last 3 minutes; drain and rinse in cold water. In a large bowl, combine the oil, Parmesan cheese, lemon juice and lemon peel; add linguine mixture and toss to coat.

Drain and discard marinade; add shrimp to linguine. Cover and refrigerate until serving. Sprinkle with basil. **Yield:** 6 servings.

Lemon-Linguine Shrimp Salad

South-of-the-Border Chowder

Prep/Total Time: 20 min.

This fast, filling soup is loaded with potatoes, sweet corn, pearl onions and smoky bacon to create a satisfying Southwestern flavor. Try pairing it with flour tortillas or tortilla chips. —Tonya Burkhard, Port Charlotte, Florida

✓ Uses less fat, sugar or salt. Includes Nutrition Facts and Diabetic Exchanges.

- 1/2 cup chopped onion
- 4 bacon strips, diced
- 2 tablespoons all-purpose flour
- 1/2 teaspoon ground cumin
- 1/2 teaspoon chili powder
- 1/8 teaspoon garlic powder
- 1 package (32 ounces) frozen Southern-style hash brown potatoes
- 2 cans (14-1/2 ounces *each*) chicken broth
- 1 can (14-3/4 ounces) cream-style corn
- 1 can (11 ounces) Mexicorn, drained
- 1 can (4 ounces) chopped green chilies
- 1/4 cup pearl onions

Sour cream and minced fresh cilantro, optional

In a Dutch oven or soup kettle, saute onion and bacon until onion is tender and bacon is crisp. Stir in the flour, cumin, chili powder and garlic powder. Bring to a boil; cook and stir for 1 minute or until thickened.

Stir in the hash brown potatoes, chicken broth, cream-style corn, Mexicorn, green chilies and pearl onions. Bring to a boil. Reduce heat; simmer, uncovered, for 10 minutes or until heated through. Garnish chowder with sour cream and minced cilantro if desired. **Yield:** 10 servings (2-1/2 quarts).

Nutrition Facts: 1 cup (calculated without optional toppings) equals 197 calories, 6 g fat (2 g saturated fat), 6 mg cholesterol, 756 mg sodium, 34 g carbohydrate, 4 g fiber, 6 g protein. **Diabetic Exchanges:** 2 starch, 1 vegetable.

Onion Orange Medley

Prep/Total Time: 20 min.

Here's a very unusual salad that's easy to prepare in a hurry. The combination of red onion and oranges is delicious and unique. If there's time, I refrigerate the salad for at least 2 hours before serving to blend the flavors.
—Edie DeSpain, Logan, Utah

- 6 medium navel oranges, peeled and sliced
- 1 medium red onion, thinly sliced and separated into rings
- 6 tablespoons vegetable oil
- 2 tablespoons white wine vinegar
- 2 tablespoons orange juice
- 1 tablespoon sugar
- 1/2 teaspoon grated orange peel
- 1/8 teaspoon ground cloves

Dash salt and pepper

In a large bowl, combine the oranges and onion. In a small bowl, whisk the oil, vinegar, orange juice, sugar,

Curry Chicken Salad Wraps

orange peel, cloves, salt and pepper until blended. Drizzle over salad; toss gently to coat. Cover and refrigerate until serving. **Yield:** 10 servings.

Curry Chicken Salad Wraps

(Pictured above)

Prep/Total Time: 25 min.

With curry powder and mango chutney, these sandwiches offer a twist on traditional chicken salad. The fresh mint and creamy dressing make them ideal for a special lunch or dinner on a warm day. For a low-carb version, wrap the salad in a large lettuce leaf instead of a tortilla.
—Robyn Cavallaro, Easton, Pennsylvania

```
1/2 cup mayonnaise
1/2 cup sour cream
1/4 cup finely chopped green onions
  2 tablespoons curry powder
  1 tablespoon mango chutney
1/2 teaspoon salt
1/2 teaspoon pepper
  1 package (10 ounces) ready-to-serve roasted
    chicken breast strips
  1 cup seedless red grapes, halved
1/2 cup julienned carrot
  6 tablespoons chopped pecans, toasted
1/4 cup thinly sliced onion
  6 lettuce leaves
  6 flour tortillas (10 inches), warmed
3/4 cup fresh mint (about 24 leaves)
```

For dressing, in a small bowl, combine the first seven ingredients. Set aside 1-1/2 cups for serving. In a large bowl, combine the chicken, grapes, carrot, pecans and onion. Stir in the remaining dressing.

Place a lettuce leaf on each tortilla; top each with 2/3 cup chicken salad and mint leaves. Roll up. Serve with reserved dressing. **Yield:** 6 servings.

Crunchy Romaine Strawberry Salad

Prep/Total Time: 30 min.

This is such an impressive salad—it's been a hit at every get-together we've attended. In addition to being pretty and colorful, it's so easy to toss together with a homemade, four-ingredient dressing. And the mouth-watering combination of tastes and textures seems to please every palate.
—Leslie Lancaster, Zachary, Louisiana

```
  1 package (3 ounces) ramen noodles
  1 cup chopped walnuts
1/4 cup butter
1/4 cup vegetable oil
1/4 cup sugar
  2 tablespoons red wine vinegar
1/2 teaspoon soy sauce
  8 cups torn romaine
1/2 cup chopped green onions
  2 cups fresh strawberries, sliced
```

Discard seasoning packet from ramen noodles or save for another use. Break noodles into small pieces. In a skillet, saute the noodles and walnuts in butter for 8-10 minutes or until golden; cool.

For dressing, in a jar with a tight-fitting lid, combine the oil, sugar, vinegar and soy sauce; shake well. Just before serving, combine the romaine, onions, strawberries and noodle mixture in a large bowl. Drizzle with dressing and toss gently. **Yield:** 12 servings.

Chapter 13

⏱ *Easy Half-Hour Entrees*

FROM Tuscan Chicken Breasts and Shrimp Cantonese to Ginger Sirloin Strips, the dishes in this chapter seem like the kind of time-consuming specialties you find at fancy restaurants. But it's true—each and every entree here can be prepared in only 30 minutes...or less!

In all, you get a whopping 47 taste-tempting main courses that are proven family-pleasers from busy households just like your own. So you can count on suppertime success whenever you prepare them.

Plus, many of these mouth-watering dishes are so chock-full and hearty, they can make a complete dinner all by themselves. You'll save even more time because you won't need to fuss with a side dish!

30-MINUTE MAINSTAYS. Crazy-Crust Sausage Pizza and Spinach Feta Pizza (recipes on p. 194).

Crazy-Crust Sausage Pizza
Spinach Feta Pizza

Crazy-Crust Sausage Pizza

(Pictured above and on page 192)

Prep/Total Time: 30 min.

This tasty pizza has an unusual crepe-like crust that's fast to fix—you simply stir up the batter and pour it in the pan. Then, just add all the tempting toppings.
—*Marie McConnell, Las Cruces, New Mexico*

  1 pound bulk Italian sausage
  1 medium onion, chopped
  1 medium green pepper, chopped
  1 can (4 ounces) mushroom stems and pieces, drained
  1 cup all-purpose flour
2/3 cup milk
  2 eggs
  1 teaspoon salt
  1 tablespoon cornmeal
  1 teaspoon dried oregano
1/4 teaspoon pepper
  1 cup pizza sauce
  1 cup (4 ounces) shredded part-skim mozzarella cheese
1/4 cup grated Parmesan cheese

In a large skillet, cook the sausage, onion, green pepper and mushrooms over medium heat until meat is no longer pink and vegetables are tender; drain.

In a bowl, combine the flour, milk, eggs and salt. Grease a 14-in. pizza pan; sprinkle with cornmeal. Pour batter into pan, tilting to cover. Spoon sausage mixture over batter; sprinkle with oregano and pepper.

Bake at 425° for 10-12 minutes or until lightly browned. Spread with pizza sauce; sprinkle with cheeses. Bake 5-10 minutes longer or until sauce is heated through and cheese is melted. **Yield:** 6-8 slices.

Spinach Feta Pizza

(Pictured above and on page 192)

Prep/Total Time: 30 min.

My husband and I love this pizza on busy work nights. We eat more vegetarian meals now, and this fills the bill deliciously. —*Connie Clegg, Frederick, Maryland*

  1 tube (10 ounces) refrigerated pizza crust
  1 tablespoon olive oil
  1 teaspoon minced garlic
  1 can (15 ounces) pizza sauce
  2 cups chopped fresh spinach
3/4 cup sliced red onion, separated into rings
  1 cup sliced fresh mushrooms
  1 cup (4 ounces) shredded part-skim mozzarella cheese
1/2 cup crumbled feta cheese
  1 teaspoon dried basil
  1 teaspoon Italian seasoning
Crushed red pepper flakes, optional

Unroll crust into a greased 15-in. x 10-in. x 1-in. baking pan; flatten dough and build up edges slightly. Brush with oil; sprinkle with garlic. Spread with pizza sauce. Layer with spinach, onion, mushrooms and cheeses. Sprinkle with basil, Italian seasoning and pepper flakes if desired. Bake at 400° for 15-18 minutes or until golden brown. **Yield:** 12 pieces.

Bacon-Wrapped Beef Patties

(Pictured below)

Prep/Total Time: 25 min.

I found this in a local newspaper 25 years ago, when I was a newlywed. My husband raved about it, and I have served it at least once a month ever since. He never tires of it!
—Lana Maskus, Wright, Kansas

    6 bacon strips
    2 eggs, beaten
  3/4 cup crushed saltines
    2 tablespoons chopped onion
1-1/2 teaspoons salt
  1/8 teaspoon pepper
    1 pound ground beef
  1/2 cup ketchup
    2 tablespoons brown sugar
  1/4 teaspoon ground mustard

Place bacon on a microwave-safe plate lined with microwave-safe paper towels. Cover with another paper towel; microwave on high for 2-3 minutes or until cooked but not crisp.

Meanwhile, in a large bowl, combine the eggs, saltines, onion, salt and pepper. Crumble beef over mixture and mix well. Shape into six patties. Wrap bacon strips around patties; secure with toothpicks. Place on a broiler pan. Broil 3-4 in. from the heat for 6 minutes.

In a small bowl, combine the ketchup, brown sugar and mustard. Turn patties; top with ketchup mixture. Broil 6-7 minutes longer or until meat is no longer pink and bacon is crisp. Remove toothpicks before serving. **Yield:** 6 servings.

Pork 'n' Penne Skillet

Bacon-Wrapped Beef Patties

Pork 'n' Penne Skillet

(Pictured above)

Prep/Total Time: 30 min.

I enjoy this one-pan skillet supper because it's quick and the cleanup is easy. But best of all, my family enjoys this flavorful and nutritious dinner.
—Dawn Goodison
Rochester, New York

    2 tablespoons all-purpose flour
    1 teaspoon chili powder
  3/4 teaspoon salt
  3/4 teaspoon pepper
    1 pound boneless pork loin chops, cut into
      strips
    2 cups sliced fresh mushrooms
    1 cup chopped onion
    1 cup chopped sweet red pepper
    1 teaspoon dried oregano
    1 teaspoon minced garlic
    1 tablespoon vegetable oil
    1 tablespoon butter
    3 cups milk
    1 can (15 ounces) tomato sauce
    2 cups uncooked penne

In a large resealable plastic bag, combine the flour, chili powder, salt and pepper. Add pork, a few pieces at a time, and shake to coat.

In a large skillet, cook the pork, mushrooms, onion, red pepper, oregano and garlic in oil and butter over medium heat for 4-6 minutes or until pork is browned.

Add the milk, tomato sauce and pasta. Bring to a boil. Reduce heat; simmer, uncovered, for 15-20 minutes or until meat juices run clear and pasta is tender. **Yield:** 8 servings.

Tuxedo Pasta

Greek Pork Pockets

Prep/Total Time: 20 min.

For a nutritious grab-and-go meal on busy summer days, I rely on these hefty handfuls for my family. With pork and only five other items in the filling, the pockets are easy to make. My kids prefer them to peanut butter and jelly any day!
—*Diane Hixon, Niceville, Florida*

✓ Uses less fat, sugar or salt. Includes Nutrition Facts and Diabetic Exchanges.

   1 pork tenderloin (1 pound), sliced
1/2 cup Caesar salad dressing
   1 teaspoon canola oil
   2 pita breads (6 inches), halved
1/2 cup chopped cucumber
   4 slices red onion, separated into rings
1/4 cup cucumber ranch salad dressing

Place the pork in a large resealable plastic bag; add Caesar dressing. Seal bag and turn to coat. In a large non-stick skillet, saute pork in oil for 7-8 minutes or until juices run clear.

Fill each pita half with pork, cucumber and onion; drizzle with cucumber dressing. **Yield:** 4 servings.

Nutrition Facts: 1 filled pita half (prepared with reduced-fat salad dressings) equals 274 calories, 9 g fat (2 g saturated fat), 64 mg cholesterol, 586 mg sodium, 19 g carbohydrate, 1 g fiber, 26 g protein. **Diabetic Exchanges:** 3 lean meat, 1 starch, 1 vegetable.

Tuxedo Pasta

(Pictured above)

Prep/Total Time: 20 min.

With chicken, pasta and colorful vegetables, this tempting medley tossed with a mild lemon and wine mixture is a complete meal and a snap to assemble. I try to keep leftover chicken or turkey on hand so that I can fix this nicely flavored dish whenever I want. If you prefer, substitute green or yellow pepper for the sweet red pepper.
—*Jackie Hannahs, Fountain, Michigan*

   2 cups uncooked bow tie pasta
   2 cups cubed cooked chicken
   1 medium zucchini, sliced
1-1/2 cups sliced fresh mushrooms
1/2 cup chopped sweet red pepper
   3 tablespoons butter, *divided*
1/4 cup lemon juice
   2 tablespoons white wine *or* chicken broth
3/4 cup shredded Parmesan cheese
   3 tablespoons minced fresh basil *or* 1
     tablespoon dried basil

Cook pasta according to package directions. Meanwhile, in a large skillet, saute the chicken, zucchini, mushrooms and red pepper in 2 tablespoons butter for 4-5 minutes or until vegetables are tender. Add the lemon juice and wine or broth. Bring to a boil. Reduce heat; cook and stir for 2 minutes or until heated through.

Drain pasta; add to skillet. Stir in Parmesan cheese, basil and remaining butter. **Yield:** 6 servings.

Honey-Ginger Chicken Stir-Fry

Prep/Total Time: 25 min.

When I was first married, we did not have a working oven or grill, so I used the stovetop for everything. After a while, I needed some new ideas and created this saucy stir-fry. I make half of it for the two of us and double it for company.
—*April Walcher, Hutchinson, Kansas*

✓ Uses less fat, sugar or salt. Includes Nutrition Facts and Diabetic Exchanges.

1/4 cup honey
   3 to 4 teaspoons soy sauce
1-1/2 teaspoons lemon juice
   1 teaspoon ground ginger
1-1/4 pounds boneless skinless chicken breasts, cut
     into 1/4-inch slices
1/2 teaspoon salt
1/4 teaspoon pepper
   1 tablespoon canola oil
   1 package (16 ounces) frozen stir-fry
     vegetable blend
   1 can (8 ounces) sliced water chestnuts,
     drained
   4 to 6 cups hot cooked rice

In a small bowl, combine the honey, soy sauce, lemon juice and ginger; set aside.

Sprinkle chicken with salt and pepper. In a large skillet or wok, stir-fry chicken in oil for 3-4 minutes or until lightly browned. Add the vegetables and water chestnuts; stir-fry 3-4 minutes longer or until the vegetables are crisp-tender.

Stir honey mixture and stir into chicken mixture. Cook for 3-5 minutes or until heated through and chicken juices run clear. Serve with rice. **Yield:** 4 servings.

Nutrition Facts: 1-1/4 cups chicken mixture with 1/2 cup rice (prepared with 3 teaspoons reduced-sodium soy sauce) equals 420 calories, 6 g fat (1 g saturated fat), 63 mg cholesterol, 554 mg sodium, 62 g carbohydrate, 6 g fiber, 29 g protein.

Crab Patties

(Pictured below)

Prep/Total Time: 20 min.

I've been whipping up batches of these delicious patties for years. They're always a hit—whether I serve them for brunch, lunch or dinner for my family or friends. Even my grandchildren love these cheesy bites.
—Paula Marchesi
Lenhartsville, Pennsylvania

    1 egg, lightly beaten
  1/4 cup dry bread crumbs
    2 tablespoons finely chopped onion
1-1/2 teaspoons prepared horseradish
1-1/2 teaspoons chopped sweet red pepper
1-1/2 teaspoons Dijon mustard
  1/8 teaspoon salt
  1/8 teaspoon cayenne pepper
  1/4 cup mayonnaise, *divided*
    6 ounces imitation crabmeat, chopped
    1 tablespoon butter
    2 English muffins, split and toasted
    4 slices tomato
  1/2 cup shredded Swiss cheese

In a large bowl, combine the first eight ingredients; stir in 2 tablespoons mayonnaise. Add the crab and mix well. Shape the mixture into four patties. In a large skillet, cook the patties in butter over medium heat for 3-4

Crab Patties

Pepper Steak Sandwiches

minutes on each side or until golden brown.

Place the English muffins on a baking sheet. Spread with remaining mayonnaise. Top with tomato, crab patties and cheese. Broil 4 in. from the heat for 2 minutes or until cheese is melted. **Yield:** 4 servings.

Pepper Steak Sandwiches

(Pictured above)

Prep/Total Time: 25 min.

My husband created these sandwiches years ago, when we had just begun dating. He fixed them for my family, and we were hooked. —Julie Tullos, Clinton, Mississippi

    1 pound frozen beef sandwich steaks, thawed
    4 teaspoons vegetable oil, *divided*
    1 medium sweet onion, chopped
  3/4 cup julienned green pepper
  1/4 teaspoon salt
  1/4 teaspoon pepper
    1 cup chopped dill pickles
  1/2 cup Italian salad dressing
  1/2 cup chopped fresh tomato
  1/4 cup chopped red onion
    5 hard rolls, split
    2 cups (8 ounces) shredded part-skim mozzarella cheese

In a large skillet, cook steaks in 2 teaspoons oil in batches over medium heat for 3-4 minutes or until no longer pink. Meanwhile, in another skillet, saute the sweet onion and green pepper in remaining oil until tender; sprinkle with salt and pepper.

In a small bowl, combine the pickles, salad dressing, tomato and red onion; set aside.

Place the roll tops, cut side up, on a baking sheet. Sprinkle with cheese. Broil 4 in. from the heat for 2 minutes or until cheese is melted. Divide steaks among roll bottoms; top with onion mixture and pickle mixture. Replace roll tops. **Yield:** 5 servings.

Smothered Chicken Breasts

Smothered Chicken Breasts

(Pictured above)

Prep/Total Time: 30 min.

After sampling this delicious dish in a restaurant, I decided to re-create it at home. Topped with bacon and cheese, it comes together with ingredients I usually have handy. Plus, it cooks in one skillet, so cleanup is a cinch. —Brenda Carpenter Warrensburg, Missouri

    4 boneless skinless chicken breast halves
      (6 ounces *each*)
1/4 teaspoon salt
1/4 teaspoon lemon-pepper seasoning
    1 tablespoon vegetable oil
    8 bacon strips
    1 medium onion, sliced
1/4 cup packed brown sugar
1/2 cup shredded Colby-Monterey Jack cheese

Sprinkle the chicken with the salt and lemon-pepper seasoning. In a large skillet, cook the chicken in oil for 13-15 minutes or until the juices run clear; remove chicken and keep warm.

In the same skillet, cook bacon over medium heat until crisp. Using a slotted spoon, remove to paper towels; drain, reserving 2 tablespoons drippings. In the drippings, saute the onion and brown sugar until onion is golden. Place two bacon strips on each chicken breast half; top with the caramelized onion and shredded cheese. **Yield:** 4 servings.

Vegetable Beef Soup

Prep/Total Time: 30 min.

Just brimming with veggies, this hearty soup will warm your family and friends right down to their toes!
—Marie Carlisle, Sumrall, Mississippi

✓ Uses less fat, sugar or salt. Includes Nutrition Facts and Diabetic Exchanges.

    4 cups cubed peeled potatoes
    6 cups water
    1 pound ground beef
    5 teaspoons beef bouillon granules
    1 can (10-3/4 ounces) condensed tomato
      soup, undiluted
    2 cups frozen corn, thawed
    2 cups frozen sliced carrots, thawed
    2 cups frozen cut green beans, thawed
    2 cups frozen sliced okra, thawed
    3 tablespoons dried minced onion

In a Dutch oven or soup kettle, bring potatoes and water to a boil. Cover and cook for 10-15 minutes or until tender. Meanwhile, in a large skillet, cook beef over medium heat until no longer pink; drain.

Add the bouillon, soup, vegetables, dried minced onion and beef to the undrained potatoes. Reduce heat; simmer, uncovered, for 8-10 minutes or until heated through, stirring occasionally. **Yield:** 14 servings (3-1/2 quarts).

Nutrition Facts: 1 cup (prepared with lean ground beef, reduced-sodium bouillon and reduced-sodium tomato soup) equals 150 calories, 3 g fat (1 g saturated fat), 16 mg cholesterol, 249 mg sodium, 23 g carbohydrate, 3 g fiber, 9 g protein. **Diabetic Exchanges:** 2 vegetable, 1 starch, 1 lean meat.

Sensational Sloppy Joes

Prep/Total Time: 30 min.

I've always liked sloppy joes but was feeling that my own recipe lacked flair. Then a co-worker shared hers, and I know I'll never go back! Grape jelly adds a hint of sweetness to the flavorful mixture, but I often use more than called for because my husband likes his extra-sweet. —Jessica Mergen, Cuba City, Wisconsin

    1 pound ground beef
1/2 cup chopped onion
1/2 cup condensed tomato soup
1/2 cup ketchup
    3 tablespoons grape jelly
    1 tablespoon brown sugar
    1 tablespoon cider vinegar
    1 tablespoon prepared mustard
1/2 teaspoon salt
1/2 teaspoon celery seed
    5 hamburger buns, split

In a large skillet, cook beef and onion over medium heat until meat is no longer pink; drain. Stir in the soup, ketchup, jelly, brown sugar, vinegar, mustard, salt and celery seed. Bring to a boil. Reduce heat; simmer, uncovered, for 10 minutes or until heated through. Serve on buns. **Yield:** 5 servings.

Warm Scallop Salad

(Pictured below)

Prep/Total Time: 20 min.

Bottled Italian dressing adds to the snappy preparation of this warm and wonderful salad. I received the recipe from a friend years ago, and it always brings raves. People never guess that this tasty dish is lower in fat and calories.
—*Gertrudis Miller, Evansville, Indiana*

✓ Uses less fat, sugar or salt. Includes Nutrition Facts and Diabetic Exchanges.

   1 pound sea scallops
   1 tablespoon canola oil
   1 medium sweet red pepper, julienned
   2 teaspoons minced garlic
 1/3 cup Italian salad dressing
   1 tablespoon water
   6 cups torn mixed salad greens
 1/2 teaspoon pepper

In a large skillet, saute scallops in oil for 2 minutes on each side or until firm and opaque. Remove and keep warm.

In the same skillet, saute red pepper and garlic for 2-3 minutes. Add salad dressing and water; cook 2-3 minutes longer, stirring occasionally. Return scallops to the pan; cook for 2-3 minutes or until heated through.

Place the greens in a salad bowl. Add scallop mixture and toss lightly; sprinkle with pepper. **Yield:** 4 servings.

Nutrition Facts: 1-1/2 cups (prepared with fat-free Italian dressing) equals 168 calories, 5 g fat (1 g saturated fat), 38 mg cholesterol, 491 mg sodium, 10 g

Artichoke Steak Salad

carbohydrate, 3 g fiber, 21 g protein. **Diabetic Exchanges:** 3 very lean meat, 2 vegetable.

Artichoke Steak Salad

(Pictured above)

Prep/Total Time: 25 min.

Keep your kitchen cool on hot summer days by using your outdoor grill to cook the steaks for this satisfying main-dish salad. Our Test Kitchen tosses the sliced beef with marinated artichoke hearts, spinach, cherry tomatoes, mushrooms and a nicely seasoned homemade vinaigrette.

   2 pounds boneless beef sirloin steaks
  12 cherry tomatoes
   1 medium red onion, sliced
   1 jar (7-1/2 ounces) marinated artichoke hearts, drained and sliced
   1 cup sliced fresh mushrooms
 1/4 cup red wine vinegar
 1/4 cup olive oil
   1 teaspoon sugar
   1 teaspoon salt
 1/2 teaspoon dried oregano
 1/2 teaspoon dried rosemary, crushed
 1/2 teaspoon pepper
 1/2 teaspoon minced garlic
   6 cups torn fresh spinach

Grill steaks, covered, over medium heat or broil 4 in. from the heat for 5-7 minutes on each side or until meat reaches desired doneness (for medium-rare, a meat thermometer should read 145°; medium, 160°; well-done, 170°).

Meanwhile, in a large bowl, combine the tomatoes, onion, artichokes and mushrooms. In a small bowl, whisk the vinegar, oil, sugar, salt, oregano, rosemary, pepper and garlic. Pour over the vegetable mixture and toss to coat.

Thinly slice the steaks across the grain. Add the beef and spinach to the vegetable mixture; toss to coat. **Yield:** 6 servings.

Warm Scallop Salad

Southwestern Pork Chops

(Pictured below)

Prep/Total Time: 30 min.

This recipe came out of necessity! I love to cook but hate to grocery shop, and one day I found myself with nothing but some pork chops, canned black beans and canned tomatoes. This is the dish I came up with, and my husband loved it. —Vicki Blaine, Plymouth, Michigan

> 1 medium onion, chopped
> 2 tablespoons olive oil, *divided*
> 1-1/2 teaspoons minced garlic
> 2 cans (14-1/2 ounces *each*) diced tomatoes, drained
> 1 can (15 ounces) black beans, rinsed and drained
> 3/4 cup chicken broth
> 1-1/2 teaspoons chili powder
> 1/2 teaspoon dried oregano
> 1/2 teaspoon ground cumin
> 1/8 teaspoon crushed red pepper flakes
> 4 bone-in pork loin chops (1/2 inch thick)
> 1/4 teaspoon salt
> 1/4 teaspoon pepper
> Hot cooked rice
> 2 tablespoons minced fresh cilantro, optional

In a large skillet, saute onion in 1 tablespoon oil for 3-4 minutes or until tender. Add garlic; saute 1-2 minutes longer or until tender. Stir in the tomatoes, beans, broth, chili powder, oregano, cumin and pepper flakes. Bring to a boil. Reduce heat; simmer, uncovered, for 4-5 minutes or until heated through.

Meanwhile, in another skillet, brown pork chops on both sides in remaining oil over medium-high heat. Sprinkle with salt and pepper. Pour tomato mixture over chops. Cover and simmer for 10-15 minutes or until

Southwestern Pork Chops

meat juices run clear. Serve with a slotted spoon over rice. Sprinkle with cilantro if desired. **Yield:** 4 servings.

Chicken Fajita Spaghetti

Prep/Total Time: 20 min.

This tasty dinner has been a great time-saver for me. I usually cut up the chicken, onion and peppers while our two young children are napping. Then, just before my husband gets home from work, I toss everything into the skillet while the pasta is cooking on another burner. —Heather Brown, Frisco, Texas

✓ Uses less fat, sugar or salt. Includes Nutrition Facts and Diabetic Exchanges.

> 8 ounces uncooked spaghetti
> 1 pound boneless skinless chicken breasts, cut into strips
> 1 tablespoon canola oil
> 1 small onion, sliced
> 1 small sweet red pepper, julienned
> 1 small sweet yellow pepper, julienned
> 1 can (4 ounces) chopped green chilies
> 1/2 cup water
> 1/2 cup taco sauce
> 1 envelope fajita seasoning mix

Cook the spaghetti according to package directions. Meanwhile, in a large skillet, saute chicken in oil for 8-10 minutes or until juices run clear; remove from the heat and keep warm.

In the same skillet, saute the onion and peppers until tender. Add the chicken, chilies, water, taco sauce and fajita seasoning; heat through. Drain spaghetti; top with chicken mixture. **Yield:** 6 servings.

Nutrition Facts: 1-1/4 cups equals 282 calories, 5 g fat (1 g saturated fat), 42 mg cholesterol, 722 mg sodium, 37 g carbohydrate, 2 g fiber, 21 g protein. **Diabetic Exchanges:** 2 starch, 2 lean meat, 1 vegetable.

Creamy Chicken with Noodles

Prep/Total Time: 30 min.

One night, I had some chicken thawed in the fridge and a limited amount of time. I started tossing things together and was pleasantly surprised by the results. My family was thrilled with this comforting combination. —Donna Akerley, Woodridge, New York

> 8 ounces uncooked egg noodles
> 6 boneless skinless chicken breast halves (4 ounces *each*)
> 1/2 teaspoon salt
> 1/4 teaspoon pepper
> 3 to 4 tablespoons olive oil, *divided*
> 2 cups sliced fresh mushrooms
> 1 teaspoon minced garlic
> 1 can (10-3/4 ounces) condensed cream of chicken soup, undiluted
> 1 can (10-3/4 ounces) condensed cream of mushroom soup, undiluted
> 3/4 cup half-and-half cream

1/4 cup marsala wine *or* chicken broth
1/4 teaspoon chili powder
1/2 cup minced fresh parsley, *divided*

Cook noodles according to package directions. Meanwhile, flatten chicken to 1/4-in. thickness. Sprinkle with salt and pepper. In a large skillet, cook chicken in 2 tablespoons oil in batches for 5-7 minutes on each side or until golden brown and juices run clear; remove and keep warm.

In the same skillet, saute mushrooms and garlic in remaining oil until tender. Stir in the soups, cream, wine or broth and chili powder until blended; heat through. Stir in 1/4 cup parsley.

Drain noodles; serve with chicken and sauce. Sprinkle with remaining parsley. **Yield:** 6 servings.

Chicken in Lime Butter

Prep/Total Time: 20 min.

A few ingredients make this moist, tender chicken something extraordinary! The flavor added by the rich, buttery sauce with a splash of lime juice is unmatched. It's been a hands-down winner at our house for over 20 years.
—Denise Segura, Draper, Utah

  **4 boneless skinless chicken breast halves
    (4 ounces *each*)
1/8 teaspoon salt
1/8 teaspoon pepper
  2 tablespoons vegetable oil
1/4 cup butter
  1 tablespoon lime juice
1/2 teaspoon dill weed
1/4 teaspoon minced chives**

Sprinkle the chicken with salt and pepper. In a large skillet, cook the chicken in oil over medium heat for 5-7 minutes on each side or until juices run clear. Remove and keep warm.

Add butter and lime juice to the skillet; cook and stir until butter is melted. Stir in dill and chives. Drizzle over chicken. **Yield:** 4 servings.

Orange Roughy Bundles

Prep/Total Time: 25 min.

Cleanup is a breeze when you grill this simple seafood supper. Each meal-in-one packet contains zucchini, red pepper and a flaky, full-flavored fish fillet. It cooks in no time and is just as delicious with flounder or sole.
—Margaret Wilson, Hemet, California

  **4 fresh *or* frozen orange roughy fillets (6
    ounces *each*), thawed
1/4 cup grated Parmesan cheese
1/8 to 1/4 teaspoon cayenne pepper
  2 medium zucchini, cut into 1/4-inch slices
  1 small sweet red pepper, julienned
1/2 teaspoon salt**

Place each fillet on a piece of heavy-duty foil (about 12-in. square). Sprinkle with Parmesan cheese and

Kielbasa Tortellini Alfredo

cayenne. Top with zucchini, red pepper and salt. Fold foil over vegetables and seal tightly. Grill, covered, over indirect heat for 8-10 minutes or until fish flakes easily with a fork. **Yield:** 4 servings.

Kielbasa Tortellini Alfredo

(Pictured above)

Prep/Total Time: 20 min.

Our Test Kitchen home economists combined just six ingredients to create this hearty and colorful main dish. The stovetop supper is easy to put together and sure to please the whole family.

  **1 package (9 ounces) refrigerated cheese *or*
    spinach tortellini
1/2 pound smoked kielbasa *or* Polish sausage,
    sliced
  1 medium sweet red pepper, julienned
  2 teaspoons vegetable oil
  1 jar (16 ounces) Alfredo sauce
  1 cup chopped tomato**

Cook the tortellini according to the package directions. Meanwhile, in a large skillet, saute the kielbasa and sweet red pepper in oil for 3 minutes or until the pepper is crisp-tender.

Drain tortellini. Stir tortellini and Alfredo sauce into skillet; heat through. Garnish with tomato. **Yield:** 4 servings.

No Peeking!

OPENING your grill's cover adds extra minutes to the cook time. Rather than taking a peek to check on your food, set a timer. Also, use a thermometer to make sure the food is cooked properly.

Tuscan Chicken Breasts

Prep/Total Time: 30 min.

I teach a college humanities class one night a week and rely on quick recipes to make dinner for my family before I race out the door. This has been a favorite that pleases everyone. —Erin Mylroie, St. George, Utah

  1 cup chopped onion
  1 cup *each* chopped sweet yellow and red peppers
  1 tablespoon olive oil
  1 tablespoon minced garlic
  4 boneless skinless chicken breast halves (4 to 6 ounces *each*)
  1 can (14-1/2 ounces) Italian diced tomatoes, drained
2/3 cup chicken broth
  1 tablespoon balsamic vinegar
3/4 teaspoon salt
1/4 teaspoon sugar
1/8 teaspoon crushed red pepper flakes
1/8 teaspoon pepper
Hot cooked pasta
1/4 cup shredded Parmesan cheese

In a large skillet, saute onion and peppers in oil for 4-5 minutes or until crisp-tender. Stir in garlic; cook 1-2 minutes longer or until vegetables are tender.

Flatten the chicken to 1/2-in. thickness; place over the vegetables. Add the tomatoes, chicken broth, vinegar, salt, sugar, pepper flakes and pepper. Bring to a boil. Reduce heat; simmer, uncovered, for 20-25 minutes or until the chicken juices run clear and the sauce is thickened. Serve with pasta. Sprinkle with Parmesan cheese. **Yield:** 4 servings.

Ginger Sirloin Strips

Ginger Sirloin Strips

(Pictured above)

Prep/Total Time: 20 min.

A wonderful blend of fruit flavors, along with just the right touch of ginger, makes this fabulous stir-fry a winner with our family. I created the recipe one night while trying to think of new ways to prepare beef strips. —Jill Cox, Lincoln, Nebraska

  1 can (14 ounces) pineapple tidbits
  1 can (11 ounces) mandarin oranges
  2 tablespoons cornstarch
1-1/2 pounds boneless beef sirloin steak, cut into strips
4-1/2 teaspoons minced fresh gingerroot
  1 tablespoon olive oil
  1 can (16 ounces) whole-berry cranberry sauce
  1 cup thinly sliced green onions
Hot cooked rice

Drain pineapple and oranges, reserving juice; set fruit aside. In a small bowl, combine cornstarch and juices until smooth; set aside.

In a large skillet or wok, stir-fry beef and ginger in oil until meat is no longer pink. Add the cranberry sauce, onions and pineapple. Stir cornstarch mixture and add to skillet; cook and stir until slightly thickened. Gently stir in oranges. Serve with rice. **Yield:** 7 servings.

Shrimp with Style

Prep/Total Time: 25 min.

I created this one day by experimenting with the items I happened to have in the fridge at the time. The recipe was a definite success—my family craves it all through the year. —Cyndi McLaughlin, Pinon Pines, California

  1 package (9 ounces) refrigerated angel hair pasta
1/2 pound sliced fresh mushrooms
1-1/2 teaspoons minced garlic
  1 cup butter, cubed
  1 pound uncooked medium shrimp, peeled and deveined
  2 packages (3 ounces *each*) julienned sun-dried tomatoes (not packed in oil)
  1 package (2-1/4 ounces) slivered almonds, toasted
1/2 cup crumbled feta cheese
1/2 cup minced fresh parsley
  3 tablespoons white wine *or* chicken broth
  2 teaspoons lemon juice
1/2 teaspoon salt
1/2 teaspoon pepper
1/2 cup shredded Parmesan cheese

Cook pasta according to package directions. Meanwhile, in a large skillet, saute mushrooms and garlic in butter for 2 minutes. Add shrimp; cook and stir for 5-7 minutes or until shrimp turn pink.

Stir in the tomatoes, almonds, feta cheese, parsley, wine or broth, lemon juice, salt and pepper; cook for 3-5 minutes or until heated through. Drain pasta and place in a serving bowl; top with shrimp mixture and Parmesan cheese. **Yield:** 5 servings.

Southwestern Egg Rolls

(Pictured below)

Prep/Total Time: 30 min.

I brought these egg rolls to our church potluck, and everybody commented on the Southwestern flavor of the filling. This recipe makes a large batch, and when I didn't have a single egg roll left to take home, I knew they'd been a success.
—Jacqueline Bower, Washington, Iowa

- 1 **pound bulk hot Italian sausage**
- 1 **can (15 ounces) black beans, rinsed and drained**
- 1 **can (11 ounces) Mexicorn, drained**
- 1 **can (10 ounces) diced tomatoes and green chilies, undrained**
- 1 **package (8.8 ounces) ready-to-serve Spanish rice**
- 19 **egg roll wrappers**

Oil for frying

In a large skillet, cook sausage over medium heat until no longer pink; drain. Stir in the beans, Mexicorn, tomatoes and rice. Bring to a boil. Reduce heat; simmer, uncovered, for 5-10 minutes or until heated through.

Place 1/3 cup sausage mixture in the center of each egg roll wrapper. Fold bottom corner over filling. Fold sides toward center over filling. Moisten remaining corner with water; roll up tightly to seal.

In an electric skillet, heat 1 in. of oil to 375°. Fry egg rolls, two at a time, for 30 seconds on each side or until golden brown. Drain on paper towels. Serve warm. **Yield:** 19 egg rolls.

Salmon with Sweet Salsa

Salmon with Sweet Salsa

(Pictured above)

Prep/Total Time: 15 min.

After years of not eating salmon, I tasted it one night at a formal dinner, where it was served with a sweet topping I really liked. After experimenting on my own, I came up with this sweet-and-spicy combo that's become a favorite. I serve it with fried rice that I pick up on my way home from work. —Rebecca Reece, Henderson, Nevada

- 4 **salmon fillets (6 ounces *each*)**
- 4 **teaspoons Creole seasoning**
- 2 **tablespoons olive oil**
- 3/4 **cup salsa**
- 1/2 **cup apricot preserves**

Sprinkle one side of salmon fillets with Creole seasoning. In a large skillet, cook salmon, seasoned side down, in oil over medium-high heat for 2 minutes. Turn salmon; reduce heat to medium and cook 8-10 minutes longer or until fish flakes easily with a fork.

Meanwhile, in a small bowl, combine salsa and preserves. Serve with salmon. **Yield:** 4 servings.

Southwestern Egg Rolls

Cran-Orange Pork Medallions

(Pictured below)

Prep/Total Time: 30 min.

Talk about versatile recipes! This is a longtime family favorite just as it is, but occasionally I jazz up the medallions with jalapeno peppers and ginger. I've also made it with peach preserves and dried cherries for a delicious change of pace. —Julie Wesson, Wilton, Wisconsin

- 1 pork tenderloin (1 pound), cut into 1-inch slices
- 1/2 teaspoon salt
- 1/2 teaspoon garlic powder
- 1/2 teaspoon ground coriander
- 1/4 teaspoon pepper
- 2 tablespoons olive oil
- 1 medium red onion, chopped
- 1/2 cup orange marmalade
- 1/4 cup orange juice
- 1/4 cup orange-flavored dried cranberries
- 2 tablespoons balsamic vinegar

Flatten pork slices to 1/4-in. thickness. Combine the salt, garlic powder, coriander and pepper; sprinkle over both sides of pork. In a large skillet, saute pork in oil for 3 minutes on each side or until juices run clear. Remove and keep warm.

In the same skillet, saute onion in pan juices for 5 minutes or until tender. Stir in the marmalade, orange juice, cranberries and vinegar. Bring to a boil. Reduce heat; return pork to skillet. Simmer, uncovered, for 5 minutes or until sauce is thickened. **Yield:** 4 servings.

Cran-Orange Pork Medallions

Steak Fajita Pasta

Prep/Total Time: 30 min.

This steak and pasta dish combines flavors my family loves with the convenience I love. Adding fresh ingredients to a packaged mix results in great homemade taste. —Veronica Callaghan, Glastonbury, Connecticut

- 1 pound beef flank steak *or* boneless beef sirloin steak
- 1 small onion, thinly sliced
- 2 tablespoons butter
- 1 can (14-1/2 ounces) diced tomatoes, drained
- 1 jar (7 ounces) roasted sweet red peppers, drained and coarsely chopped
- 1-1/3 cups water
- 1/4 teaspoon hot pepper sauce
- 1 package (4.8 ounces) angel hair pasta with herbs
- 2/3 cup half-and-half cream

Place steak on a broiler pan. Broil 4 in. from the heat for 5-7 minutes on each side or until meat reaches desired doneness (for medium-rare, a meat thermometer should read 145°; medium, 160°; well-done, 170°).

Meanwhile, in a large skillet, saute onion in butter until tender. Add tomatoes and peppers; saute 1 minute longer. Add water and pepper sauce. Bring to a boil; stir in pasta with contents of seasoning packet. Return to a boil. Reduce heat to medium; cook, uncovered, for 5-6 minutes or until pasta is tender, stirring frequently.

Stir in cream; heat through. Thinly slice beef; serve over pasta. **Yield:** 4 servings.

Editor's Note: This recipe was tested with Pasta Roni.

Southwest Corn Bread Bake

Prep/Total Time: 30 min.

You'll warm up cool nights when you fix this tasty casserole loaded with hearty beans and corn, then topped with corn bread. —Christine Geyer, Coralville, Iowa

- 1 can (15-1/2 ounces) chili beans, undrained
- 1 can (8-3/4 ounces) whole kernel corn, drained
- 2 tablespoons chopped onion
- 1/2 teaspoon ground cumin
- 1/2 cup all-purpose flour
- 1/2 cup cornmeal
- 2 tablespoons sugar
- 1-1/4 teaspoons baking powder
- 1/4 teaspoon salt
- 1/2 cup plus 1 tablespoon milk
- 1-1/2 teaspoons canola oil

In a bowl, combine the chili beans, corn, onion and cumin. Transfer to an 8-in. square baking dish coated with nonstick cooking spray. In another bowl, combine the dry ingredients. Combine milk and oil; stir into the dry ingredients just until moistened.

Drop by tablespoons over chili mixture; carefully spread over the top. Bake, uncovered, at 350° for 20-25 minutes or until golden brown. **Yield:** 4 servings.

Cherry-Topped Chicken

Prep/Total Time: 15 min.

Looking for a main course that's easy to make on busy weeknights, but special enough to serve company? This recipe fills the bill. It's super-simple to put together, so we enjoy it at least once a week. —Tabetha Moore
New Braunfels, Texas

✓ Uses less fat, sugar or salt. Includes Nutrition Facts and Diabetic Exchanges.

    4 boneless skinless chicken breast halves
      (4 ounces *each*)
    1 tablespoon canola oil
  1/2 cup cherry preserves
  1/4 teaspoon ground allspice

Flatten chicken to 1/4-in. thickness. In a large skillet, cook chicken in oil over medium heat for 5 minutes on each side or until juices run clear.

Meanwhile, in a small microwave-safe bowl, combine the cherry preserves and allspice until blended. Heat in the microwave until warmed. Serve over chicken. **Yield:** 4 servings.

Nutrition Facts: 1 chicken breast half with 2 tablespoons preserves equals 252 calories, 6 g fat (1 g saturated fat), 63 mg cholesterol, 55 mg sodium, 26 g carbohydrate, trace fiber, 23 g protein. **Diabetic Exchanges:** 3 very lean meat, 2 fruit, 1/2 fat.

Speedy Weeknight Chili

Prep/Total Time: 30 min.

Great-tasting and fuss-free, this chili recipe is terrific. I use my food processor to chop up the vegetables, which really cuts down the preparation time. I think this is also a good chili to choose if you're watching your weight—just substitute ground turkey breast for the beef.
—Cynthia Hudson, Greenville, South Carolina

1-1/2 pounds ground beef
    2 small onions, chopped
  1/2 cup chopped green pepper
    1 teaspoon minced garlic
    2 cans (16 ounces *each*) kidney beans, rinsed
      and drained
    2 cans (14-1/2 ounces *each*) stewed tomatoes
    1 can (28 ounces) crushed tomatoes
    1 bottle (12 ounces) beer *or* nonalcoholic beer
    1 can (6 ounces) tomato paste
  1/4 cup chili powder
  3/4 teaspoon dried oregano
  1/2 teaspoon hot pepper sauce
  1/4 teaspoon sugar
  1/4 teaspoon salt
  1/4 teaspoon pepper

In a large saucepan or Dutch oven, cook the beef, onions, green pepper and garlic over medium heat until meat is no longer pink; drain.

Add remaining ingredients; bring to a boil. Reduce the heat; simmer, uncovered, for 10 minutes. **Yield:** 15 servings.

Stuffed Grilled Chicken

Stuffed Grilled Chicken

(Pictured above)

Prep/Total Time: 30 min.

As a single working mom with two kids, I look for recipes that are fast and simple. I changed some of the ingredients in the original recipe for this chicken dish to speed it up, and my family often requests it for dinner. —Candi VanMeveren
Lamberton, Minnesota

✓ Uses less fat, sugar or salt. Includes Nutrition Facts and Diabetic Exchanges.

  1/2 cup chopped onion
  1/2 teaspoon minced garlic
    5 tablespoons butter, *divided*
  3/4 cup seasoned bread crumbs
    4 boneless skinless chicken breast halves
      (4 ounces *each*)
    1 teaspoon grated lemon peel

In a small skillet, saute onion and garlic in 3 tablespoons butter for 2-3 minutes or until tender. Remove from the heat; stir in bread crumbs. Carefully cut a pocket in each chicken breast half. Fill with bread crumb mixture; secure with metal or soaked wooden skewers.

In a small microwave-safe bowl, melt remaining butter; stir in lemon peel. Grill chicken, covered, over medium heat or broil 4 in. from the heat for 6-8 minutes on each side or until juices run clear, basting frequently with lemon butter. **Yield:** 4 servings.

Nutrition Facts: 1 chicken breast half (prepared with reduced-fat butter) equals 275 calories, 11 g fat (6 g saturated fat), 88 mg cholesterol, 465 mg sodium, 17 g carbohydrate, 1 g fiber, 27 g protein. **Diabetic Exchanges:** 3-1/2 lean meat, 1 starch.

Spicy Ham 'n' Broccoli Pasta

Parmesan Baked Cod
Prep/Total Time: 25 min.

You'll need just five ingredients for this goof-proof way to keep oven-baked fish moist. My mom is one of the best cooks in the world, and she shared this recipe with me. I've come to rely on it for a fast and fabulous dinner. —Mary Hoppe
Pewaukee, Wisconsin

✓ Uses less fat, sugar or salt. Includes Nutrition Facts and Diabetic Exchanges.

   4 cod fillets (4 ounces *each*)
2/3 cup mayonnaise
1/4 cup grated Parmesan cheese
1/4 cup chopped green onions
   1 teaspoon Worcestershire sauce

Place fillets in an 8-in. square baking dish coated with nonstick cooking spray. In a small bowl, combine mayonnaise, cheese, onions and Worcestershire. Spoon over fish. Bake, uncovered, at 400° for 15-20 minutes or until fish flakes easily with a fork. **Yield:** 4 servings.
  Nutrition Facts: 1 fillet (prepared with reduced-fat mayonnaise and reduced-fat Parmesan cheese) equals 247 calories, 15 g fat (2 g saturated fat), 57 mg cholesterol, 500 mg sodium, 7 g carbohydrate, trace fiber, 20 g protein. **Diabetic Exchanges:** 3 very lean meat, 3 fat.

Spicy Ham 'n' Broccoli Pasta
(Pictured above)
Prep/Total Time: 25 min.

I love pasta but get tired of serving it with tomato sauce all the time. My family really enjoys the different and delicious combination of ham and olives in this easy dish. It goes together quickly and is a great way to use up left-over ham. I serve it with a tossed salad and garlic bread.
—Valerie Smith, Aston, Pennsylvania

   8 ounces uncooked bow tie pasta
2-1/2 cups frozen broccoli florets
   1 medium onion, halved and thinly sliced
   1 teaspoon minced garlic
   2 cups cubed deli ham
   1 can (2-1/4 ounces) sliced ripe olives, drained
1/4 cup olive oil
1/2 teaspoon salt
1/2 teaspoon Italian seasoning
1/2 teaspoon crushed red pepper flakes
1/2 cup grated Parmesan cheese

In a large saucepan, cook pasta according to package directions, adding the broccoli, onion and garlic during the last 5-7 minutes. Cook until pasta and broccoli are tender; drain. In a large serving bowl, combine the ham, olives and pasta mixture.
  In a small bowl, combine the oil, salt, Italian seasoning and red pepper flakes. Pour over the pasta mixture. Sprinkle with grated Parmesan cheese and toss to coat. **Yield:** 4-5 servings.

Pork Tenderloin Medallions
Prep/Total Time: 30 min.

I'm always on the lookout for elegant dishes like this one, which features coated pork in a sensational mushroom sauce. —Diane Peterson, Hudsonville, Michigan

   1 pound pork tenderloin
1/4 cup all-purpose flour
1/2 teaspoon salt
1/4 teaspoon pepper
   1 egg
   2 tablespoons water
3/4 cup dry bread crumbs
   3 tablespoons butter
   1 tablespoon olive oil
1/4 pound sliced fresh mushrooms
   2 tablespoons white wine *or* chicken broth
   2 tablespoons additional chicken broth
1/2 teaspoon lemon juice
   1 tablespoon minced fresh parsley
Hot cooked pasta, optional

Cut pork into 12 pieces; flatten to 1/4-in. thickness. In a shallow bowl, combine flour, salt and pepper. In another bowl, beat egg and water. Place bread crumbs in a third bowl. Coat pork with flour mixture, dip in egg and then coat with crumbs.
  In a large skillet over medium-low heat, cook pork in butter and oil for 6-7 minutes on each side or until juices run clear. Remove and keep warm.
  Add the mushrooms, wine or broth and additional

broth to skillet; stir to loosen browned bits. Bring to a boil; cook until liquid is reduced by half, stirring occasionally. Stir in lemon juice and parsley; cook 2-3 minutes longer or until heated through. Pour over pork. Serve with pasta if desired. **Yield:** 3-4 servings.

Chicken Rice Dish

(Pictured below)

Prep/Total Time: 25 min.

Asparagus and a hint of lemon dress up this all-in-one chicken and rice dish. It's both refreshing and filling.
—ReBecca Vandiver, Bethany, Oklahoma

✓ Uses less fat, sugar or salt. Includes Nutrition Facts and Diabetic Exchanges.

      2 cups water
      2 cups cut fresh asparagus (1-inch diagonal pieces)
      1 package (6 ounces) long grain and wild rice mix
  1/4 cup butter, *divided*
  3/4 pound boneless skinless chicken breasts, cut into 1-inch strips
      1 teaspoon minced garlic
  1/4 teaspoon salt
      1 medium carrot, shredded
      2 tablespoons lemon juice
  1/2 teaspoon grated lemon peel, optional

In a large saucepan, combine the water, asparagus, rice mix with contents of seasoning packet and 2 tablespoons butter. Bring to a boil; reduce heat. Cover and simmer for 10-15 minutes or until the water is absorbed.

   Meanwhile, in a large skillet, saute the chicken, garlic and salt in remaining butter until juices run clear. Add the carrot, lemon juice and lemon peel if desired; cook

Mushroom-Swiss Lamb Chops

and stir for 1-2 minutes or until heated through. Stir into rice mixture. **Yield:** 4 servings.

   Nutrition Facts: 1-1/4 cups (prepared with reduced-fat butter) equals 247 calories, 7 g fat (4 g saturated fat), 54 mg cholesterol, 668 mg sodium, 29 g carbohydrate, 2 g fiber, 20 g protein. **Diabetic Exchanges:** 2 lean meat, 1-1/2 starch, 1 vegetable.

Mushroom-Swiss Lamb Chops

(Pictured above)

Prep/Total Time: 30 min.

Looking for something effortless but impressive to serve company on a busy day? These lamb chops make a really nice, last-minute meal for guests. Using prepared salad dressing is the key—it adds instant flavor.
—Candy McMenamin
Lexington, South Carolina

      4 lamb loin chops (2 inches thick and about 8 ounces *each*)
  1/2 teaspoon salt
  1/2 teaspoon pepper
      2 cups sliced fresh mushrooms
      2 tablespoons butter
  1/4 cup Russian salad dressing
  1/2 cup shredded Swiss cheese

Sprinkle both sides of lamb chops with salt and pepper. Place on a broiler pan. Broil 4-6 in. from the heat for 10-15 minutes on each side or until meat reaches desired doneness (for medium-rare, a meat thermometer should read 145°; medium, 160°; well-done, 170°).

   Meanwhile, in a large skillet, saute mushrooms in butter for 5-6 minutes or until tender. Stir in salad dressing. Bring to a boil; cook until liquid is reduced by half. Sprinkle cheese over lamb chops; broil 1-2 minutes longer or until cheese is melted. Serve with mushroom mixture. **Yield:** 4 servings.

Chicken Rice Dish

Pepper Jack Chicken Pasta

(Pictured below)

Prep/Total Time: 25 min.

My wife, Jennie, is a wonderful cook and generally skeptical about my kitchen experiments. But she likes this recipe well enough to give me temporary kitchen privileges…and even encouraged me to enter a Quick Cooking contest! If you can't find the pepper Jack soup, just substitute cheddar cheese or nacho cheese soup.

—Mike Kirschbaum, Cary, North Carolina

    3 cups uncooked mostaccioli
1/4 cup chopped onion
1/4 cup chopped sweet red pepper
1/2 teaspoon minced garlic
    1 tablespoon vegetable oil
    1 can (10-3/4 ounces) condensed
        Southwest-style pepper Jack soup, undiluted
    1 package (9 ounces) ready-to-use
        Southwestern chicken strips
3/4 cup water
    1 can (15 ounces) black beans, rinsed and
        drained
1/4 cup shredded Monterey Jack cheese, optional

Cook mostaccioli according to package directions. Meanwhile, in a large skillet, saute the onion, red pepper and garlic in oil until tender. Stir in the soup, chicken and water. Bring to a boil. Reduce heat; cover and simmer for 8 minutes.

Stir in beans; heat through. Drain mostaccioli and place in a serving bowl; top with chicken mixture. Sprinkle with cheese if desired. **Yield:** 6 servings.

Pepper Jack Chicken Pasta

Deli Monte Cristos

Prep/Total Time: 10 min.

In the mood for something other than the usual Reuben or grilled cheese? This was a famous sandwich in the islands years ago. We make it often, and I always get requests for more. I'm happy to oblige since the recipe is so fast to fix.

—Darlene Van Wie, Clayton, New York

    4 slices rye bread
    4 thin slices deli ham
    2 thin slices deli turkey
    2 tablespoons deli coleslaw
    2 tablespoons Thousand Island salad dressing
    2 slices Swiss cheese
    2 eggs

On two slices of bread, layer a slice of ham and turkey, coleslaw, salad dressing and cheese. Top with remaining ham and bread. In a shallow bowl, whisk the eggs. Dip both sides of sandwiches in eggs.

In a nonstick skillet coated with nonstick cooking spray, cook sandwiches over medium heat for 2-3 minutes on each side or until bread is toasted and cheese is melted. **Yield:** 2 servings.

Maple Cranberry Chicken

Prep/Total Time: 25 min.

With just four ingredients, these moist and flavorful chicken breasts are a breeze to cook on the grill. The tart cranberry sauce contrasts nicely with the sweet maple syrup.

—Margaret Wilson, Hemet, California

1/2 cup maple syrup
    1 can (16 ounces) whole-berry cranberry
        sauce, *divided*
    6 boneless skinless chicken breast halves
        (4 ounces *each*)
1/2 teaspoon salt

In a small bowl, combine syrup and 3/4 cup cranberry sauce; set aside. Sprinkle chicken with salt.

If grilling the chicken, coat grill rack with nonstick cooking spray before starting the grill. Grill chicken, covered, over medium heat or broil 4 in. from the heat for 6-8 minutes on each side or until juices run clear, basting frequently with syrup mixture. Serve with remaining cranberry sauce. **Yield:** 6 servings.

Sunday Pork Chops

Prep/Total Time: 25 min.

I love this recipe because it tastes like a "real" Sunday supper, but I don't have to spend my whole Sunday making it. Instead, I can bike or work in my garden all day and still wind up the weekend with this home-cooked, sit-down meal for my family. *—Trisha Kruse, Eagle, Idaho*

    1 tablespoon brown sugar
1/4 teaspoon garlic powder

Beef Fillets with Grilled Vegetables

oil. Grill tomatoes and onion, uncovered, over medium heat for 4-5 minutes on each side or until onion is crisp-tender. Grill romaine for 30 seconds on each side or until heated through. Wrap vegetables in foil and set aside.

Drain and discard marinade. Grill fillets, covered, over medium heat for 7-8 minutes on each side or until meat reaches desired doneness (for medium-rare, a meat thermometer should read 145°; medium, 160°; well-done, 170°), basting occasionally with butter. Serve with grilled vegetables. Sprinkle with salt and remaining pepper. **Yield:** 4 servings.

Turkey and Gravy Baskets

(Pictured below)

Prep/Total Time: 20 min.

Using store-bought items, you can put this special entree on the table anytime. Our Test Kitchen home economists combined fresh veggies with packaged cooked turkey and gravy, then spooned the mixture into puff pastry shells from the freezer section for a pretty presentation.

    1 package (10 ounces) frozen puff pastry shells
    2 cups fresh broccoli florets
  1/2 cup chopped onion
  1/2 cup chopped sweet red pepper
    4 teaspoons canola oil
    1 package (18 ounces) refrigerated turkey breast slices in gravy
  1/2 cup turkey gravy

Bake four pastry shells according to package directions; save remaining shells for another use. Meanwhile, in a large skillet, saute the broccoli, onion and red pepper in oil for 5 minutes or until crisp-tender.

Cut turkey slices into bite-size pieces; add to skillet with gravy from package and additional gravy. Heat through. Serve in pastry shells. **Yield:** 4 servings.

    4 bone-in pork loin chops (1 inch thick and 6 ounces *each*)
    1 tablespoon olive oil
    1 can (11 ounces) Mexicorn, undrained
1-1/3 cups reduced-sodium chicken broth
    1 package (6 ounces) corn bread stuffing mix
    2 tablespoons butter

Combine brown sugar and garlic powder; rub over both sides of pork chops. In a large skillet, brown chops in oil on both sides over medium heat. Remove from the pan.

In the same skillet, combine the Mexicorn, broth, stuffing mix and butter; top with pork chops. Cover and cook for 10-12 minutes or until meat is tender. **Yield:** 4 servings.

Beef Fillets with Grilled Vegetables

(Pictured above)

Prep/Total Time: 30 min.

Here's a super entree that's not only quick, but it also leaves you with no pots or pans to clean! Basting the beef with butter seals in the meat's juices and adds flavor. And romaine lettuce is a must because the leaves can stand up to grilling.   —Cindie Haras, Boca Raton, Florida

    4 beef tenderloin fillets (1-1/2 inches thick and 4 ounces *each*)
    3 teaspoons pepper, *divided*
  1/2 cup Caesar salad dressing
    8 to 12 romaine leaves
    2 medium tomatoes, cut into 1-inch slices
    1 medium onion, sliced
    3 tablespoons olive oil
    2 tablespoons butter, melted
  1/2 teaspoon salt

Rub fillets with 2 teaspoons pepper; place in a large re-sealable plastic bag. Add salad dressing; seal bag and turn to coat. Refrigerate for 10 minutes.

Meanwhile, brush romaine, tomatoes and onion with

Turkey and Gravy Baskets

Shrimp Cantonese

Shrimp Cantonese

(Pictured above)

Prep/Total Time: 30 min.

This recipe proves that you don't have to sacrifice good taste when you need something fast. The nutritious stir-fry features tender shrimp, fresh spinach and packaged veggies. —Bobby Taylor, Michigan City, Indiana

✓ Uses less fat, sugar or salt. Includes Nutrition Facts and Diabetic Exchanges.

    2 tablespoons cornstarch
1-1/4 cups chicken broth
  1/4 cup soy sauce
  1/4 teaspoon pepper
    2 cups sliced onions
    2 cups sliced celery
    2 tablespoons butter
  3/4 pound uncooked medium shrimp, peeled
       and deveined
    8 ounces fresh spinach, torn
    1 package (16 ounces) frozen Oriental mixed
       vegetables, thawed
Hot cooked rice

In a small bowl, combine the cornstarch and chicken broth until smooth. Add the soy sauce and pepper; mix well. Set aside.

In a large skillet or wok, stir-fry onions and celery in butter for 2-3 minutes or until tender. Add shrimp; cook and stir until shrimp turn pink. Add spinach and mixed vegetables; stir-fry 4-6 minutes longer or until spinach is tender.

Stir broth mixture and stir into shrimp mixture. Bring to a boil; cook and stir for 2 minutes or until thickened. Serve with rice. **Yield:** 6 servings.

Nutrition Facts: 1 cup (prepared with reduced-sodium broth, reduced-sodium soy sauce and reduced-fat butter; calculated without rice) equals 131 calories, 3 g fat (2 g saturated fat), 91 mg cholesterol, 732 mg sodium, 13 g carbohydrate, 4 g fiber, 13 g protein. **Diabetic Exchanges:** 2 very lean meat, 2 vegetable, 1/2 fat.

Unstuffed Peppers

Prep/Total Time: 30 min.

If you like stuffed peppers, you'll love this speedy version. It offers the great flavor of the original but takes only half an hour. —Beth DeWyer, Du Bois, Pennsylvania

    1 cup uncooked instant rice
    1 pound ground beef
    2 medium green peppers, cut into 1-inch
       pieces
  1/2 cup chopped onion
    1 jar (26 ounces) marinara sauce
1-1/2 teaspoons salt-free seasoning blend
  1/2 cup shredded Italian cheese blend
  1/2 cup seasoned bread crumbs
    1 tablespoon olive oil

Cook rice according to package directions. Meanwhile, in a large skillet, cook the beef, green peppers and onion over medium-high heat for 10-12 minutes or until meat is no longer pink; drain. Stir in the rice, marinara sauce and seasoning blend. Stir in cheese.

Transfer to a greased 2-qt. baking dish. Toss bread crumbs and oil; sprinkle over the top. Bake at 350° for 8-10 minutes or until heated through and topping is golden brown. **Yield:** 6 servings.

Club Sandwiches

Prep/Total Time: 25 min.

I am a busy wife, mother, grandmother and great-grandmother who loves to sew and cook. Stacked with deli meat, bacon, avocado and more, this sandwich is one of my all-time favorites and makes a satisfying meal all by itself. —Janet Miller, Midland, Texas

  1/2 cup mayonnaise
    4 French rolls, split
    1 cup shredded lettuce
    8 slices tomato
    1 medium ripe avocado, peeled and sliced
  1/4 cup prepared Italian salad dressing
  1/2 teaspoon coarsely ground pepper
   12 cooked bacon strips
  1/2 pound sliced deli turkey
  1/2 pound sliced deli ham
    4 slices Swiss cheese

Spread mayonnaise over cut sides of rolls. On roll bottoms, layer lettuce, tomato and avocado. Drizzle with dressing; sprinkle with pepper. Layer with bacon, turkey, ham and cheese. Replace roll tops. **Yield:** 4 servings.

Chicken-Stuffed Tomatoes

(Pictured below)

Prep/Total Time: 20 min.

I turn garden-fresh tomatoes into a sensational summer meal by filling them with this creamy chicken salad. I thought of this recipe when I had a lot of home-grown produce on hand, and I've enjoyed it many times.
—Nancy MacLeod
Boynton Beach, Florida

- 4 medium tomatoes
- 1 cooked rotisserie chicken, skin removed and cubed (2-3/4 cups)
- 1/2 cup shredded carrot
- 1/4 cup chopped green onions
- 1/3 cup mayonnaise
- 1/3 cup ranch salad dressing
- 1/4 cup chopped walnuts

Cut a thin slice off the top of each tomato. Scoop out pulp, leaving 1/2-in. shells. Invert tomatoes onto paper towels to drain.

In a small bowl, combine the chicken, carrot and onions. Combine mayonnaise and ranch dressing; stir into chicken mixture. Spoon into tomatoes. Sprinkle with walnuts. **Yield:** 4 servings.

Chicken-Stuffed Tomatoes

Turkey Lo Mein

Turkey Lo Mein

(Pictured above)

Prep/Total Time: 30 min.

I love Chinese dishes but hate chopping all the veggies. So I use convenient frozen vegetable combos and ready-made sauce for this tasty dish that's quick and easy. It's versatile enough to make the most of whatever items I have in the kitchen.
—Christi Paulton, Phelps, Wisconsin

✓ Uses less fat, sugar or salt. Includes Nutrition Facts and Diabetic Exchanges.

- 8 ounces uncooked linguine
- 2 pounds turkey breast tenderloins, cut into 1/4-inch strips
- 2 tablespoons canola oil, *divided*
- 1/2 pound sliced fresh mushrooms
- 2 cups frozen pepper and onion stir-fry
- 2/3 cup stir-fry sauce

Cook linguine according to package directions. Meanwhile, in a large skillet or wok, stir-fry turkey in batches in 1 tablespoon hot oil for 5-6 minutes or until no longer pink. Remove and keep warm.

In the same pan, stir-fry mushrooms in remaining oil for 3 minutes. Add the pepper and onion mixture; stir-fry for 2-3 minutes or until vegetables are tender. Add turkey and stir-fry sauce; cook and stir for 2-3 minutes or until heated through. Drain linguine; add to turkey mixture and toss to coat. **Yield:** 8 servings.

Nutrition Facts: 1 cup equals 284 calories, 6 g fat (1 g saturated fat), 56 mg cholesterol, 775 mg sodium, 27 g carbohydrate, 2 g fiber, 33 g protein. **Diabetic Exchanges:** 3 very lean meat, 2 starch.

Chapter 14

⏱ *Delectable Desserts*

GO AHEAD—indulge! You'll always have time for a scrumptious, to-die-for dessert when you choose from the fuss-free but fabulous treats here.

Need kid-pleasing goodies for an event at school? Bake a batch of popular Oatmeal Kiss Cookies. Want a special standout for your Christmas dinner? Whip up irresistible Pumpkin Cream Trifle. Crave a sweet recipe for busy weekdays? Turn to spiced Apple Crumble.

Because all of these tantalizing delights were shared by our home economists and other on-the-go cooks, you know that each tempting treat can easily fit into an active lifestyle. So why not fix one tonight? Your family is sure to love it!

LUSCIOUS LAYERS. Caramel Chocolate Cake (p. 224).

Caramel Butter-Pecan Bars

1 can (21 ounces) apple pie filling
1 tablespoon brown sugar
1 tablespoon lemon juice
1/2 teaspoon ground cinnamon
4 brown sugar-cinnamon toaster pastries, crumbled
1 tablespoon butter, melted
Vanilla ice cream

In a large bowl, combine the pie filling, brown sugar, lemon juice and cinnamon. Transfer to a greased 8-in. square baking dish. Combine toaster pastries and butter; sprinkle over apple mixture. Bake at 350° for 20-25 minutes or until bubbly. Serve warm with ice cream. **Yield:** 6 servings.

Berry Cute Santas

(Pictured below)

Prep/Total Time: 30 min.

We make these edible elves every Christmas. They go together in a twinkling, and children have a ball assembling them while you finish making dinner. It's fun to put a Santa at each place setting on the table. —Crystal Duncan Fayetteville, Arkansas

1 loaf (10-3/4 ounces) frozen pound cake, thawed
1 package (8 ounces) cream cheese, softened
1/2 cup confectioners' sugar
12 red-frilled toothpicks
12 large strawberries, cut in half widthwise
24 miniature semisweet chocolate chips
12 fudge-covered cream-filled chocolate sandwich cookies

Cut twelve 1-in. cubes from pound cake (save remaining cake for another use). For icing, in a small mixing bowl, beat cream cheese and confectioners' sugar on high speed until light and fluffy. Cut a small hole in the corner of a pastry or plastic bag; insert a #18 star tip. Fill bag with icing.

For each Santa, thread a frilled toothpick through a pointed strawberry half, then through a pound cake cube and a second strawberry half.

For eyes, place dabs of icing on the bottoms of two chocolate chips; press onto cake. Pipe icing to form beards and to add fur brims below strawberry hats. Place each Santa on a cookie; serve immediately. **Yield:** 1 dozen.

Berry Cute Santas

Caramel Butter-Pecan Bars

(Pictured above)

Prep: 10 min. **Bake:** 15 min. + cooling

These rich and nutty bars are to die for! The chocolate layer takes a little while to harden, so I fix them ahead of time. —Mary Jean Hlavac, McFarland, Wisconsin

2 cups all-purpose flour
1 cup packed brown sugar
3/4 cup cold butter
1-1/2 cups chopped pecans
1 jar (12 ounces) caramel ice cream topping, warmed
1 package (11-1/2 ounces) milk chocolate chips

In a bowl, combine flour and brown sugar; cut in butter until crumbly. Press into an ungreased 13-in. x 9-in. x 2-in. baking dish. Top with pecans. Drizzle caramel topping evenly over pecans.

Bake at 350° for 15-20 minutes or until caramel is bubbly. Place on a wire rack. Sprinkle with chocolate chips. Let stand for 5 minutes.

Carefully spread chips over caramel layer. Cool at room temperature for at least 6 hours or until chocolate is set. Cut into bars. **Yield:** 4 dozen.

Apple Crumble

Prep/Total Time: 30 min.

Convenient toaster pastries lend scrumptious flavor to this quick and easy crumble. It's been a lifesaver when my three young boys are begging for something sweet. —Michelle Kenney, Sabina, Ohio

Chewy Coconut Cookies

Prep: 20 min. **Bake:** 15 min. per batch

Last year, I wanted to invent my own recipe. So I sat down with my mom and came up with a cookie I knew I would really like. It's crisp on the outside, moist and chewy inside, and flavored with peanut butter. —Nick Robeson
Warren, Pennsylvania

  3/4 cup butter-flavored shortening
  1/2 cup peanut butter
    1 cup sugar
    1 cup packed brown sugar
    3 eggs
  1/2 cup mashed ripe banana
    1 teaspoon vanilla extract
  1/2 teaspoon almond extract
2-1/2 cups all-purpose flour
    1 teaspoon baking soda
    1 teaspoon salt
  1/2 teaspoon baking powder
    1 cup flaked coconut

In a large mixing bowl, cream the shortening, peanut butter and sugars. Add eggs, one at a time, beating well after each addition. Beat in the banana and extracts.

Combine the flour, baking soda, salt and baking powder; gradually add to creamed mixture. Stir in coconut.

Drop by heaping teaspoonfuls 2 in. apart onto lightly greased baking sheets. Bake at 350° for 12-14 minutes or until edges are lightly browned. Remove to wire racks. **Yield:** about 5-1/2 dozen.

Topped Cheesecake Squares

(Pictured at right)

Prep: 30 min. **Bake:** 30 min. + chilling

Our Test Kitchen staff dressed up the same cheesecake squares in three delightfully different ways. You might be hard-pressed to pick your favorite variety!

1-1/4 cups chocolate wafer crumbs
  1/4 cup butter, melted
    2 packages (8 ounces *each*) cream cheese, softened
  2/3 cup plus 2 tablespoons sugar, *divided*
    2 eggs, lightly beaten
1-1/2 teaspoons vanilla extract, *divided*
  1/4 teaspoon almond extract
    1 cup (8 ounces) sour cream
CHOCOLATE STRAWBERRIES:
    2 ounces dark chocolate candy bar
    3 fresh strawberries
    1 square (1 ounce) white baking chocolate
CARAMEL TOPPING:
    6 caramels
    1 tablespoon heavy whipping cream
Whipped cream
    1 tablespoon sliced almonds, toasted
BERRY TOPPING:
  1/4 cup seedless raspberry jam
    6 fresh raspberries
    6 fresh blackberries
    6 fresh blueberries

In a bowl, combine crumbs and butter. Press firmly onto bottom of an 8-in. square baking dish. In a small mixing bowl, beat cream cheese and 2/3 cup sugar until smooth. Add eggs; beat on low speed just until combined. Stir in 1/2 teaspoon vanilla extract and almond extract. Pour over the crust. Bake at 325° for 45-55 minutes or until set.

Cool for 5 minutes. Meanwhile, in a small bowl, combine the sour cream and the remaining sugar and vanilla. Spread over filling; bake 5 minutes longer. Cool on a wire rack for 1 hour. Refrigerate for at least 5 hours or overnight.

In a small microwave-safe bowl, melt candy bar at 50% power; stir until smooth. Dip bottoms of strawberries in chocolate and place on a waxed paper-lined baking sheet to set. Microwave white chocolate, uncovered, at 50% power until melted; stir until smooth. Drizzle over strawberries. Refrigerate until serving.

Just before serving, cut cheesecake into nine squares. Place chocolate strawberries on three squares.

For caramel topping, in a small microwave-safe bowl, combine caramels and cream. Microwave, uncovered, on high for 45 seconds, stirring once. Spoon over three cheesecake squares. Top with a dollop of whipped cream. Sprinkle with almonds.

For berry topping, in a small microwave-safe bowl, combine jam and berries. Microwave, uncovered, on high for 45 seconds, stirring once. Spoon over remaining squares. **Yield:** 9 servings.

Editor's Note: This recipe was tested in a 1,100-watt microwave.

Topped Cheesecake Squares

Cookie Angels

crushed Life Savers. Use decorating gels to add faces. **Yield:** 1-1/2 dozen.

Cappuccino Cheesecake Pie

Prep: 20 min. + standing **Bake:** 40 min. + chilling

With a rich mocha filling and cute chocolate garnish, this yummy pie is delightful on Valentine's Day or any time at all. —*Elisa Pellegriti, Florida, New York*

    2 packages (8 ounces *each*) cream cheese,
      softened
1/2 cup sugar
    1 envelope mocha cappuccino mix (1/4 cup)
    2 eggs, lightly beaten
1/4 cup milk
    1 extra-servings-size graham cracker crust
      (9 ounces)
GARNISH:
1/4 cup semisweet chocolate chips
1/2 teaspoon shortening

In a large mixing bowl, beat the cream cheese, sugar and cappuccino mix until smooth. Add eggs and milk; beat just until combined. Pour into the crust. Bake at 325° for 40-45 minutes or until the center is almost set. Cool on a wire rack for 1 hour. Refrigerate for 3 hours or overnight.

In a small microwave-safe bowl, melt chocolate chips and shortening; stir until smooth. Spread into a 4-in. square on a sheet of waxed paper. Let stand at room temperature until firm, about 1 hour.

Using a small heart-shaped cookie cutter, cut out eight hearts from the hardened chocolate. Top each serving of cheesecake pie with a chocolate heart. Refrigerate leftovers. **Yield:** 8 servings.

Cookie Angels

(Pictured above)

Prep: 35 min. **Bake:** 10 min. per batch + cooling

For busy hostesses who prefer the convenience of make-ahead holiday treats, our Test Kitchen created an angel to carol best wishes at each place setting on the table.

  2/3 cup butter-flavored shortening
  1/4 cup sugar
    1 egg
1-1/2 cups all-purpose flour
  1/2 teaspoon baking powder
  1/2 teaspoon salt
   36 miniature pretzels
    1 can (16 ounces) vanilla frosting, *divided*
  1/4 cup confectioners' sugar
Brown paste food coloring
   18 yellow Life Savers
   10 green Life Savers, crushed
Decorating gels

In a small mixing bowl, cream shortening and sugar; beat in egg. Combine the flour, baking powder and salt; stir into creamed mixture. Set aside 1/2 cup of dough; divide remaining dough into three portions.

On a lightly floured surface, roll out each portion into a 6-in. circle; cut each into six wedges to form bodies. Transfer to ungreased baking sheets. For angel heads, roll teaspoonfuls of reserved dough into 18 balls; lightly press onto pointed end of each wedge. Press a pretzel into each side for wings.

Bake at 350° for 10-12 minutes or until lightly browned. Remove to wire racks to cool completely.

For hair, beat 1/4 cup vanilla frosting and confectioners' sugar until smooth; tint with food coloring. Press dough through a garlic press. Trim strands as desired; place on heads. For halos, attach yellow Life Savers.

Frost gowns with remaining frosting; sprinkle with

Apple and Pear Topping

Prep/Total Time: 15 min.

Dress up a dish of vanilla ice cream or a slice of pound cake with these saucy seasoned apple and pear slices. The warm, comforting topping takes only minutes but has wonderful apple pie flavor. —*Cora Garcia Pomona, California*

✓ Uses less fat, sugar or salt. Includes Nutrition Facts and Diabetic Exchanges.

    3 large apples, peeled and sliced
    1 medium pear, peeled and sliced
1/2 cup packed brown sugar
    4 tablespoons water, *divided*
    1 teaspoon ground cinnamon
1/8 teaspoon ground nutmeg
1/8 teaspoon ground cloves
    1 tablespoon all-purpose flour
    1 teaspoon vanilla extract
Vanilla ice cream

In a large skillet, combine the apples, pear, brown sugar, 2 tablespoons water, cinnamon, nutmeg and cloves. Cook and stir over medium heat for 4-7 minutes or until the apple and pear slices are tender.

In a small bowl, combine flour and remaining water until smooth; stir into skillet. Bring to a boil; cook and stir for 1 minute or until thickened. Remove from the heat; stir in vanilla. Serve over ice cream. Refrigerate leftovers. **Yield:** 3 cups.

Nutrition Facts: 1/2 cup (calculated with 1/2 cup reduced-fat ice cream) equals 197 calories, 2 g fat (1 g saturated fat), 6 mg cholesterol, 45 mg sodium, 45 g carbohydrate, 2 g fiber, 2 g protein. **Diabetic Exchanges:** 2 fruit, 1 starch.

Oatmeal Kiss Cookies

(Pictured below)

Prep: 35 min. **Bake:** 10 min. per batch

This is always a nice change of pace from the usual peanut butter cookie. Kids like to help unwrap the kisses.
—Anna Mary Knier, Mt. Joy, Pennsylvania

    1/2 cup butter, softened
    1/2 cup shortening
      1 cup sugar
      1 cup packed brown sugar
      2 eggs
      2 cups all-purpose flour
      1 teaspoon baking soda
      1 teaspoon salt
  2-1/4 cups quick-cooking oats
      1 cup chopped nuts
     72 milk chocolate kisses

In a mixing bowl, cream the butter, shortening and sugars. Add eggs, one at a time, beating well after each addition. Combine the flour, baking soda and salt; gradually add to the creamed mixture. Stir in the oats and

Cookie Fruit Baskets

nuts. Roll into 1-in. balls. Place 2 in. apart on ungreased baking sheets.

Bake at 375° for 10-12 minutes or until lightly browned. Immediately press a chocolate kiss in the center of each cookie. Remove to wire racks. **Yield:** 6 dozen.

Cookie Fruit Baskets

(Pictured above)

Prep: 15 min. **Bake:** 10 min. per batch + cooling

When visiting a friend, I helped organize her recipe collection into scrapbooks. When I found this recipe, I asked to copy it. I took the elegant dessert to my bridge club luncheon and heard many oohs and aahs.
—Theresa Myslicki
North Fort Myers, Florida

    1/4 cup butter
    1/4 cup packed brown sugar
    1/4 cup light corn syrup
  3-1/2 tablespoons all-purpose flour
    1/2 cup ground pecans
    1/2 teaspoon vanilla extract
Vanilla ice cream and fresh raspberries and
  blueberries

In a small saucepan, melt butter over low heat. Stir in brown sugar and corn syrup; cook and stir until mixture comes to a boil. Remove from the heat. Stir in flour. Fold in pecans and vanilla. Drop by tablespoonfuls 3 in. apart onto parchment paper-lined baking sheets.

Bake at 325° for 8-10 minutes or until golden brown. Cool for 30-60 seconds; peel cookies off paper. Immediately drape cookies over inverted 6-oz. custard cups; cool completely.

Scoop ice cream into baskets; top with raspberries and blueberries. **Yield:** 12 servings.

Oatmeal Kiss Cookies

Coconut Ice Cream Torte

Coconut Ice Cream Torte

(Pictured above)

Prep: 15 min. + freezing

Guests will ooh and aah when you bring out this fabulous ice cream torte ringed with snack-size Mounds bars. But this is one showstopper our Test Kitchen staff created with busy hostesses in mind. It's super-easy, feeds a crowd and can be made days ahead for convenience.

      18 macaroons, crushed
    1/4 cup butter, melted
    3/4 cup hot fudge ice cream topping
      26 snack-size Mounds *or* Almond Joy candy bars
       1 quart vanilla ice cream, softened
       1 quart strawberry ice cream, softened
    1/4 cup sliced almonds, toasted

In a small bowl, combine cookie crumbs and butter. Press onto the bottom of a greased 10-in. springform pan. Freeze for 15 minutes.

In a microwave-safe bowl, heat hot fudge topping on high for 15-20 seconds or until pourable; spread over crust. Arrange candy bars around the edge of pan. Freeze for 15 minutes. Spread vanilla ice cream over fudge topping; freeze for 30 minutes.

Spread strawberry ice cream over vanilla layer; sprinkle with almonds. Cover and freeze until firm. May be frozen for up to 2 months. Remove from the freezer 10 minutes before serving. Remove sides of pan. **Yield:** 13 servings.

Editor's Note: If Almond Joy candy bars are used, arrange bars with almond side facing inward toward the center of the pan.

Nesting Chicks

(Pictured below)

Prep/Total Time: 30 min.

Want a fun treat for a spring bake sale or Easter gathering? Our home economists hatched these cute cereal nests topped with jelly beans and marshmallow chicks.

       1 package (10-1/2 ounces) miniature marshmallows
       2 tablespoons butter
       1 teaspoon water
       4 drops green food coloring
    1-1/2 cups flaked coconut
       6 cups Corn Pops
     1/2 cup jelly beans
      16 Peeps

Nesting Chicks

In a large saucepan, combine marshmallows and butter. Cook and stir over low heat until melted and smooth. Meanwhile, in a small resealable plastic bag, combine water and food coloring. Add coconut; seal bag and shake to tint. Set aside.

Place the cereal in a large bowl; add marshmallow mixture and stir until combined. Press into greased muffin cups. Remove nests from cups; top with tinted coconut, jelly beans and Peeps. **Yield:** 16 servings.

Pumpkin Cream Trifle

Prep: 30 min. **Bake:** 45 min. + cooling

I created this crowd-pleasing dessert for my sister's wedding shower a week before Thanksgiving, when I had pumpkin on the brain. It relies on convenience foods for speed, but the taste says "I slaved." I'm always asked for the recipe.
—*Gayle Holdman, Highland, Utah*

       1 package (18-1/4 ounces) spice cake mix
       1 package (3.4 ounces) instant vanilla pudding mix
       1 cup canned pumpkin
     1/2 cup water
     1/2 cup vegetable oil
       3 eggs
       1 teaspoon ground cinnamon
     1/2 teaspoon ground ginger
       2 cups cold milk
       2 packages (3.4 ounces *each*) instant cheesecake pudding mix
       2 cups whipped topping

1 cup chopped pecans, toasted
3/4 cup English toffee bits *or* almond brickle chips

In a large mixing bowl, combine the first eight ingredients. Transfer to a greased 13-in. x 9-in. x 2-in. baking pan. Bake at 350° for 45-50 minutes or until a toothpick inserted near the center comes out clean. Cool on a wire rack.

In a large bowl, whisk the milk and pudding mixes for 2 minutes. Let stand for 2 minutes or until soft-set. Fold in the whipped topping.

Cut cake into 1-in. cubes. In a 3-qt. glass serving bowl or trifle bowl, layer a third of the cake cubes, pudding mixture, pecans and toffee bits. Repeat layers twice. Refrigerate until serving. **Yield:** 15-20 servings.

Nectarine Plum Cobbler

Prep: 30 min. **Bake:** 30 min.

For this cobbler, I reworked the dough portion of the original recipe and used buttermilk instead. My family just loves it. —Darlene Jackson, The Pas, Manitoba

1-1/4 cups sugar, *divided*
   2 tablespoons cornstarch
  3/4 cup unsweetened apple juice
   5 cups sliced peeled fresh plums
   5 cups sliced peeled nectarines *or* peaches
2-1/2 cups all-purpose flour
   3 teaspoons baking powder
  1/2 teaspoon baking soda
  1/2 teaspoon salt
  1/2 cup cold butter
1-1/2 cups buttermilk
Vanilla ice cream, optional

In a large saucepan, combine 3/4 cup sugar and cornstarch. Gradually stir in apple juice until smooth. Stir in plums and nectarines. Cook and stir until mixture comes to a boil; cook 1-2 minutes longer or until thickened and bubbly. Reduce heat; simmer, uncovered, for 5 minutes.

Remove from the heat; cool for 10 minutes. Pour into a greased 13-in. x 9-in. x 2-in. baking dish.

In a large bowl, combine the flour, baking powder, baking soda, salt and remaining sugar. Cut in butter until crumbly. Make a well in the center; stir in buttermilk just until a soft dough forms. Drop by tablespoonfuls over fruit mixture. Bake at 375° for 30-35 minutes or until golden brown. Serve warm with ice cream if desired. **Yield:** 10-12 servings.

Almond Coconut Bars

(Pictured above right)

Prep: 15 min. **Bake:** 20 min. + chilling

These goodies are perfect to take to a picnic or potluck supper. I think they taste like Almond Joy candy bars.
—Dolores Skrout, Summerhill, Pennsylvania

1-1/2 cups graham cracker crumbs
  1/2 cup butter, melted
   1 can (14 ounces) sweetened condensed milk

Almond Coconut Bars

   1 package (7 ounces) flaked coconut
   2 cups (12 ounces) semisweet chocolate chips
  1/2 cup peanut butter
  24 whole almonds

In a small bowl, combine the graham cracker crumbs and butter. Press into an ungreased 13-in. x 9-in. x 2-in. baking pan. Combine milk and coconut; carefully spread over crust. Bake at 350° for 18-20 minutes or until lightly browned.

In a microwave-safe bowl, combine the chocolate chips and peanut butter. Microwave on high for 1 minute; stir. Microwave 30-60 seconds longer or until chips are melted; stir until smooth. Spread over warm bars. Garnish with almonds. Refrigerate for 1 hour before cutting. **Yield:** 2 dozen.

Parchment Possibilities

LINING a baking pan with parchment paper when baking a cake ensures that the cake won't stick to the pan. To try this technique the next time you're in the kitchen, follow this simple method:

First, cut the parchment paper to fit the bottom of the cake pan. Grease the pan lightly before placing the paper in the pan.

Next, spoon your cake batter over the paper in the pan. If any batter happens to run underneath the paper, the baked cake will still release easily from the greased pan.

Immediately after the cake is inverted onto a cooling rack, carefully peel off the parchment paper.

Raspberry Coconut Truffles
Cocoa Mint Truffles
Peanut Butter Truffles

Raspberry Coconut Truffles

(Pictured above)

Prep: 30 min. + freezing

Toasted coconut lends an attractive look and sweet nutty taste to these rich bites from our Test Kitchen staff. They're sure to be the star of any holiday get-together.

> 1 cup raspberry cream-filled dark chocolate pieces
> 3/4 cup whipped topping
> 3 tablespoons seedless raspberry preserves
> 1/8 teaspoon rum extract
> 1/2 cup flaked coconut, toasted

In a small saucepan, melt chocolate pieces over low heat. Transfer to a small mixing bowl and cool to lukewarm, about 7 minutes. Beat in whipped topping, preserves and extract. Place in the freezer for 15 minutes or until firm enough to form into balls.

Shape into 1-in. balls; roll in coconut. Store in an airtight container in the refrigerator. **Yield:** 1-1/2 dozen.

Editor's Note: This recipe was tested with Hershey's Premier Dark Chocolate Baking Pieces filled with Raspberry Creme.

Cocoa Mint Truffles

(Pictured above)

Prep: 30 min. + freezing

These lovely truffles are decadent but oh-so-simple to do. Our home economists gave them a rich mint flavor inside and a powdered cocoa coating outside.

> 3/4 cup semisweet chocolate chips
> 6 mint Andes candies
> 3/4 cup whipped topping

> 2 tablespoons baking cocoa
> 1/8 teaspoon instant coffee granules

In a small saucepan, melt chocolate chips and candies over low heat. Transfer to a small mixing bowl and cool to lukewarm, about 7 minutes. Beat in whipped topping. Place in the freezer for 15 minutes or until firm enough to form into balls.

In a small bowl, combine cocoa and coffee granules. Shape chocolate mixture into 1-in. balls; roll in cocoa mixture. Store in an airtight container in the refrigerator. **Yield:** 16 servings.

Peanut Butter Truffles

(Pictured at left)

Prep: 30 min. + freezing

The smooth, yummy filling in these Test Kitchen treats will make them a hit with peanut butter lovers of all ages. Sprinkling them with chopped peanuts provides the pretty finishing touch.

> 1 cup peanut butter and milk chocolate chips
> 3/4 cup whipped topping
> 1 cup milk chocolate chips
> 1 tablespoon shortening
> 1/4 cup chopped salted peanuts

In a small saucepan, melt peanut butter and chocolate chips over low heat. Transfer to a small mixing bowl and cool to lukewarm, about 7 minutes. Beat in whipped topping. Place in the freezer for 15 minutes or until firm enough to form into balls.

Shape into 1-in. balls. In a small microwave-safe bowl, melt milk chocolate chips and shortening; stir until smooth. Dip balls in chocolate and place on a waxed paper-lined baking sheet. Sprinkle with peanuts. Refrigerate until firm. Store in an airtight container in the refrigerator. **Yield:** 16 servings.

Editor's Note: This recipe was tested with peanut butter and milk chocolate chips that come together in one bag (not the swirled chips). If your store does not carry them, buy peanut butter chips and milk chocolate chips individually, using 1/2 cup of each.

Sweet Potato Pie

Prep: 25 min. **Bake:** 45 min. + cooling

Pie crust mix, canned sweet potatoes and sweetened condensed milk hurry along this comforting, classic dessert. The simple but special deep-dish pie gives a down-home finish to meals and is perfect garnished with whipped topping and nuts.
—Paul Azzone, Shoreham, New York

> 1-2/3 cups pie crust mix
> 1/4 cup chopped pecans
> 3 to 4 tablespoons cold water
> 3 eggs
> 2 cans (15 ounces *each*) sweet potatoes, drained
> 1 can (14 ounces) sweetened condensed milk

1-1/2 to 2 teaspoons pumpkin pie spice
    1 teaspoon vanilla extract
  1/2 teaspoon salt
Whipped topping and additional chopped pecans,
    toasted, optional

In a small bowl, combine pie crust mix and pecans. Gradually add water, tossing with a fork until dough forms a ball. Roll out to fit a 9-in. deep-dish pie plate. Transfer pastry to pie plate. Flute edges; set aside.

In a food processor or blender, combine the eggs, sweet potatoes, milk, pumpkin pie spice, vanilla and salt; blend until smooth. Pour into pastry.

Bake at 425° for 15 minutes. Reduce heat to 350°; bake 30-35 minutes longer or until a knife inserted near the center comes out clean. Cool on a wire rack. Garnish with whipped topping and toasted pecans if desired. **Yield:** 8 servings.

Raspberry Coconut Cake

Prep: 20 min. **Bake:** 25 min. + cooling

This seemed like a festive dessert to fix for the holidays, so I decided to try it out on my co-workers. They loved it!
—Joanie Ward, Brownsburg, Indiana

  1 **package (18-1/4 ounces) white cake mix**
  3 **cups flaked coconut,** *divided*
  6 **squares (1 ounce** *each***) white baking**
    chocolate
1/4 **cup heavy whipping cream**
3/4 **cup seedless raspberry jam**
  1 **cup butter, softened**
  1 **cup confectioners' sugar**

Prepare cake batter according to package directions; fold in 2/3 cup coconut. Pour into two greased 9-in. round baking pans. Bake at 350° for 25-30 minutes or until a toothpick inserted near the center comes out clean. Cool for 10 minutes before removing from pans to wire racks to cool completely.

In a microwave-safe bowl, combine white chocolate and cream. Microwave, uncovered, on high for 1 minute or until chocolate is almost melted; stir until smooth. Cool to room temperature. In a small bowl, combine jam and 1 cup coconut. Spread over one cake layer; top with second layer.

In a small mixing bowl, cream butter and confectioners' sugar until light and fluffy; gradually beat in white chocolate mixture. Spread over top and sides of cake. Toast remaining coconut; sprinkle over cake. **Yield:** 12 servings.

Editor's Note: This recipe was tested in a 1,100-watt microwave.

Thankful Turkey Table Favors

(Pictured above right)

Prep/Total Time: 25 min.

I have fond memories of my daughters putting together these cute gobblers to welcome relatives to our table.
—Theresa Bjorklund, Nicollet, Minnesota

Thankful Turkey Table Favors

1-1/2 **cups plus 1 tablespoon chocolate frosting,**
    divided
  24 **fudge-striped cookies**
  72 **pieces candy corn**
  24 **milk chocolate kisses**
  24 **red-hot candies**

Spread 1-1/2 cups chocolate frosting on the bottoms of the fudge-striped cookies. For the tail feathers, insert three pieces of candy corn in a fan shape into frosting on each cookie. Place a chocolate kiss on each cookie for the body. For the wattles, attach a red-hot to the side of each chocolate kiss with a dab of the remaining frosting. **Yield:** 2 dozen.

Lemon Oat Bars

Prep: 10 min. **Bake:** 35 min. + cooling

A sweet oat mixture does double duty as crust and topping for these refreshing lemon bars. One of my college roommates gave me this recipe many years ago, and I've been making it for my family for years. It seems there's always time to whip up a pan of these tangy treats, since they require just 10 minutes of prep work.
—Margaret Scoresby, Mosinee, Wisconsin

1-1/2 **cups all-purpose flour**
    1 **cup old-fashioned oats**
    1 **cup packed brown sugar**
  1/2 **teaspoon salt**
  1/4 **teaspoon ground cinnamon**
  2/3 **cup cold butter**
    1 **can (14 ounces) sweetened condensed milk**
  1/2 **cup lemon juice**
1-1/2 **teaspoons grated lemon peel**

For the crust and topping, in a large bowl, combine the flour, oats, brown sugar, salt and cinnamon; cut in the butter until crumbly. Press 3 cups into a greased 9-in. square baking pan; set the remaining oat mixture aside. Bake at 350° for 10 minutes.

In a small bowl, combine the sweetened condensed milk, lemon juice and lemon peel. Pour over the crust. Sprinkle with the reserved oat mixture. Bake for 25-30 minutes or until the edges are brown. Cool on a wire rack. **Yield:** 9 servings.

Caramel Peanut Fantasy

(Pictured below)

Prep: 30 min. + chilling

Packed with peanuts and gooey with caramel, this do-ahead treat from our Test Kitchen is one sweet dream of a dessert to serve company. With an easy cookie crust, it goes together in a snap...and will disappear just as fast!

  2 cups vanilla wafer crumbs
1/3 cup butter, melted
 20 caramels
 15 miniature Snickers candy bars
1/2 cup caramel ice cream topping
1/2 cup heavy whipping cream, *divided*
  2 cups salted peanuts, chopped
3/4 cup semisweet chocolate chips

In a small bowl, combine wafer crumbs and butter. Press onto the bottom of a greased 9-in. springform pan. Place on a baking sheet. Bake at 350° for 8-10 minutes. Cool on a wire rack.

In a heavy saucepan, combine caramels, candy bars, caramel topping and 1/4 cup cream; cook and stir over low heat until smooth and blended. Remove from the heat; stir in peanuts. Spread over crust. Cover and refrigerate for 1 hour.

In a saucepan or microwave, melt chocolate chips and remaining cream. Spread over caramel layer. Cover and refrigerate for 1 hour or until serving. Refrigerate leftovers. **Yield:** 12 servings.

Chocolate Almond Fondue

Prep/Total Time: 20 min.

Since fondue has become popular again, I've had fun searching out recipes that are fast and especially delicious. This luscious variation for fruit and cubed cake is a favorite. —Angela Hutton, Kapolei, Hawaii

3/4 cup heavy whipping cream
  2 milk chocolate candy bars (5 ounces *each*), chopped
  1 jar (7 ounces) marshmallow creme

Caramel Peanut Fantasy

  3 squares (1 ounce *each*) white baking chocolate, chopped
1/4 cup chopped almonds, toasted
  3 tablespoons amaretto *or* 1/2 teaspoon almond extract
Assorted fresh fruit and pound cake cubes

In a heavy saucepan, heat cream over low heat until warmed. Add the candy bars, marshmallow creme and white chocolate; stir until melted. Stir in almonds and amaretto or almond extract. Transfer to a fondue pot and keep warm. Serve with fruit and cake cubes. **Yield:** about 4 cups.

Patriotic Banana Split

Prep/Total Time: 15 min.

For a lip-smacking salute to summer, our home economists created a cross between a banana split and a fruit salad. A scoop of melon, berries and a creamy topping produce a red, white and blue finale to any meal. And best of all, you won't have to worry about your dessert melting!

☑ Uses less fat, sugar or salt. Includes Nutrition Facts and Diabetic Exchanges.

  4 ounces cream cheese
1/2 cup marshmallow creme
  1 tablespoon lemon juice
  1 teaspoon grated lemon peel
1/2 medium seedless watermelon
  6 large ripe bananas, quartered
1/3 cup fresh blueberries
1/3 cup granola cereal without raisins

In a mixing bowl, beat the cream cheese, marshmallow creme, lemon juice and peel until smooth; set aside. Using an ice cream scoop, scoop six balls from watermelon (save remaining melon for another use). In shallow dessert bowls, arrange four banana quarters; top with a watermelon ball. Spoon cream cheese topping over melon. Sprinkle with blueberries and cereal. Serve immediately. **Yield:** 6 servings.

Nutrition Facts: One serving (prepared with reduced-fat cream cheese and reduced-fat cereal) equals 254 calories, 6 g fat (3 g saturated fat), 14 mg cholesterol, 91 mg sodium, 50 g carbohydrate, 4 g fiber, 4 g protein. **Diabetic Exchanges:** 3 fruit, 1 fat, 1/2 starch.

Apple Snack Cake

(Pictured above right)

Prep: 15 min. **Bake:** 35 min. + cooling

A package of quick bread mix is the secret behind this speedy spice cake. Moist and flecked with bits of apple, it's excellent for dessert or as a breakfast treat with a cup of coffee. —Marilyn Terman, Columbus, Ohio

1/2 cup butter, softened
1/2 cup packed brown sugar
  3 eggs
  1 teaspoon vanilla extract
  1 package (15.4 ounces) nut quick bread mix

Cranberry Shortbread Bars
Apple Snack Cake

1 teaspoon ground cinnamon
2 medium tart apples, peeled and finely
   chopped
1/2 cup raisins
ICING:
  3/4 cup confectioners' sugar
  1/4 teaspoon ground cinnamon
  2 tablespoons butter, melted
  1/4 teaspoon vanilla extract
  3 to 5 tablespoons milk

In a large mixing bowl, cream butter and brown sugar. Beat in eggs and vanilla. Add quick bread mix and cinnamon; beat until combined. Fold in apples and raisins.

Transfer to a greased 13-in. x 9-in. x 2-in. baking dish. Bake at 350° for 35-40 minutes or until a toothpick inserted near the center comes out clean. Cool on a wire rack.

In a small bowl, combine the confectioners' sugar, cinnamon, butter, vanilla and enough milk to achieve desired consistency. Drizzle over cake. **Yield:** 12-15 servings.

Cranberry Shortbread Bars

(Pictured above)

Prep: 20 min. **Bake:** 30 min. + cooling

Our Test Kitchen staff combined walnuts, cranberries, coconut and white chocolate to come up with these colorful and tasty bars. With a glass of milk, they make the perfect snack after an afternoon of outdoor activities.

1 cup butter, softened
1/2 cup confectioners' sugar
1 egg
1-1/2 cups all-purpose flour
1/2 cup flaked coconut
1/8 teaspoon salt
1/2 cup sugar
1/2 cup packed brown sugar
3 tablespoons cornstarch
1 package (12 ounces) fresh *or* frozen
   cranberries
1 cup unsweetened apple juice
1 cup chopped walnuts
2 squares (1 ounce *each*) white baking
   chocolate, melted

In a large mixing bowl, cream butter and confectioners' sugar. Beat in egg. Combine the flour, coconut and salt; gradually add to creamed mixture. Set aside 1 cup for topping. Spread remaining mixture into a greased 13-in. x 9-in. x 2-in. baking dish. Bake at 425° for 10 minutes.

Meanwhile, in a small saucepan, combine the sugars and cornstarch. Stir in cranberries and apple juice. Bring to a boil. Reduce heat; cook and stir for 5 minutes or until thickened. Remove from the heat; stir in walnuts.

Spread over crust. Sprinkle with reserved crumb mixture. Bake for 20-25 minutes or until golden brown and bubbly. Cool on a wire rack. Drizzle with white chocolate. Cut into bars. **Yield:** 2 dozen.

Caramel Chocolate Cake

with 3/4 cup pudding mixture. Top with remaining cake layer; spread remaining pudding mixture over top and sides of cake. Spoon pecan mixture around top edge. Store in the refrigerator. **Yield:** 10-12 servings.

Fudge-Filled Brownie Bars

Prep: 10 min. **Bake:** 30 min. + cooling

I always have the ingredients to put together these soft, chewy bars. They've been a hit at many gatherings.
—Nola Burski, Lakeville, Minnesota

```
1-1/2 cups all-purpose flour
  3/4 cup packed brown sugar
  3/4 cup butter, softened
    1 egg yolk
  3/4 teaspoon vanilla extract
FILLING:
    1 package fudge brownie mix (13-inch x
      9-inch pan size)
    1 egg
  1/3 cup water
  1/3 cup vegetable oil
TOPPING:
    1 package (11-1/2 ounces) milk chocolate
      chips, melted
  3/4 cup chopped walnuts, toasted
```

In a large bowl, combine the first five ingredients. Press onto the bottom of a greased 15-in. x 10-in. x 1-in. baking pan. Bake at 350° for 15-18 minutes or until golden brown.

Meanwhile, in a large bowl, combine the filling ingredients. Spread over hot crust. Bake for 15 minutes or until set. Cool on a wire rack for 30 minutes.

Spread melted chocolate over filling; sprinkle with walnuts. Cool completely. Cut into bars. **Yield:** 4 dozen.

Berry-Topped Stars

Prep: 45 min. **Bake:** 10 min. + cooling

Our home economists needed just six items, including store-bought cookie dough, to fix these sweet treats. They're sure to be the star at your Fourth of July celebrations, but they're great for any summer occasion.

```
    1 tube (18 ounces) refrigerated sugar cookie
      dough, softened
  1/4 cup all-purpose flour
    1 package (8 ounces) cream cheese, softened
  1/3 cup confectioners' sugar
   24 small fresh strawberries, thinly sliced
    1 cup fresh blueberries
```

In a small mixing bowl, combine cookie dough and flour until combined. Roll on a lightly floured surface to 1/4-in. thickness. Cut with a floured 3-in. star-shaped cookie cutter.

Place 1 in. apart on ungreased baking sheets. Bake at 350° for 8-10 minutes or until edges are golden brown. Cool for 1 minute before removing to wire racks to cool completely.

For frosting, in a small mixing bowl, beat cream

Caramel Chocolate Cake

(Pictured above and on page 212)

Prep: 25 min. + cooling **Bake:** 30 min. + cooling

Here, German chocolate cake from a boxed mix gets a special treatment when spread with an easy butterscotch frosting and accented with a caramel-nut topping. I love to make this cake for guests and to take to potlucks.
—Gloria Guadron, Washington, Indiana

```
  3/4 cup packed brown sugar
    6 tablespoons butter, cubed
    2 tablespoons plus 1 cup cold milk, divided
  1/2 cup chopped pecans
    1 package (18-1/4 ounces) German chocolate
      cake mix
    1 package (3.4 ounces) instant butterscotch
      pudding mix
    2 cups whipped topping
```

In a small saucepan, combine the brown sugar, butter and 2 tablespoons milk. Cook and stir over low heat until sugar is dissolved. Increase heat to medium. Do not stir. Cook for 3-6 minutes or until bubbles form in center of mixture and color is amber brown. Remove from the heat; stir in pecans. Cool to room temperature, stirring occasionally.

Meanwhile, prepare and bake cake according to package directions for two 9-in. round baking pans. Cool for 10 minutes before removing from pans to wire racks to cool completely.

In a bowl, whisk pudding mix and remaining milk until smooth. Fold in whipped topping. Cover and refrigerate until thickened, about 20 minutes.

Place one cake layer on a serving platter; spread

cheese and confectioners' sugar until smooth. Set aside 1-2 tablespoons. Spread remaining frosting over cookies. Place strawberry slices on each cookie. Place four to five blueberries in each cookie center, using reserved frosting to attach them. Store in the refrigerator. **Yield:** 2 dozen.

Cinnamon Apple Tart

(Pictured below)

Prep: 15 min. **Bake:** 20 min. + cooling

I got the idea for this delicious dessert from a lovely woman who's a fabulous cook. It's so simple to make—and cleanup is just as easy! The tart is wonderful after dinner, but you could also serve it for your next brunch alongside eggs and bacon.
—Stacie Blemings, Califon, New Jersey

    1 large apple, peeled and chopped
    1 teaspoon lemon juice
    1 sheet refrigerated pie pastry
    2 tablespoons apple jelly
    2 tablespoons sugar
  1/4 cup cinnamon baking chips
  1/3 cup sliced almonds
    1 teaspoon milk
ICING:
    1 cup confectioners' sugar
  1/4 teaspoon almond extract
    1 to 2 tablespoons milk

In a small bowl, toss apple with lemon juice; set aside. On a lightly floured surface, roll pastry into a 14-in. cir-

Salty Peanut Squares

cle. Transfer to a parchment paper-lined baking sheet. Spread jelly to within 2 in. of edges. Sprinkle with apple mixture, sugar, baking chips and almonds. Fold up edges of pastry over filling, leaving center uncovered. Brush folded pastry with milk.

Bake at 400° for 20-25 minutes or until golden brown. Use parchment paper to slide tart onto a wire rack to cool. In a small bowl, combine confectioners' sugar, extract and enough milk to achieve desired consistency. Drizzle over tart. **Yield:** 6 servings.

Salty Peanut Squares

(Pictured above)

Prep: 15 min. + cooling

If your family likes corn chips, they'll love the sweet and salty blend in these fast-to-fix bars. They make great take-along treats for picnics or tailgate parties. Plus, they're so easy that kids may want to make their own batch.
—Wanda Borgen, Minot, North Dakota

    1 package (10 ounces) corn chips, slightly crushed, *divided*
    1 cup unsalted peanuts, *divided*
    1 cup light corn syrup
    1 cup sugar
    1 cup peanut butter
  1/2 cup milk chocolate chips, melted

Place half of the corn chips and peanuts in a greased 13-in. x 9-in. x 2-in. pan; set aside. In a saucepan, bring the corn syrup and sugar to a boil. Stir in the peanut butter until blended. Drizzle half over the corn chip mixture in the pan.

Add remaining corn chips and peanuts to remaining syrup; stir until combined. Spoon over mixture in the pan; press down lightly. Drizzle with melted chocolate. Cool before cutting. **Yield:** 2 dozen.

Cinnamon Apple Tart

Chapter 15

IMAGINE coming home from work and having an assembled chicken potpie ready to pop in the oven...or marinated flank steak all set to broil...or home-made soup that requires just a few minutes on the stove.

All of those convenient recipes and many more are right here in this handy chapter! By putting together these dishes a day, weeks or even months in advance, they'll be available to you and your family when you need them the most.

Just do a bit of planning and prepare any of these fantastic foods—from main courses to desserts—when you have a few minutes to spare in the kitchen. Then savor the sensational, home-cooked results later on!

READY-MADE MEAL. Convenient Chicken Potpies (p. 235).

Marinated Beef Stir-Fry

(Pictured below)

Prep: 15 min. + marinating **Cook:** 15 min.

I love this quick-and-easy stir-fry because everything but the cooking can be done in advance. It's great with sourdough bread and a fresh tomato and cucumber salad. Or, serve it with warm flour tortillas and your favorite hot sauce.
—*Marian Johnson, Brawley, California*

✓ Uses less fat, sugar or salt. Includes Nutrition Facts and Diabetic Exchanges.

1/2 cup dry red wine *or* beef broth
6 tablespoons olive oil, *divided*
1 teaspoon chili powder
1 teaspoon minced garlic
1/2 teaspoon ground cumin
1/4 teaspoon salt
1/4 teaspoon ground ginger
1/4 teaspoon pepper
1/2 pound beef flank steak, cut into 1/8-inch strips
1 medium onion, cut into thin strips
1/2 cup julienned zucchini
1/2 cup julienned carrot
1/2 cup *each* julienned green and sweet red peppers

In a large resealable plastic bag, combine the wine or broth, 4 tablespoons oil, chili powder, garlic, cumin, salt, ginger and pepper; add beef. Seal bag and turn to coat; refrigerate for at least 12 hours.

In a large skillet or wok, stir-fry the onion, zucchini, carrot and peppers in remaining oil for 4-5 minutes or until crisp-tender. Remove and keep warm.

Drain and discard marinade. Stir-fry beef for 5-6 minutes or until no longer pink; drain. Return vegetables to the pan; stir-fry for 2-3 minutes or until heated through. **Yield:** 3 servings.

Nutrition Facts: 1 cup (prepared with reduced-sodium broth) equals 268 calories, 20 g fat (4 g saturated fat), 32 mg cholesterol, 112 mg sodium, 10 g carbohydrate, 3 g fiber, 14 g protein. **Diabetic Exchanges:** 2 lean meat, 2 vegetable, 2 fat.

Marinated Beef Stir-Fry

Colorful Chicken Casserole

Prep: 25 min. **Bake:** 30 min.

Chicken and pasta combine with a variety of vegetables for this all-in-one entree. I make one for dinner and keep the other in the freezer for unexpected company.
—*Bernice Morris, Marshfield, Missouri*

✓ Uses less fat, sugar or salt. Includes Nutrition Facts and Diabetic Exchanges.

1 cup chopped celery
1 cup chopped green pepper
3/4 cup chopped onion
2 tablespoons butter
1 cup chicken broth
1 cup frozen corn
1 cup frozen peas
1 teaspoon salt, optional
1/4 teaspoon pepper
3 cups cubed cooked chicken
1 package (7 ounces) ready-cut spaghetti *or* elbow macaroni, cooked and drained
1 jar (4-1/2 ounces) sliced mushrooms, drained
1 cup (4 ounces) shredded cheddar cheese

In a large skillet, saute celery, green pepper and onion in butter until tender. Add broth, corn, peas, salt if desired and pepper; heat through.

Stir in chicken and spaghetti. Divide between two 8-in. square baking dishes coated with nonstick cooking spray. Top with mushrooms and cheese.

Cover and freeze one casserole for up to 3 months. Cover and bake the second casserole at 350° for 20 minutes. Uncover and bake 10 minutes longer or until heated through.

To use frozen casserole: Bake at 350° for 35 minutes. Uncover and bake 15 minutes longer or until heated through. **Yield:** 2 casseroles (4 servings each).

Nutrition Facts: 1 cup (prepared with reduced-fat butter, reduced-sodium broth and reduced-fat cheese; calculated without salt) equals 295 calories, 9 g fat (4 g saturated fat), 62 mg cholesterol, 334 mg sodium, 30 g carbohydrate, 3 g fiber, 25 g protein. **Diabetic Exchanges:** 3 lean meat, 1-1/2 starch, 1 vegetable.

Beans and Franks Bake

Prep: 20 min. **Bake:** 40 min.

I've prepared this casserole several times, and it's always a hit. The kid-pleasing combo has a sweet flavor from the baked beans and corn bread topping. Plus, cooking everything together cuts down on pans to wash.
—*Roxanne VanGelder, Rochester, New Hampshire*

2 packages (8-1/2 ounces *each*) corn bread/muffin mix
1 can (28 ounces) baked beans
4 hot dogs, halved and sliced
1/2 pound sliced bacon, cooked and crumbled
1 cup ketchup
1/2 cup packed brown sugar
1/2 cup chopped onion
2 cups (8 ounces) shredded part-skim mozzarella cheese

Prepare the corn bread batter according to the package directions; set aside. In a large bowl, combine the baked beans, hot dogs, bacon, ketchup, brown sugar and onion. Transfer to two greased 8-in. square baking dishes. Sprinkle with the mozzarella cheese; top with the corn bread batter.

Cover and freeze one casserole for up to 3 months. Bake the second casserole, uncovered, at 350° for 40-45 minutes or until a toothpick inserted near the center comes out clean.

To use frozen casserole: Remove from the freezer 30 minutes before baking. Cover and bake at 350° for 40 minutes. Uncover; bake 15-20 minutes longer or until heated through. **Yield:** 2 casseroles (4 servings each).

Veggie Calzones

Sausage Egg Casserole

Prep: 20 min. + chilling **Bake:** 40 min.

When we have friends stay overnight, I usually serve this tasty breakfast bake, and everyone enjoys it.
        —Ramona Bubb, Reedsville, Pennsylvania

1 pound bulk Italian sausage
1/3 cup chopped onion
1 celery rib, chopped
6 eggs
2 cups milk
1/2 to 1 teaspoon salt
1 teaspoon spicy brown mustard
4 cups seasoned stuffing cubes, toasted
1 cup (4 ounces) shredded cheddar cheese

In a large skillet, cook the sausage, onion and celery over medium heat until meat is no longer pink and vegetables are tender; drain and set aside. In a large mixing bowl, beat the eggs, milk, salt and mustard. Stir in the stuffing cubes, cheese and sausage mixture. Transfer to a greased 11-in. x 7-in. x 2-in. baking dish. Cover and refrigerate overnight.

Remove from the refrigerator 30 minutes before baking. Cover and bake at 350° for 30 minutes. Uncover; bake 10 minutes longer or until a knife inserted near the center comes out clean. **Yield:** 6 servings.

Veggie Calzones

(Pictured above right)

Prep: 25 min. + rising **Bake:** 35 min.

Bread dough makes it a breeze to assemble these savory turnovers. They freeze well, and once frozen, they can be heated in half an hour.   *—Lee Ann Arey, Gray, Maine*

1/2 pound fresh mushrooms, chopped
1 medium onion, chopped
1 medium green pepper, chopped
2 tablespoons vegetable oil
3 plum tomatoes, seeded and chopped
1 can (6 ounces) tomato paste
1 cup (4 ounces) shredded Monterey Jack cheese
1 cup (4 ounces) shredded part-skim mozzarella cheese
1/2 cup grated Parmesan cheese
2 loaves (1 pound *each*) frozen bread dough, thawed
1 egg
1 tablespoon water

In a large skillet, saute the mushrooms, onion and green pepper in oil until tender. Add tomatoes; cook and stir for 3 minutes. Stir in tomato paste; set aside. Combine cheeses and set aside.

On a lightly floured surface, divide dough into eight pieces. Roll each piece into a 7-in. circle. Spoon a scant 1/2 cup of vegetable mixture and 1/4 cup of cheese mixture over one half of each circle. Brush edges of dough with water; fold dough over filling and press edges with a fork to seal. Place calzones 3 in. apart on greased baking sheets. Cover and let rise in a warm place for 20 minutes.

Beat egg and water; brush over calzones. Bake at 375° for 15 minutes. Cool desired number of calzones; freeze for up to 3 months. Bake the remaining calzones 18-22 minutes longer or until golden brown. Serve immediately.

To use frozen calzones: Place 2 in. apart on a greased baking sheet. Bake at 350° for 30-35 minutes or until golden brown. **Yield:** 8 servings.

Hamburger Noodle Bake

Spaghetti Casserole

Prep: 15 min. **Bake:** 25 min.

These comforting casseroles take advantage of convenience products like canned spaghetti and jarred mushrooms. Kids love how cheesy they are, you'll love how you can serve one today and freeze the other for a busy night.
—*Pat Richter, Lake Placid, Florida*

1-1/2 pounds ground beef
    1 cup chopped green pepper
1/2 cup chopped onion
    1 teaspoon minced garlic
    1 teaspoon salt
1/2 teaspoon pepper
    3 cans (14-3/4 ounces *each*) prepared spaghetti
    1 jar (6 ounces) sliced mushrooms, drained
    1 can (2-1/4 ounces) sliced ripe olives, drained
    2 cups (8 ounces) shredded cheddar cheese
    1 cup grated Parmesan cheese

In a large skillet, cook the beef, green pepper, onion, garlic, salt and pepper over medium-high heat for 10-12 minutes or until meat is no longer pink; drain. Stir in the spaghetti, mushrooms and olives.

Transfer to two greased 8-in. square baking dishes. Sprinkle with cheddar and Parmesan cheeses. Cover and freeze one casserole for up to 3 months. Bake remaining casserole, uncovered, at 350° for 25-30 minutes or until bubbly and golden brown.

To use frozen casserole: Remove from the freezer 30 minutes before baking (do not thaw). Cover and bake at 350° for 1 hour. Uncover; bake 15-20 minutes longer or until heated through. **Yield:** 2 casseroles (4 servings each).

Hamburger Noodle Bake

(Pictured above)

Prep: 20 min. **Bake:** 35 min.

This is an old family favorite I frequently made when my boys were growing up. There were never any leftovers!
—*Patricia Teller, Lewiston, Idaho*

    5 cups uncooked egg noodles
    2 pounds ground beef
    1 cup chopped onion
1/2 cup chopped green pepper
    2 cans (10-3/4 ounces *each*) condensed tomato soup, undiluted
    2 cups (8 ounces) shredded cheddar cheese
1-1/2 cups water
1/2 cup chili sauce
1-1/2 cups soft bread crumbs
    3 tablespoons butter, melted

Cook noodles according to package directions until almost tender; drain. In a large skillet, cook the beef, onion and green pepper over medium-high heat for 10-12 minutes or until meat is no longer pink; drain. Stir in the noodles, soup, cheese, water and chili sauce. Transfer to two greased 8-in. square baking dishes.

Toss the bread crumbs and butter; sprinkle over casseroles. Bake one casserole, uncovered, at 350° for 35-40 minutes or until bubbly and golden. Cover and freeze remaining casserole for up to 3 months.

To use frozen casserole: Remove from the freezer 30 minutes before baking (do not thaw). Cover and bake at 350° for 60 minutes. Uncover; bake 10-15 minutes longer or until heated through. **Yield:** 2 casseroles (4 servings each).

Stuffed Sourdough Sandwiches

Prep/Total Time: 30 min.

These delicious stuffed sandwiches are a snap to put together. Some can be baked as soon as they're assembled, while the rest can be frozen for a quick dinner later.
—*Shannon Hansen, Oxnard, California*

1-1/2 pounds ground beef
1/2 cup chopped onion
    1 can (15 ounces) tomato sauce
    1 can (4 ounces) chopped green chilies
1/2 cup chopped fresh mushrooms
    2 tablespoons chili powder
    2 tablespoons sliced ripe olives
1/4 teaspoon garlic salt
    1 cup (4 ounces) shredded cheddar cheese
    8 sourdough rolls

In a large skillet, cook beef and onion over medium heat until meat is no longer pink; drain. Add the tomato sauce, chilies, mushrooms, chili powder, olives and garlic salt. Bring to a boil. Reduce heat; simmer, uncovered, for 10 minutes or until heated through. Add cheese; cook and stir until melted.

Cut 1/4 in. off the top of each roll; set aside. Carefully hollow out the bottom of each roll, leaving a 1/4-in. shell (discard the removed bread or save for another use). Fill each roll with about 1/2 cup meat mixture. Replace bread tops.

Individually wrap four sandwiches tightly in foil; freeze for up to 3 months. Place remaining sandwiches on a baking sheet. Bake at 350° for 10-15 minutes or until heated through.

To use frozen sandwiches: Thaw in the refrigerator overnight. Place foil-wrapped sandwiches on baking sheets. Bake at 350° for 20-25 minutes or until heated through. **Yield:** 8 servings.

Chocolate Chip Pancakes

(Pictured below)

Prep: 15 min. **Cook:** 5 min. per batch

Mornings will get off to a great start with these yummy double-chocolate pancakes from our Test Kitchen home economists. Whip up a batch on the weekend, and you'll have a quick-and-easy breakfast the whole family will rave about for days to come.

    2 cups biscuit/baking mix
    2 tablespoons instant chocolate drink mix
    2 teaspoons baking powder
    1 egg
    1 cup milk
    1/2 cup sour cream
    1/4 cup miniature semisweet chocolate chips
Maple syrup and butter, optional

In a large bowl, combine the biscuit mix, drink mix and baking powder. Combine the egg, milk and sour cream; stir into dry ingredients just until moistened. Fold in chocolate chips.

Pour batter by 1/4 cupfuls onto a greased hot grid-

Fruit Slush

dle. Turn when bubbles form on top; cook until second side is golden brown. Serve some with maple syrup and butter if desired.

Cool remaining pancakes. Arrange in a single layer on baking sheets. Freeze overnight or until frozen. Transfer to a resealable plastic bag. May be frozen for up to 2 months.

To use frozen pancakes: Place on a lightly greased baking sheet. Bake at 400° for 4-6 minutes or until heated through. Serve with syrup and butter if desired. **Yield:** 11 pancakes.

Chocolate Chip Pancakes

Fruit Slush

(Pictured above)

Prep: 20 min. + freezing

I'm a busy mom, and when I'm expecting company, I do all that I can beforehand. This sweet citrus slush is easy to make ahead of time and tastes so refreshing.
—Martha Miller, Fredericksburg, Ohio

    3 cups water
    1 cup sugar
    1 can (20 ounces) crushed pineapple,
      undrained
    1 can (6 ounces) frozen orange juice
      concentrate, thawed
    1 medium ripe peach, chopped *or* 2/3 cup
      sliced frozen peaches, thawed and chopped

In a large saucepan over medium heat, bring water and sugar to a boil. Remove from the heat. Cool for 10 minutes.

Add the pineapple, orange juice concentrate and peach; stir well. Pour into a freezer container; freeze for at least 12 hours or overnight. May be frozen for up to 3 months. Remove from freezer 1 hour before serving. **Yield:** 6-8 servings.

Double Meat Loaf

(Pictured below)

Prep: 15 min. **Bake:** 55 min.

This tender meat loaf featuring both beef and pork is a delicious entree for weekdays or when company comes.
—*Shirley Snyder, Payson, Arizona*

    1 egg
    1 cup beef broth
 1/2 cup quick-cooking oats
    1 tablespoon dried minced onion
    2 teaspoons dried parsley flakes
    1 teaspoon salt
 1/2 teaspoon pepper
1-1/2 pounds lean ground beef
    1 pound bulk pork sausage
    1 can (8 ounces) tomato sauce

In a large bowl, combine the first seven ingredients. Crumble beef and sausage over mixture; mix well. Pat into two greased 8-in. x 4-in. x 2-in. loaf pans. Top with tomato sauce.

Cover and freeze one meat loaf for up to 3 months. Bake the remaining loaf, uncovered, at 350° for 55-60 minutes or until a meat thermometer reads 160°.

To use frozen meat loaf: Thaw in the refrigerator overnight. Bake as directed. **Yield:** 2 loaves (4-6 servings each).

Mashed Potato Cups

(Pictured below)

Prep: 15 min. **Bake:** 15 min.

The original recipe for this side dish was doubled to make an extra batch to freeze. It's a nice alternative to the standard potatoes or rice. If you like, sprinkle the potatoes with Parmesan cheese and basil or oregano.
—*Jill Hancock, Nashua, New Hampshire*

Double Meat Loaf
Mashed Potato Cups

    6 cups hot mashed potatoes (without added milk and butter)
 1/2 cup milk
 1/4 cup butter
    1 teaspoon salt
 1/8 teaspoon pepper
1-1/3 cups plus 2 tablespoons shredded Colby-Monterey Jack cheese, *divided*
    2 tablespoons minced fresh parsley

In a large mixing bowl, combine the mashed potatoes, milk, butter, salt and pepper. Stir in 1-1/3 cups cheese. Grease two 6-portion muffin pans; divide potato mixture between pans. Sprinkle with remaining cheese; top with parsley.

Cover and freeze one pan for up to 3 months. Bake the remaining pan, uncovered, at 350° for 15-20 minutes or until heated through and cheese is melted.

To use frozen potato cups: Thaw in the refrigerator. Bake as directed. **Yield:** 2 pans (6 servings each).

Enchiladas El Paso

Prep: 20 min. **Bake:** 30 min.

These lightly seasoned enchiladas have a mild taste that's sure to please even the pickiest palates. I found this recipe years ago, and it quickly became a favorite. It's even better when prepared one day and served the next.
—*Loraine Meyer, Bend, Oregon*

✓ Uses less fat, sugar or salt. Includes Nutrition Facts and Diabetic Exchanges.

    1 pound ground beef
 1/2 cup chopped onion
    1 can (14-1/2 ounces) diced tomatoes, drained
    1 can (6 ounces) tomato paste
 1/2 cup water
    3 teaspoons chili powder
1-1/4 teaspoons salt
 1/4 teaspoon pepper
 10 flour tortillas (8 inches), warmed
    2 cups (8 ounces) shredded cheddar cheese

In a large skillet, cook the ground beef and onion over medium heat until the meat is no longer pink; drain. Stir in the tomatoes, tomato paste, water, chili powder, salt and pepper.

Spoon about 1/3 cup meat sauce down the center of each tortilla. Top each with 2 tablespoons cheese. Roll up and place seam side down in an ungreased 13-in. x 9-in. x 2-in. baking dish. Top with the remaining meat sauce and cheese.

Cover and refrigerate overnight. Or cover and bake at 375° for 25 minutes. Uncover; bake 3-5 minutes longer or until heated through.

To use refrigerated enchiladas: Remove from the refrigerator 30 minutes before baking. Bake as directed. **Yield:** 10 servings.

Nutrition Facts: 1 enchilada (prepared with lean ground beef, no-salt-added tomato paste, fat-free tortillas and reduced-fat cheese) equals 283 calories, 8 g fat (5 g saturated fat), 38 mg cholesterol, 799 mg sodium,

34 g carbohydrate, 3 g fiber, 19 g protein. **Diabetic Exchanges:** 2 lean meat, 2 vegetable, 1-1/2 starch.

Turkey Meatball Soup

(Pictured at right)

Prep/Total Time: 30 min.

Our home economists combined ready-made turkey meatballs with fresh and frozen vegetables to come up with this nicely seasoned soup. Small families can enjoy half of it now and freeze the rest for later, but bigger families may want to double the recipe so there will be plenty left over for a second meal.

  3 cups cut fresh green beans
  2 cups fresh baby carrots
  2 cups chicken broth
  1 teaspoon dried oregano
  1 teaspoon dried basil
  1 teaspoon minced garlic
  2 cans (14-1/2 ounces *each*) Italian stewed
    tomatoes
  1 package (12 ounces) refrigerated fully
    cooked Italian turkey meatballs
  2 cups frozen corn

In a large saucepan or soup kettle, combine the first six ingredients. Bring to a boil. Reduce heat; cover and simmer for 10 minutes.

Add the tomatoes, meatballs and corn. Cover and cook over medium-low heat for 10 minutes or until meatballs are heated through. Serve immediately or transfer to freezer containers. May be frozen for up to 3 months.

To use frozen soup: Thaw in the refrigerator overnight. Transfer to a soup kettle. Cover and cook over medium heat until heated through. **Yield:** 6 servings.

Cajun-Style Brunch Bake

Prep: 10 min. + chilling **Bake:** 45 min. + standing

It's so convenient to fix this hearty breakfast casserole the night before, refrigerate it until morning and just pop it in the oven. The recipe was given to me by a co-worker and has turned out to be a family hit! I adapted it to our tastes, adding onion, potato and Cajun seasoning.
—Kathie Deusser, Church Point, Louisiana

  6 eggs, lightly beaten
  2 cups milk
  1 pound sliced bacon, cooked and crumbled
  6 slices bread, cubed
  1 medium potato, peeled and diced
  1 cup (4 ounces) shredded cheddar cheese
1/2 cup finely chopped onion
  1 to 1-1/2 teaspoons Cajun seasoning
  1 teaspoon salt

In a large bowl, combine all ingredients; mix well. Transfer to a greased 11-in. x 7-in. x 2-in. baking dish. Cover and refrigerate overnight.

Remove from the refrigerator 30 minutes before baking. Bake, uncovered, at 350° for 45-50 minutes or until

Turkey Meatball Soup

a knife inserted near the center comes out clean. Let stand for 10 minutes before cutting. **Yield:** 6 servings.

Mocha Punch

Prep: 15 min. + chilling

Looking for an easy alternative to the usual fruit-based punches? Try this smooth, creamy drink from our home economists. It's almost like sipping a chocolate shake.

  6 cups water
1/2 cup sugar
1/2 cup instant chocolate drink mix
1/4 cup instant coffee granules
1/2 gallon vanilla ice cream
1/2 gallon chocolate ice cream
  1 cup heavy whipping cream, whipped
Chocolate curls, optional

In a large saucepan, bring water to a boil. Remove from the heat. Add sugar, drink mix and coffee; stir until dissolved. Transfer to a large bowl. Cover and refrigerate for 4 hours or overnight.

About 30 minutes before serving, pour mixture into a large punch bowl. Add scoops of ice cream; stir until partially melted. Garnish with dollops of whipped cream and chocolate curls if desired. **Yield:** 20-25 servings (about 5 quarts).

Make-Ahead Appetizers

My family doesn't eat a lot of bread, so I often have extra slices. To avoid waste, I started cutting them with small cookie cutters. I place the cut shapes on waxed paper and put them in a freezer bag.

When guests drop in, I can grab the frozen bread shapes, top them with butter, garlic and cheese, then broil them for a few minutes for hot snacks in a snap.
—Christina Creech, Oakdale, California

Flank Steak with Orange Sauce

Flank Steak with Orange Sauce

(Pictured above)

Prep: 15 min. + marinating **Broil:** 15 min.

Tender flank steak is treated to an orange marinade with a peppery kick in this full-flavored recipe from our Test Kitchen home economists.

- 3/4 cup orange juice
- 1/4 cup honey
- 1 tablespoon lime juice
- 1 tablespoon soy sauce
- 1/2 teaspoon coarsely ground pepper
- 1 tablespoon vegetable oil
- 1 teaspoon minced fresh gingerroot
- 1 beef flank steak (1 pound)

In a small bowl, combine the first six ingredients. Cover and refrigerate 1/2 cup for serving. Add oil and ginger to the remaining orange sauce; pour into a large resealable bag. Add the flank steak; seal bag and turn to coat. Refrigerate for at least 1 hour or overnight.

Drain and discard marinade. Place steak on a broiler pan. Broil 4 in. from the heat for 7-8 minutes on each side or until meat reaches desired doneness (for medium-rare, a meat thermometer should read 145°; medium, 160°; well-done, 170°).

Meanwhile, in a small saucepan, warm reserved orange sauce until heated through. Thinly slice steak across the grain; serve with sauce. **Yield:** 4 servings.

South-of-the-Border Quiche

(Pictured at right)

Prep: 20 min. **Bake:** 35 min. + standing

Every holiday, we have brunch, and that's when I serve these quiches. The recipe is my family's most requested.
—*Paula Marchesi, Lenhartsville, Pennsylvania*

- 2 unbaked pastry shells (9 inches)
- 2 teaspoons chili powder
- 1 teaspoon ground cumin
- 1-1/2 cups (6 ounces) shredded cheddar cheese
- 1-1/2 cups (6 ounces) shredded Monterey Jack cheese
- 1 cup (4 ounces) shredded sharp cheddar cheese
- 8 eggs
- 2 cups half-and-half cream
- 2 cans (4 ounces *each*) chopped green chilies
- 2 cans (2-1/4 ounces *each*) sliced ripe olives, drained
- 1/4 cup chopped green onions
- 2 tablespoons minced fresh cilantro
- 1/2 teaspoon salt
- 1/2 teaspoon pepper
- Salsa and sour cream, optional

Line unpricked pastry shells with a double thickness of heavy-duty foil. Bake at 400° for 5 minutes. Remove foil; bake 5 minutes longer.

Sprinkle chili powder and cumin over pastry shells; sprinkle with cheeses. In a bowl, whisk the eggs, cream, chilies, olives, onions, cilantro, salt and pepper. Pour evenly over cheese.

Cover and freeze one quiche up to 3 months. Cover edges of remaining quiche loosely with foil; place on a baking sheet. Bake at 400° for 35-40 minutes or until a knife inserted near the center comes out clean. Let stand for 10 minutes before cutting. Serve with salsa and sour cream if desired.

To use frozen quiche: Remove from the freezer 30 minutes before baking (do not thaw). Cover edges of crust loosely with foil; place on a baking sheet. Bake at 400° for 55-60 minutes or until a knife inserted near the center comes out clean. Let stand for 10 minutes before cutting. **Yield:** 2 quiches (6 servings each).

South-of-the-Border Quiche

Chicken Macaroni Casserole

Prep: 20 min. + chilling **Bake:** 50 min.

I received this recipe from a ladies' circle years ago and have shared it many times. The overnight casserole is a real crowd-pleaser, and I know, because my family is a crowd! —Martha St. Clair, Salem, Illinois

- 3 cups cubed cooked chicken
- 2 cups uncooked elbow macaroni
- 2 cups (8 ounces) shredded cheddar cheese
- 2 cans (14-1/2 ounces *each*) chicken broth
- 2 cans (10-3/4 ounces *each*) condensed cream of mushroom soup, undiluted
- 1 can (8 ounces) sliced water chestnuts, drained
- 1 jar (6 ounces) sliced mushrooms
- 1/3 cup finely chopped onion
- 1/4 cup chopped green pepper
- 1 jar (2 ounces) sliced pimientos, drained
- 1 tablespoon soy sauce
- 4 cups herb-flavored stuffing mix
- 1/2 cup butter, melted

In a large bowl, combine the first 11 ingredients. Transfer to a greased 13-in. x 9-in. x 2-in. baking dish. Refrigerate overnight.

Remove from the refrigerator 30 minutes before baking. Toss the stuffing mix with butter; sprinkle over casserole. Bake, uncovered, at 350° for 50-55 minutes or until heated through. **Yield:** 10 servings.

Chocolate Cranberry Cheesecake

Prep: 15 min. **Bake:** 30 min. + chilling

To me, the ultimate dessert any time of the year is cheesecake. I worked at a specialty bakery that offered 23 different cheesecakes, but not a chocolate cranberry variety like this one. —Darlene Brenden, Salem, Oregon

- 1-1/3 cups chocolate wafer crumbs
- 1/4 cup sugar
- 1/4 cup butter, melted
- FILLING:
- 2 packages (8 ounces *each*) cream cheese, softened
- 1/2 cup sugar
- 3/4 cup sour cream
- 1 tablespoon cornstarch
- 2 eggs, lightly beaten
- 1 cup whole-berry cranberry sauce
- 1/4 cup hot fudge ice cream topping, warmed

In a small bowl, combine wafer crumbs, sugar and butter. Press onto the bottom and 1 in. up the sides of a greased 9-in. springform pan; set aside.

In a large mixing bowl, beat cream cheese and sugar until smooth. Add sour cream and cornstarch; beat well. Add eggs; beat on low speed just until combined. Fold in cranberry sauce. Pour into crust. Place pan on a baking sheet.

Bake at 325° for 30-35 minutes or until center is almost set. Cool on a wire rack for 10 minutes. Carefully

Convenient Chicken Potpies

run a knife around edge of pan to loosen; cool 1 hour longer. Refrigerate overnight. Remove sides of pan. Pipe dessert plates with fudge topping; top with cheesecake. Refrigerate leftovers. **Yield:** 10-12 servings.

Convenient Chicken Potpies

(Pictured above and on page 226)

Prep/Total Time: 30 min.

I created this recipe because my husband and I love chicken potpie, but most recipes take too long and are too high in fat and calories. I can throw this together at a moment's notice. —Sharon Bailey, Brick, New Jersey

✓ Uses less fat, sugar or salt. Includes Nutrition Facts and Diabetic Exchanges.

- 4 cups cubed cooked chicken
- 4 cups frozen mixed vegetables, thawed
- 2 cans (18-1/2 ounces *each*) ready-to-serve cream of potato soup
- 1 package (15 ounces) refrigerated pie pastry

In a large bowl, combine the chicken, vegetables and soup. Divide between two 9-in. pie plates. Roll out pastry to fit top of pies. Cut slits in pastry. Place over filling; trim, seal and flute edges.

Bake one potpie at 400° for 25-30 minutes or until golden. Cover and freeze remaining potpie for up to 3 months.

To use frozen potpie: Remove from the freezer 30 minutes before baking (do not thaw). Cover edges of crust loosely with foil; place on a baking sheet. Bake at 425° for 30 minutes. Reduce heat to 350°; remove foil. Bake 60-65 minutes longer or until golden. **Yield:** 2 potpies (6 servings each).

Nutrition Facts: 1 serving (prepared with reduced-fat soup) equals 327 calories, 13 g fat (5 g saturated fat), 48 mg cholesterol, 364 mg sodium, 34 g carbohydrate, 4 g fiber, 18 g protein. **Diabetic Exchanges:** 2 starch, 2 lean meat, 1 vegetable, 1 fat.

Chapter 16

⊕ *Casseroles and Stovetop Suppers*

POPPING a quick casserole in the oven and stirring up speedy fare on the stovetop are two of the easiest ways to put dinner on the table pronto.

If you like to use these fast supper strategies, you're sure to appreciate the outstanding entrees here. Each delicious dish either is a snap to assemble before baking or comes together in a rush on the range.

Just pull out a baking pan to prepare family-pleasers such as Pizza Casserole and Ham 'n' Cheese Pasta. Or grab a skillet to serve favorites like Chicken with Garlic Sauce and Calypso Pork 'n' Garbanzos.

Whichever cooking method you choose, you'll soon have a busy-day dinner well in hand!

ALL-IN-ONE MEAL. Penne and Smoked Sausage (p. 240).

Rich 'n' Cheesy Macaroni

8 ounces process American cheese, cubed
1-1/3 cups small-curd cottage cheese
2/3 cup sour cream
2 cups (8 ounces) shredded sharp cheddar cheese
1-1/2 cups soft bread crumbs

Cook macaroni according to package directions; drain. Place in a greased 2-1/2-qt. baking dish. In a saucepan, melt 4 tablespoons butter. Stir in flour, salt and sugar until smooth. Gradually stir in milk. Bring to a boil; cook and stir for 2 minutes or until thickened.

Reduce heat; stir in American cheese until melted. Stir in cottage cheese and sour cream. Pour over macaroni. Sprinkle with cheddar cheese. Melt remaining butter and toss with bread crumbs; sprinkle over top. Bake, uncovered, at 350° for 30 minutes or until golden brown. **Yield:** 6-8 servings.

Alfredo Chicken 'n' Biscuits

(Pictured below)

Prep: 20 min. **Bake:** 20 min.

Chock-full of veggies and topped off with dill-seasoned biscuits, this delicious chicken casserole will warm you through and through. It's fun to assemble and has an excellent flavor. —Cheryl Miller, Fort Collins, Colorado

2 cups chopped fresh broccoli
1-1/2 cups sliced fresh carrots
1 cup chopped onion
2 tablespoons olive oil
2 cups cubed cooked chicken
1 carton (10 ounces) refrigerated Alfredo sauce
1 cup biscuit/baking mix
1/3 cup milk
1/4 teaspoon dill weed

Catchall Casseroles

IS YOUR FAMILY fond of comforting casseroles? If so, you've turned to the right place. Hot from the oven, these delicious baked dishes are guaranteed to please...and don't take long to assemble before you pop them in the oven.

While the casserole cooks, toss together a simple green salad and whip up an easy dessert. You'll have a complete supper that'll fill 'em up fast.

Rich 'n' Cheesy Macaroni

(Pictured above)

Prep: 30 min. **Bake:** 30 min.

With three different kinds of cheese, this rich bake puts a tasty twist on traditional macaroni and cheese.
—Erin Frakes, Rock Island, Illinois

2-1/2 cups uncooked elbow macaroni
6 tablespoons butter, *divided*
1/4 cup all-purpose flour
1 teaspoon salt
1 teaspoon sugar
2 cups milk

Alfredo Chicken 'n' Biscuits

In a large skillet, saute the broccoli, carrots and onion in oil until crisp-tender. Stir in the chicken and Alfredo sauce; heat through. Transfer to a lightly greased 8-in. square baking dish.

In a small bowl, combine the baking mix, milk and dill just until moistened. Drop by rounded tablespoonfuls onto chicken mixture. Bake, uncovered, at 400° for 18-22 minutes or until bubbly and biscuits are golden brown. **Yield:** 4 servings.

Ham 'n' Cheese Pasta

(Pictured above)

Prep: 15 min. **Bake:** 30 min.

My mother would prepare this yummy pasta dish whenever there was leftover ham. Horseradish gives it a nice tangy taste. I quickened the preparation by using process cheese instead of making a cheese sauce from scratch, and now my children love it, too. —Karen Kopp
Indianapolis, Indiana

  8 ounces uncooked medium pasta shells
  1 pound process cheese (Velveeta), cubed
1/2 cup milk
  2 tablespoons ketchup
  1 tablespoon prepared horseradish
  2 cups cubed fully cooked ham
  1 package (8 ounces) frozen peas, thawed

Cook the pasta shells according to the package directions. Meanwhile, in a microwave-safe bowl, combine the process cheese and milk. Cover and microwave on high for 2 minutes; stir. Heat 1-2 minutes longer or until smooth, stirring twice. Stir in the ketchup and horseradish until blended.

Drain pasta and place in a large bowl. Stir in the ham, peas and cheese sauce. Transfer to a greased 2-qt. baking dish. Cover and bake at 350° for 30-35 minutes or until bubbly. **Yield:** 4 servings.

Tuna Noodle Casserole

Prep: 15 min. **Bake:** 30 min.

For old-fashioned comfort food, I think this classic tuna casserole ranks in the top 10! It's quick and easy to fix yet makes a complete meal for two. —Kris Lehman
South Milwaukee, Wisconsin

   1 medium onion, chopped
   2 teaspoons butter
   1 tablespoon all-purpose flour
1/2 teaspoon salt
1/4 teaspoon pepper
   1 cup milk
   2 cups cooked wide egg noodles
   1 can (6 ounces) tuna, drained and flaked
2/3 cup frozen peas, thawed
1/4 cup crushed cornflakes

In a saucepan, saute onion in butter until tender. Stir in the flour, salt and pepper until blended. Gradually add milk. Bring to a boil; cook and stir for 2 minutes or until thickened. Stir in the noodles, tuna and peas.

Transfer to a greased 1-qt. baking dish. Sprinkle with cornflakes. Bake, uncovered, at 350° for 30-35 minutes or until bubbly around the edges. **Yield:** 2 servings.

Penne and Smoked Sausage

Penne and Smoked Sausage

(Pictured above and on page 236)

Prep: 15 min. **Bake:** 30 min.

This must-try casserole tastes so good when it's hot and bubbly from the oven. The cheddar french-fried onions add a cheesy, crunchy touch. —Margaret Wilson
Hemet, California

 2 cups uncooked penne *or* medium tube pasta
 1 pound smoked sausage *or* fully cooked kielbasa, cut into 1/4-inch slices
1-1/2 cups milk
 1 can (10-3/4 ounces) condensed cream of celery soup, undiluted
1-1/2 cups cheddar french-fried onions, *divided*
 1 cup (4 ounces) shredded part-skim mozzarella cheese, *divided*
 1 cup frozen peas

Cook pasta according to package directions. Meanwhile, in a large skillet, brown sausage over medium heat for 5 minutes; drain. In a large bowl, combine milk and soup. Stir in 1/2 cup onions, 1/2 cup cheese, peas and sausage. Drain pasta; stir into sausage mixture.

Transfer to a greased 13-in. x 9-in. x 2-in. baking dish. Cover and bake at 375° for 25-30 minutes or until bubbly. Sprinkle with remaining onions and cheese. Bake, uncovered, 3-5 minutes longer or until cheese is melted. **Yield:** 6 servings.

Creamy Seafood Casserole

Prep: 15 min. **Bake:** 25 min.

I think this is one of the very best recipes I received from my mother. It's not only easy and delicious, it's convenient because it can be made the night before. The next day, you just pop it in the oven. The recipe calls for a topping of crushed crackers, but you could also use potato chips. —Mary Brown, Whitman, Massachusetts

 1 pound flounder fillets, cut into 1-1/2-inch pieces
 1 pound uncooked medium shrimp, peeled and deveined
 1 can (10-3/4 ounces) condensed cream of shrimp soup, undiluted
1/4 cup milk
 1 cup crushed butter-flavored crackers (about 25 crackers)
1/4 cup grated Parmesan cheese
 1 teaspoon paprika
 2 tablespoons butter, melted

Arrange fish and shrimp in a greased 11-in. x 7-in. x 2-in. baking dish. Combine soup and milk; pour over seafood. Combine the cracker crumbs, Parmesan cheese, paprika and butter; sprinkle over top.

Bake, uncovered, at 350° for 25-30 minutes or until the fish flakes easily with a fork and shrimp turn pink. **Yield:** 6-8 servings.

Tater Beef Bake

(Pictured below)

Prep: 25 min. **Bake:** 35 min.

I combine two childhood classics—sloppy joes and Tater Tots—to create this home-style dinner that youngsters gobble up.   —Karla Wiederholt, Cuba City, Wisconsin

1-1/2 pounds ground beef
1-1/4 cups water
   2 envelopes sloppy joe sauce mix
   1 can (6 ounces) tomato paste
3-1/2 cups frozen cut green beans
   1 can (4 ounces) mushroom stems and pieces, drained
   6 cups frozen Tater Tots
   1 cup (4 ounces) shredded cheddar cheese

In a Dutch oven, cook beef over medium heat until no longer pink; drain. Stir in water and sauce mix. Bring to a boil. Reduce heat; simmer, uncovered, for 3-5 minutes or until thickened. Add tomato paste; stir until blended. Add green beans and mushrooms.

Transfer to a greased 13-in. x 9-in. x 2-in. baking dish. Top with Tater Tots. Bake, uncovered, at 350° for 30 minutes. Sprinkle with cheese; bake 5-10 minutes longer or until heated through and cheese is melted. **Yield:** 6-8 servings.

Crunchy Turkey Casserole

(Pictured above right)

Prep: 15 min. **Bake:** 40 min.

Chow mein noodles and nuts lend crunch to this creamy bake. Keep it handy when you have holiday leftovers.
—Joanne Shewchuk, St. Benedict, Saskatchewan

Crunchy Turkey Casserole

Tater Beef Bake

   2 cups cubed cooked turkey
   1 can (15 ounces) whole baby corn, drained and cut into 1/2-inch pieces
   1 can (10-3/4 ounces) condensed cream of mushroom soup, undiluted
   1 cup (4 ounces) shredded cheddar cheese
   1 cup chopped celery
   1 cup chow mein noodles, *divided*
1/2 cup sliced fresh mushrooms
1/2 cup slivered almonds, *divided*
1/2 cup chopped green pepper

In a large bowl, combine the turkey, corn and soup. Stir in the cheese, celery, 1/4 cup noodles, mushrooms, 1/4 cup almonds and green pepper. Pour into a greased 2-qt. baking dish.

Cover and bake at 350° for 30 minutes. Uncover; sprinkle with remaining noodles and almonds. Bake 10-15 minutes longer or until heated through. **Yield:** 6 servings.

Freezing Peppers

In my locale, produce is trucked in from elsewhere and is costly. So I buy green peppers and other varieties on sale, cut them into 1-inch pieces and quick-freeze them on cookie sheets for a few hours. Then I put them in bags and pop them in the freezer. Later, when I need them, the peppers are as good as the day I bought them.
—Diane Cunningham
Vanderhoof, British Columbia

Pizza Casserole

(Pictured below)

Prep: 25 min. **Bake:** 25 min. + standing

Looking for a satisfying, all-in-one dish the whole family will enjoy? You can rely on this flavorful pizza bake.
—Nancy Zimmerman, Cape May Court House, New Jersey

  3/4 cup chopped onion
    1 *each* medium sweet red and yellow pepper, diced
    1 tablespoon olive oil
    1 medium zucchini, halved lengthwise and sliced
    1 teaspoon minced garlic
    2 cans (14-1/2 ounces *each*) diced tomatoes, drained
  3/4 pound smoked sausage, sliced
    1 can (6 ounces) tomato paste
    1 teaspoon salt
    1 teaspoon Italian seasoning
  1/2 teaspoon pepper
  1/4 cup grated Parmesan cheese, *divided*
    2 cups (8 ounces) shredded part-skim mozzarella cheese
    1 tube (11 ounces) refrigerated breadsticks

In a large skillet, saute onion and peppers in oil for 2-3 minutes or until almost tender. Add zucchini and garlic; saute 4-6 minutes longer or until vegetables are tender. Stir in the tomatoes, sausage, tomato paste, salt, Italian seasoning, pepper and 2 tablespoons Parmesan cheese. Bring to a boil. Reduce heat; simmer, uncovered, for 8-10 minutes or until heated through.

Spoon half of the sausage mixture into a greased 13-in. x 9-in. x 2-in. baking dish. Sprinkle with mozzarella cheese; top with remaining sausage mixture. Separate breadsticks; arrange in a lattice pattern over the top. Sprinkle with remaining Parmesan cheese.

Bake, uncovered, at 375° for 25-30 minutes or until topping is golden brown and filling is bubbly. Let stand for 10 minutes before serving. **Yield:** 6-8 servings.

Cheese-Topped Beef Bake

Prep: 20 min. **Bake:** 25 min.

I found two easy recipes with some similar ingredients and decided to combine them. The result is this delicious casserole that gets raves every time.
—Debbie Schwab
De Pere, Wisconsin

    1 package (16 ounces) medium pasta shells
    1 pound ground beef
    1 jar (26 ounces) spaghetti sauce
    1 envelope taco seasoning
    1 carton (8 ounces) spreadable chive and onion cream cheese
    1 cup (8 ounces) sour cream
    1 cup (4 ounces) shredded cheddar cheese

Cook pasta according to package directions. Meanwhile, in a large skillet, cook beef over medium heat until no longer pink; drain. Stir in the spaghetti sauce and taco seasoning. In a small bowl, combine cream cheese and sour cream; set aside.

Drain the pasta; stir into beef mixture. Transfer to a greased 13-in. x 9-in. x 2-in. baking dish. Spread with cream cheese mixture; sprinkle with cheddar cheese. Bake, uncovered, at 350° for 25-30 minutes or until cheese is melted. **Yield:** 8-10 servings.

Hearty Chicken Casserole

Prep: 25 min. **Bake:** 10 min.

I discovered this recipe in a cookbook we received as a wedding gift and altered it to suit my family's tastes.
—Janet Applin, Gladstone, Michigan

2-1/2 cups frozen mixed vegetables
  1/2 cup chopped onion
  1/2 cup butter, *divided*
  1/3 cup all-purpose flour
  1/2 teaspoon dried sage leaves
  1/2 teaspoon pepper
  1/4 teaspoon salt
    2 cups chicken broth
  3/4 cup milk
    3 cups cubed cooked chicken
    1 can (14-1/2 ounces) sliced potatoes, drained and quartered
    2 cups seasoned stuffing cubes

Cook the mixed vegetables according to the package directions; drain. Meanwhile, in a large saucepan, saute the onion in 1/4 cup butter for 2-3 minutes or until tender. Stir in the flour, sage, pepper and salt until blended. Gradually add the chicken broth and milk. Bring to a boil; cook and stir until thickened. Stir in the chicken,

Pizza Casserole

potatoes and mixed vegetables; heat through.

Transfer to a greased 13-in. x 9-in. x 2-in. baking dish. Melt the remaining butter; toss with stuffing cubes. Sprinkle over chicken mixture. Bake, uncovered, at 450° for 10-12 minutes or until heated through. **Yield:** 6 servings.

Ham and Potato Bake

Prep: 20 min. **Bake:** 35 min.

This is comfort food at its easiest! I keep the ingredients on hand because my family loves this dish, and it's so simple to prepare. —Gianna Strauss, Seguin, Texas

    4 medium red potatoes, thinly sliced
  1/2 cup chopped onion
  1/2 cup chopped celery
    1 tablespoon butter
1-1/2 cups cubed fully cooked ham
    6 slices process American cheese, cut into
      1/2-inch strips
    1 can (10-3/4 ounces) condensed cream of
      chicken soup, undiluted

Place potatoes in a large saucepan and cover with water. Bring to a boil. Reduce heat; cover and simmer for 10 minutes or until tender. Drain. In a large skillet, saute onion and celery in butter until tender. Stir in potatoes.

In a greased 2-qt. baking dish, layer half of the potato mixture, ham and cheese. Top with remaining potato mixture and ham; spread with soup. Arrange remaining cheese strips in a lattice pattern over the top. Bake, uncovered, at 350° for 35-40 minutes or until heated through. **Yield:** 4 servings.

Baked Sole and Spinach

Prep: 25 min. **Bake:** 30 min.

A cheesy pasta layer is topped with fish, spinach and almonds to make this meal-in-one. It's a nice change of pace. —Anna Fuery, Taftville, Connecticut

    1 package (8 ounces) egg noodles
    3 tablespoons butter
    3 tablespoons all-purpose flour
    3 cups milk
1-1/2 cups (6 ounces) shredded cheddar cheese,
      divided
    1 tablespoon lemon juice
    1 teaspoon salt
    1 teaspoon ground mustard
    1 teaspoon Worcestershire sauce
  1/8 teaspoon ground nutmeg
  1/8 teaspoon pepper
    2 packages (10 ounces *each*) frozen chopped
      spinach, thawed and squeezed dry
1-1/2 pounds sole fillets
  1/4 cup slivered almonds, toasted

Cook noodles according to package directions. Meanwhile, in a large saucepan, melt butter. Stir in flour until smooth; gradually add milk. Bring to a boil; cook and stir for 2 minutes or until thickened.

Stir in 1 cup cheese, lemon juice, salt, mustard,

Ham and Swiss Casserole

Worcestershire sauce, nutmeg and pepper until cheese is melted. Set aside half of the cheese sauce. Drain noodles; add to the remaining sauce.

Transfer to a greased 13-in. x 9-in. x 2-in. baking dish. Top with the spinach, sole, reserved cheese sauce and remaining cheese; sprinkle with almonds. Bake, uncovered, at 375° for 30-35 minutes or until fish flakes easily with a fork. **Yield:** 6 servings.

Ham and Swiss Casserole

(Pictured above)

Prep: 15 min. **Bake:** 30 min.

Here's a delightfully rich and creamy dinner. My family can't get enough of the easy-to-fix sauce, and it's a great way to use up leftover ham from a holiday meal. —Julie Jackman, Bountiful, Utah

    8 ounces uncooked penne *or* medium tube
      pasta
    2 envelopes country gravy mix
    1 package (10 ounces) frozen chopped
      spinach, thawed and squeezed dry
    2 cups (8 ounces) shredded Swiss cheese
    2 cups cubed fully cooked ham
4-1/2 teaspoons ground mustard

Cook pasta according to package directions. Meanwhile, in a large saucepan, cook gravy mix according to package directions. Stir in the spinach, cheese, ham and mustard. Drain the pasta; stir into ham mixture.

Transfer to a greased 13-in. x 9-in. x 2-in. baking dish. Cover and bake at 350° for 20 minutes. Uncover; bake 10-15 minutes longer or until heated through. **Yield:** 8 servings.

Lemon Garlic Shrimp

Stovetop Suppers

IT'S EASY to pull dinner together quickly when all of the ingredients combine in a skillet or saucepan. Here, you'll find rangetop recipes that will come in handy again and again when time's tight.

Not only are these stovetop suppers fast to fix on hectic weeknights, they're proven family-pleasers. So go ahead—just pull out a skillet or saucepan, turn on a burner and start cooking!

Lemon Garlic Shrimp

(Pictured above)

Prep/Total Time: 30 min.

Shrimp, red pepper and a tasty lemon sauce dress up a boxed broccoli rice mix in this quick main course. I found the recipe years ago and have served it numerous times, always with success. —Lynn Corsaro, Florence, Colorado

✓ Uses less fat, sugar or salt. Includes Nutrition Facts and Diabetic Exchanges.

  1 package (6-1/2 ounces) broccoli au gratin rice and vermicelli mix
  1 pound uncooked medium shrimp, peeled and deveined

  1 medium sweet red pepper, julienned
  3 green onions, cut into 1/2-inch pieces
  1 teaspoon minced garlic
  1/2 teaspoon Italian seasoning
  1 tablespoon butter
  2 teaspoons cornstarch
  1/2 cup chicken broth
  1 tablespoon lemon juice
  1 teaspoon grated lemon peel, *divided*

Prepare rice mix according to package directions. Meanwhile, in a large skillet, saute the shrimp, red pepper, onions, garlic and Italian seasoning in butter until shrimp turn pink.

In a small bowl, combine the cornstarch, broth and lemon juice until smooth; stir into shrimp mixture. Bring to a boil; cook and stir for 1-2 minutes or until thickened. Stir 1/2 teaspoon lemon peel into prepared rice. Serve with shrimp mixture; sprinkle with remaining lemon peel. **Yield: 4 servings.**

Nutrition Facts: 1 serving (prepared with reduced-fat butter and reduced-sodium broth) equals 321 calories, 10 g fat (5 g saturated fat), 186 mg cholesterol, 907 mg sodium, 35 g carbohydrate, 2 g fiber, 24 g protein. **Diabetic Exchanges:** 3 lean meat, 2 starch, 1 vegetable.

Calypso Pork 'n' Garbanzos

Prep/Total Time: 30 min.

With this recipe, I can prepare both a zippy pork entree and a tasty vegetable side dish with little effort.
  —Ellen Burr, Los Angeles, California

  1 pound pork tenderloin, cut into 1-inch pieces
  1 tablespoon chili powder
  3 tablespoons olive oil, *divided*
  1 cup julienned sweet red pepper
  3/4 cup chopped onion
  1 can (15 ounces) garbanzo beans *or* chickpeas, rinsed and drained
  1 cup salsa
  1 teaspoon salt

Place the pork in a large bowl; sprinkle with chili powder. Drizzle with 1 tablespoon oil; toss to coat. In a large skillet, brown pork in remaining oil over medium heat for 5-6 minutes or until no longer pink. Remove and keep warm.

In the same skillet, saute red pepper and onion for 3-4 minutes or until crisp-tender. Stir in the beans, salsa, salt and pork; cook for 3-4 minutes or until heated through. **Yield: 4 servings.**

Meatball Stroganoff

Prep/Total Time: 25 min.

You'll need just four ingredients to fix this simple supper that makes the most of convenience products. This is a super-easy way to make a "comfort food" dinner for your family. To save time, defrost the meatballs in the microwave. —Sarita Powers, Waynesboro, Virginia

    1 jar (12 ounces) home-style beef gravy
1/2 cup sour cream
    1 package (12 ounces) frozen fully cooked
        meatballs, thawed
Hot cooked egg noodles

In a large saucepan, combine gravy and sour cream. Bring to a boil; stir in meatballs. Reduce heat; cook, uncovered, for 15-20 minutes or until heated through, stirring occasionally. Serve over noodles. **Yield:** 4 servings.

Shrimp 'n' Black Bean Chili

(Pictured below)

Prep/Total Time: 25 min.

It's not spicy, but this flavorful chili is sure to warm you up on chilly winter evenings. Since the recipe calls for cooked shrimp and canned goods, it's very quick to fix.
—Elizabeth Hunt, Kirbyville, Texas

✓ Uses less fat, sugar or salt. Includes Nutrition Facts and Diabetic Exchanges.

1/2 cup chopped onion
1/2 cup chopped green pepper
    1 tablespoon canola oil
    1 can (15 ounces) black beans, rinsed and
        drained
    1 can (14-1/2 ounces) diced tomatoes,
        undrained
    1 cup chicken broth
1/3 cup picante sauce
    1 teaspoon ground cumin
1/2 teaspoon dried basil
    1 pound cooked medium shrimp, peeled and
        deveined
Hot cooked rice, optional

In a large saucepan, saute onion and green pepper in oil for 4-5 minutes or until crisp-tender. Stir in the beans,

Ribbons and Bows Dinner

tomatoes, broth, picante sauce, cumin and basil. Reduce heat; simmer, uncovered, for 10-15 minutes or until heated through.

Add shrimp; simmer 3-4 minutes longer or until heated through. Serve with rice if desired. **Yield:** 6 servings.

Nutrition Facts: 1 cup (prepared with reduced-sodium chicken broth; caiculated without rice) equals 190 calories, 4 g fat (1 g saturated fat), 115 mg cholesterol, 504 mg sodium, 18 g carbohydrate, 5 g fiber, 20 g protein. **Diabetic Exchanges:** 3 very lean meat, 1 starch.

Ribbons and Bows Dinner

(Pictured above)

Prep/Total Time: 25 min.

Our Test Kitchen stirred up a winner with this savory combination. Pork tenderloin "ribbons," pasta "bows" and fresh broccoli and cauliflower are wrapped in a creamy Alfredo sauce for an all-in-one meal that's easy as can be.

4-1/2 cups uncooked bow tie pasta
    2 pork tenderloins (3/4 pound *each*), cut into
        2-inch strips
    3 tablespoons olive oil, *divided*
    2 cups fresh broccoli florets
    2 cups fresh cauliflowerets
    1 jar (17 ounces) Alfredo sauce
2-1/2 teaspoons dried basil
3/4 teaspoon garlic salt
1/4 teaspoon white pepper

Cook pasta according to package directions. Meanwhile, in a large skillet, cook pork in 1 tablespoon oil over medium heat until no longer pink; remove and keep warm. In the same pan, saute the broccoli and cauliflower in remaining oil until crisp-tender.

Drain pasta; stir into the skillet. Add the Alfredo sauce, pork, basil, garlic salt and pepper. Cook and stir until heated through. **Yield:** 6 servings.

Shrimp 'n' Black Bean Chili

Creamy Chicken and Pasta

(Pictured below)

Prep/Total Time: 30 min.

This rich chicken-and-pasta main dish flavored with wine and garlic is popular at my home. The whole family really enjoys it. —Elaine Moser, Spokane, Washington

- 2 cups uncooked penne *or* medium tube pasta
- 2 cups sliced fresh mushrooms
- 1 cup sliced green onions
- 2 tablespoons butter
- 1/2 cup white wine *or* chicken broth
- 1 teaspoon minced garlic
- 1 tablespoon all-purpose flour
- 1/3 cup water
- 1 cup heavy whipping cream
- 2 cups cubed cooked chicken
- 2 tablespoons capers, drained
- 1/4 teaspoon salt
- 1/8 teaspoon pepper
- Shredded Parmesan cheese

Cook pasta according to package directions. Meanwhile, in a large skillet, saute mushrooms and onions in butter for 4-5 minutes or until tender. Add wine or broth and garlic. Bring to a boil; cook until liquid is reduced by half, about 5 minutes.

Combine flour and water until smooth; gradually add to mushroom mixture. Bring to a boil. Reduce heat; cook and stir for 2 minutes or until thickened. Stir in cream. Bring to a boil. Reduce heat; simmer, uncovered, for 4-5 minutes or until heated through.

Drain pasta. Add the pasta, chicken, capers, salt and pepper to cream sauce. Cook for 3-4 minutes or until heated through. Sprinkle with Parmesan cheese. **Yield:** 5 servings.

Creamy Chicken and Pasta

Chicken with Garlic Sauce

Prep/Total Time: 30 min.

A creamy sauce drapes nicely over this golden chicken, zucchini and pasta. The recipe was given to me by a friend, and my kids request it as a special treat. —Sharon Hamlin, Kirkville, New York

- 6 boneless skinless chicken breast halves (6 ounces *each*)
- 2 tablespoons vegetable oil
- 2 tablespoons butter
- 1/2 teaspoon salt
- 1/2 teaspoon pepper
- 4 medium zucchini, cut into 1/4-inch slices
- 3 tablespoons chopped onion
- SAUCE:
- 2 tablespoons butter
- 3 tablespoons all-purpose flour
- 1-1/2 teaspoons minced garlic
- 1-1/4 cups water
- 2 teaspoons chicken bouillon granules
- 4 ounces cream cheese, cubed
- Hot cooked pasta

In a large skillet, cook chicken in oil and butter over medium heat for 8-9 minutes on each side or until juices run clear. Sprinkle with salt and pepper. Remove chicken and keep warm. In the same skillet, saute zucchini and onion for 4-5 minutes or until tender.

Meanwhile, in a large saucepan, melt butter. Stir in flour and garlic until smooth. Gradually add water and bouillon. Bring to a boil; cook and stir for 2 minutes or until thickened. Reduce heat; add cream cheese. Stir until smooth and heated through. Serve over chicken, vegetables and pasta. **Yield:** 6 servings.

Jambalaya Skillet

Prep/Total Time: 30 min.

This full-flavored dish is quick, easy and delicious. It remains a real standby recipe for me. I can always turn out a tasty batch in a hurry for unexpected guests, yet it's a little different from many spur-of-the-moment meals. —Norlene Razak, Kyle, Texas

✓ Uses less fat, sugar or salt. Includes Nutrition Facts and Diabetic Exchanges.

- 1/2 pound boneless skinless chicken breast, cubed
- 2 tablespoons butter
- 1 pound smoked kielbasa *or* Polish sausage, halved lengthwise and cut into 1/4-inch slices
- 1 can (14-1/2 ounces) stewed tomatoes
- 1 cup chicken broth
- 1 medium green pepper, diced
- 1 medium onion, diced
- 1-1/2 cups uncooked instant rice
- 1/2 teaspoon salt, optional
- 1/2 teaspoon hot pepper sauce

In a large skillet, cook the chicken in butter over medium heat until no longer pink. Add the kielbasa, tomatoes, broth, green pepper and onion; bring to a boil. Stir in the rice, salt if desired and hot pepper sauce. Remove from the heat; cover and let stand 5 minutes. **Yield:** 6 servings.

Nutrition Facts: 1 cup (prepared with reduced-fat butter, turkey sausage and reduced-sodium chicken broth; calculated without salt) equals 311 calories, 10 g fat (4 g saturated fat), 68 mg cholesterol, 742 mg sodium, 30 g carbohydrate, 2 g fiber, 24 g protein. **Diabetic Exchanges:** 3 very lean meat, 2 starch, 1 fat.

Creamy Shells and Chicken

Prep/Total Time: 30 min.

This is a great weekday chicken dinner. Using a packaged pasta side dish mix really hurries along the prep. While it simmers, I can throw together a salad or steam some broccoli, and a tasty meal is ready in a flash.
—*Trisha Kruse, Eagle, Idaho*

1/2 pound boneless skinless chicken breasts, cut into 1-inch strips
1/4 teaspoon salt
1/4 teaspoon pepper
 2 tablespoons vegetable oil, *divided*
 2 tablespoons butter, *divided*
1/2 cup chopped onion
1/2 cup chopped green pepper
1/2 cup chopped sweet red pepper
1-1/3 cups water
1/2 cup milk
 1 package (4.9 ounces) creamy garlic shells
Shredded Parmesan cheese

Sprinkle chicken with salt and pepper. In a large skillet, cook chicken over medium heat in 1 tablespoon oil and 1 tablespoon butter for 4-5 minutes or until juices run clear. Remove and keep warm.

In the same skillet, saute onion and peppers in remaining oil and butter for 4-5 minutes or until crisp-tender. Stir in the water, milk and shells. Bring to a boil. Reduce heat; simmer, uncovered, for 10-12 minutes or until pasta is tender, stirring occasionally.

Stir in chicken; cook 2-3 minutes longer or until heated through. Sprinkle with Parmesan cheese. **Yield:** 3 servings.

Ground Beef Zucchini Skillet

Prep/Total Time: 25 min.

My mom gave me this recipe when I was searching for entrees with ground beef and veggies that my kids would eat. I serve it with garlic bread. —*Carol Kurpjuweit Humansville, Missouri*

1 pound ground beef
1 tablespoon dried minced onion
1 teaspoon minced garlic
1 can (15-1/4 ounces) whole kernel corn, drained
1 can (14-1/2 ounces) diced tomatoes, undrained
1 medium zucchini, halved and sliced

Polish Sausage and Veggies

1 jar (4-1/2 ounces) sliced mushrooms, drained
1 teaspoon dried basil
1 teaspoon dried oregano
1/4 teaspoon salt
1/4 teaspoon pepper
1/4 cup grated Parmesan cheese

In a skillet, cook the beef, onion and garlic over medium heat until meat is no longer pink; drain. Stir in the corn, tomatoes, zucchini, mushrooms, basil, oregano, salt and pepper. Cover and simmer for 10-15 minutes or until heated through and zucchini is tender. Sprinkle with Parmesan cheese. **Yield:** 6 servings.

Polish Sausage and Veggies

(Pictured above)

Prep/Total Time: 30 min.

I was looking for something different to prepare with Polish sausage, so I created this entree one afternoon. My family liked it so much that I've made it time and again since. —*Rita Kodet, Chula Vista, California*

4 cups cubed peeled potatoes (about 2-1/2 pounds)
1 pound smoked Polish sausage, cut into 1/4-inch slices
1/2 cup chopped onion
1/2 cup julienned sweet yellow pepper
1/2 cup julienned sweet red pepper
1-1/2 teaspoons Cajun seasoning
1 tablespoon vegetable oil
1 tablespoon butter

In a large skillet over medium heat, cook the potatoes, sausage, onion, peppers and Cajun seasoning in oil and butter for 15-20 minutes or until potatoes are tender, stirring occasionally. **Yield:** 6 servings.

Chapter 17

⏱ *Fast, Delicious...and Nutritious*

IT'S ALMOST too good to be true—but it is! Every recipe in this lightened-up chapter is not only fixed in a flash, it's also ideal for folks who are watching their diet.

Savor an array of delicious, speedy specialties that trim off calories, fat, salt and sugar. To find dietary information about any dish, just check the Nutrition Facts section at the end of the recipe.

You'll find guilt-free foods that can take you through the entire day, from hearty Breakfast Bake and delectable Morning Cinnamon Rolls to Zesty Grilled Chicken and tempting Banana Chocolate Parfaits.

(All the good-for-you foods in this book are flagged with a red checkmark in the indexes beginning on page 316.)

GUILT-FREE FLAVOR. Sausage Bean Soup (p. 258), Grecian Gold Medal Wraps (p. 259) and Parmesan Vegetable Toss (p. 258).

All recipes in this chapter use less fat, sugar or salt and include Nutrition Facts and Diabetic Exchanges.

Balsamic Chicken and Peppers

(Pictured above)

Prep/Total Time: 25 min.

I like using a colorful mix of peppers to brighten this skillet specialty—and a little balsamic vinegar to flavor the tender chicken. —Valerie Moore, Stilwell, Kansas

    4 boneless skinless chicken breast halves
      (4 ounces *each*)
1/4 teaspoon pepper
1/8 teaspoon salt
    2 tablespoons olive oil, *divided*
    1 *each* medium sweet yellow, red and orange
      peppers, julienned
    1 small onion, sliced
    2 tablespoons balsamic vinegar

Sprinkle chicken with pepper and salt. In a large skillet, cook chicken in 1 tablespoon oil for 4-6 minutes on each side or until no longer pink; drain. Remove chicken and keep warm.

In same skillet, saute peppers and onion in remaining oil for 3-4 minutes or until tender. Return chicken to pan. Add vinegar; heat through. **Yield:** 4 servings.

Nutrition Facts: 1 chicken breast half with 1 cup peppers equals 220 calories, 10 g fat (2 g saturated fat), 63 mg cholesterol, 133 mg sodium, 9 g carbohydrate, 2 g fiber, 24 g protein. **Diabetic Exchanges:** 3 very lean meat, 2 vegetable, 1-1/2 fat.

Grapefruit Spinach Salad

(Pictured above)

Prep/Total Time: 15 min.

A splash of citrus adds zest to this special spinach salad from our home economists. To cut prep time, use a jar of grapefruit segments from your grocer's produce section.

    2 large pink grapefruit
4-1/2 cups torn fresh spinach *or* mixed greens
    1 cup sliced celery
1/2 cup dried cherries
1/4 cup olive oil
    5 teaspoons red wine vinegar
1/2 teaspoon sugar
1/8 teaspoon salt
Dash pepper

Cut each grapefruit in half horizontally. With a sharp knife, cut around each section to loosen fruit; remove fruit segments and set aside. Squeeze grapefruit halves, reserving 1 tablespoon juice. In a large salad bowl, combine spinach, celery, cherries and grapefruit segments.

In a jar with a tight-fitting lid, combine the remaining

ingredients and reserved juice; shake well. Pour over salad and toss to coat. Serve immediately. **Yield:** 6 servings.

Nutrition Facts: 1/2 cup equals 166 calories, 9 g fat (1 g saturated fat), 0 cholesterol, 94 mg sodium, 21 g carbohydrate, 3 g fiber, 3 g protein. **Diabetic Exchanges:** 1-1/2 fat, 1 vegetable, 1 fruit.

Banana Chocolate Parfaits

Prep/Total Time: 20 min.

The flavors of chocolate and banana pair wonderfully in this Test Kitchen treat. With chocolate pudding and a crunchy cookie topping, these creamy and pretty parfaits are sure to satisfy any sweet-tooth craving.

   3 medium bananas, sliced
1/4 cup lemon juice
   2 cups cold fat-free milk
   1 package (1.4 ounces) sugar-free instant chocolate pudding mix
   1 cup (8 ounces) reduced-fat sour cream
1-1/2 cups reduced-fat whipped topping
   8 chocolate wafers, crushed

In a small bowl, combine bananas and lemon juice; let stand for 5 minutes. In another bowl, whisk the milk and pudding mix for 2 minutes. Refrigerate for 5 minutes. Stir in sour cream.

Drain bananas. Place half of the banana slices in eight parfait glasses; layer with pudding mixture, whipped topping, chocolate wafer crumbs and remaining banana slices. Refrigerate until serving. **Yield:** 8 servings.

Nutrition Facts: 1 parfait equals 183 calories, 6 g fat (5 g saturated fat), 11 mg cholesterol, 236 mg sodium, 27 g carbohydrate, 2 g fiber, 5 g protein. **Diabetic Exchanges:** 1 starch, 1 fruit, 1 fat.

Whole Wheat Pancakes

Prep/Total Time: 25 min.

To fix a large batch of tender pancakes for my five children, I rely on this fuss-free recipe. It calls for whole wheat flour and buttermilk, which make the pancakes very filling but also very light. Serve them with hot chocolate for a breakfast that's sure to delight little ones.
                    —Line Walter, Wayne, Pennsylvania

   2 cups whole wheat flour
1/2 cup toasted wheat germ
   1 teaspoon baking soda
1/2 teaspoon salt
   2 eggs
   3 cups 1% buttermilk
   1 tablespoon canola oil

In a large bowl, combine the flour, wheat germ, baking soda and salt. In another bowl, whisk the eggs, buttermilk and oil. Stir into dry ingredients just until blended.

Pour batter by 1/4 cupfuls onto a hot griddle coated with nonstick cooking spray; turn when bubbles form on top of pancakes. Cook until second side is golden brown. **Yield:** 20 pancakes.

Nutrition Facts: 2 pancakes equals 157 calories, 4 g

fat (1 g saturated fat), 45 mg cholesterol, 335 mg sodium, 24 g carbohydrate, 4 g fiber, 9 g protein. **Diabetic Exchanges:** 1-1/2 starch, 1 fat.

Flavorful Summer Squash

(Pictured below)

Prep/Total Time: 25 min.

I jazz up sauteed squash with plenty of red onion, garlic and dried herbs for garden-fresh goodness. Sprinkled with mozzarella, it makes a colorful and delicious side dish.
                    —Andrea Yacyk, Brigantine, New Jersey

   3 medium yellow summer squash, sliced
   2 medium zucchini, sliced
   1 medium red onion, sliced and separated into rings
   1 teaspoon minced garlic
   1 tablespoon olive oil
   1 teaspoon dried parsley flakes
   1 teaspoon dried basil
1/2 teaspoon dried oregano
1/2 teaspoon dried thyme
1/4 teaspoon salt
1/2 cup shredded part-skim mozzarella cheese

In a large nonstick skillet, saute the yellow squash, zucchini, onion and garlic in oil until crisp-tender, stirring occasionally.

Stir in the parsley, basil, oregano, thyme and salt. Remove from the heat. Sprinkle with cheese; cover and let stand until cheese is melted. **Yield:** 6 servings.

Nutrition Facts: 2/3 cup equals 83 calories, 4 g fat (1 g saturated fat), 5 mg cholesterol, 147 mg sodium, 9 g carbohydrate, 3 g fiber, 5 g protein. **Diabetic Exchanges:** 2 vegetable, 1/2 fat.

Flavorful Summer Squash

Light Strawberry Pie

(Pictured below)

Prep: 25 min. + chilling

This beautiful, ruby-red pie offers both luscious taste and make-ahead convenience. Folks rave about this dessert without realizing that it's a low-sugar recipe. When they find out, they love the fact that they can indulge guilt-free.
—*Lou Wright, Rockford, Illinois*

    1 can (8 ounces) unsweetened crushed
      pineapple
    1 package (.8 ounce) sugar-free cook-and-
      serve vanilla pudding mix
    1 package (.3 ounce) sugar-free strawberry
      gelatin
    3 cups sliced fresh strawberries
    1 reduced-fat graham cracker crust (8 inches)
  1/2 cup reduced-fat whipped topping

Drain pineapple, reserving juice in a 2-cup measuring cup. Set pineapple aside. Add enough water to juice to measure 1-1/2 cups; transfer to a saucepan. Whisk in the pudding mix and gelatin until combined. Bring to a boil; cook and stir for 1-2 minutes or until thickened. Stir in pineapple. Remove from the heat; cool for 10 minutes.

Add the strawberries; toss gently to coat. Pour into crust. Refrigerate until set, about 3 hours. Garnish each piece with 1 tablespoon whipped topping. Refrigerate leftovers. **Yield:** 8 servings.

Nutrition Facts: 1 piece equals 159 calories, 4 g fat (2 g saturated fat), 0 cholesterol, 172 mg sodium, 29 g carbohydrate, 2 g fiber, 2 g protein. **Diabetic Exchanges:** 1 starch, 1 fruit, 1/2 fat.

Light Strawberry Pie

Zesty Grilled Chicken

Prep: 10 min. + marinating **Grill:** 15 min.

On hot summer days, this yummy grilled chicken is terrific. I usually have the ingredients for the spicy marinade on hand. —*Missy Herr, Quarryville, Pennsylvania*

      6 tablespoons white vinegar
      3 tablespoons canola oil
      2 tablespoons ketchup
      2 teaspoons dried parsley flakes
  1-1/2 teaspoons garlic salt
    1/2 teaspoon paprika
    1/4 teaspoon dried oregano
    1/8 teaspoon hot pepper sauce
    1/8 teaspoon Worcestershire sauce
      1 bay leaf
      4 boneless skinless chicken breast halves (6
        ounces *each*)

In a large resealable plastic bag, combine the first 10 ingredients; add chicken. Seal bag and turn to coat; refrigerate for 4-8 hours, turning occasionally.

Drain and discard marinade. Grill chicken, covered, over medium heat for 6-8 minutes on each side or until juices run clear. **Yield:** 4 servings.

Nutrition Facts: 1 chicken breast half equals 208 calories, 7 g fat (1 g saturated fat), 94 mg cholesterol, 275 mg sodium, 1 g carbohydrate, trace fiber, 34 g protein. **Diabetic Exchanges:** 5 very lean meat, 1/2 fat.

Baked Eggplant Italiano

Prep: 30 min. **Bake:** 30 min.

I created this as a substitute for lasagna. Using veggies and reduced-fat cheeses really cuts calories but doesn't sacrifice flavor. —*Traci Chatterton, Windsor, New York*

      2 small eggplants, peeled and cut into
        1/2-inch slices
      3 tablespoons olive oil, *divided*
      1 teaspoon garlic powder
      1 teaspoon salt, *divided*
    1/2 teaspoon pepper, *divided*
      2 small tomatoes, finely chopped
      1 small onion, finely chopped
      1 tablespoon Italian seasoning
      2 teaspoons minced garlic
      1 package (6 ounces) fresh baby spinach
      1 cup reduced-fat ricotta cheese
      1 cup (4 ounces) shredded part-skim
        mozzarella cheese, *divided*
      1 egg, lightly beaten
      2 cups garden-style pasta sauce

Brush both sides of eggplant slices with 2 tablespoons oil; sprinkle with garlic powder, 1/2 teaspoon salt and 1/4 teaspoon pepper. Grill, covered, over medium heat or broil 4-6 in. from the heat for 2-3 minutes on each side. Set aside.

In a large skillet, saute tomatoes, onion, Italian seasoning, garlic, and remaining salt and pepper in remaining oil. Add spinach; stir until wilted. Combine ricotta,

1/2 cup mozzarella and egg; stir into tomato mixture.

Arrange eggplant in a single layer in a 13-in. x 9-in. x 2-in. baking dish coated with nonstick cooking spray. Top with tomato mixture and pasta sauce. Sprinkle with remaining mozzarella. Bake, uncovered, at 350° for 30-35 minutes or until bubbly. Let stand for 5 minutes before serving. **Yield:** 6 servings.

Nutrition Facts: 1 serving equals 275 calories, 15 g fat (4 g saturated fat), 60 mg cholesterol, 885 mg sodium, 25 g carbohydrate, 7 g fiber, 13 g protein. **Diabetic Exchanges:** 2 vegetable, 2 fat, 1 starch, 1 lean meat.

Turkey-Melon Pasta Salad

Prep/Total Time: 25 min.

Bow tie pasta, turkey and watermelon combine in this breezy medley. It's delicious with tall glasses of lemonade or iced tea. —R. Jean Rand, Edina, Minnesota

        2 cups uncooked bow tie pasta
    1-1/2 cups cubed cooked turkey breast
    1-1/2 cups diced seedless watermelon
      1/2 cup sliced celery
        2 tablespoons chopped green onion
      1/4 cup fat-free plain yogurt
        2 tablespoons reduced-fat mayonnaise
        2 tablespoons lime juice
    1-3/4 teaspoons sugar

Cook pasta according to package directions. Meanwhile, in a large bowl, combine the turkey, watermelon, celery and onion; set aside.

In a small bowl, whisk the yogurt, mayonnaise, lime juice and sugar until smooth. Drain pasta and rinse in cold water; stir into turkey mixture. Drizzle with the yogurt mixture and toss to coat. Refrigerate until serving. **Yield:** 4 servings.

Nutrition Facts: 1-1/2 cups equals 202 calories, 4 g fat (1 g saturated fat), 48 mg cholesterol, 113 mg sodium, 23 g carbohydrate, 1 g fiber, 20 g protein. **Diabetic Exchanges:** 2 lean meat, 1 starch, 1/2 fruit.

Roasted Pork Tenderloin And Vegetables

(Pictured above right)

Prep: 10 min. **Bake:** 30 min.

My mother-in-law served this easy-to-prepare dinner at a family gathering. The roasted veggies are so good…even kids like them. —Coleen Martin, Brookfield, Wisconsin

        2 pork tenderloins (3/4 pound *each*)
        2 pounds red potatoes, quartered
        1 pound carrots, halved and cut into 2-inch
            pieces
        1 medium onion, cut into wedges
        1 tablespoon olive oil
        2 teaspoons dried rosemary, crushed
        1 teaspoon rubbed sage
      1/2 teaspoon salt
      1/4 teaspoon pepper

Roasted Pork Tenderloin and Vegetables

Place the pork in a shallow roasting pan coated with nonstick cooking spray; arrange the potatoes, carrots and onion around pork. Drizzle with oil. Combine the seasonings; sprinkle over meat and vegetables.

Bake, uncovered, at 450° for 30-40 minutes or until a meat thermometer reads 160°, stirring vegetables occasionally. **Yield:** 6 servings.

Nutrition Facts: One serving (3 ounces cooked meat with 1 cup vegetables) equals 331 calories, 7 g fat (2 g saturated fat), 67 mg cholesterol, 299 mg sodium, 40 g carbohydrate, 5 g fiber, 28 g protein. **Diabetic Exchanges:** 3 lean meat, 2 starch, 1 vegetable.

Fruity Cooler

Prep/Total Time: 15 min.

This sparkly and refreshing beverage is super-easy to make. With colorful fruit floating on top, it's pretty for a special dinner. —Bernadette Bennett, Waco, Texas

        1 quart white grape juice, chilled
        1 can (12 ounces) lemon-lime soda, chilled
        1 cup sliced fresh *or* frozen strawberries
      1/2 cup fresh *or* frozen sliced peaches
        1 medium orange, halved and sliced
    Ice cubes, optional

In a 2-qt. punch bowl or pitcher, combine grape juice, soda and fruit. Serve with ice if desired. **Yield:** 8 servings.

Nutrition Facts: 1 cup (prepared with diet soda) equals 88 calories, trace fat (trace saturated fat), 0 cholesterol, 12 mg sodium, 21 g carbohydrate, 1 g fiber, 1 g protein. **Diabetic Exchange:** 1-1/2 fruit.

Breakfast Bake

(Pictured below)

Prep: 15 min. **Bake:** 50 min.

I wanted to have scrambled eggs and hash browns one morning, and this is the all-in-one casserole I created. My wife loved it! —Howard Rogers, El Paso, Texas

1-1/2 cups egg substitute
1/2 cup fat-free milk
3-1/2 cups frozen O'Brien hash brown potatoes, thawed
1-1/3 cups shredded reduced-fat cheddar cheese, *divided*
1/2 cup chopped sweet onion
4 tablespoons crumbled cooked bacon, *divided*
1/2 teaspoon salt
1/2 teaspoon salt-free seasoning blend
1/4 teaspoon chili powder
4 green onions, chopped

In a large bowl, whisk the egg substitute and milk. Stir in the hash browns, 1 cup cheese, onion, 2 tablespoons bacon, salt, seasoning blend and chili powder. Pour into an 8-in. square baking dish coated with non-stick cooking spray.

Bake at 350° for 45-50 minutes or until a knife inserted near the center comes out clean. Sprinkle with the remaining cheese and bacon. Bake 3-5 minutes longer or until cheese is melted. Sprinkle with green onions. Let stand for 5 minutes before cutting. **Yield:** 6 servings.

Nutrition Facts: 1 piece equals 219 calories, 6 g fat (4 g saturated fat), 22 mg cholesterol, 682 mg sodium, 25 g carbohydrate, 3 g fiber, 17 g protein. **Diabetic Exchanges:** 2 lean meat, 1-1/2 starch.

Lemon-Dill Steamed Vegetables

Prep/Total Time: 20 min.

For a pretty side dish, try this lovely combination of fresh vegetables tossed with a buttery, well-seasoned sauce. —Page Alexander, Baldwin City, Kansas

Breakfast Bake

3/4 pound fresh baby carrots
4 medium new potatoes, quartered
6 fresh brussels sprouts, halved
2 tablespoons butter, melted
1 tablespoon lemon juice
1/2 teaspoon salt
1/2 teaspoon dill weed
1/8 teaspoon pepper

Place the vegetables in a steamer basket; place in a large saucepan over 1 in. of water. Bring to a boil; cover and steam for 10-12 minutes or until crisp-tender.

In a large serving bowl, combine the butter, lemon juice, salt, dill and pepper. Add the vegetables and toss to coat. Serve immediately. **Yield:** 6 servings.

Nutrition Facts: 3/4 cup (prepared with reduced-fat butter) equals 158 calories, 2 g fat (1 g saturated fat), 7 mg cholesterol, 278 mg sodium, 32 g carbohydrate, 4 g fiber, 4 g protein. **Diabetic Exchanges:** 1-1/2 starch, 1 vegetable.

Rich Parsley Biscuits

Prep/Total Time: 30 min.

These honey-flavored bites are delectable alongside soup at lunch or dinner, but they're also perfect for brunch. —Margaret Wilt, Ridley Park, Pennsylvania

2-1/4 cups all-purpose flour
3 teaspoons baking powder
1/4 teaspoon baking soda
4 ounces cold reduced-fat cream cheese
4-1/2 teaspoons cold reduced-fat butter
2/3 cup reduced-sodium chicken broth
1/2 cup minced fresh parsley
1/2 cup honey

In a large bowl, combine the flour, baking powder and baking soda. Cut in cream cheese and butter until mixture resembles coarse crumbs. Stir in the broth, parsley and honey just until moistened.

Turn onto a lightly floured surface; knead 8-10 times. Pat or roll out to 1/2-in. thickness; cut with a floured 2-1/2-in. biscuit cutter.

Place 2 in. apart on a baking sheet coated with non-stick cooking spray. Bake at 450° for 8-10 minutes or until golden brown. Serve warm. **Yield:** 16 biscuits.

Nutrition Facts: 1 biscuit equals 123 calories, 2 g fat (1 g saturated fat), 7 mg cholesterol, 159 mg sodium, 23 g carbohydrate, 1 g fiber, 3 g protein. **Diabetic Exchange:** 1-1/2 starch.

Pineapple Salsa

(Pictured above right)

Prep/Total Time: 20 min.

Serve this mouth-watering salsa with tortilla chips as a snack...or draped over grilled chicken or fish for a jazzed-up entree. —Suzi LaPar, Wahiawa, Hawaii

2 cups diced fresh pineapple
2 medium tomatoes, seeded and diced

3/4 cup diced sweet onion
1/4 cup minced fresh cilantro
  1 jalapeno pepper, seeded and diced
  1 tablespoon olive oil
  1 teaspoon ground coriander
3/4 teaspoon ground cumin
1/2 teaspoon salt
1/2 teaspoon minced garlic
Baked tortilla chips

In a large bowl, combine the first 10 ingredients. Cover and refrigerate until serving. Serve with tortilla chips. **Yield:** 3-1/2 cups.

  Editor's Note: When cutting or seeding hot peppers, use rubber or plastic gloves to protect your hands. Avoid touching your face.

  Nutrition Facts: 1/4 cup (calculated without chips) equals 29 calories, 1 g fat (trace saturated fat), 0 cholesterol, 87 mg sodium, 5 g carbohydrate, 1 g fiber, trace protein. **Diabetic Exchange:** Free food.

Fantastic Fish Tacos

(Pictured above)

Prep/Total Time: 25 min.

Searching for a healthier substitute for fried fish tacos, I came up with this refreshingly light seafood entree. It's been a hit with both my friends and family. The orange roughy fillets are so mild that even non-fish eaters are pleasantly surprised by them. —*Jennifer Palmer
Rancho Cucamonga, California*

1/2 cup fat-free mayonnaise
  1 tablespoon lime juice
  2 teaspoons fat-free milk
1/3 cup dry bread crumbs
  2 tablespoons salt-free lemon-pepper seasoning
  1 egg, lightly beaten
  1 teaspoon water
  1 pound orange roughy fillets, cut into 1-inch strips
  4 corn tortillas (6 inches), warmed
  1 cup coleslaw mix
  2 medium tomatoes, diced
  1 cup (4 ounces) shredded reduced-fat Mexican cheese blend
  1 tablespoon minced fresh cilantro

In a small bowl, combine the mayonnaise, lime juice and milk; cover and refrigerate until serving.

  In a shallow bowl, combine bread crumbs and lemon-pepper. In another shallow bowl, combine egg and water. Dip fish in egg mixture, then roll in crumbs.

  In a large nonstick skillet coated with nonstick cooking spray, cook fish over medium-high heat for 3-4 minutes on each side or until it flakes easily with a fork. Spoon onto tortillas; top with coleslaw mix, tomatoes, cheese and cilantro. Drizzle with mayonnaise mixture. **Yield:** 4 servings.

  Nutrition Facts: 1 taco equals 314 calories, 10 g fat (4 g saturated fat), 99 mg cholesterol, 659 mg sodium, 32 g carbohydrate, 3 g fiber, 30 g protein. **Diabetic Exchanges:** 3 lean meat, 2 starch.

Morning Cinnamon Rolls

(Pictured below)

Prep/Total Time: 25 min.

Convenient crescent roll dough hurries along these yummy glazed rolls. I found the recipe in a cookbook and slimmed it down by using sugar substitute instead of sugar. With hot coffee, these buns are a guilt-free morning treat.
—Helen Lipko, Martinsburg, Pennsylvania

    1 tube (8 ounces) refrigerated reduced-fat
      crescent rolls
Sugar substitute equivalent to 1/2 cup sugar,
    divided
  1/2 teaspoon ground cinnamon
  1/4 cup confectioners' sugar
    1 tablespoon fat-free milk

Unroll crescent dough into a rectangle; seal seams and perforations. Combine half of the sugar substitute and the cinnamon; sprinkle over dough. Roll up jelly-roll style, starting with a long side; seal edge. Cut into eight slices.

Place the rolls cut side down in a 9-in. round baking pan coated with nonstick cooking spray. Bake at 375° for 12-15 minutes or until golden brown. In a small bowl, combine the confectioners' sugar, milk and remaining sugar substitute; drizzle over the warm rolls. **Yield:** 8 servings.

Editor's Note: This recipe was tested with Splenda Sugar Blend for Baking.

Nutrition Facts: 1 roll equals 123 calories, 5 g fat (1 g saturated fat), trace cholesterol, 234 mg sodium, 18 g carbohydrate, trace fiber, 2 g protein. **Diabetic Exchanges:** 1 starch, 1 fat.

Morning Cinnamon Rolls

Hearty Pork Chops

Prep: 10 min. + marinating **Grill:** 15 min.

Just six ingredients are needed for the make-ahead marinade that lends great taste to these chops from our Test Kitchen. Whip up the mixture the night before to trim time from the next day's dinner.

  2/3 cup lemon-lime soda
  1/2 cup soy sauce
  1/4 cup honey
    1 teaspoon dried thyme
  3/4 teaspoon dried rosemary, crushed
  1/4 teaspoon pepper
    6 bone-in pork loin chops (3/4 inch thick and 7
      ounces *each*)

In a large resealable plastic bag, combine the first six ingredients; add the pork chops. Seal the bag and turn to coat; refrigerate for 4 hours or overnight, turning bag occasionally.

Drain and discard marinade. Grill pork, covered, over medium heat 6-8 minutes on each side or until juices run clear. **Yield:** 6 servings.

Nutrition Facts: 1 pork chop (prepared with diet soda and reduced-sodium soy sauce) equals 227 calories, 8 g fat (3 g saturated fat), 86 mg cholesterol, 387 mg sodium, 5 g carbohydrate, trace fiber, 31 g protein. **Diabetic Exchange:** 4 lean meat.

Spinach Chicken Roll-Ups

Prep: 20 min. **Bake:** 30 min.

This rave-winning recipe is one that I have adapted over time. It dresses up meals very well for company or special occasions yet is nice for busy weeknights, too.
—Chris Duncan, Ellensburg, Washington

    2 boneless skinless chicken breast halves
      (6 ounces *each*)
  1/2 cup fresh baby spinach, chopped
  1/4 cup shredded part-skim mozzarella cheese
    2 tablespoons butter, *divided*
  1/4 cup seasoned bread crumbs
    1 tablespoon all-purpose flour
  1/8 teaspoon salt
  1/8 teaspoon pepper
  1/4 cup chicken broth
  1/4 cup milk

Flatten chicken to 1/4-in. thickness; layer with spinach and cheese. Roll up and secure with toothpicks. In a shallow microwave-safe bowl, melt 1 tablespoon butter. Place bread crumbs in another bowl. Dip chicken in butter, then roll in crumbs.

Place the chicken seam side down in an 8-in. square baking dish coated with nonstick cooking spray. Bake, uncovered, at 375° for 30-35 minutes or until the chicken juices run clear.

In a small saucepan, melt remaining butter. Stir in the flour, salt and pepper until smooth. Gradually add broth and milk. Bring to a boil; cook and stir for 1-2 minutes or until thickened. Discard toothpicks from roll-ups;

serve with sauce. **Yield:** 2 servings.

Nutrition Facts: 1 roll-up (prepared with reduced-fat butter and reduced-sodium broth) equals 360 calories, 14 g fat (7 g saturated fat), 126 mg cholesterol, 679 mg sodium, 15 g carbohydrate, 1 g fiber, 43 g protein. **Diabetic Exchanges:** 4 lean meat, 1 starch, 1 fat.

Vegetable Pizza

Prep/Total Time: 30 min.

An assortment of fresh veggies gives this delicious meatless pizza plenty of flavor. I often add a few sliced black olives to the mix. —Beverly Little, Marietta, Georgia

    1 tube (13.8 ounces) refrigerated pizza crust
 1/2 cup sliced fresh mushrooms
 1/2 cup chopped onion
 1/2 cup chopped fresh broccoli
 1/2 cup chopped green pepper
 1/2 cup chopped fresh baby spinach
    1 cup meatless spaghetti sauce
    2 plum tomatoes, thinly sliced
    2 cups (8 ounces) shredded part-skim
      mozzarella cheese

Unroll pizza crust into a 15-in. x 10-in. x 1-in. baking pan coated with nonstick cooking spray; flatten dough and build up edges slightly. Bake at 400° for 8 minutes.

Meanwhile, in a nonstick skillet coated with nonstick cooking spray, saute the mushrooms, onion, broccoli, green pepper and spinach until crisp-tender.

Spread spaghetti sauce over crust. Top with sauteed vegetables, tomatoes and cheese. Bake for 15-20 minutes or until crust is golden brown and cheese is melted. Let stand for 10 minutes before serving. **Yield:** 8 slices.

Nutrition Facts: 1 piece equals 263 calories, 10 g fat (6 g saturated fat), 33 mg cholesterol, 644 mg sodium, 24 g carbohydrate, 2 g fiber, 18 g protein. **Diabetic Exchanges:** 2 vegetable, 1-1/2 lean meat, 1 starch, 1 fat.

Applesauce Oat Bran Muffins

Prep: 20 min. **Bake:** 20 min.

I sprinkle a tempting topping of cinnamon, sugar and walnuts on these moist muffins. They're best served warm from the oven. —Beth Struble, Bryan, Ohio

    1 cup oat bran
    1 cup all-purpose flour
 1/4 cup plus 1 tablespoon sugar, *divided*
    2 teaspoons baking powder
 1/2 teaspoon salt
    2 eggs
    1 cup unsweetened applesauce
    3 tablespoons canola oil
    3 tablespoons fat-free milk
 1/4 cup raisins
 1/4 cup chopped walnuts
 1/2 teaspoon ground cinnamon

In a large bowl, combine the oat bran, flour, 1/4 cup sugar, baking powder and salt. In another bowl, beat the eggs, applesauce, oil and milk. Stir into dry ingredients

Fruit Smoothies

just until moistened. Fold in raisins.

Fill muffin cups coated with nonstick cooking spray three-fourths full. Combine the walnuts, cinnamon and remaining sugar; sprinkle over batter. Bake at 400° for 16-20 minutes or until a toothpick comes out clean. Cool for 5 minutes before removing from pan to a wire rack. Serve warm. **Yield:** 1 dozen.

Nutrition Facts: 1 muffin equals 156 calories, 6 g fat (1 g saturated fat), 35 mg cholesterol, 179 mg sodium, 24 g carbohydrate, 2 g fiber, 4 g protein. **Diabetic Exchanges:** 1-1/2 starch, 1 fat.

Fruit Smoothies

(Pictured above)

Prep/Total Time: 5 min.

I came up with this six-ingredient recipe when experimenting in the kitchen one day. The smoothies are refreshing and make a wholesome, nutrition-packed snack. They're also a great way to get going in the morning. —Bryce Sickich, New Port Richey, Florida

 3/4 cup fat-free milk
 1/2 cup orange juice
 1/2 cup unsweetened applesauce
    1 small ripe banana, halved
 1/2 cup frozen unsweetened raspberries
    7 to 10 ice cubes

In a blender, combine all ingredients; cover and process until smooth. Pour into chilled glasses; serve immediately. **Yield:** 3 servings.

Nutrition Facts: 1 cup equals 97 calories, trace fat (trace saturated fat), 1 mg cholesterol, 33 mg sodium, 22 g carbohydrate, 2 g fiber, 3 g protein. **Diabetic Exchange:** 1-1/2 fruit.

Sausage Bean Soup

(Pictured below and on page 249)

Prep/Total Time: 30 min.

This hearty soup is so simple to assemble with ingredients that are usually on hand, and it's delicious to boot.

—Gail Wilkerson, House Springs, Missouri

4 cups water
1 medium potato, peeled and chopped
6 brown-and-serve turkey sausage links
   (1 ounce *each*)
2 cans (16 ounces *each*) kidney beans, rinsed
   and drained
1 can (28 ounces) diced tomatoes, undrained
1 cup chopped onion
1 medium green pepper, chopped
1 bay leaf
1/2 teaspoon *each* garlic salt, seasoned salt,
   pepper and dried thyme

In a large saucepan, bring water and potato to a boil. Cover and cook for 10-15 minutes or until tender (do not drain). Meanwhile, crumble sausage into a skillet; cook over medium heat until browned. Drain if necessary. Add to saucepan.

Stir in the remaining ingredients. Bring to a boil. Reduce heat; simmer, uncovered, for 8-10 minutes or until heated through, stirring occasionally. Discard bay leaf. **Yield:** 10 servings.

Nutrition Facts: 1 cup equals 160 calories, 3 g fat (1 g saturated fat), 14 mg cholesterol, 515 mg sodium, 24 g carbohydrate, 6 g fiber, 10 g protein. **Diabetic Exchanges:** 1 starch, 1 lean meat, 1/2 fat.

Parmesan Vegetable Toss

(Pictured below on page 248)

Prep/Total Time: 15 min.

I've enjoyed this crunchy vegetable medley in a creamy dressing on many occasions. It's ready in a flash and easy to double for special events. I like to stir a little sugar into the dressing before tossing it with the veggies.

—Marian Seuferling, Louisburg, Kansas

2 cups fresh broccoli florets
2 cups fresh cauliflowerets
1 small red onion, thinly sliced
1/4 cup fat-free mayonnaise
1/4 cup fat-free ranch salad dressing
5 teaspoons shredded Parmesan cheese
1/4 teaspoon dried basil
1 cup chopped lettuce
1 can (8 ounces) sliced water chestnuts,
   drained
1/2 cup Caesar salad croutons

In a large bowl, combine the broccoli, cauliflower and onion. In a small bowl, combine the mayonnaise, ranch salad dressing, shredded Parmesan cheese and basil. Drizzle over vegetable mixture; toss to coat. Chill until serving.

Just before serving, add the lettuce and water chestnuts; toss to coat. Sprinkle with Caesar salad croutons. **Yield:** 6 servings.

Nutrition Facts: 3/4 cup equals 84 calories, 2 g fat (1 g saturated fat), 2 mg cholesterol, 283 mg sodium, 16 g carbohydrate, 3 g fiber, 3 g protein. **Diabetic Exchange:** 3 vegetable.

**Sausage Bean Soup
Grecian Gold Medal Wraps
Parmesan Vegetable Toss**

Grecian Gold Medal Wraps

(Pictured below left and on page 248)

Prep/Total Time: 20 min.

For a healthy dish, I created these sandwiches with fat-free yogurt and whole wheat tortillas. Because the Greek olives have lots of flavor, you don't need to use many.
—Margee Berry, Trout Lake, Washington

- 1/2 cup canned white kidney *or* cannellini beans, rinsed and drained
- 1/3 cup crumbled feta cheese
- 1/3 cup fat-free plain yogurt
- 1/4 cup chopped red onion
- 2 teaspoons lemon juice
- 2 small tomatoes, chopped
- 4 whole wheat tortillas (8 inches), warmed
- 1 package (6 ounces) ready-to-serve grilled chicken breast strips
- 2/3 cup torn romaine
- 2 tablespoons chopped pitted Greek olives

In a small bowl, mash beans with a fork. Stir in the feta cheese, yogurt, onion and lemon juice. Fold in tomatoes. Spread 1/4 cup onto each tortilla. Top with chicken, romaine and olives; roll up. **Yield:** 4 servings.

Nutrition Facts: 1 wrap equals 213 calories, 5 g fat (2 g saturated fat), 33 mg cholesterol, 777 mg sodium, 31 g carbohydrate, 4 g fiber, 17 g protein. **Diabetic Exchanges:** 2 starch, 1 very lean meat, 1/2 fat.

Salisbury Steak with Gravy

(Pictured above right)

Prep: 15 min. **Bake:** 50 min.

This light recipe was shared at a Weight Watchers meeting I attended, and my whole family really enjoys it. I like that it's so quick to fix, too! I need just 15 minutes to prepare the tasty steak patties before popping them in the oven.
—Danelle Weiher, Verndale, Minnesota

- 1/2 cup fat-free milk
- 14 fat-free saltines, crushed
- 2 tablespoons dried minced onion
- 2 teaspoons dried parsley flakes
- 1 pound lean ground beef
- 1 jar (12 ounces) fat-free beef gravy
- 2 tablespoons ketchup
- 2 teaspoons Worcestershire sauce
- 1/4 teaspoon pepper

In a large bowl, combine the milk, saltines, onion and parsley. Crumble beef over mixture and mix well. Shape into four patties. Place in an 8-in. square baking dish coated with nonstick cooking spray.

In a small bowl, combine the gravy, ketchup, Worcestershire and pepper; pour over patties. Bake, uncovered, at 350° for 50-55 minutes or until meat is no longer pink. **Yield:** 4 servings.

Nutrition Facts: 1 serving equals 266 calories, 9 g fat (4 g saturated fat), 77 mg cholesterol, 727 mg sodium,

Festive Rice Medley
Salisbury Steak with Gravy

21 g carbohydrate, 1 g fiber, 24 g protein. **Diabetic Exchanges:** 3 lean meat, 1-1/2 starch.

Festive Rice Medley

(Pictured above)

Prep/Total Time: 15 min.

I punch up the flavor and nutrition of this versatile rice side dish with fresh cilantro and brightly colored peppers. The medley can be served with so many different main courses, from salisbury steak to chicken, pork and seafood.
—Vicki Zobal
Georgetown, Texas

- 1-1/2 cups uncooked instant rice
- 1/4 cup chopped sweet red pepper
- 1/4 cup chopped sweet yellow pepper
- 2 teaspoons canola oil
- 2 tablespoons minced fresh cilantro
- 2 tablespoons chopped green onion
- 1/2 teaspoon minced garlic
- 1/4 teaspoon salt
- 1/4 teaspoon paprika, optional

Cook rice according to package directions. In a large skillet, saute the peppers in oil for 2-3 minutes or until tender. Add the cilantro, onion, garlic and salt. Stir in the rice and paprika if desired. Cook for 2-3 minutes or until heated through. **Yield:** 5 servings.

Nutrition Facts: 1/2 cup equals 130 calories, 2 g fat (trace saturated fat), 0 cholesterol, 121 mg sodium, 25 g carbohydrate, 1 g fiber, 2 g protein. **Diabetic Exchange:** 1-1/2 starch.

Chapter 18

☀ *Microwave Magic*

WHY LIMIT your microwave oven to "zapping" last night's leftovers? The impressive recipes here prove it's true—this handy appliance can do much more for time-crunched cooks!

Just page through this chapter, and you'll see exceptional main dishes, standout sides... even special desserts. Each one comes together by popping ingredients in the microwave and hitting the "start" button.

Your family and guests will find it hard to believe that delicious foods like Garden-Style Beef Lasagna, Buttery Garlic Potatoes and luscious Caramel Apple Dip came straight from the microwave.

So keep it in mind for busy weeknights, holiday dinner parties...any time at all.

FIXED IN A FLASH. Cheese-Topped Meat Loaves (p. 264).

Apricot Chicken

run clear, stirring once. Let stand for 3 minutes. Serve with rice. **Yield:** 4 servings.

Baked Potatoes with Topping

(Pictured on the cover)

Prep/Total Time: 25 min.

I like to perk up ordinary baked potatoes with this rich topping. It's a fast way to make spuds a little more special, whether you're serving dinner guests or just want to surprise your family on a weeknight with a yummy treat.   —Alice DePauw Defuniak Springs, Florida

    6 large baking potatoes
1/3 cup butter, softened
    6 green onions, sliced
1/4 cup mayonnaise
    2 tablespoons crumbled cooked bacon
1-1/2 cups (6 ounces) shredded cheddar cheese

Scrub and pierce potatoes; place on a microwave-safe plate. Microwave, uncovered, on high for 20-23 minutes or until tender, turning once.

Meanwhile, in a small bowl, combine the butter, onions, mayonnaise and bacon; set aside. Cut an X in the top of each potato; fluff pulp with a fork. Top each with 3 tablespoons of butter mixture. Sprinkle with cheese. **Yield:** 6 servings.

Spiced Peach Chutney

Prep/Total Time: 25 min.

If you like chutney, you'll enjoy this tasty twist on traditional versions. The quick-to-cook condiment, jazzed up with onion and fresh cilantro, is great on grilled meats and chicken. It won't take long to prepare this recipe using the microwave.
—Shirley Glaab, Hattiesburg, Mississippi

1/2 cup chopped onion
    2 teaspoons olive oil
1-1/2 cups chopped peeled fresh peaches
1/3 cup raisins
    2 tablespoons brown sugar
1/4 teaspoon ground cinnamon
1/8 teaspoon salt
1/8 teaspoon ground cloves
Pinch cayenne pepper
    1 tablespoon minced fresh cilantro
    1 teaspoon cider vinegar

In a microwave-safe bowl, combine onion and oil. Cover and cook on high for 2 to 2-1/2 minutes or until onion is tender.

Add peaches, raisins, sugar, cinnamon, salt, cloves and cayenne. Cover; cook at 50% power for 5 minutes. Uncover and cook 4-5 minutes longer or until thickened. Stir in cilantro and vinegar. Cool. Serve at room temperature. Store in refrigerator. **Yield:** 1-1/4 cups.

Editor's Note: These recipes were tested in an 1,100-watt microwave.

Apricot Chicken

(Pictured above)

Prep/Total Time: 15 min.

This is one of my favorite ways to fix chicken in a hurry. Everybody loves the flavor, and leftovers are just as good the next day.   —Vicki Ruiz, Twin Falls, Idaho

1/2 cup apricot preserves
    2 tablespoons soy sauce
    1 tablespoon chicken broth *or* sherry
    1 tablespoon vegetable oil
    1 tablespoon cornstarch
    1 teaspoon minced garlic
1/4 teaspoon ground ginger
    1 pound boneless skinless chicken breasts, cut into strips
    1 medium green pepper, chopped
1/2 cup salted cashews
Hot cooked rice

In a large bowl, combine the first seven ingredients. Add chicken and toss to coat. Transfer to a shallow microwave-safe dish. Cover and microwave on high for 3 minutes, stirring once.

Add green pepper and cashews. Cover and microwave on high for 2-4 minutes or until chicken juices

Buttery Garlic Potatoes

Prep/Total Time: 15 min.

My husband and three boys love oven-roasted potatoes. But I work full-time, so I usually don't have time to fix them. I whipped up this speedy microwave recipe with red potatoes and seasonings instead, and it was a hit.
—Heidi Iacovetto, Phippsburg, Colorado

   6 small red potatoes, quartered
1/4 cup butter, melted
   1 teaspoon seasoned salt
   1 teaspoon paprika
   1 teaspoon dried parsley flakes
   1 teaspoon minced garlic

Place the potatoes in a 2-qt. microwave-safe dish. In a small bowl, combine the butter, seasoned salt, paprika, parsley and garlic; pour over potatoes and toss to coat.

Microwave, uncovered, on high for 8-10 minutes or until potatoes are tender, stirring frequently. **Yield:** 4 servings.

Toffee-Crunch Coffee Sundaes

(Pictured below)

Prep/Total Time: 15 min.

This foolproof fudge sauce has a secret ingredient: coffee ice cream. I created it one day when I was out of heavy cream and wanted to make hot fudge sauce for company. Layered with ice cream and candy bars, this dessert delighted my guests. —Beth Royals, Richmond, Virginia

   1 cup (6 ounces) semisweet chocolate chips
   1 quart coffee ice cream, *divided*
   1 tablespoon light corn syrup

Toffee-Crunch Coffee Sundaes

Asparagus with Lemon Sauce

1/2 cup chopped Heath candy bars (about 1-1/2 bars)
Whipped cream
Additional Heath candy bars, cut into triangles, optional

In a microwave-safe bowl, combine the chocolate chips, 1/2 cup ice cream and corn syrup. Microwave on high for 45 seconds or until smooth. Spoon 1/3 cup of ice cream into each of four parfait glasses. Top each with 2 tablespoons chocolate sauce and 1 tablespoon chopped candy bars. Repeat layers. Top with remaining ice cream. Garnish with whipped cream and additional candy bars if desired. **Yield:** 4 servings.

Asparagus with Lemon Sauce

(Pictured above)

Prep/Total Time: 15 min.

We didn't have an oven or stove in our first years of marriage, so we relied heavily on our microwave. This side dish of asparagus in a creamy lemon sauce was always a favorite. —Janice Gerbitz, Woodland, California

   3 cups cut fresh asparagus (2-inch pieces)
   1 can (8 ounces) sliced water chestnuts, drained
1/4 cup cream cheese, softened
   2 tablespoons water
   2 tablespoons milk
1/2 teaspoon grated lemon peel
   1 tablespoon sliced almonds, toasted

Place asparagus and water chestnuts in a shallow microwave-safe dish; add 1/2 in. of water. Cover and microwave on high for 6-8 minutes or until asparagus is crisp-tender; drain and keep warm.

In a small microwave-safe bowl, combine the cream cheese, water, milk and lemon peel. Cover and microwave on high for 1 to 1-1/2 minutes or until heated through, stirring occasionally. Pour over asparagus mixture; sprinkle with almonds. **Yield:** 4 servings.

Cod Delight

(Pictured below)

Prep/Total Time: 10 min.

I used to bake cod in the oven, but the microwave gets it on the table sooner. When I serve this delicious main course to company, everyone likes it and requests the recipe right away. —Nancy Daugherty, Cortland, Ohio

✓ Uses less fat, sugar or salt. Includes Nutrition Facts and Diabetic Exchanges.

      1 pound cod fillets
  1/2 cup chopped tomatoes
  1/3 cup finely chopped onion
      2 tablespoons water
      2 tablespoons canola oil
4-1/2 teaspoons lemon juice
      1 teaspoon dried parsley flakes
  1/2 teaspoon minced garlic
  1/2 teaspoon minced fresh basil
  1/8 teaspoon salt
      1 teaspoon seafood seasoning

Place the cod fillets in a shallow microwave-safe dish. In a small bowl, combine the tomatoes, onion, water, oil, lemon juice, parsley, garlic, basil and salt; spoon over cod. Sprinkle with seafood seasoning. Cover and microwave on high for 6 minutes or until fish flakes easily with a fork. **Yield:** 4 servings.

Nutrition Facts: 1 serving equals 154 calories, 8 g fat (1 g saturated fat), 43 mg cholesterol, 304 mg sodium, 3 g carbohydrate, 1 g fiber, 18 g protein. **Diabetic Exchanges:** 3 very lean meat, 1 fat.

Cheese-Topped Meat Loaves

Cheese-Topped Meat Loaves

(Pictured above and on page 260)

Prep/Total Time: 20 min.

These tender, mini meat loaves are terrific when you're cooking for two. I found the recipe 20 years ago and have enjoyed it ever since. —Lois Kinneberg, Phoenix, Arizona

      1 egg
      2 tablespoons plus 1/3 cup picante sauce, *divided*
  1/4 cup old-fashioned oats
      1 teaspoon dried minced onion
  1/4 teaspoon chili powder
  1/8 teaspoon salt
  1/2 pound ground beef
  1/4 cup shredded cheddar cheese

In a small bowl, combine the egg, 2 tablespoons picante sauce, oats, onion, chili powder and salt. Crumble beef over mixture and mix well. Shape into two 4-in. x 2-in. loaves; place in a microwave-safe dish. Cover and microwave on high for 5-6 minutes or until a meat thermometer reads 160°.

Place the remaining picante sauce in a small microwave-safe bowl; cover and microwave on high for 30 seconds. Pour over meat loaves. Sprinkle with cheese; cover and microwave on high for 45 seconds or until cheese is melted. **Yield:** 2 servings.

Microwave Broccoli Chicken Bake

Prep/Total Time: 20 min.

Creamy and comforting, this meal-in-one casserole is guaranteed to satisfy hearty appetites. It came from a cookbook that my senior high school class compiled. —Leanna Johnston, Omaha, Nebraska

      1 cup uncooked instant rice
  1/2 cup butter

Cod Delight

1 package (10 ounces) frozen chopped broccoli, thawed
6 ounces process cheese (Velveeta), cubed
1/3 cup chopped onion
1/4 cup chopped celery
1/4 cup chopped green pepper
1/2 teaspoon garlic powder
1 can (10-3/4 ounces) condensed cream of mushroom soup, undiluted
2 cups cubed cooked chicken

Microwave rice according to package directions; set aside. Place butter in a microwave-safe 2-1/2-qt. dish; cover and microwave on high for 2 minutes or until melted. Add the broccoli, cheese, onion, celery, green pepper and garlic powder.

Cover and microwave on high for 2-4 minutes or until the vegetables are crisp-tender. Stir in the cream of mushroom soup, chicken and rice. Cover and microwave at 70% power for 2 minutes or until heated through. **Yield:** 4-6 servings.

Potato Chip Clusters

(Pictured below)

Prep: 15 min. + chilling

These sweet-and-salty goodies make for merry munching during holiday trips or parties. The candy clusters travel well in containers without melting or getting soft.
—Donna Brockett, Kingfisher, Oklahoma

9 squares (1 ounce *each*) white baking chocolate
2 cups crushed potato chips
1/2 cup chopped pecans

In a large microwave-safe bowl, melt white chocolate. Stir in potato chips and pecans. Drop by tablespoonfuls onto waxed paper-lined baking sheets. Refrigerate until set. **Yield:** about 3 dozen.

Spicy Chocolate Bark

(Pictured below)

Prep: 15 min. + chilling

You'll warm hearts with this quick confection that has a bit of a peppery bite at the end. Our Test Kitchen home economists needed only four ingredients to stir up this tasty gift idea. Folks who like spicy foods just may put it at the top of their Christmas wish lists!

1 pound milk chocolate candy coating, chopped
1/2 cup chopped cashews, toasted
1/2 cup chopped pecans, toasted
1/2 teaspoon cayenne pepper

In a large microwave-safe bowl, melt candy coating. Stir in the nuts and cayenne. Spread onto a waxed paper-lined baking sheet. Refrigerate for 20 minutes. Break into small pieces. Store in an airtight container in the refrigerator. **Yield:** about 1-1/2 pounds.

Spicy Chocolate Bark
Potato Chip Clusters

Lemon-Pepper Vegetables

Nutty Salmon

Prep/Total Time: 15 min.

I've been making this fast salmon entree for 20 years. It couldn't be easier or more delicious, and I always get compliments...even from people who usually don't care for fish! —Vicki Ruiz, Twin Falls, Idaho

1/2 cup slivered almonds
1/4 cup butter, cubed
1/4 cup lemon juice
1/4 teaspoon salt
1/8 teaspoon pepper
1-1/2 pounds salmon fillets

Place almonds in a small microwave-safe bowl; add butter. Cover and microwave on high for 3-4 minutes or until almonds are browned, stirring twice. Add lemon juice, salt and pepper.

Place the salmon in an 8-in. square microwave-safe dish; top with almond mixture. Cover and microwave on high for 5-7 minutes or until fish flakes easily with a fork. Let stand for 5 minutes before serving. **Yield:** 4 servings.

Lemon-Pepper Vegetables

(Pictured above)

Prep/Total Time: 20 min.

Our Test Kitchen home economists tossed together this mildly seasoned, fresh-tasting side dish that's sure to brighten up any dinner table.

✓ Uses less fat, sugar or salt. Includes Nutrition Facts and Diabetic Exchanges.

1 pound fresh green beans, trimmed and cut into 2-inch pieces
2 tablespoons water
1 small yellow summer squash, cut into 1/2-inch slices
1 cup halved cherry tomatoes
2 tablespoons butter
3/4 teaspoon lemon-pepper seasoning
1/4 teaspoon Italian seasoning

In a large microwave-safe bowl, combine green beans and water. Cover and microwave on high for 5-6 minutes or until crisp-tender.

Stir in squash. Cover and microwave on high for 2 minutes. Add tomatoes. Cover and cook 30 seconds longer or until heated through; drain. Gently stir in the butter and seasonings. **Yield:** 6 servings.

Nutrition Facts: 2/3 cup (prepared with reduced-fat butter) equals 49 calories, 2 g fat (1 g saturated fat), 7 mg cholesterol, 88 mg sodium, 7 g carbohydrate, 3 g fiber, 2 g protein. **Diabetic Exchanges:** 1 vegetable, 1/2 fat.

Tangy Meat Sauce

(Pictured below)

Prep/Total Time: 25 min.

This is the best meat sauce I've ever tried. It's economical, timely and absolutely scrumptious! I often make batches for new moms because it can be kept in the freezer for future meals. —Adalia Schweitzer Hamilton, Ontario

1/2 pound lean ground beef
1/2 cup chopped onion
1/2 cup chopped green pepper
1/2 teaspoon minced garlic
1 can (15 ounces) tomato sauce
1 can (6 ounces) tomato paste

Tangy Meat Sauce

1 tablespoon sugar
1 tablespoon red wine vinegar
1/2 teaspoon salt
1/2 teaspoon dried basil
1/4 teaspoon dried oregano
Hot cooked spaghetti

Crumble beef into a 2-qt. microwave-safe dish. Add the onion, green pepper and garlic; mix well. Cover and microwave on high for 5-6 minutes or until meat is no longer pink and vegetables are tender, stirring frequently; drain.

Stir in the tomato sauce, tomato paste, sugar, vinegar, salt, basil and oregano. Cover and microwave at 70% power for 6-8 minutes or until heated through, stirring once. Serve over spaghetti. **Yield:** 3 cups.

Shrimp-Stuffed Sole

Prep/Total Time: 15 min.

If you like stuffed fish, you'll want to keep this recipe on hand. It's a breeze to assemble and cooks in just a few minutes in the microwave. —Robert Bishop
Lexington, Kentucky

4 sole fillets, halved lengthwise
1 tablespoon lemon juice
1/8 teaspoon onion salt *or* onion powder
1/4 cup butter, melted, *divided*
1 can (6 ounces) small shrimp, rinsed and drained
1/3 cup milk
1/4 cup finely chopped celery
2 teaspoons minced fresh parsley
1 cup cubed bread, toasted
Dash paprika

Sprinkle sole with lemon juice and onion salt; set aside. Pour 2 tablespoons butter into an 8-in. square microwave-safe dish. Add shrimp, milk, celery and parsley. Cover and microwave on high for 1 to 1-1/2 minutes or until celery is tender. Stir in bread.

Spoon shrimp mixture onto fillets. Starting with a short side, roll up each and secure with toothpicks. Place in a greased shallow microwave-safe dish. Brush with remaining butter; sprinkle with paprika.

Cover and microwave on high for 4-6 minutes or until fish flakes easily with a fork. Let stand for 5 minutes. Discard toothpicks. **Yield:** 4 servings.

Caramel Apple Dip

Prep/Total Time: 15 min.

This warm caramel dip is so simple and yummy. People always think I slaved over the stove to prepare it and are amazed to find that I made it in the microwave. —Becky Heiner, West Valley City, Utah

1 package (14 ounces) caramels
20 large marshmallows
1/2 cup butter, melted
1/3 cup heavy whipping cream
Apple slices

Chicken Enchilada Dip

Place caramels in a microwave-safe bowl. Microwave, uncovered, on high for 1 minute. Add marshmallows; microwave for 1 minute or until marshmallows are melted, stirring occasionally. Whisk in butter and cream until combined. Serve with apple slices. Refrigerate leftovers. **Yield:** 2-1/2 cups.

Chicken Enchilada Dip

(Pictured above)

Prep/Total Time: 20 min.

A friend of mine brought this appetizer to our house for a dinner party. Everyone loved the zesty, cheesy dip so much that no one was hungry for supper! He graciously shared the recipe, and I've served it many times, always with rave reviews. —Leah Davis, Morrow, Ohio

2 cups shredded cooked chicken
1 can (10-3/4 ounces) condensed cream of chicken soup, undiluted
1 cup (4 ounces) shredded cheddar cheese
1 can (5 ounces) evaporated milk
1/2 cup chopped celery
1/3 cup finely chopped onion
1 can (4 ounces) chopped green chilies
1 envelope taco seasoning
Tortilla chips

In a 2-qt. microwave-safe dish, combine the first eight ingredients. Microwave, uncovered, on high for 4-5 minutes; stir. Microwave, uncovered, 3-4 minutes longer or until heated through. Serve with tortilla chips. **Yield:** 3 cups.

Microwave Potato Salad

(Pictured below)

Prep: 20 min. + chilling

Microwaving potatoes for this tasty salad is a handy time-saver...and keeps your stove from heating up your kitchen on hot days. I changed the original recipe by adding roasted peppers and olives. Chop your ingredients while the potatoes cook, and it's ready to chill in minutes!
—*Bonnie Carelli, Charlton Heights, West Virginia*

- 7 cups cubed red potatoes (about 2 pounds)
- 1 cup water
- 1-1/2 cups (6 ounces) shredded sharp cheddar cheese
- 1 cup mayonnaise
- 4 hard-cooked eggs, chopped
- 3/4 cup pimiento-stuffed olives, halved
- 3/4 cup chopped roasted sweet red peppers
- 1/2 cup sliced green onions
- 1/2 teaspoon pepper

Place the potatoes in a shallow 2-qt. microwave-safe dish; add water. Cover and microwave on high for 9-11 minutes or until tender, stirring once. Drain and rinse in cold water.

In a large bowl, combine the remaining ingredients. Add potatoes and gently toss to coat. Cover and refrigerate for at least 1 hour before serving. **Yield:** 10 servings.

Chicken in a Hurry

Chicken in a Hurry

(Pictured above)

Prep: 20 min. **Cook:** 10 min.

I cook meat and veggies in my microwave all the time, but these stuffed chicken breasts filled with green chilies and cheese are a stress-free favorite. —*Barbara Frasier Fyffe, Alabama*

- 4 boneless skinless chicken breast halves (6 ounces *each*)
- 3 tablespoons butter, softened
- 3 tablespoons sharp American cheese spread
- 2 tablespoons chopped green chilies
- 2 teaspoons dried minced onion
- 1/4 teaspoon salt
- 1/4 cup butter, melted
- 1 cup seasoned bread crumbs

Flatten chicken to 1/4-in. thickness. In a small bowl, combine the butter, cheese spread, chilies, onion and salt. Spread 2 tablespoons on each chicken breast half; roll up and secure with toothpicks. Place butter and bread crumbs in separate shallow bowls. Dip chicken rolls in butter, then coat with crumbs.

Place in a greased 8-in. square microwave-safe dish. Cover and microwave on high for 10 minutes or until chicken juices run clear. Discard toothpicks. **Yield:** 4 servings.

Garden-Style Beef Lasagna

Prep: 25 min. **Cook:** 30 min. + standing

This fabulous, classic dish uses no-cook noodles. People who have tried the lasagna rave about it and ask me for the recipe. They're always surprised that it wasn't baked in the oven. —*Micaela Miller, Corinth, Texas*

Microwave Potato Salad

1-1/2 pounds lean ground beef
3/4 cup chopped onion
1 teaspoon minced garlic
1-1/2 cups garden-style pasta sauce
1 can (15 ounces) tomato sauce
2 tablespoons dried parsley flakes, *divided*
1 teaspoon dried oregano
2 cups (16 ounces) small-curd cottage cheese
1/2 cup grated Parmesan cheese, *divided*
1 egg
1 teaspoon dried basil
6 no-cook lasagna noodles
2 cups (8 ounces) shredded part-skim
mozzarella cheese, *divided*

Crumble the ground beef into a microwave-safe dish. Add the onion and garlic; mix well. Cover and microwave on high for 3 minutes; stir. Cook 2-3 minutes longer or until the meat is no longer pink. Stir in garden-style pasta sauce, tomato sauce, 1 tablespoon parsley and oregano; cover and microwave for 2 minutes or until heated through. Set aside.

Combine cottage cheese, 1/4 cup Parmesan cheese, egg, basil and remaining parsley. Spread 1-1/3 cups meat sauce in a greased microwave-safe 11-in. x 7-in. x 2-in. baking dish. Layer with three noodles, 1 cup cheese mixture and 1/2 cup mozzarella cheese. Repeat layers. Top with remaining meat sauce.

Cover loosely and microwave at 50% power for 15-18 minutes or until noodles are tender. Sprinkle with remaining mozzarella and Parmesan. Microwave, uncovered, 5 minutes longer or until cheese is melted. Let stand for 15 minutes. **Yield:** 6-8 servings.

Fruit and Caramel Brie

(Pictured below)

Prep/Total Time: 15 min.

I'm a stay-at-home mother with two boys, and I enjoy cooking, especially appetizers. It must run in the family—my mom served appetizers and desserts exclusively for several Christmas Eve celebrations! This sweet-and-savory Brie recipe is particularly easy to put together.
—Tracy Schuhmacher, Penfield, New York

1 round (8 ounces) Brie cheese, rind removed
1/3 cup caramel ice cream topping
1/4 cup dried cranberries
1/4 cup chopped dried apples
1/4 cup chopped walnuts
1 loaf (1 pound) French bread baguette, sliced
and toasted

Place Brie in a microwave-safe bowl. In a small bowl, combine the caramel topping, cranberries, apples and walnuts. Spread over Brie.

Microwave, uncovered, on high for 60-90 seconds or until cheese is heated through and slightly melted. Serve with toasted baguette slices. **Yield:** 8 servings.

Fruit and Caramel Brie

Chapter 19

☉ *Swift Snacks & Easy Appetizers*

WHO HAS TIME to assemble taste-tempting and impressive hors d'oeuvres for special occasions...or to fix wholesome, satisfying snacks when hunger hits before dinner? You do!

Your guests will be thrilled when you offer appetizers such as Slow Cooker Mexican Dip, Olive Bruschetta and Shrimp Tartlets. And any time the kids crave something after school, they'll love Peanut Butter Pinwheels, Cheese Puffs and Flavored Oyster Crackers.

All of these mouth-watering munchies are quick to fix. So whether you're serving an elegant holiday dinner, hosting a Super Bowl bash or just spending time at home with family, you'll want to look right here.

QUICK BITES. Jalapeno Cheese Spread and Bacon Pinwheels (recipes on p. 276).

Tomato Bacon Cups

Tomato Bacon Cups

(Pictured above)

Prep: 20 min. **Bake:** 10 min. per batch

These savory biscuits made with convenient refrigerated dough have a flavorful tomato and bacon filling. I first sampled them at a friend's house one Thanksgiving and just had to get the recipe. I've whipped up batches of the rich, cheesy bites for special events and gatherings ever since, and they always disappear fast. —Paige English
Portland, Oregon

   1 small tomato, finely chopped
1/2 cup mayonnaise
1/2 cup real bacon bits
1/2 cup shredded Swiss cheese
   1 small onion, finely chopped
   1 teaspoon dried basil
   1 tube (12 ounces) refrigerated buttermilk
      biscuits, separated into 10 biscuits

In a small bowl, combine the tomato, mayonnaise, bacon, cheese, onion and basil; set aside. Split each biscuit into three layers; press each layer into an ungreased miniature muffin cup.

  Spoon the tomato mixture into the miniature muffin cups. Bake at 450° for 8-10 minutes or until golden brown. Serve warm. **Yield:** 2-1/2 dozen.

Barbecue Wings

Prep/Total Time: 30 min.

Growing up near Buffalo, New York, I was familiar with the famous buffalo wing and decided to try my hand at creating my own recipe. Spicy and sweet with a hint of celery, these wings always go fast when I take them to parties. Serve them with carrots, celery and blue cheese dressing for dipping, and you can't go wrong!
—Sara Yarrington, Salem, New Hampshire

Oil for deep-fat frying
   1 package (40 ounces) chicken wingettes,
      thawed
1/2 cup barbecue sauce
   1 tablespoon butter
   1 teaspoon celery seed
   1 teaspoon hot pepper sauce

In an electric skillet or deep-fat fryer, heat oil to 375°. Fry chicken wings, a few at a time, for 8 minutes or until golden brown and juices run clear, turning occasionally. Drain on paper towels.

  In a small microwave-safe bowl, combine the barbecue sauce, butter, celery seed and hot pepper sauce. Cover and microwave on high for 1 minute or until heated through. Place the chicken wings in a large bowl; add sauce and toss to coat. **Yield:** 6 servings.

Spinach Dip in Red Cabbage

(Pictured below)

Prep/Total Time: 15 min.

A hollowed-out cabbage makes a bright, eye-catching serving dish for this tangy spinach dip. I found the recipe in a cookbook of easy appetizers, and I receive many compliments when I serve it on a platter full of colorful veggies.
—Patricia Johnson, Kingfield, Maine

✓ Uses less fat, sugar or salt. Includes Nutrition Facts and Diabetic Exchanges.

    1 large head red cabbage
    1 package (10 ounces) frozen chopped
      spinach, thawed and squeezed dry
    1 cup (8 ounces) sour cream
    1 cup mayonnaise
  1/2 cup chopped green onions
  1/2 cup minced fresh parsley
    2 teaspoons lemon juice
  1/2 teaspoon dill weed
Assorted fresh vegetables

Gently peel back outer leaves of cabbage. Slice 1/2 in. from bottom of cabbage so it sits flat. Cut a 3-in. circle in the top of the cabbage; hollow out a third of the cabbage to form a bowl (save removed cabbage for another use).

In a large bowl, combine the spinach, sour cream, mayonnaise, onions, parsley, lemon juice and dill. Spoon into cabbage bowl just before serving. Serve with vegetables. **Yield:** 3 cups.

Nutrition Facts: 2 tablespoons (prepared with reduced-fat sour cream and fat-free mayonnaise) equals 38 calories, 1 g fat (1 g saturated fat), 4 mg cholesterol, 106 mg sodium, 6 g carbohydrate, 2 g fiber, 2 g protein. **Diabetic Exchange:** 1 vegetable.

Cran-Apple Salsa

Spinach Dip in Red Cabbage

Cran-Apple Salsa

(Pictured above)

Prep/Total Time: 15 min.

Here's a festive twist on traditional holiday cranberry relish. This salsa packs a sweet-tart blend of fresh flavors and goes together in moments. Plus, the color is beautiful! We think it's the perfect snack for the Christmas season.
—Jody Bauer, Balaton, Minnesota

✓ Uses less fat, sugar or salt. Includes Nutrition Facts and Diabetic Exchanges.

    1 package (12 ounces) fresh *or* frozen
      cranberries, thawed
    3 medium apples, cut into wedges
    1 medium sweet red pepper, cut into pieces
    1 small red onion, chopped
  1/2 cup sugar
  1/3 cup unsweetened apple juice
    3 tablespoons minced fresh cilantro
    2 tablespoons chopped jalapeno pepper
    1 teaspoon grated lime peel
Tortilla chips

In a food processor, process the cranberries, apples, red pepper and onion in batches until coarsely pureed. Transfer to a serving bowl; stir in the sugar, apple juice, cilantro, jalapeno and lime peel. Refrigerate until serving. Serve with tortilla chips. **Yield:** 5 cups.

Editor's Note: When cutting or seeding hot peppers, use rubber or plastic gloves to protect your hands. Avoid touching your face.

Nutrition Facts: 1/4 cup (calculated without chips) equals 45 calories, trace fat (trace saturated fat), 0 cholesterol, 1 mg sodium, 12 g carbohydrate, 1 g fiber, trace protein. **Diabetic Exchange:** 1 fruit.

Calzone Pinwheels

(Pictured below)

Prep/Total Time: 30 min.

Once you try these mini calzone spirals, you may never go back to traditional ones. Not only do these pretty bites take advantage of convenient refrigerator crescent rolls, but they can be made ahead and popped in the oven right before guests arrive. No one can stop after eating just one!

—*Lisa K. Smith, Bryan, Ohio*

  1/2 cup ricotta cheese
     1 teaspoon Italian seasoning
  1/4 teaspoon salt
  1/2 cup shredded part-skim mozzarella cheese
  1/2 cup diced pepperoni
  1/4 cup grated Parmesan cheese
  1/4 cup chopped fresh mushrooms
  1/4 cup finely chopped green pepper
     2 tablespoons finely chopped onion
     1 package (8 ounces) refrigerated crescent rolls
     1 jar (14 ounces) pizza sauce, warmed

In a small bowl, combine the ricotta, Italian seasoning and salt. Stir in the mozzarella, pepperoni, Parmesan, mushrooms, green pepper and onion. Separate crescent dough into four rectangles; seal perforations.

Spread the cheese mixture over each rectangle to within 1/4 in. of edges. Roll up jelly-roll style, starting with a short side; pinch the seams to seal. Cut each into four slices.

Place cut side down on greased baking sheets. Bake at 375° for 10-15 minutes or until golden brown. Serve warm with pizza sauce. Refrigerate leftovers. **Yield:** 16 appetizers.

Calzone Pinwheels

Chicken Chili Nachos

Prep/Total Time: 25 min.

Guests will huddle around the buffet table at halftime when you put out heaping plates of these spicy chicken nachos.

—*Karen Horning, Rockford, Illinois*

     1 pound boneless skinless chicken breasts, cubed
     1 can (10 ounces) diced tomatoes and green chilies, undrained
     1 can (16 ounces) kidney beans, rinsed and drained
     1 can (15-1/2 ounces) chili beans, undrained
     1 teaspoon paprika
     1 teaspoon ground cumin
  1/2 teaspoon cayenne pepper
     1 package (13-1/2 ounces) tortilla chips
1-1/2 cups (6 ounces) shredded Mexican cheese blend, *divided*

In a large skillet coated with nonstick cooking spray, saute chicken until no longer pink. Add tomatoes; cook over medium-high heat for 3 minutes or until tomato juice is reduced. Stir in beans, paprika, cumin and cayenne; cook for 5 minutes or until heated through.

Arrange the tortilla chips on two large microwave-safe plates; sprinkle each with 1/4 cup cheese. Top with chicken mixture and remaining cheese. Microwave, uncovered, on high for 25-30 seconds or until cheese is melted. **Yield:** 8 servings.

Barbecued Peanuts

Prep: 10 min. **Bake:** 25 min. + cooling

These zippy, coated peanuts are great for football parties, movie nights and even after-school snacks. I like to prepare them during the holidays to give as presents, too. For variety, try barbecue sauces of different flavors.

—*Abbey Boyle, Tampa, Florida*

  1/3 cup barbecue sauce
     2 tablespoons butter, melted
     1 teaspoon garlic powder
  1/4 to 1/2 teaspoon cayenne pepper
     1 jar (16 ounces) dry roasted peanuts

In a large bowl, combine sauce, butter, garlic powder and cayenne. Add peanuts; stir until evenly coated. Transfer to a greased 13-in. x 9-in. x 2-in. baking pan. Bake, uncovered, at 325° for 25-30 minutes, stirring every 10 minutes. Spread on waxed paper; cool completely. Store in an airtight container. **Yield:** 3 cups.

Sweet-Tooth Snacks

Have a cheesecake craving? Sandwich flavored cream cheese spread, such as strawberry, between two graham crackers. It tastes amazingly like the real thing!

—*Jan Schmid, Hibbing, Minnesota*

Baked Chicken Nachos

Baked Chicken Nachos

(Pictured above)

Prep: 20 min. **Bake:** 15 min.

Here's a colorful party appetizer that's delicious and so simple. Rotisserie (or leftover) chicken makes it quick, and the seasonings and splash of lime juice provide fantastic flavor. In fact, my husband likes these nachos so much that he often requests them for dinner. —Gail Cawsey
Fawnskin, California

    2 medium sweet red peppers, diced
    1 medium green pepper, diced
    3 teaspoons vegetable oil, *divided*
    1 can (15 ounces) black beans, rinsed and drained
    1 teaspoon minced garlic
    1 teaspoon dried oregano
  1/4 teaspoon ground cumin
  1/2 pound cooked rotisserie chicken, shredded
4-1/2 teaspoons lime juice
  1/8 teaspoon salt
  1/8 teaspoon pepper
7-1/2 cups tortilla chips
    8 ounces pepper Jack cheese, shredded
  1/4 cup thinly sliced green onions
  1/2 cup minced fresh cilantro
    1 cup (8 ounces) sour cream
    2 to 3 teaspoons diced pickled jalapeno peppers, optional

In a skillet, saute peppers in 1-1/2 teaspoons oil for 3 minutes or until crisp-tender; transfer to a bowl. In the same skillet, saute beans, garlic, oregano and cumin in remaining oil for 3 minutes or until heated through.

Meanwhile, combine chicken, lime juice, salt and pepper. In a greased 13-in. x 9-in. x 2-in. baking dish, layer half of the tortilla chips, pepper mixture, bean mixture, chicken mixture, cheese, onions and cilantro. Repeat layers. Bake, uncovered, at 350° for 15-20 minutes or until heated through. Serve with sour cream and jalapenos if desired. **Yield:** 16 servings.

Jalapeno Cheese Spread
Bacon Pinwheels

Jalapeno Cheese Spread

(Pictured above and on page 270)

Prep/Total Time: 10 min.

I keep the ingredients for this wonderful cheese spread on hand so I can serve it anytime. The jalapenos give this appetizer a bit of a kick, and it's always a hit at parties.
—Patricia Kitts, Dickinson, Texas

✓ Uses less fat, sugar or salt. Includes Nutrition Facts and Diabetic Exchanges.

    1 package (8 ounces) cream cheese, softened
    3 tablespoons canned jalapeno slices, drained and chopped
    3 tablespoons chopped pecans, toasted
Bagel chips *or* **assorted crackers**

Place the block of cream cheese on a serving plate; sprinkle the cream cheese with the jalapenos and toasted pecans. Serve cheese spread with bagel chips or assorted crackers. **Yield:** 8 servings.

Nutrition Facts: 2 tablespoons spread (prepared with reduced-fat cream cheese; calculated without the bagel chips or crackers) equals 91 calories, 8 g fat (4 g saturated fat), 20 mg cholesterol, 195 mg sodium, 2 g carbohydrate, trace fiber, 3 g protein. **Diabetic Exchange:** 1-1/2 fat.

Bacon Pinwheels

(Pictured above and on page 271)

Prep/Total Time: 30 min.

With a rich cream cheese, mushroom and bacon filling, these golden rolls are a mouth-watering addition to any buffet table. *—Janne Rowe, Wichita, Kansas*

    6 bacon strips, diced
    6 ounces cream cheese, softened
1/2 cup mayonnaise
    1 can (4 ounces) mushroom stems and pieces, drained
1/2 teaspoon garlic powder
    1 tube (8 ounces) refrigerated crescent rolls

In a large skillet, cook bacon over medium heat until crisp. Using a slotted spoon, remove to paper towels to drain. In a small mixing bowl, beat cream cheese and mayonnaise. Add the mushrooms, garlic powder and bacon.

Separate crescent dough into four rectangles; seal perforations. Spread cream cheese mixture over each rectangle to within 1/4 in. of edges. Roll up jelly-roll style, starting with a short side; pinch seams to seal. Cut each into six slices.

Place slices cut side down on greased baking sheets. Bake at 375° for 10-12 minutes or until golden brown. Serve warm. Refrigerate leftovers. **Yield:** 2 dozen.

Mini Spinach Frittatas

(Pictured below)

Prep/Total Time: 30 min.

These mini frittatas are a cinch to make, taste delicious and always attract attention. They're a must if you're tired of the same old party fare! You can double the recipe for a crowd and freeze the bites for added convenience.
—Nancy Statkevicus, Tucson, Arizona

 1 cup ricotta cheese
3/4 cup grated Parmesan cheese
2/3 cup chopped fresh mushrooms
 1 package (10 ounces) frozen chopped
  spinach, thawed and squeezed dry
 1 egg
1/2 teaspoon dried oregano
1/4 teaspoon salt
1/4 teaspoon pepper
 24 slices pepperoni

In a small bowl, combine the first eight ingredients. Place a slice of pepperoni in each of 24 greased miniature muffin cups. Fill the muffin cups three-fourths full with the cheese mixture.
 Bake at 375° for 20-25 minutes or until a toothpick comes out clean. Carefully run a knife around edges of muffin cups to loosen. Serve warm. **Yield:** 2 dozen.

Three-Pepper Veggie Tray

(Pictured above right)

Prep/Total Time: 25 min.

In no time at all, you can put together this colorful platter of crisp, fresh vegetables from our home economists. Instead of offering veggie dip, serve a trio of salad dressings in dishes of varying heights for added interest.

Mini Spinach Frittatas

Three-Pepper Veggie Tray

 2 pints cherry tomatoes
 1 package (16 ounces) fresh baby carrots
 2 *each* medium green, sweet red and yellow
  peppers, cut into strips
 2 medium bunches broccoli, cut into florets
 2 medium cucumbers, sliced
Assorted salad dressings

Arrange vegetables on a serving platter. Serve with dressings. **Yield:** 24 servings.

1-2-3 Snack Mix

Prep/Total Time: 5 min.

This colorful, kid-friendly trail mix provides protein and energy by the handful on action-packed summer days. It's great for long car trips, too! The recipe really is as quick as one-two-three because it requires just a trio of ingredients—fun fish-shaped crackers, tangy dried cranberries and crunchy cashews. *—Sue Sherman, Toledo, Ohio*

 1 package (7.2 ounces) miniature cheddar
  cheese fish-shaped crackers
 1 package (6 ounces) dried cranberries
1-1/4 cups salted cashews

In a large bowl, combine the fish-shaped crackers, dried cranberries and cashews. Store in an airtight container. **Yield:** 6 cups.

medium heat until golden brown. Drain on paper towels. Serve warm with marinara sauce if desired. **Yield:** 12 servings.

Cheese Puffs

(Pictured below)

Prep: 15 min. **Bake:** 15 min. per batch

I found this recipe in one of my mother's old cookbooks and updated the flavor by adding cayenne and mustard. Perfect for busy days, these golden puffs go together in minutes and disappear just as quickly at parties.
—*Jamie Wetter, Boscobel, Wisconsin*

    1 cup water
    2 tablespoons butter
  1/2 teaspoon salt
  1/8 teaspoon cayenne pepper
    1 cup all-purpose flour
    4 eggs
1-1/4 cups shredded Gruyere *or* Swiss cheese
    1 tablespoon Dijon mustard
  1/4 cup grated Parmesan cheese

In a large saucepan, bring water, butter, salt and cayenne to a boil. Add flour all at once and stir until a smooth ball forms. Remove from the heat. Immediately transfer to a mixing bowl. Add eggs, one at a time, beating well after each addition. Continue beating until mixture is smooth and shiny. Stir in Gruyere and mustard.

Drop by rounded teaspoonfuls 2 in. apart onto greased baking sheets. Sprinkle with Parmesan cheese. Bake at 425° for 15-20 minutes or until golden brown. Serve warm or cold. **Yield:** 4 dozen.

Cheese Puffs

Rosemary Cheese Patties

(Pictured above)

Prep/Total Time: 25 min.

We're a family that loves snacks, and I combined some of our favorite ingredients in this convenient, simple and delicious recipe. Great for entertaining, it can be prepared ahead of time and browned just before your guests arrive. It's also easy to double for a crowd.
—*Judy Armstrong, Prairieville, Louisiana*

    1 package (8 ounces) cream cheese, softened
    1 cup grated Parmesan cheese
  3/4 cup seasoned bread crumbs, *divided*
    2 eggs
1-1/2 to 2 teaspoons minced fresh rosemary
1-1/2 teaspoons minced garlic
  1/8 to 1/4 teaspoon cayenne pepper
    2 tablespoons olive oil
Marinara sauce, warmed, optional

In a small mixing bowl, combine the cream cheese, Parmesan cheese, 1/4 cup bread crumbs, eggs, rosemary, garlic and cayenne. Place the remaining crumbs in a shallow bowl. Shape heaping tablespoonfuls of cheese mixture into 1-1/2-in. balls; flatten to 1/2-in. thickness. Coat with bread crumbs.

In a large skillet, brown patties in oil in batches over

Rosemary Cheese Patties

Three-Bean Salsa

Prep: 25 min. + chilling

Here's a simple recipe for a big batch of fabulous, chunky salsa. It's fast, fresh, low in fat and high in fiber. The jalapenos add a nice kick, but you could leave those out if you and your family prefer salsa that's on the milder side.
—Regina Gutierrez, San Antonio, Texas

✓ Uses less fat, sugar or salt. Includes Nutrition Facts and Diabetic Exchanges.

- 1 can (16 ounces) kidney beans, rinsed and drained
- 1 can (15-1/4 ounces) whole kernel corn, drained
- 1 can (15 ounces) garbanzo beans *or* chickpeas, rinsed and drained
- 1 can (15 ounces) black beans, rinsed and drained
- 2 cups chopped fresh tomatoes
- 2 to 3 jalapeno peppers, seeded and chopped
- 1/4 cup chopped green onions
- 1/4 cup lime juice
- 2 tablespoons minced fresh cilantro
- 2 teaspoons ground cumin
- 1 teaspoon salt
- 1/4 teaspoon pepper
Tortilla chips

In a large bowl, combine the first 12 ingredients; toss to coat. Chill for at least 30 minutes before serving. Serve with tortilla chips. Refrigerate leftovers. **Yield:** 8 cups.

Editor's Note: When cutting or seeding hot peppers, use rubber or plastic gloves to protect your hands. Avoid touching your face.

Nutrition Facts: 1/4 cup (calculated without chips) equals 97 calories, 1 g fat (trace saturated fat), 0 cholesterol, 354 mg sodium, 17 g carbohydrate, 4 g fiber, 5 g protein. **Diabetic Exchange:** 1 starch.

Nutty Fruit 'n' Cheese Tray

(Pictured above right)

Prep/Total Time: 30 min.

Our home economists used packaged cheese cubes to speed up this lovely display. To save even more time, add plain nuts instead of the Candied Walnuts (recipe at right).

- 1 fresh pineapple
- 3 cups (12 ounces) cubed Colby-Monterey Jack cheese
- 3 cups (12 ounces) cubed cheddar cheese
- 3 cups (12 ounces) cubed Swiss cheese
- 3 cups (12 ounces) cubed pepper Jack cheese
- 1 pound green grapes
- 1 pound seedless red grapes
- 1 medium honeydew, peeled, seeded and cubed
- 1 medium cantaloupe, peeled, seeded and cubed

Nutty Fruit 'n' Cheese Tray Candied Walnuts

- 1 pound fresh strawberries
Candied Walnuts, optional

Slice pineapple in half horizontally. Cut top half into 1-in. wedges, leaving intact. Transfer to a platter. Peel and cube remaining pineapple. Arrange cheeses, fruits and nuts, if desired, on platter. **Yield:** 24 servings.

Candied Walnuts

(Pictured above)

Prep/Total Time: 20 min.

Ordinary nuts become a taste sensation with this easy stovetop recipe from our Test Kitchen. They're terrific on a Nutty Fruit 'n' Cheese Tray (recipe at left).

- 1/2 cup packed brown sugar
- 2 tablespoons vegetable oil
- 2 tablespoons balsamic vinegar
- 1/8 teaspoon pepper
- 2 cups walnut halves

In a large skillet, combine the brown sugar, oil, vinegar and pepper. Cook and stir over medium heat until blended. Add walnuts; cook and stir 6-8 minutes longer or until well coated and sugar is melted. Spread on foil to cool. Store in an airtight container. **Yield:** 2 cups.

Bread Bowl Seafood Dip

(Pictured below)

Prep: 15 min. **Bake:** 45 min.

Every Christmas Eve, our family shares a special hors d'oeuvres supper, and this seafood dip is a menu staple. I got the recipe from a friend who made it for my daughter's wedding shower. The appetizer is so rich, elegant and creamy—and a huge hit at parties any time of year.
—Terry Flewelling, Lacombe, Alberta

```
    1 package (8 ounces) cream cheese, softened
  1/2 cup mayonnaise
1-1/2 teaspoons Dijon mustard
    1 can (6 ounces) small shrimp, rinsed and
      drained
    1 can (6 ounces) crabmeat, drained, flaked
      and cartilage removed
  2/3 cup shredded Monterey Jack cheese, divided
  1/2 cup chopped green onions
    1 round loaf (1 pound) sourdough bread
```
Assorted fresh vegetables

In a mixing bowl, beat the cream cheese, mayonnaise and mustard. Stir in the shrimp, crab, 1/3 cup Monterey Jack cheese and onions. Cut the top fourth off the loaf of bread; carefully hollow out bottom, leaving a 1/2-in. shell. Cube removed bread; set aside.

Spoon the seafood mixture into the bread shell. Sprinkle mixture with remaining Monterey Jack cheese. Wrap tightly in heavy-duty foil and place on a baking sheet.

Sugar 'n' Spice Nuts

Bake at 350° for 25 minutes. Unwrap; bake 20-25 minutes longer or until cheese is melted and dip is heated through. Serve with vegetables and reserved bread cubes. **Yield:** 2-1/4 cups.

Sugar 'n' Spice Nuts

(Pictured above)

Prep/Total Time: 30 min.

My daughters…grandkids…everyone looks forward to this mouth-watering mix of crunchy nuts and dried cranberries when they're home for the holidays. Tucked in colorful tins, this snack also makes a handy last-minute gift for busy hostesses or drop-in visitors. —Joan Klinefelter
Utica, Illinois

```
1/4 cup packed brown sugar
1/2 teaspoon ground cinnamon
1/4 teaspoon cayenne pepper
  1 egg white
  1 cup salted cashews
  1 cup pecan halves
  1 cup dry roasted peanuts
1/2 cup dried cranberries
```

In a small bowl, combine the brown sugar, cinnamon and cayenne; set aside. In a large bowl, whisk the egg white; add nuts and cranberries. Sprinkle with sugar mixture and toss to coat. Spread in a single layer on a greased baking sheet.

Bake at 300° for 18-20 minutes or until golden brown, stirring once. Cool before storing in an airtight container. **Yield:** 3-1/2 cups.

Bread Bowl Seafood Dip

Coconut Fried Shrimp

Prep/Total Time: 20 min.

For a tropical taste company will find delightful, serve this crunchy coconut-coated shrimp with a sweet sauce. It's an impressive appetizer and can even be served as a main course. —Debbi Barate, Seward, Pennsylvania

  1 pound uncooked jumbo shrimp (about 12), peeled and deveined
1/4 cup all-purpose flour
  2 egg whites, lightly beaten
1-1/3 cups flaked coconut
Oil for deep-fat frying
  1 jar (12 ounces) pineapple preserves
  1 tablespoon frozen nonalcoholic pina colada mix, thawed

Starting with the tail, make a slit down the inner curve of each shrimp; press lightly to flatten. In three separate shallow bowls, place the flour, egg whites and coconut. Coat the shrimp with flour; dip into egg whites, then coat with the coconut.

In an electric skillet or deep-fat fryer, heat oil to 375°. Fry shrimp, a few at a time, for 1 to 1-1/2 minutes on each side or until golden brown. Drain on paper towels.

In a small bowl, combine preserves and pina colada mix. Serve with shrimp. **Yield:** 4 servings.

Fruit and Cheese Kabobs

Prep/Total Time: 20 min.

Our Test Kitchen staff, many of whom are busy mothers themselves, came up with this fresh and fruity snack idea. The summery skewers are easy to make ahead and carry to the ballpark, beach or playing field. Plus, kids will love dipping them in the cinnamon-spiced yogurt.

☑ Uses less fat, sugar or salt. Includes Nutrition Facts and Diabetic Exchanges.

  1 pint fresh strawberries, halved
1-1/2 cups green grapes
  1 package (8 ounces) cheddar and Monterey Jack cheese cubes
  1 cup (8 ounces) vanilla yogurt
1/2 cup sour cream
  2 tablespoons honey
1/2 teaspoon ground cinnamon

On 12 wooden skewers, alternately thread the halved strawberries, grapes, cheddar cheese cubes and Monterey Jack cheese cubes.

For the dip, in a small bowl, combine the vanilla yogurt, sour cream, honey and cinnamon. Serve kabobs and dip immediately or refrigerate. **Yield:** 12 kabobs (1-1/2 cups dip).

Nutrition Facts: 2 kabobs with 1/4 cup dip (prepared with reduced-fat cheese, fat-free yogurt and reduced-fat sour cream) equals 233 calories, 10 g fat (7 g saturated fat), 34 mg cholesterol, 361 mg sodium, 26 g carbohydrate, 2 g fiber, 13 g protein. **Diabetic Exchanges:** 1-1/2 lean meat, 1-1/2 fruit, 1 fat.

Grilled Jerk Chicken Wings

(Pictured below)

Prep/Total Time: 30 min.

I've been making this recipe for parties ever since I can remember. It's simple to fix, doesn't take a lot of ingredients or time and is always a favorite with my guests. You can change it up for different groups by varying the seasonings. —Caren Adams, Fontana, California

1/2 cup Caribbean jerk seasoning
  18 fresh chicken wingettes (2 to 3 pounds)
  2 cups honey barbecue sauce
1/3 cup packed brown sugar
  2 teaspoons prepared mustard
  1 teaspoon ground ginger

Coat grill rack with nonstick cooking spray before starting the grill. Place jerk seasoning in a large resealable plastic bag; add chicken wings, a few at a time, and shake to coat. In a small bowl, combine the barbecue sauce, brown sugar, mustard and ginger; set aside.

Grill chicken wings, covered, over medium heat for 12-16 minutes, turning occasionally. Brush with sauce. Grill, uncovered, 8-10 minutes longer or until juices run clear, basting and turning several times. **Yield:** 6 servings.

Editor's Note: Caribbean jerk seasoning may be found in the spice aisle of your grocery store.

Grilled Jerk Chicken Wings

Shrimp Tartlets

(Pictured below)

Prep/Total Time: 30 min.

These mini tart shells are filled with a cream cheese mixture, then topped off with seafood sauce and shrimp for a picture-perfect look and delightful taste. They make great appetizers and could even be served as a quick, light meal.
—Gina Hutchison, Smithville, Missouri

✓ Uses less fat, sugar or salt. Includes Nutrition Facts and Diabetic Exchanges.

    1 package (8 ounces) cream cheese, softened
1-1/2 teaspoons Worcestershire sauce
    1 to 2 teaspoons grated onion
    1 teaspoon garlic salt
  1/8 teaspoon lemon juice
    2 packages (2.1 ounces *each*) frozen miniature phyllo tart shells
  1/2 cup seafood sauce
   30 cooked medium shrimp, peeled and deveined

In a small mixing bowl, combine the first five ingredients. Spoon into tart shells. Top with seafood sauce and shrimp. Refrigerate until serving. **Yield:** 2-1/2 dozen.

Nutrition Facts: 3 tartlets (prepared with reduced-fat cream cheese) equals 149 calories, 8 g fat (3 g saturated fat), 48 mg cholesterol, 434 mg sodium, 11 g carbohydrate, trace fiber, 8 g protein. **Diabetic Exchanges:** 1-1/2 fat, 1 starch.

Shrimp Tartlets

Flavored Oyster Crackers

Prep/Total Time: 25 min.

Our Test Kitchen needed just four simple ingredients to create these crunchy bits you'll want to munch by the handful—or use as tasty toppers on soups and salads.

    2 packages (10 ounces *each*) oyster crackers
  1/2 cup vegetable oil
  1/4 cup grated Parmesan cheese
    1 envelope savory herb with garlic soup mix

Place the crackers in a large bowl. Combine the oil, Parmesan cheese and soup mix; pour over crackers and toss gently.

Transfer to two ungreased 15-in. x 10-in. x 1-in. baking pans. Bake at 350° for 5-7 minutes, stirring once. Cool. Store in an airtight container. **Yield:** 12 cups.

Slow Cooker Mexican Dip

Prep: 15 min. **Cook:** 1-1/2 hours

My husband and I love to entertain, and this irresistible, seven-ingredient dip is always a hit. It couldn't be much easier to prepare, and using our slow cooker leaves us free to visit with our guests. After all, that's the purpose of a party!
—Heather Courtney, Ames, Iowa

1-1/2 pounds ground beef
    1 pound bulk hot Italian sausage
    1 cup chopped onion
    1 package (8.8 ounces) ready-to-serve Spanish rice
    1 can (16 ounces) refried beans
    1 can (10 ounces) enchilada sauce
    1 pound process cheese (Velveeta), cubed
    1 package tortilla chip scoops

In a Dutch oven, cook the beef, sausage and onion over medium heat until meat is no longer pink; drain. Heat rice according to package directions.

In a 3-qt. slow cooker, combine the meat mixture, rice, beans, enchilada sauce and cheese. Cover and cook on low for 1-1/2 to 2 hours or until cheese is melted. Serve with tortilla scoops. **Yield:** 8 cups.

Yummy Guacamole

Prep/Total Time: 20 min.

I've been making this for years, and my family just loves it. It's a recipe I've been happy to stick with because it's so easy and never fails to please guacamole lovers. You may want to make a double batch since it goes fast! —Terri Kearns
Oklahoma City, Oklahoma

    2 medium ripe avocados, peeled and pitted
    3 tablespoons mayonnaise
    1 plum tomato, chopped
    1 jalapeno pepper, seeded and chopped
    2 tablespoons minced fresh cilantro
    1 tablespoon lemon juice

1/4 teaspoon salt
Corn chips

In a small bowl, mash the avocados and mayonnaise until smooth. Stir in the tomato, jalapeno, cilantro, lemon juice and salt. Serve with corn chips. **Yield:** 1-1/2 cups.

Editor's Note: When cutting or seeding hot peppers, use rubber or plastic gloves to protect your hands. Avoid touching your face.

Peanut Butter Pinwheels

Prep/Total Time: 5 min.

With four little ones, my time is limited. I came across this easy and tasty snack while searching on-line for wholesome munchies for children. The pinwheels are really quick to prepare and filling enough to hold the kids until dinner.
—Mary Haluch, Ludlow, Massachusetts

✓ Uses less fat, sugar or salt. Includes Nutrition Facts and Diabetic Exchanges.

 4 tablespoons creamy peanut butter
 2 flour tortillas (8 inches)
 2 teaspoons honey
 1/2 cup granola

Spread peanut butter over each tortilla; drizzle with honey and sprinkle with granola. Roll up; cut into slices. Serve immediately. **Yield:** 16 appetizers.

Nutrition Facts: 4 pinwheels (prepared with reduced-fat peanut butter and reduced-fat granola) equals 217 calories, 8 g fat (1 g saturated fat), 0 cholesterol, 247 mg sodium, 32 g carbohydrate, 2 g fiber, 8 g protein. **Diabetic Exchanges:** 2 starch, 1 lean meat.

Olive Bruschetta

Prep/Total Time: 30 min.

This colorful classic can be made several days ahead of time. I think it actually tastes better if prepared in advance so all the fresh flavors can blend together. It's best served at room temperature with a crusty loaf of toasted French bread or your favorite crackers. *—Linda Austin*
Lake Hopatcong, New Jersey

✓ Uses less fat, sugar or salt. Includes Nutrition Facts and Diabetic Exchanges.

 2 cups grape tomatoes, quartered
 2 celery ribs, chopped
 1/2 cup shredded carrot
 1/4 cup sliced ripe olives
 1/4 cup sliced pimiento-stuffed olives
 1/4 cup minced fresh flat-leaf parsley
 1/4 cup chopped red onion
 1 teaspoon minced garlic
 3 tablespoons olive oil
 2 tablespoons balsamic vinegar
 1/4 teaspoon salt
 1/8 teaspoon pepper

Garlic-Onion Cheese Spread

 1 loaf (1 pound) French bread baguette, sliced and toasted

In a large bowl, combine the first eight ingredients. In a small bowl, combine the oil, vinegar, salt and pepper; pour over vegetables and toss to coat. Serve on toasted baguette slices. **Yield:** 2-1/2 dozen.

Nutrition Facts: 2 appetizers equals 169 calories, 7 g fat (1 g saturated fat), 0 cholesterol, 296 mg sodium, 25 g carbohydrate, 2 g fiber, 3 g protein. **Diabetic Exchanges:** 1-1/2 starch, 1 fat.

Garlic-Onion Cheese Spread

(Pictured above)

Prep/Total Time: 10 min.

Whenever there's an event at church, my friends remind me to bring this cheese spread. Once you start eating it on crackers, it's hard to stop! The sweet and savory mixture is also delicious as a dip for fresh vegetables.
—Michelle DeFriez, Grand Blanc, Michigan

✓ Uses less fat, sugar or salt. Includes Nutrition Facts and Diabetic Exchanges.

 2 packages (8 ounces *each*) cream cheese, softened
 2 to 3 tablespoons apricot preserves
 3 green onions (green portion only), chopped
 3 tablespoons crumbled cooked bacon
 1/2 to 1 teaspoon minced garlic
Dash pepper
Assorted crackers

In a small mixing bowl, beat cream cheese and preserves until blended. Stir in the onions, bacon, garlic and pepper. Refrigerate until serving. Serve with crackers. **Yield:** 2-1/4 cups.

Nutrition Facts: 2 tablespoons (prepared with reduced-fat cream cheese) equals 44 calories, 3 g fat (2 g saturated fat), 10 mg cholesterol, 72 mg sodium, 2 g carbohydrate, trace fiber, 2 g protein. **Diabetic Exchange:** 1 fat.

Chapter 20

TOO BUSY for complicated, time-consuming cooking techniques? Follow the lead of our Test Kitchen home economists! They have all sorts of creative shortcuts and tips to speed up meal making—and you'll see a number of them right here.

Learn how to quickly whip up marvelous meringue...grill outdoors like an expert...bake special dinner rolls in a snap... create delightful desserts with pie fillings and cake mixes...and win raves with a bounty of fresh raspberries.

Every mini "class" in this chapter includes handy how-to photos and complete directions to make the process as easy as can be. In no time at all, you'll be cooking like a pro!

EASY ELEGANCE. Raspberry Butter Torte (p. 290).

Flank Steak Pinwheels

CREAM CHEESE SAUCE:
　1 package (3 ounces) cream cheese, softened
1/4 cup milk
　1 tablespoon butter
1/4 teaspoon pepper
1/2 cup crumbled blue cheese

Place bacon strips on a microwave-safe plate lined with microwave-safe paper towels. Cover with another paper towel; microwave on high for 2-3 minutes or until partially cooked.

Meanwhile, cut steak horizontally from a long side to within 1/2 in. of opposite side. Open meat so it lies flat; cover with plastic wrap. Flatten to 1/4-in. thickness.

Remove the plastic. Place the spinach over the steak to within 1 in. of the edges; top with the red peppers. With the grain of the meat going from left to right, roll up jelly-roll style. Wrap the bacon strips around the beef; secure with toothpicks. Slice beef across the grain between the bacon into eight slices.

Grill, covered, over medium heat for 5-7 minutes on each side or until meat reaches desired doneness (for medium-rare, a meat thermometer should read 145°; medium, 160°; well-done, 170°). Discard toothpicks.

In a small saucepan, combine the cream cheese, milk, butter and pepper. Cook and stir over low heat just until smooth (do not boil). Stir in blue cheese. Serve with pinwheels. **Yield:** 4 servings.

Editor's Note: This recipe was tested in a 1,100-watt microwave.

Grilling Like a Pro

CAN'T STAND the heat? Get out of the kitchen and into your backyard. On warm summer days, grilling is a fast, fun and easy way to cook. Instead of serving the usual burgers and hot dogs, wow family and friends with these delicious outdoor dishes.

In this section, the home economists in our Test Kitchen walk you through several grilling methods that result in fabulous alfresco fare such as stuffed pork chops, steak pinwheels and more.

Just follow the simple tips, handy step-by-step directions and how-to photos also provided here, and you'll be grilling like an expert all summer long.

Flank Steak Pinwheels

(Pictured above and on the cover)

Prep: 30 min. **Grill:** 10 min.

The key to these pretty pinwheels from our Test Kitchen lies in their butterfly treatment. Because the steaks are flattened, marinade isn't needed. Instead, they're stuffed with veggies, then draped with a cheese sauce.

　8 bacon strips
　1 beef flank steak (1-1/2 pounds)
　4 cups fresh baby spinach
　1 jar (7 ounces) roasted sweet red peppers, drained

Preparing Pinwheels

WHEN making Flank Steak Pinwheels (recipe below left), use the following technique:

Make a lengthwise cut horizontally through the steak to within 1/2 inch of the opposite side, without cutting through it. Open the meat so that it lies flat. Then flatten with a meat mallet as directed.

With the grain going left to right, roll up the stuffed steak jelly-roll style. Wrap bacon strips around the beef and secure with toothpicks.

Cut across the meat's grain between bacon slices to make eight pinwheel slices.

Grilled Marjoram Corn

Prep: 20 min. + soaking **Grill:** 25 min.

We love grilled veggies, and this recipe is a family favorite. The ears of sweet corn are soaked in their husks first for perfect steaming, then served with a tasty marjoram butter. —Sue Gronholz, Beaver Dam, Wisconsin

    6 large ears sweet corn in husks
    1 tablespoon minced fresh marjoram *or* 1
      teaspoon dried marjoram
  1/2 teaspoon lime juice
  1/2 cup butter, softened, *divided*
  3/4 teaspoon salt, *divided*
   24 fresh marjoram sprigs

Soak corn in cold water for 20 minutes. Meanwhile, in a small bowl, combine the minced marjoram, lime juice, 1/3 cup butter and 1/4 teaspoon salt; set aside.

Carefully peel back corn husks to within 1 in. of bottom; remove silk. Combine the remaining butter and salt; spread over corn. Top with marjoram sprigs. Rewrap corn in husks and secure with kitchen string.

Grill corn, covered, over medium heat for 25-30 minutes or until tender, turning occasionally. Remove marjoram sprigs. Serve corn with reserved butter mixture. **Yield:** 6 servings.

Dilly Salmon

(Pictured above right)

Prep: 10 min. + marinating **Grill:** 15 min.

This fillet gets tangy flavor from a marinade and basting sauce seasoned with Dijon mustard and fresh dill. When it comes to recipes for grilled salmon, I think this is one of the best! I'm always happy to share it. —Karla Sprague
Hilton Head Island, South Carolina

    1 cup Dijon mustard
  2/3 cup white wine *or* chicken broth
  1/2 cup packed brown sugar
  1/4 cup cider vinegar
    3 tablespoons soy sauce
    1 cup vegetable oil
  1/2 cup minced fresh dill
    1 teaspoon pepper
    1 salmon fillet (1 inch thick and 3 pounds),
      cut in half widthwise

In a bowl, whisk the mustard, wine or broth, brown sugar, vinegar and soy sauce until well blended. Gradually whisk in oil. Stir in dill and pepper. Place salmon in a shallow glass dish. Pour 2 cups marinade over salmon. Cover and refrigerate for 1 hour. Cover and refrigerate remaining marinade for basting.

Coat grill rack with nonstick cooking spray before starting grill. Drain and discard marinade. Place salmon skin side down on grill. Grill, covered, over medium-hot heat for 5 minutes. Baste with some of reserved marinade. Grill 7-9 minutes longer or until fish flakes easily with a fork, basting occasionally. **Yield:** 8-12 servings.

Dilly Salmon

Apple Country Ribs

Prep: 10 min. + marinating **Grill:** 40 min.

For a lip-smacking main course at your next backyard event, try these super-tender boneless ribs created in our Test Kitchen. They're treated to a sweet apple juice and herb combination that's sure to have your guests asking for seconds...as well as the recipe!

  3/4 cup unsweetened apple juice
  1/2 cup beer *or* nonalcoholic beer
  1/2 cup vegetable oil
  1/4 cup packed brown sugar
    1 tablespoon Worcestershire sauce
    1 tablespoon minced garlic
    1 teaspoon salt
    1 teaspoon dried thyme
    1 teaspoon pepper
  1/2 teaspoon cayenne pepper
    3 pounds boneless country-style pork ribs

For the marinade, in a small bowl, combine the first 10 ingredients. Pour 1-1/2 cups marinade into a large resealable plastic bag; add the ribs. Seal the bag and turn to coat the ribs; refrigerate for 5 hours or overnight, turning once. Cover and refrigerate the remaining marinade for basting.

Prepare grill for indirect heat. Drain and discard marinade. Grill ribs, covered, over indirect medium heat for 10 minutes on each side. Baste with some of the reserved marinade. Grill 20-25 minutes longer or until juices run clear and meat is tender, turning and basting occasionally. **Yield:** 12 servings.

Cherry-Stuffed Pork Chops

Cherry-Stuffed Pork Chops

(Pictured above)

Prep: 20 min. **Grill:** 20 min.

Grilled chops have a lovely stuffing of couscous, cherries and seasonings in this Test Kitchen main dish. Served with asparagus or a salad, it's perfect for special occasions but speedy enough for everyday family suppers.

    1 package (5.6 ounces) couscous with toasted pine nuts
    6 boneless pork loin chops (1 inch thick and 6 ounces *each*)
1/2 cup dried cherries
    1 tablespoon brown sugar

    1 tablespoon butter, melted
1/2 teaspoon minced fresh gingerroot
1/2 teaspoon garlic powder
1/2 teaspoon pepper

Prepare couscous according to package directions. Meanwhile, cut a deep slit in each pork chop, forming a pocket. Stir the cherries, brown sugar, butter and ginger into prepared couscous. Stuff 1/3 cup into each chop; secure with toothpicks. Sprinkle with garlic powder and pepper.

    Grill pork chops, covered, over medium heat for 10-12 minutes on each side or until a meat thermometer reads 160°. Discard toothpicks. **Yield:** 6 servings.

Pointers to Pockets

WHEN creating the pockets in the Cherry-Stuffed Pork Chops (recipe above), use a paring knife to make a slit in the chop's fatty side. Cut almost to the other side but not through the chop. Spoon the stuffing mixture into the pocket and secure the opening with toothpicks.

Pineapple Sirloin Kabobs

Prep: 20 min. + marinating **Grill:** 10 min.

These skewers are so simple—and even more delicious than you can imagine. With chunks of steak, pineapple, onion and mushrooms, the kabobs are a complete dinner all by themselves. —Beverly Folks, Roswell, Georgia

    1 can (8 ounces) unsweetened pineapple chunks
1/2 cup water
1/2 cup soy sauce
    1 teaspoon garlic powder
1/2 teaspoon salt
1/4 teaspoon ground ginger
1/4 teaspoon paprika
    1 pound boneless beef sirloin steak, cut into 1-inch pieces
  16 medium fresh mushrooms

1 large onion, cut into chunks
1 medium green pepper, cut into 1-inch pieces
1/2 cup butter, melted

Drain pineapple, reserving juice; refrigerate the pineapple. In a large resealable plastic bag, combine the water, soy sauce, garlic powder, salt, ginger, paprika and reserved pineapple juice; add steak. Seal bag and turn to coat; refrigerate for at least 30 minutes.

Drain and discard marinade. On metal or soaked wooden skewers, alternately thread the steak, mushrooms, onion, green pepper and pineapple. Grill, covered, over medium-hot heat or broil 4-6 in. from the heat for 4-5 minutes on each side or until meat reaches desired doneness, basting frequently with melted butter. **Yield:** 4 servings.

Beef Tenderloin with Mushroom Sauce

Prep/Total Time: 20 min.

Grilled to perfection, these peppered steaks are draped with a wine-and-mushroom sauce for spectacular results. While the meat is cooking on the grill, the sauce comes together quickly in a skillet on the stovetop.
—Teresa Seaman, Pickerington, Ohio

4 beef tenderloin steaks (1-1/2 inches thick and 6 ounces *each*)
1 tablespoon coarsely ground pepper
1/2 pound sliced fresh mushrooms
1/2 teaspoon minced garlic
1/3 cup butter, cubed
2 tablespoons all-purpose flour
1 cup beef broth
3/4 cup dry red wine *or* additional beef broth
1/8 teaspoon salt

Rub steaks with pepper. Grill, covered, over medium heat or broil 4 in. from the heat for 6-8 minutes on each side or until meat reaches desired doneness (for medium-rare, a meat thermometer should read 145°; medium, 160°; well-done, 170°).

Meanwhile, in a large skillet, saute mushrooms and garlic in butter for 3-4 minutes or until tender. Stir in flour until blended. Gradually stir in the broth, wine or additional broth and salt. Bring to a boil; cook and stir for 2-3 minutes or until thickened. Serve with steaks. **Yield:** 4 servings.

Pineapple Shrimp Packets

(Pictured above right)

Prep/Total Time: 25 min.

Your family and friends will be thrilled to receive these individual grilled shrimp packets. The foil makes cleanup a breeze.
—Nancy Zimmerman
Cape May Court House, New Jersey

6 canned pineapple slices
1-1/2 pounds uncooked medium shrimp, peeled and deveined

Pineapple Shrimp Packets

1/3 cup chopped sweet red pepper
1/3 cup packed brown sugar
1 tablespoon seafood seasoning
3 tablespoons butter, cubed

For each packet, place a pineapple slice on a double thickness of heavy-duty foil (about 12 in. square). Top with the shrimp and sweet red pepper. Combine the brown sugar and seafood seasoning; sprinkle over the shrimp. Dot with butter. Fold the foil around the mixture and seal tightly.

Grill, covered, over medium heat for 10-15 minutes or until shrimp turn pink. **Yield:** 6 servings.

Full-Flavor Packets

GRILLING with foil packets lets you make individual meals you can tailor to suit a variety of tastes. To create the packets swiftly:

• Center one serving on a double thickness of heavy foil.
• Bring sides of foil together and double fold with 1-inch folds, making sure to leave room for heat circulation at the top.
• Double fold the ends with 1-inch folds.
• After the foil packets are grilled, open both ends to let the steam escape and then open the top of each packet. Serve food out of packets or on plates.

Raspberry Butter Torte

Raspberry Butter Torte

(Pictured at left and on page 284)

Prep: 30 min. **Bake:** 30 min. + cooling

Raspberry pie filling and homemade chocolate frosting jazz up a packaged cake mix for this picture-perfect torte created by our Test Kitchen.

        1 package (18-1/2 ounces) butter recipe
            golden cake mix
    1/4 cup chopped almonds, toasted
        2 cups heavy whipping cream
        1 cup confectioners' sugar
    1/4 cup baking cocoa
    1-1/2 teaspoons rum extract
        2 cups raspberry filling
Chocolate curls
Toasted sliced almonds, optional

Prepare cake batter according to package directions; fold in almonds. Pour into two greased and floured 9-in. round baking pans. Bake as directed. Cool for 10 minutes before removing from pans to wire racks to cool completely.

For frosting, in a small mixing bowl, beat cream until it begins to thicken. Add the confectioners' sugar, cocoa and extract; beat until stiff peaks form.

Split each cake into two horizontal layers. Place one layer on a plate; spread with 1/2 cup berry filling and 1/2 cup frosting. Repeat with remaining cake layers. Place remaining frosting in a pastry bag with a #195 star tip. Decorate top and sides of cake as desired.

Garnish with chocolate curls and sliced almonds if desired. Store in the refrigerator. **Yield:** 12-14 servings.

Editor's Note: For the cake pictured at left, we piped about 1/2 cup frosting around the cake between layers and 1-1/2 cups on top.

Pie Filling Possibilities

FEEL like you don't have time to whip up impressive desserts for special occasions or as a surprise after weekday meals? Let our Test Kitchen home economists come to the rescue!

Here, they reveal the versatility of one handy ingredient—canned pie filling. This convenient store-bought product streamlines assembly for not only pies, but also many other tempting treats. Give it a try in any of the five delectable, easy dessert recipes featured here.

Preparing these treats—from a "berry" luscious torte to a delightfully different pizza—is as easy as pie. And your guests will never guess the secret ingredient you used to trim the preparation time.

Peanut Butter Crumb Apple Pie

Prep: 10 min. **Bake:** 20 min. + cooling

I use time-saving apple pie filling and a prepared pie crust for this scrumptious, streusel-topped dessert.
—Billie Moss, Walnut Creek, California

Quick Chocolate Curls

ADDING a pretty chocolate garnish to Raspberry Butter Torte (recipe at top) is a cinch. Use a vegetable peeler to "peel" curls from a solid block of chocolate. To keep the strips intact, allow them to fall gently onto a plate or a single layer of waxed paper. If you get only shavings, your chocolate may be too hard, so warm it slightly.

1 can (21 ounces) apple pie filling
1 teaspoon lemon juice
1 pastry shell (9 inches), baked
1/2 cup all-purpose flour
1/3 cup packed brown sugar
1 to 3 teaspoons grated lemon peel
1/2 teaspoon ground cinnamon
1/4 teaspoon ground nutmeg
6 tablespoons chunky peanut butter
2 tablespoons cold butter

Combine pie filling and lemon juice; spoon into pastry shell. In a large bowl, combine flour, brown sugar, lemon peel, cinnamon and nutmeg; cut in peanut butter and butter until crumbly. Sprinkle over filling. Bake at 400° for 20-22 minutes or until topping is lightly browned. Cool on wire rack. **Yield:** 6-8 servings.

Layered Lemon Pie

Prep/Total Time: 25 min.

This is a crowd-pleasing ending for almost any meal. The creamy lemon filling is always a hit with my husband. —Elizabeth Yoder, Belcourt, North Dakota

1 package (8 ounces) cream cheese, softened
1/2 cup sugar
1 can (15-3/4 ounces) lemon pie filling
1 carton (8 ounces) frozen whipped topping, thawed
1 graham cracker crust (9 inches)

In a small mixing bowl, beat cream cheese and sugar until smooth. Beat in half of the pie filling. Fold in the whipped topping. Spoon into crust. Spread with remaining pie filling. Refrigerate for 15 minutes or until serving. Refrigerate leftovers. **Yield:** 8 servings.

Deep-Fried Cherry Pies

Prep/Total Time: 30 min.

With a flaky homemade crust, these stuffed pies make a quick dessert. We love them after dinner or as a snack. —Monica Larkin, Shinnston, West Virginia

1 cup all-purpose flour
1/4 teaspoon baking powder
1/4 teaspoon salt
2 tablespoons shortening
1/3 cup boiling water
1 cup cherry pie filling
Oil for deep-fat frying
1/4 cup maple syrup
1/4 cup whipped topping

In a small bowl, combine the flour, baking powder and salt. Cut in shortening until mixture resembles coarse crumbs. Stir in water just until moistened. Turn onto a lightly floured surface; knead 8-10 times.

Divide dough into four portions; roll each into an 8-in. circle. Place 1/4 cup of pie filling in the center of each circle. Fold dough over filling; secure with toothpicks.

In an electric skillet, heat 1 in. of oil to 375°. Fry pies,

folded side down, in the oil for 2-3 minutes or until lightly browned. Turn and fry 2-3 minutes longer. Drain on paper towels. Remove the toothpicks. Serve with syrup and whipped topping. **Yield:** 4 servings.

Peaches 'n' Cream Pizza

(Pictured below)

Prep: 15 min. **Bake:** 30 min. + cooling

For this sweet pizza, a crispy crust is topped with almond-flavored cream cheese and peach pie filling. —Linda Patrick, Houston, Texas

1 tube (8 ounces) refrigerated crescent roll dough
1 package (8 ounces) cream cheese, softened
1/2 cup sugar
1/2 teaspoon almond extract
1 can (21 ounces) peach pie filling
1/2 cup all-purpose flour
1/4 cup packed brown sugar
3 tablespoons cold butter
1/2 cup sliced almonds

Separate crescent dough into eight triangles. Press onto a greased 12-in. pizza pan; seal seams. Bake at 375° for 8-10 minutes or until edges are golden. Cool slightly on a wire rack.

In a small mixing bowl, beat cream cheese, sugar and extract until smooth. Spread over crust. Top with pie filling. In a small bowl, combine flour and brown sugar; cut in butter until crumbly. Sprinkle over peaches. Top with nuts. Bake for 20-25 minutes or until golden brown. Cool. Refrigerate leftovers. **Yield:** 12-16 servings.

Peaches 'n' Cream Pizza

Easter Meringue Cups

Picture-Perfect Meringues

LIGHT-AS-AIR MERINGUES are the stuff cooks' dreams are made of. The combination of egg whites and sugar that's stiffly beaten for meringues bakes into sweet, crisp shells and cookies. But for all too many cooks, meringues just don't turn out right.

Here, our Test Kitchen pros provide tips and simple recipes for you to try. In no time, you'll be whipping up memorable meringues with ease.

When preparing meringues:
• Keep an eye on the weather. Meringues can absorb moisture on a humid day and become limp and sticky.
• Bring egg whites to room temperature so that they'll reach the greatest volume when beaten.
• Place egg whites in a clean glass or metal mixing bowl (not plastic). Be sure there's no trace of grease, egg yolk or fat on the bowl or beaters, which will prevent the whites from foaming.
• Once soft peaks form, add sugar gradually to achieve the most volume.
• You'll know the sugar is dissolved when the mixture feels silky-smooth between your fingertips.

For best results:
• Pipe meringue shells and cookies from a pastry bag for a decorative look.
• Once meringues are baked, turn the oven off and leave them inside. After an hour, meringues will be firm and dry.
• Fill crisp, dry meringue shells just before serving to prevent the filling from softening them.

Easter Meringue Cups

(Pictured above)

Prep: 25 min. + standing **Bake:** 45 min. + cooling

These crunchy shells with a lemon filling will make guests ooh and aah. Our home economists topped the cups with fresh fruit for a colorful finish.

    3 egg whites
1/2 teaspoon vanilla extract
1/4 teaspoon cream of tartar
3/4 cup sugar
1/2 cup lemon curd

1 cup sliced fresh strawberries
2 medium kiwifruit, peeled and sliced
1/2 cup fresh raspberries
1/3 cup mandarin oranges
1/3 cup cubed fresh pineapple

Place egg whites in a large mixing bowl; let stand at room temperature for 30 minutes. Beat egg whites, vanilla and cream of tartar on medium speed until soft peaks form. Gradually beat in sugar, 1 tablespoon at a time, on high until stiff peaks form.

Drop meringue into eight mounds on a parchment paper-lined baking sheet. Shape into 3-in. cups with the back of a spoon.

Bake at 275° for 45-50 minutes or until set and dry. Turn off oven and do not open door; leave meringues in oven for 1 hour. Spread cups with lemon curd and fill with fruit. **Yield:** 8 servings.

Meringue Drops

(Pictured at right)

Prep: 25 min. + standing **Bake:** 20 min. + cooling

These pretty pastel cookies from our Test Kitchen are a fun way to brighten a springtime luncheon, holiday buffet, baby or bridal shower...any occasion at all!

3 egg whites
1/2 teaspoon vanilla extract
1/4 teaspoon cream of tartar
Food coloring, optional
3/4 cup sugar
White pearl or coarse sugar, optional

Place egg whites in a large mixing bowl; let stand at room temperature for 30 minutes. Beat egg whites, vanilla, cream of tartar and food coloring if desired on medium

Meringue Drops

speed until soft peaks form. Gradually beat in sugar, 1 tablespoon at a time, on high until stiff peaks form.

Cut a small hole in the corner of a pastry or plastic bag; insert #3 star pastry tip. Fill the bag with meringue. Pipe 2-in. circles or shapes 2 in. apart onto parchment paper-lined baking sheets. Sprinkle with pearl sugar if desired.

Bake at 300° for 20-25 minutes or until set and dry. Turn off oven and do not open door; leave meringues in oven for 1 hour. Store in an airtight container. **Yield:** about 2 dozen.

Making Meringue Cups

Beat the egg white mixture as the recipe directs until soft peaks form.

TIP: To test for soft peaks, lift the beaters from the egg whites. The peaks of egg white should curl down.

Add sugar as the recipe directs until stiff peaks form and sugar is dissolved.

TIP: To test for stiff peaks, lift the beaters from the whites. The peaks of egg white should stand straight up so that if you tilt the bowl, the whites don't slide around.

Drop the meringue into mounds on a parchment paper-lined baking sheet. Then shape into 3-in. cups with the back of a spoon.

After drying meringues in the oven and cooling completely, carefully remove them from the paper to add the filling.

TIP: You can store the meringue shells in an airtight container with waxed paper between the layers for up to 2 days at room temperature.

Raspberry Orange Torte

Rave-Winning Raspberries

GORGEOUS, ruby-red raspberries are perfect for popping in your mouth as a snack, tossing into fruit salads and garnishing desserts. But what can you do with a bounty of these juicy gems picked from your backyard patch...or purchased at the local farmers market or grocery store?

Here, our home economists show you how to press the berries, which results in a puree that has all the wonderful berry flavor with none of the seeds. Use this technique when making thick Raspberry Sauce, refreshing Raspberry Lime Slush or elegant Raspberry Orange Torte.

Any of these treats would complement a summer meal. But you can even use frozen berries in the recipes, so you can enjoy them any time of year!

Raspberry Orange Torte
(Pictured above)

Prep: 25 min. **Bake:** 30 min. + cooling

Guests are sure to be dazzled by this super-moist dessert that's ideal for special occasions. Our home economists spread a rich orange cream filling between the cake layers for a luscious look and taste.

    1 package (18-1/4 ounces) white cake mix
    1 package (10 ounces) frozen sweetened
       raspberries, thawed
    2 cups heavy whipping cream
    1 carton (8 ounces) Mascarpone cheese
3/4 cup sugar
    2 tablespoons orange juice
1/2 teaspoon grated orange peel
    2 cups fresh raspberries

Prepare and bake cake according to package directions, using two greased 9-in. round baking pans. Cool on a wire rack for 1 hour.

Press the sweetened raspberries through a sieve; discard the seeds. Set the raspberry puree aside. In a small mixing bowl, beat the heavy whipping cream until stiff peaks form. In a large mixing bowl, beat the Mascarpone cheese, sugar, orange juice and orange peel. Fold in the whipped cream.

Split each cake into two horizontal layers. Place the bottom layer on a serving plate. Brush with about 1/4 cup raspberry puree. Spread with about 1 cup cream mixture; top with 1/2 cup fresh raspberries. Repeat the layers three times. Refrigerate until serving. **Yield:** 10-12 servings.

Raspberry Sauce

Prep: 10 min. **Cook:** 40 min.

Spoon this smooth sauce from our Test Kitchen over waffles or pancakes for a fabulous breakfast. Or try it over vanilla ice cream or slices of purchased pound cake for an easy-as-can-be but elegant dessert.

2 cups fresh *or* frozen raspberries
1-3/4 cups plus 1 tablespoon water, *divided*
1/3 cup sugar
2 tablespoons cornstarch

In a saucepan, combine the raspberries, 1-3/4 cups water and sugar. Bring to a boil. Reduce heat; simmer, uncovered, for 30 minutes.

Mash raspberry mixture and strain through a fine sieve into a 2-cup measuring cup; discard seeds. Add water if needed to make 2 cups puree. Return to the saucepan.

Combine cornstarch and remaining water until smooth; gradually stir into raspberry mixture. Bring to a boil over medium heat, stirring constantly. Cook and stir 1 minute longer. Remove from the heat; cool. Store in the refrigerator. **Yield:** 2 cups.

Raspberry Lime Slush

(Pictured at right)

Prep: 15 min. + freezing

For a cool ending to a meal, our home economists scooped this bright pink slush into stemmed glasses, then drizzled it with ginger ale. The lime adds a little zing for a sweet-tart taste that's especially refreshing.

3/4 cup sugar
2 cups water, *divided*
1 cup fresh *or* frozen raspberries, thawed
1/2 cup lime juice
3 cups ginger ale, chilled

In a small saucepan, combine sugar and 1/2 cup water. Cook and stir over high heat until sugar is completely dissolved. Remove from the heat. Press raspberries through a sieve; discard seeds.

In a large bowl, combine the raspberry puree, sugar syrup, lime juice and remaining water. Transfer to a 1-qt. freezer container. Cover and freeze for 12 hours, stirring occasionally. May be frozen for up to 3 months.

To serve, combine the raspberry mixture and ginger ale in a 2-qt. pitcher. Or for one serving, combine 1/2 cup raspberry mixture and 1/2 cup ginger ale in a glass. **Yield:** 6 servings.

Key Steps to Torte

WHEN making Raspberry Orange Torte (recipe on p. 294), try the following techniques:

Use the back of a spoon to press the berries through a sieve.

Place toothpicks around a cake layer as a guide when splitting with a serrated knife.

Use a pastry brush to spread the raspberry puree on a split cake layer.

Raspberry Lime Slush

Raspberry Butter

In a small bowl, combine all ingredients. Serve immediately. Refrigerate leftovers. **Yield:** about 3/4 cup.

Parsley Butter

Prep/Total Time: 5 min.

1/2 cup butter, softened
  1 tablespoon minced fresh tarragon *or* 1 teaspoon dried tarragon
  1 tablespoon minced fresh parsley *or* 1 teaspoon dried parsley flakes
1/2 teaspoon minced chives
1/4 teaspoon minced garlic
Dash pepper

In a small bowl, combine all ingredients. Serve immediately. Refrigerate leftovers. **Yield:** 1/2 cup.

Tarragon Butter

Prep/Total Time: 5 min.

1/2 cup butter, softened
1/4 cup fresh tarragon leaves, chopped
1/8 teaspoon lemon juice
Dash salt and pepper

In a small bowl, combine all ingredients. Serve immediately. Refrigerate leftovers. **Yield:** 1/2 cup.

Maple Butter

Prep/Total Time: 5 min.

3/4 cup butter, softened
1/2 cup maple syrup

In a small bowl, combine butter and syrup. Serve immediately. Refrigerate leftovers. **Yield:** about 1 cup.

Spiced Honey Butter

Prep/Total Time: 5 min.

1/2 cup butter, softened
1/4 cup honey
  1 teaspoon grated orange peel
1/2 teaspoon ground cinnamon

In a small bowl, combine all ingredients. Serve immediately. Refrigerate leftovers. **Yield:** 3/4 cup.

Herb Butter

Prep/Total Time: 5 min.

1/2 cup butter, softened
  1 tablespoon minced fresh parsley
1-1/2 teaspoons minced garlic
  1 teaspoon Italian seasoning
1/4 teaspoon crushed red pepper flakes

In a small bowl, combine all ingredients. Serve immediately. Refrigerate leftovers. **Yield:** 1/2 cup.

Special Rolls And Spreads

SAY GOOD-BYE to the hours of kneading and preparation that perfect yeast breads often require. The fantastic rolls here start with a package of 36 frozen dinner rolls, so they're a cinch to whip up.

Once thawed and shaped, they'll rise until doubled, leaving you time to do other things. Serve them with one of the Test Kitchen butters on this page for a delicious yet easy finish.

Raspberry Butter

(Pictured above)

Prep/Total Time: 5 min.

1/2 cup butter, softened
1/3 cup fresh *or* frozen raspberries
  2 tablespoons confectioners' sugar
Dash lemon juice

Swirl Roll

Combine two dinner rolls into a ball. On a lightly floured surface, roll the ball into a 12-inch rope. Holding one end of the rope, wrap dough in a circle into a greased muffin cup to form a coil as shown above. Pinch end to seal. Repeat with remaining dough. Cover and let rise until doubled. Bake at 350° for 15-20 minutes until golden brown. **Yield:** 18 rolls.

Cloverleaf Rolls

Cut each dinner roll in half; shape into seventy-two 1-1/2-inch balls. Make each ball smooth by pulling the edges under. Place three balls, smooth side up, in a greased muffin cup as shown above. Repeat with remaining dough. Cover and let rise until doubled. Bake at 350° for 15-20 minutes until golden brown. **Yield:** 24 rolls.

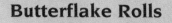

Butterflake Rolls

Combine two dinner rolls into a ball. Place the ball into a greased muffin cup. With scissors, make four or five deep cuts into the ball as shown above, leaving the bottom of the roll attached. Brush butter into each cut. Repeat with remaining dough. Cover and let rise until doubled. Bake at 350° for 15-20 minutes until golden brown. **Yield:** 18 rolls.

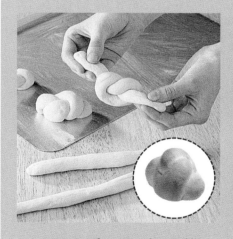

Knot-Shaped Rolls

On a lightly floured surface, roll each dinner roll into a 9-inch rope. Tie each rope into a knot as shown above. Tuck and pinch ends under. Place rolls 2 inches apart on greased baking sheets. Cover and let rise until doubled. Bake at 350° for 15-20 minutes until golden brown. **Yield:** 36 rolls.

Twist Rolls

On a lightly floured surface, roll each dinner roll into a 12-inch rope. Fold each rope in half and twist ends around each other as shown above. Tuck ends under. Place the rolls 2 inches apart on greased baking sheets. Cover and let rise until doubled. Bake at 350° for 15-20 minutes until golden brown. **Yield:** 36 rolls.

S-Shaped Rolls

On a lightly floured surface, roll each dinner roll into a 9-inch rope. Shape each rope into an S, then coil each end until it touches the center as shown above. Place 2 inches apart on greased baking sheets. Cover and let rise until doubled. Bake at 350° for 15-20 minutes until golden brown. **Yield:** 36 rolls.

Tricks with Cake Mix

DEVOTING a full day to holiday baking is an annual event for many families, with decorated treats covering the kitchen table and lining the countertops when they're done.

When time is tight, spending an entire day in the kitchen is not always an option. But even busy bakers can create festive desserts when they turn to recipes like these that call for time-saving cake mixes.

Whether you're looking for a sweet ending to a family meal, an eye-catching addition to a cookie tray or a fun take-along to a classroom party, you're sure to find something here that will surprise and delight.

Cupcake Christmas Tree

(Pictured above)

Prep: 45 min. **Bake:** 20 min. + cooling

Here's a minty treatment for chocolate cupcakes, which can be arranged in a tree shape for a pretty presentation. The star on the top of the tree and cute gift packages beneath are a breeze to make with colorful candies.
—Heather McKinley, Mechanic Falls, Maine

   1 package (18-1/4 ounces) devil's food cake mix
1-1/2 cups mint chocolate chips
   6 tablespoons butter, softened
2-2/3 cups confectioners' sugar
   4 to 5 tablespoons milk
  1/2 teaspoon vanilla extract
  1/4 teaspoon peppermint extract
   1 teaspoon baking cocoa
  1/4 teaspoon green paste food coloring
Candy-coated milk chocolate miniature kisses
   2 chocolate stars
 12 Starburst candies

Prepare cake batter according to package directions; fold in chips. Fill foil-lined muffin cups two-thirds full. Bake at 350° for 18-24 minutes or until a toothpick comes out clean. Cool for 5 minutes before removing from pans to wire racks to cool completely.

For frosting, in a mixing bowl, cream butter and confectioners' sugar. Stir in milk and extracts. Transfer 2 tablespoons to a small bowl; stir in cocoa. Stir green food coloring into remaining frosting.

Frost 21 cupcakes with green frosting; arrange in a pyramid to form a tree. Decorate all but the top cupcake with miniature kisses for lights. Frost two cupcakes with chocolate frosting and place at base of tree for trunk; top each with a chocolate star. Save remaining cupcake for another use.

With a rolling pin, roll two yellow Starburst candies flat; cut with 2-in. and 1-1/2-in. star-shaped cookie cutters. Press smaller star onto larger star; place on cupcake at top of tree.

For presents, roll five Starburst candies into 3-in. x 3/4-in. rectangles; cut each rectangle into four 3-in.-long strips. Place two strips crosswise on one whole Starburst candy; press together at base to attach.

For bow, form two strips into figure eights; press the strips together in the center and press onto the wrapped candy (see tip box at bottom).

Repeat with remaining strips and remaining four whole Starburst candies. Place presents beneath cupcake tree. **Yield:** 23 servings.

Peppermint Angel Roll

Prep: 30 min. **Bake:** 15 min. + freezing

This is a very festive, fancy-looking dessert for Christmas. The angel food cake makes it less heavy than many traditional holiday recipes. My husband loves it, and I love it because it's so simple and convenient during a hectic season! —Holly Dicke, Plain City, Ohio

    1 package (16 ounces) angel food cake mix
    1 tablespoon confectioners' sugar
  1/2 gallon peppermint ice cream, softened
    1 jar (11-3/4 ounces) hot fudge ice cream
      topping, warmed
Miniature candy canes and additional confectioners' sugar, optional

Prepare cake batter according to package directions. Line a greased 15-in. x 10-in. x 1-in. baking pan with waxed paper and grease the paper. Spread batter evenly into pan. Bake at 350° for 15-20 minutes or until cake springs back when lightly touched.

Cool for 5 minutes. Turn cake onto a kitchen towel dusted with confectioners' sugar. Gently peel off waxed paper. Roll up cake in the towel jelly-roll style, starting with a short side. Cool completely on a wire rack.

Unroll cake and spread ice cream over cake to within 1/2 in. of edges. Roll up again. Cover and freeze until firm.

Cut into slices; drizzle with hot fudge topping. If desired, garnish with candy canes and dust with confectioners' sugar. **Yield:** 10 servings.

Stamped by Design Cookies

(Pictured above right)

Prep: 25 min. **Bake:** 10 min. per batch + cooling

I came up with this recipe when I wanted a different type of frosted cookie to give as a gift at Christmastime. These chocolaty goodies have an indentation in the center that's filled in with colorful icing, creating a fun "stamped" effect. —Sherry Lee, Columbus, Ohio

Stamped by Design Cookies

    1 package (18-1/4 ounces) chocolate *or* white cake mix
    2 eggs
  1/4 cup vegetable oil
Sugar
1-1/2-in. cookie cutters
ICING:
    2 cups confectioners' sugar
    2 to 3 tablespoons milk
Assorted food coloring, optional

In a large mixing bowl, beat the cake mix, eggs and oil. Roll the dough into 1-in. balls; place 2 in. apart on greased baking sheets. Flatten each ball with a glass dipped in sugar.

Bake at 350° for 6-8 minutes or until the tops are set. Lightly press a 1-1/2-in. cookie cutter onto cookies, making a slight indentation in center of each. Remove to wire racks to cool completely.

In a small bowl, whisk the confectioners' sugar and enough milk to achieve a drizzling consistency. Tint with food coloring if desired. Place icing in a small heavy-duty resealable plastic bag; cut a small hole in a corner of bag. Carefully pipe icing into the indentations on cookies. **Yield:** 6 dozen.

Wrapping Up Candy Presents

CREATE the cute candy gifts for the Cupcake Christmas Tree (recipe on p. 298) in a few simple steps:

1   2   3   4

DO YOU LIKE to try a wide variety of recipes? Maybe you enjoy creating different kinds of dishes using the same ingredient. Either way, this theme-related chapter is for you!

We've gathered an assortment of similar types of foods and grouped them together, so you can turn to the ones that interest you most. You'll find fare featuring zippy zucchini... cool cucumbers...tempting tomatoes...sensational strawberries and a bounty of basil.

Plus, you'll see a range of recipes for cream puff shells, a delightful pie and homemade mixes that make great gifts for Christmastime.

Just take a look through this creative collection, and you're bound to become inspired!

"BERRY" VERSATILE. Strawberry Apple Pie, Sweet Pasta Salad and Strawberry Pork Chops (all recipes on p. 302)

Strawberry Pork Chops

Sensational Strawberries

RIPE with flavor and packed with nutrition, ruby-red strawberries are one of the first celebrations of summertime. These versatile berries are wonderful tucked into everything from hearty entrees to salads and desserts.

Here, we've featured a bumper crop of juicy, just-picked strawberry recipes sure to add a luscious taste of summer to your warm-weather menus.

Strawberry Pork Chops

(Pictured above and on page 300)

Prep/Total Time: 20 min.

These strawberry-topped pork chops from our Test Kitchen home economists are easy enough for weeknight dinners but special enough for guests.

✓ Uses less fat, sugar or salt. Includes Nutrition Facts.

- 3/4 cup raspberry vinaigrette
- 2 tablespoons chopped green onion
- 1 tablespoon brown sugar
- 1/4 teaspoon paprika
- 1/4 teaspoon Worcestershire sauce
- 2 teaspoons dried rosemary, crushed
- 1/2 to 1 teaspoon pepper
- 4 bone-in pork loin chops (1 inch thick and 6 ounces *each*)
- 1 tablespoon canola oil
- 2 cups sliced fresh strawberries (1/4-inch slices)

In a small bowl, combine the vinaigrette, onion, brown sugar, paprika and Worcestershire sauce; set aside. Combine rosemary and pepper; rub over both sides of chops.

In a large skillet, cook chops in oil over medium-high heat for 5-6 minutes on each side or until browned. Pour vinaigrette mixture over meat; cook 3-4 minutes longer or until pork juices run clear.

Remove chops and keep warm. Add strawberries to the cooking juices and toss to coat; serve with pork chops. **Yield:** 4 servings.

Nutrition Facts: 1 pork chop with 2 tablespoons sauce (prepared with fat-free raspberry vinaigrette) equals 365 calories, 18 g fat (5 g saturated fat), 83 mg cholesterol, 259 mg sodium, 25 g carbohydrate, 2 g fiber, 28 g protein.

Strawberry Apple Pie

(Pictured on page 300)

Prep: 15 min. **Bake:** 45 min.

I ran out of apples when baking an apple pie to bring to my in-laws'. I substituted berries for the rest of the apples, and it was a hit!   —*Dianne Ebke, Plymouth, Nebraska*

- 3-1/2 cups thinly sliced peeled Granny Smith apples (about 3 medium)
- 1-1/4 cups sliced fresh strawberries
- 1 tablespoon lemon juice
- 1/2 cup sugar
- 3 to 4 tablespoons all-purpose flour

Pastry for double-crust pie (9 inches)
TOPPING:
- 1/2 teaspoon sugar
- 1/8 teaspoon ground cinnamon

Whipped topping, optional

In a large bowl, combine apples and strawberries; drizzle with lemon juice. Combine sugar and flour; sprinkle over fruit and toss lightly.

Line a 9-in. pie plate with bottom pastry; trim even with edge of plate. Add filling. Roll out remaining pastry to fit top of pie; place over filling. Trim, seal and flute edges. Cut slits in top. Combine sugar and cinnamon; sprinkle over pastry. Cover edges loosely with foil.

Bake at 450° for 10 minutes. Reduce heat to 350°; remove foil and bake 35-40 minutes longer or until crust is golden brown and filling is bubbly. Cool on a wire rack. Garnish with whipped topping if desired. **Yield:** 6-8 servings.

Sweet Pasta Salad

(Pictured on page 301)

Prep/Total Time: 25 min.

I tried this delightful salad at a pool party and begged the hostess for the recipe. Since then, I've served it many times.   —*Joan Hallford, North Richland Hills, Texas*

- 3 cups uncooked penne *or* medium tube pasta
- 1/2 cup heavy whipping cream
- 2 tablespoons confectioners' sugar
- 1/2 teaspoon vanilla extract

2 cups sliced fresh strawberries, *divided*
1 teaspoon canola oil
1/3 cup flaked coconut, toasted
4 cups torn salad greens
1/2 cup chopped walnuts, toasted

Cook pasta according to package directions. Meanwhile, combine cream, sugar, vanilla and 1/2 cup berries in a blender or food processor; cover and process until smooth and slightly thickened, about 30 seconds.

Drain the pasta; rinse in cold water. Place in a large bowl; add oil and toss to coat. Add coconut and remaining strawberries; toss gently. Place the greens in a serving bowl; top with pasta mixture. Drizzle with dressing and sprinkle with walnuts. **Yield:** 6-8 servings.

Berries 'n' Cream French Toast

Prep/Total Time: 25 min.

My husband and I sampled this French toast at a bed-and-breakfast where we celebrated our anniversary. It's so easy to prepare. —Lesa Hefner, Elk City, Oklahoma

2 packages (3 ounces *each*) cream cheese, softened
1/2 cup marshmallow creme
1/2 teaspoon vanilla extract
2 cups sliced fresh *or* frozen strawberries
1/4 cup sugar
1-1/2 teaspoons cornstarch
1 tablespoon cold water
3 eggs
3/4 cup milk
8 slices French bread (1 inch thick)

In a small mixing bowl, beat the cream cheese, marshmallow creme and vanilla until smooth; set aside.

In a small saucepan, bring berries and sugar to a boil. Reduce heat; simmer, uncovered, for 10 minutes. Combine cornstarch and cold water until smooth; stir into berry mixture. Return to a boil; cook and stir for 2 minutes or until thickened. Remove from heat; keep warm.

In a shallow bowl, whisk the eggs and milk; dip both sides of bread in egg mixture. On a lightly greased hot griddle, cook bread over medium heat for 2 minutes on each side or until golden brown. To serve, spread each piece of French toast with cream cheese mixture; top with strawberry syrup. **Yield:** 4 servings.

Strawberry Cake Roll

(Pictured at right)

Prep: 45 min. **Bake:** 10 min. + chilling

This dessert is scrumptious and has an added bonus—the waxed paper-lined pan makes for speedy cleanup!
—Carrie Vazzano, Rolling Meadows, Illinois

✓ Uses less fat, sugar or salt. Includes Nutrition Facts and Diabetic Exchanges.

4 eggs, *separated*
2/3 cup sugar, *divided*
1 tablespoon milk

1/4 teaspoon grated lemon peel
1/2 cup all-purpose flour
1/4 teaspoon cream of tartar
FILLING:
1 carton (8 ounces) Mascarpone cheese
2 tablespoons lemon juice
2 tablespoons sugar
2 cups sliced fresh strawberries
2 teaspoons confectioners' sugar

Place egg whites in a small mixing bowl; let stand at room temperature for 30 minutes. Coat a 15-in. x 10-in. x 1-in. baking pan with nonstick cooking spray; line with waxed paper and coat the paper with nonstick cooking spray. Set aside.

In a large mixing bowl, beat yolks, 1/3 cup sugar, milk and lemon peel. Gradually stir in flour. Add cream of tartar to egg whites; beat on medium speed until soft peaks form. Gradually beat in remaining sugar, 1 tablespoon at a time, on high until stiff glossy peaks form and sugar is dissolved. Gradually fold into yolk mixture.

Carefully spread into prepared pan. Bake at 375° for 10-12 minutes or until cake springs back when lightly touched. Cool for 5 minutes. Turn cake onto a kitchen towel dusted with confectioners' sugar. Gently peel off waxed paper. Roll up cake in the towel jelly-roll style, starting with a long side. Cool completely on a wire rack.

In a small bowl, combine Mascarpone cheese and lemon juice. Unroll cake; spread filling evenly over cake to within 1/2 in. of edges. Sprinkle with sugar and top with strawberries; roll up again. Cover; chill for 1 hour before serving. Dust with confectioners' sugar. Refrigerate leftovers. **Yield:** 12 servings.

Nutrition Facts: 1 slice equals 190 calories, 11 g fat (5 g saturated fat), 95 mg cholesterol, 33 mg sodium, 21 g carbohydrate, 1 g fiber, 4 g protein. **Diabetic Exchanges:** 2 fat, 1 starch, 1/2 fruit.

Strawberry Cake Roll

Greek Garden Appetizer

1/2 teaspoon minced garlic
1/4 teaspoon dried oregano
1/4 teaspoon pepper
1-1/2 cups chopped cucumber
1 cup chopped seeded tomatoes
1/4 cup chopped green onions
2 tablespoons sliced ripe olives
Miniature pita pockets

In a large bowl, combine the cream cheese, feta, yogurt, garlic, oregano and pepper. Spread into a 9-in. pie plate. Sprinkle with cucumber, tomatoes, onions and olives. Serve with pita bread. Refrigerate leftovers. **Yield:** 4 cups.

Lemon Vinaigrette Salad

Prep/Total Time: 15 min.

For a lovely accompaniment to most any meal, try this pretty medley from our home economists. It's drizzled with a from-scratch vinaigrette that's ready in minutes.

1 head Boston *or* Bibb lettuce, separated into leaves
1 large tomato, sliced
1 small cucumber, sliced
1/4 cup olive oil
2 tablespoons lemon juice
2 teaspoons snipped fresh dill
1/4 teaspoon salt
1/8 teaspoon pepper

Arrange the lettuce on four salad plates. Top with tomato and cucumber slices. In a jar with a tight-fitting lid, combine the oil, lemon juice, dill, salt and pepper; shake well. Drizzle over salads. **Yield:** 4 servings.

Salmon with Cucumber Sauce

Prep/Total Time: 25 min.

A thick and creamy white sauce with chopped cucumber is the refreshing topping for broiled salmon fillets in this tasty main dish. Special enough for company, it also makes a fast weeknight supper...and always gets rave reviews.
—Shirley Glaab, Hattiesburg, Mississippi

1 cup chopped peeled cucumber
1/2 cup mayonnaise
1/2 cup sour cream
1-1/2 teaspoons lemon juice
1/4 teaspoon grated onion
1/4 teaspoon dill weed
1/8 teaspoon coarsely ground pepper
Dash salt
4 salmon fillets (6 ounces *each*)

For sauce, in a bowl, combine the first eight ingredients. Refrigerate until serving. Broil salmon 4-6 in. from the heat for 10-15 minutes or until fish flakes easily with a fork. Serve with cucumber sauce. **Yield:** 4 servings (1-1/2 cups sauce).

Creative Cucumbers

CRISP, refreshing cucumbers add a summery touch to everyday menus. Here, you'll find that juicy veggie featured in several delicious, fast-to-fix dishes. They're so easy to assemble, they're bound to leave you feeling cool as a cucumber!

Greek Garden Appetizer

(Pictured above)

Prep/Total Time: 15 min.

This impressive dip, made with flavored cream cheese, feta and yogurt, is perfect for summer gatherings. With its simple topping of olives, cucumber and tomatoes, it's a snap to whip up and tastes great with miniature pita pockets.
—Del Mason, Martensville, Saskatchewan

1 carton (8 ounces) spreadable garden vegetable cream cheese
2 cups (8 ounces) crumbled feta cheese
1/4 cup plain yogurt

Walnut Zucchini Muffins
Vegetarian White Bean Soup

Zippy Zucchini

ZERO IN on zucchini! The easy recipes here make the most of this versatile squash. Try one or all of these dishes to use up your garden produce.

Walnut Zucchini Muffins

(Pictured above)

Prep: 15 min. **Bake:** 20 min.

Shredded zucchini adds moistness to these tender muffins dotted with raisins and chopped walnuts.
—*Harriet Stichter, Milford, Indiana*

    1 cup all-purpose flour
  3/4 cup whole wheat flour
  2/3 cup packed brown sugar
    2 teaspoons baking powder
  3/4 teaspoon ground cinnamon
  1/2 teaspoon salt
    2 eggs
  3/4 cup milk
  1/2 cup butter, melted
    1 cup shredded zucchini
    1 cup chopped walnuts
  1/2 cup raisins

In a large bowl, combine first six ingredients. In another bowl, whisk eggs, milk and butter; stir into dry ingredients just until moistened. Fold in zucchini, nuts and raisins.

Fill greased muffin cups three-fourths full. Bake at 375° for 18-20 minutes or until a toothpick comes out clean. Cool for 5 minutes before removing from pan to a wire rack. **Yield:** 1 dozen.

Vegetarian White Bean Soup

(Pictured above)

Prep/Total Time: 30 min.

The home economists in our Test Kitchen simmered up this fresh-tasting meatless soup. Hearty with two kinds of beans, it makes a satisfying entree that's good for you, too.

✓ Uses less fat, sugar or salt. Includes Nutrition Facts and Diabetic Exchanges.

    2 small zucchini, quartered lengthwise and sliced
    1 cup *each* chopped onion, celery and carrot
    2 tablespoons canola oil
    3 cans (14-1/2 ounces *each*) vegetable broth
    1 can (15-1/2 ounces) great northern beans, rinsed and drained
    1 can (15 ounces) white kidney *or* cannellini beans, rinsed and drained
    1 can (14-1/2 ounces) diced tomatoes, undrained
  1/2 teaspoon dried thyme
  1/2 teaspoon dried oregano
  1/4 teaspoon pepper

In a large saucepan or Dutch oven, saute the zucchini, onion, celery and carrot in oil for 5-7 minutes or until crisp-tender. Add the remaining ingredients. Bring to a boil. Reduce heat; cover and simmer for 15 minutes or until vegetables are tender. **Yield:** 7 servings.

Nutrition Facts: 1-1/2 cups equals 171 calories, 5 g fat (trace saturated fat), 0 cholesterol, 1,047 mg sodium, 25 g carbohydrate, 7 g fiber, 8 g protein. **Diabetic Exchanges:** 1 starch, 1 very lean meat, 1 vegetable, 1 fat.

Orzo with Zucchini and Feta

Prep/Total Time: 20 min.

This pasta dish is simple to prepare and never fails to please. I double and sometimes triple the recipe when hosting a get-together. —Andrea Jones, McKinney, Texas

✓ Uses less fat, sugar or salt. Includes Nutrition Facts and Diabetic Exchanges.

    1 cup uncooked orzo pasta
    1 medium zucchini, cut into 1/4-inch pieces
    2 tablespoons water
  3/4 cup crumbled feta cheese
    4 teaspoons olive oil
    2 teaspoons dried oregano
Salt and pepper to taste

Cook orzo according to package directions. Meanwhile, in a small microwave-safe bowl, combine zucchini and water. Cover and cook on high for 1 minute or until crisp-tender; drain.

Drain orzo; place in a bowl. Add zucchini, feta cheese, oil, oregano, salt and pepper; toss to coat. Serve warm or chilled. **Yield:** 5 servings.

Nutrition Facts: 1 cup (prepared with reduced-fat feta; calculated without salt) equals 216 calories, 6 g fat (2 g saturated fat), 6 mg cholesterol, 226 mg sodium, 32 g carbohydrate, 2 g fiber, 9 g protein. **Diabetic Exchanges:** 2 starch, 1 very lean meat, 1/2 fat.

Zucchini Brownies

(Pictured below)

Prep: 20 min. **Bake:** 35 min. + cooling

A fast peanut butter and chocolate frosting tops off these moist brownies. They're a sweet way to use homegrown squash. —Allyson Wilkins, Amherst, New Hampshire

Zucchini Brownies

    1 cup butter, softened
1-1/2 cups sugar
    2 eggs
  1/2 cup plain yogurt
    1 teaspoon vanilla extract
2-1/2 cups all-purpose flour
  1/4 cup baking cocoa
    1 teaspoon baking soda
  1/2 teaspoon salt
    2 cups shredded zucchini
FROSTING:
  2/3 cup semisweet chocolate chips
  1/2 cup creamy peanut butter

In a large mixing bowl, cream butter and sugar. Add eggs, one at a time, beating well after each addition. Beat in yogurt and vanilla. Combine the flour, cocoa, baking soda and salt; gradually add to creamed mixture. Fold in zucchini.

Pour into a greased 13-in. x 9-in. x 2-in. baking pan. Bake at 350° for 35-40 minutes or until a toothpick inserted near the center comes out clean.

For the frosting, combine the chocolate chips and peanut butter in a small saucepan. Cook and stir over low heat until smooth. Spread the frosting over the warm brownies. Cool on a wire rack. Cut into bars. **Yield:** about 1-1/2 dozen.

Stuffed Zucchini Boats

Prep/Total Time: 30 min.

If your garden always yields an abundance of zucchini— and you're tired of the same old zucchini bread—try this flavorful entree. The zucchini is stuffed with a savory mixture of ground beef, onion, garlic, soy sauce and cheese. I received the recipe from a friend at work, and it's become a favorite. —Michael Weaver, Norman, Oklahoma

    4 medium zucchini
  1/2 pound ground beef
  1/4 cup chopped onion
1-1/2 teaspoons minced garlic
  1/4 cup water
    2 tablespoons soy sauce
    4 ounces pepper Jack cheese, shredded

Cut each zucchini in half lengthwise; cut a thin slice off the bottoms so the zucchini halves sit flat. Scoop out pulp, leaving 1/4-in. shells. Place shells in an ungreased 13-in. x 9-in. x 2-in. microwave-safe dish. Cover and microwave on high for 3 minutes or until crisp-tender; drain and set aside.

In a large skillet, cook beef, onion and garlic over medium heat for 4-5 minutes or until meat is no longer pink; drain. Stir in water and soy sauce. Bring to a boil. Reduce heat; simmer, uncovered, for 3-4 minutes or until heated through.

Fill each shell with 2 tablespoons meat mixture. Microwave, uncovered, on high for 2-3 minutes. Sprinkle with cheese; microwave 1-2 minutes longer or until zucchini is tender and cheese is melted. **Yield:** 4 servings.

Editor's Note: This recipe was tested in a 1,100-watt microwave.

Cauliflower Tomato Medley

Tasty Tomatoes

BURSTING with flavor, juicy tomatoes make any dish mouth-watering. The fresh-picked recipes here are sure to delight your family and friends.

Cauliflower Tomato Medley

(Pictured above)

Prep/Total Time: 30 min.

This dish is a great way to dress up a head of cauliflower and use up tomatoes. It goes nicely with most meat and fish entrees. —Lena Post, St. Albert, Alberta

   1 medium head cauliflower (about 2 pounds), broken into florets
   6 bacon strips, diced
1-1/2 cups soft bread crumbs
   3 medium tomatoes, cut into wedges
   2 tablespoons sliced green onion
1-1/2 teaspoons snipped fresh dill *or* 1/2 teaspoon dill weed
  1/4 teaspoon salt
Dash pepper
  3/4 cup shredded cheddar cheese

Place cauliflower in a large saucepan; add 1 in. of water. Bring to a boil. Reduce heat; cover and simmer for 5-10 minutes or until crisp-tender.

Meanwhile, in a large skillet, cook bacon over medium heat until crisp. Using a slotted spoon, remove to paper towels. Drain, reserving 3 tablespoons drippings.

Toss bacon and bread crumbs with drippings; set aside.

Drain cauliflower. Arrange the tomatoes in a greased shallow 2-qt. baking dish. Sprinkle with onion, dill, salt and pepper. Top with cauliflower and bacon mixture.

Cover and bake at 400° for 10 minutes. Uncover; sprinkle with cheese. Bake 5 minutes longer or until cheese is melted. **Yield:** 6 servings.

Two-Tomato Pasta

Prep/Total Time: 25 min.

Plum and cherry tomatoes are put to delicious use in this simple toss. It's my favorite pasta dish featuring fresh tomatoes. —Mary Ann Hansen, St. Cloud, Minnesota

   8 ounces uncooked bow tie pasta
  1/2 cup chopped onion
   1 tablespoon olive oil
   2 teaspoons minced garlic
   2 teaspoons all-purpose flour
   1 can (5-1/2 ounces) evaporated milk
   6 plum tomatoes, cut into quarters
   2 cups cherry tomatoes, halved
  1/2 cup shredded Parmesan cheese
  1/2 teaspoon salt
  1/4 teaspoon pepper
   6 fresh basil leaves, torn

Cook pasta according to package directions. Meanwhile, in a large skillet, saute onion in oil until tender. Add garlic; saute 1-2 minutes longer.

Combine flour and milk until smooth; gradually add to skillet. Bring to a boil; cook and stir for 2 minutes or until thickened. Add the tomatoes, Parmesan cheese, salt and pepper. Reduce heat; cook and stir until cheese is melted. Drain pasta; stir into tomato mixture. Sprinkle with basil. **Yield:** 9 servings.

Guacamole Chicken Salad

Prep/Total Time: 25 min.

As a registered nurse with a hectic schedule, I try to pre-pare recipes that are fast, but I also keep nutritional needs in mind. This easy and tasty dish definitely meets all of my criteria. The flavor-packed chicken salad is served with home-baked, seasoned tortilla chips. —*Carmen Bolar*
Bronx, New York

SEASONED TORTILLA CHIPS:
    4 flour tortillas (8 inches)
    1/2 teaspoon garlic powder
    1/2 teaspoon seasoned salt
    1/4 teaspoon curry powder
SALAD:
    2 large ripe avocados, peeled and cubed
    2 large tomatoes, diced
 1-1/2 cups cubed cooked chicken
    1/3 cup chopped onion
    1 jalapeno pepper, chopped
    2 tablespoons minced fresh cilantro
    1 tablespoon lime juice
    1 teaspoon minced garlic
    1/8 teaspoon salt

Spritz one side of each tortilla with nonstick cooking spray. Combine the garlic powder, seasoned salt and curry powder; sprinkle over tortillas. Cut each into four wedges. Place on ungreased baking sheets. Bake at 400° for 6-8 minutes or until crisp.

Meanwhile, in a large bowl, combine the salad ingredients; toss gently. Serve salad with the seasoned tortilla chips. **Yield:** 4 servings.

Editor's Note: When cutting or seeding hot peppers, use rubber or plastic gloves to protect your hands. Avoid touching your face.

Cilantro Tomato Bruschetta

(Pictured below)

Prep/Total Time: 25 min.

This is a no-fuss recipe all of my family and friends love. The flavors blend together for a great-tasting appetizer that goes well with many main dishes. —*Lisa Kane*
Shorewood, Wisconsin

    1 pound French bread, cut into 1-inch slices
    1/2 cup olive oil, *divided*
    1 tablespoon balsamic vinegar
    3 small tomatoes, seeded and chopped
    1/4 cup finely chopped onion
    1/4 cup fresh cilantro leaves, coarsely chopped
    1/4 teaspoon salt
    1/4 teaspoon pepper
    1/4 cup shredded part-skim mozzarella cheese

Place bread on an ungreased baking sheet; brush with 1/4 cup oil. Bake at 325° for 10-12 minutes or until golden brown.

Meanwhile, in a small bowl, whisk the vinegar and remaining oil. Stir in the tomatoes, onion, cilantro, salt and pepper. Spoon about 1 tablespoon onto each slice of bread. Sprinkle with cheese. Serve immediately. **Yield:** 12 servings.

Cilantro Tomato Bruschetta

Sorbet Cream Puffs

In a large saucepan, bring water, butter and salt to a boil. Add flour all at once and stir until a smooth ball forms. Remove from the heat; let stand for 5 minutes. Add eggs, one at a time, beating well after each addition. Continue beating until mixture is smooth and shiny.

Drop by 2 rounded tablespoonfuls 3 in. apart onto greased baking sheets. In a small bowl, whisk the milk and egg yolk; brush over puffs. Bake at 400° for 30-35 minutes or until golden brown. Remove to wire racks. Immediately split puffs open; remove tops and set aside. Discard soft dough from inside. Cool puffs. Freeze for up to 3 months.

To use frozen cream puff shells: Remove from the freezer 15 minutes before filling. **Yield:** 16 cream puff shells.

Sorbet Cream Puffs

(Pictured at left)

Prep/Total Time: 10 min.

Simple and pretty as a picture, these dainty, refreshing treats garnished with berries will melt any resistance to dessert! Best of all, they couldn't be easier to make.

> 1 cup mixed fresh berries
> 1 tablespoon sugar
> 2 cups peach sorbet
> 4 cream puff shells
> Whipped cream

In a small bowl, combine berries and sugar. Place a scoop of sorbet in each cream puff shell; dollop with whipped cream. Replace tops. Serve with berry mixture. **Yield:** 4 servings.

Ham Salad Puffs

(Pictured on page 310)

Prep/Total Time: 15 min.

Flecked with pimientos and chives, this flavorful ham salad has toasted pecans, sweet-tart pineapple and chewy raisins. It's a tangy twist on traditional ham salad.

> 1-1/2 cups diced fully cooked ham
> 1/2 cup unsweetened crushed pineapple, drained and patted dry
> 1/4 cup golden raisins
> 1/4 cup chopped pecans, toasted
> 1 tablespoon diced pimientos, drained
> 3 tablespoons mayonnaise
> 1 tablespoon ranch salad dressing
> 1 tablespoon sour cream
> 1 tablespoon minced chives
> 1/8 teaspoon pepper
> 4 cream puff shells

In a large bowl, combine the first five ingredients. In a small bowl, combine the mayonnaise, ranch dressing, sour cream, chives and pepper. Pour over ham mixture and toss gently to coat. Refrigerate until serving. Just before serving, spoon 1/2 cup ham salad into each cream puff shell; replace tops. **Yield:** 4 servings.

Puff Possibilities

NEED SOMETHING a little special to keep handy for unexpected guests? Dazzle them with these delightful cream puff recipes from our Test Kitchen.

Bake a batch of tender cream puff shells and pop them in the freezer. When you'd like to use them, take out the amount you need and let them thaw for 15 minutes while you fix a refreshing filling. Then serve treats that taste as impressive as they look.

Cream Puff Shells

Prep: 20 min. **Bake:** 30 min. + cooling

Talk about convenience! This easy recipe yields 16 buttery cream puff shells that freeze beautifully for up to 3 months. Take just the number you need from the freezer...they thaw in minutes. And they taste as yummy as the day you baked them.

> 1-1/4 cups water
> 3/4 cup butter
> 1/4 teaspoon salt
> 1-1/4 cups all-purpose flour
> 5 eggs
> 2 tablespoons milk
> 1 egg yolk

Shrimp 'n' Slaw Puffs

(Pictured below)

Prep/Total Time: 15 min.

Coleslaw mix and bottled dressing cut the prep time for this colorful and delicious salad. That leaves you more time to set an elegant luncheon table, pick some fresh flowers or visit with guests.

    8 ounces frozen cooked small shrimp, thawed and chopped
    2 cups coleslaw mix
    2 tablespoons chopped green onion
    2 tablespoons chopped sweet yellow pepper
1/4 cup coleslaw salad dressing
    1 tablespoon capers, drained and patted dry
    1 teaspoon snipped fresh dill *or* 1/4 teaspoon dill weed
1/4 teaspoon salt
1/4 teaspoon pepper
    4 cream puff shells

In a large bowl, combine the shrimp, coleslaw mix, onion and yellow pepper. In a small bowl, combine the coleslaw dressing, capers, dill, salt and pepper. Pour over shrimp mixture and toss gently to coat. Refrigerate until serving. Just before serving, spoon 1/2 cup shrimp salad into each cream puff; replace tops. **Yield:** 4 servings.

Turkey Salad Puffs

(Pictured below)

Prep/Total Time: 20 min.

Fresh mango, red grapes and lemon juice add a delightful splash of summer to this sweet and savory turkey salad seasoned with lemon-pepper and garlic. With celery and toasted nuts, the salad also has a pleasing crunch that contrasts nicely with the tender cream puff shells.

1-1/2 cups cubed cooked turkey breast
  1/2 cup chopped peeled mango
  1/4 cup quartered seedless red grapes
  1/4 cup pine nuts, toasted
    2 tablespoons chopped celery
    5 tablespoons mayonnaise
    1 teaspoon lemon juice
  1/2 teaspoon lemon-pepper seasoning
  1/4 teaspoon garlic powder
    4 cream puff shells

In a large bowl, combine the turkey, mango, grapes, pine nuts and celery. In a small bowl, combine the mayonnaise, lemon juice, lemon-pepper seasoning and garlic powder. Pour over the turkey mixture and toss gently to coat. Refrigerate until serving. Just before serving, spoon 1/2 cup turkey salad into each cream puff shell; replace tops. **Yield:** 4 servings.

Ham Salad Puffs (p. 309)
Shrimp 'n' Slaw Puffs
Turkey Salad Puffs

Italian Veggie Skillet

Bountiful Basil

FRAGRANT and refreshing, basil is a natural for seasoning Italian food. But don't stop there! Your family is sure to enjoy all of the tasty recipes here.

Italian Veggie Skillet

(Pictured above)

Prep/Total Time: 25 min.

Although I'm retired, I like recipes that are fast to prepare. This side dish is ready in no time and incorporates many of the vegetables and herbs from our garden. The taste is so refreshing, especially on a warm summer evening. —Josephine Piro
Easton, Pennsylvania

  1 medium yellow summer squash, cut into 1/4-inch slices
1/2 cup sliced fresh mushrooms
  1 tablespoon olive oil
  1 cup cherry tomatoes, halved
1/2 teaspoon salt
1/2 teaspoon minced garlic
  2 tablespoons minced fresh parsley
1-1/2 teaspoons minced fresh rosemary *or* 1/2 teaspoon dried rosemary, crushed
1-1/2 teaspoons minced fresh thyme *or* 1/2 teaspoon dried thyme
1-1/2 teaspoons plus 2 tablespoons minced fresh basil, *divided*
  2 tablespoons sliced green onion
  2 tablespoons grated Parmesan cheese

In a large skillet, saute squash and mushrooms in oil for 4-5 minutes or until tender. Add the tomatoes, salt and garlic. Reduce heat; simmer, uncovered, for 6-8 minutes.

Stir in the parsley, rosemary, thyme and 1-1/2 teaspoons basil; cook 1-2 minutes longer or until heated through. Transfer to a serving bowl. Sprinkle with onion and remaining basil; lightly toss. Sprinkle with Parmesan cheese. **Yield:** 2-3 servings.

Creamy Tomato Fettuccine

Prep/Total Time: 20 min.

In Hawaii, I sampled a wonderful fettuccine dish that was served with a secret sauce. When I asked about it, I was told how to make this great recipe. I can whip it up in just minutes. —Darlene Brenden, Salem, Oregon

  1 can (14-1/2 ounces) stewed tomatoes
1/2 cup heavy whipping cream
1/4 cup minced fresh parsley
1-1/2 teaspoons minced fresh basil
  4 cups hot cooked fettuccine
1/3 cup grated Parmesan cheese

In a large saucepan, bring tomatoes to a boil. Reduce heat. Stir in the cream, parsley and basil; heat through. Toss with fettuccine; sprinkle with Parmesan cheese. **Yield:** 4 servings.

BLT Salad

(Pictured below)

Prep/Total Time: 25 min.

In my family of six, it's hard to find a vegetable or salad everyone will eat, but they all raved about this one. With basil from my garden, this medley is simple to make but has a mouth-watering taste. —Susie Clayton
South St. Paul, Minnesota

    1 pound sliced bacon, cut into 1-inch pieces
1/4 cup butter, cubed
    4 slices white bread, crusts removed and cut
       into 1-inch cubes
1/2 cup mayonnaise
    3 to 5 tablespoons minced fresh basil
    2 tablespoons red wine vinegar
1/2 teaspoon pepper
1/2 teaspoon minced garlic
    6 cups torn romaine
1-1/2 cups grape tomatoes

In a large skillet, cook bacon over medium heat until crisp. Using a slotted spoon, remove to paper towels; drain, reserving 2 tablespoons drippings. Set bacon and drippings aside. In another large skillet, melt butter. Add bread cubes; cook over medium heat for 4-5 minutes or until golden brown, stirring frequently. Remove to paper towels; cool.

For dressing, whisk the mayonnaise, basil, vinegar, pepper, garlic and reserved drippings. In a large bowl, combine romaine, tomatoes and bacon. Drizzle with dressing and toss to coat. Top with croutons. **Yield:** 8 servings.

BLT Salad

Artichoke-Basil Pasta Sauce

Prep/Total Time: 20 min.

I received this recipe from my college roommate, and it quickly became one of my favorites. Fresh basil gives the zesty sauce just the right flavor. —Janet Bischof
Sumter, South Carolina

☑ Uses less fat, sugar or salt Includes Nutrition
Facts and Diabetic Exchanges.

    1 jar (6-1/2 ounces) marinated artichoke
       hearts
    1 cup chopped onion
    1 cup sliced fresh mushrooms
1/2 teaspoon minced garlic
    1 can (14-1/2 ounces) diced tomatoes,
       undrained
    1 cup water
    1 can (6 ounces) tomato paste
    2 tablespoons minced fresh basil *or* 2
       teaspoons dried basil
    1 teaspoon sugar
1/2 teaspoon salt, optional
Hot cooked pasta

Drain artichokes, reserving marinade; set artichokes aside. In a large saucepan, saute the onion, mushrooms and garlic in reserved marinade for 2-3 minutes or until tender.

Stir in the artichokes, tomatoes, water, tomato paste, basil, sugar and salt if desired. Bring to a boil. Reduce heat; simmer, uncovered, for 5-10 minutes or until heated through. Serve over pasta. **Yield:** 5 servings.

Nutrition Facts: 1 cup sauce (prepared without salt; calculated without pasta) equals 124 calories, 6 g fat (1 g saturated fat), 0 cholesterol, 258 mg sodium, 18 g carbohydrate, 4 g fiber, 3 g protein. **Diabetic Exchanges:** 3 vegetable, 1 fat.

Pan-Glazed Chicken

Prep/Total Time: 20 min.

Honey and balsamic vinegar lend a sweet flavor to chicken in this stovetop supper. Served over rice, the tangy combination makes a delicious meal on a busy night.
—Margaret Wilson, Hemet, California

    1 package (6 ounces) instant long grain and
       wild rice mix
    4 boneless skinless chicken breast halves
       (4 ounces *each*)
1/4 teaspoon salt
1/4 teaspoon pepper
    2 teaspoons olive oil
    2 tablespoons balsamic vinegar
    1 tablespoon honey
    2 teaspoons dried basil

Prepare rice according to package directions. Meanwhile, sprinkle chicken with salt and pepper. In a large skillet, cook chicken in oil over medium-high heat for 5 minutes on each side or until juices run clear.

Combine the vinegar, honey and basil; pour over

chicken. Cook for 1-2 minutes or until sauce is heated through. Serve with rice. **Yield:** 4 servings.

Lemon Basil Cookies

Prep: 10 min. **Bake:** 10 min. per batch

These light, basil-flecked cookies are a breeze to fix with lemon cake mix, flaked coconut and chopped pecans.
—Pam Frankenfield, Halethorpe, Maryland

    1 package (8 ounces) cream cheese, softened
1/4 cup butter, softened
    1 egg yolk
    1 teaspoon lemon juice
    1 package (18-1/4 ounces) lemon cake mix
1/4 cup flaked coconut
1/4 cup chopped pecans
    1 tablespoon dried basil
1/2 teaspoon grated lemon peel

In a large mixing bowl, beat cream cheese and butter until fluffy. Beat in egg yolk and lemon juice. Gradually add cake mix. Stir in the coconut, pecans, basil and lemon peel.

Drop by teaspoonfuls 2 in. apart onto greased baking sheets. Bake at 350° for 10-14 minutes or until golden brown. Cool for 2 minutes before removing to wire racks. **Yield:** 3-1/2 dozen.

Basil Burgers

Prep/Total Time: 25 min.

Served on onion rolls with cream cheese and sliced avocado, these burgers are a refreshing change of pace.
—Jill Christopher, Grants Pass, Oregon

    2 tablespoons minced fresh basil *or* 2
      teaspoons dried basil
    1 tablespoon olive oil
1/2 teaspoon minced garlic
1/2 teaspoon salt
1/2 teaspoon pepper
1-1/2 pounds ground beef
1/4 cup cream cheese, softened
    4 onion rolls, split and toasted
    4 slices red onion
    1 medium ripe avocado, peeled and sliced

In a bowl, combine first five ingredients. Crumble beef over mixture and mix well. Shape into four patties. Grill, uncovered, over medium-hot heat for 5-7 minutes on each side or until juices run clear. Spread cream cheese over cut side of roll tops. Place burgers, onion and avocado on roll bottoms; replace tops. **Yield:** 4 servings.

Basil Red Pepper Sandwiches

(Pictured above right)

Prep/Total Time: 25 min.

Our Test Kitchen added basil leaves to this hot, hearty sandwich that features tangy olives, roasted red pepper and melted mozzarella cheese.

Basil Red Pepper Sandwiches

    1 loaf (1 pound) unsliced Italian bread
    1 to 2 teaspoons grated lemon peel
    2 tablespoons plus 1 teaspoon olive oil, *divided*
    8 ounces sliced part-skim mozzarella cheese
    4 large pieces roasted sweet red pepper,
      patted dry
  12 fresh basil leaves
1/2 cup chopped pitted green olives

Cut the top half off the loaf of bread; carefully hollow out top and bottom, leaving a 3/4-in. shell (save removed bread for another use).

In a small bowl, combine the lemon peel and 2 tablespoons oil. Spread over the cut side of the bread top. Drizzle the remaining oil inside the bread bottom; layer with the mozzarella cheese, red pepper, basil and olives. Replace bread top. Wrap in foil. Bake at 350° for 10-12 minutes or until cheese is melted. Slice before serving. **Yield:** 4 servings.

Cooling Cookies

When making cookies, I like to place a single sheet of waxed paper over the wire rack before putting the cookies on the rack. I've found that this prevents soft cookies from falling between the slots as they cool, and it also gives the treats a nice, smooth underside.
—Janice Huelsmann, Trenton, Illinois

Dream Pie

TAKE ONE simple pie recipe, add a few twists to the ingredient list and what do you get? Three lovely desserts that taste equally scrumptious! Requiring just 10 minutes of prep time each, you can make one or whip up all three for a sweet spring buffet.

Basic Dream Pie

Prep: 10 min. + chilling

Choose from three flavors of unsweetened soft drink mix to create the colorful variations of this light, creamy pie from our Test Kitchen. Be sure to check the chart in the box below for add-ins, drizzle accents and fruit garnishes.

 1 tablespoon water
 1 envelope unsweetened soft drink mix
 1 tablespoon add-in (see tip box below)
 2 packages (3 ounces *each*) cream cheese, softened
 1 cup confectioners' sugar
 1 teaspoon vanilla extract
1-1/2 cups heavy whipping cream, whipped
 1 graham cracker crust (9 inches)
 2 tablespoons drizzle accent (see tip box)
Fruit garnish (see tip box)

In a small bowl, combine the water and soft drink mix until dissolved. Stir in add-in.

In a mixing bowl, beat the cream cheese, confectioners' sugar, vanilla and soft drink mixture until fluffy. Fold in whipped cream. Spread into crust. Chill for at least 1 hour or until set.

Decorate dessert plates with drizzle accent; top each with a piece of pie. Add fruit garnish. Refrigerate leftovers. **Yield:** 6-8 servings.

Dream Pie Variations

Unsweetened soft drink mix	Add-in	Drizzle accent	Fruit garnish
Strawberry	Strawberry ice cream topping	Hot fudge, warmed	Fresh strawberries
Lemonade	Lemonade concentrate	Seedless raspberry jam, warmed	Lemon slice
Orange	Orange juice	White baking chocolate (1 ounce), melted	Quartered orange slice

Spicy Oatmeal Cookie Mix

In a small bowl, combine the first five ingredients. In a 1-qt. glass jar, layer the flour mixture, brown sugar, sugar, oats, chips and coconut, packing well between each layer. Cover and store in a cool, dry place for up to 6 months. **Yield:** 1 batch (4 cups).

To prepare cookies: In a mixing bowl, beat the butter, egg and vanilla. Add cookie mix and mix well. Drop by rounded teaspoonfuls 2 in. apart onto ungreased baking sheets. Bake at 350° for 9-11 minutes or until golden brown. Cool for 2 minutes before removing to wire racks. **Yield:** about 3-1/2 dozen.

Hearty Pasta Soup Mix

(Pictured below)

Prep: 15 min. **Cook:** 1-1/4 hours

Warm up loved ones on frosty winter nights with a dinner using this stick-to-the-ribs soup mix. Presented in a bow-tied jar, it looks as good as it tastes.

   1/2 cup dry split peas
     2 tablespoons chicken bouillon granules
   1/2 cup dry lentils
     2 tablespoons dried minced onion
     1 teaspoon dried basil
     1 teaspoon dried parsley flakes
     1 envelope savory herb with garlic soup mix *or* vegetable soup mix
     2 cups uncooked tricolor spiral pasta
ADDITIONAL INGREDIENTS:
   10 cups water
     3 cups cubed cooked chicken
     1 can (28 ounces) diced tomatoes, undrained

In a 1-qt. glass container, layer the first seven ingredients in the order listed. Place the spiral pasta in a 1-qt. resealable plastic bag; add to the jar. Seal tightly. **Yield:** 1 batch (4 cups).

To prepare soup: Remove pasta from top of jar and set aside. Place water in a Dutch oven; stir in soup mix. Bring to a boil. Reduce heat; cover and simmer for 45 minutes. Add the chicken, tomatoes and pasta. Cover and simmer for 15-20 minutes longer or until pasta, peas and lentils are tender. **Yield:** 14 servings (3-1/2 quarts).

Merry Mixes

WRAP UP the Christmas season's best with these quick pantry presents from our Test Kitchen. Teachers, neighbors and other lucky folks will appreciate these sweet cookie mixin's and savory soup fixin's layered in a jar and ready to go. Just include a list of the few extra ingredients and prep instructions on the tag...no wrapping required!

Spicy Oatmeal Cookie Mix

(Pictured above)

Prep: 15 min. **Bake:** 10 min. per batch

Brown sugar and spice and everything nice—like cinnamon, coconut, oats and chips—are packaged together in these pretty jars of yummy, ready-to-bake cookies!

     1 cup all-purpose flour
     1 teaspoon ground cinnamon
   3/4 teaspoon baking soda
   1/4 teaspoon salt
   1/8 teaspoon ground nutmeg
   1/2 cup packed brown sugar
   1/2 cup sugar
     1 cup old-fashioned oats
     1 cup swirled milk chocolate and caramel chips
   1/2 cup flaked coconut
ADDITIONAL INGREDIENTS:
   1/2 cup butter, softened
     1 egg
   3/4 teaspoon vanilla extract

Hearty Pasta Soup Mix

General Recipe Index

This handy index lists every recipe by food category, major ingredient and/or cooking method, so you can easily locate recipes to suit your needs.

✓Recipe includes Nutrition Facts and Diabetic Exchanges

✓Recipe includes Nutrition Facts and Diabetic Exchanges

✓Recipe includes Nutrition Facts and Diabetic Exchanges

✓Recipe includes Nutrition Facts and Diabetic Exchanges

✓*Recipe includes Nutrition Facts and Diabetic Exchanges*

✓Recipe includes Nutrition Facts and Diabetic Exchanges

✓Recipe includes Nutrition Facts and Diabetic Exchanges

✓Recipe includes Nutrition Facts and Diabetic Exchanges

✓Recipe includes Nutrition Facts and Diabetic Exchanges

✓Recipe includes Nutrition Facts and Diabetic Exchanges

✓*Recipe includes Nutrition Facts and Diabetic Exchanges*

✓Recipe includes Nutrition Facts and Diabetic Exchanges

✓*Recipe includes Nutrition Facts and Diabetic Exchanges*

✓Recipe includes Nutrition Facts and Diabetic Exchanges

✓Recipe includes Nutrition Facts and Diabetic Exchanges

✓Recipe includes Nutrition Facts and Diabetic Exchanges

Alphabetical Index

This handy index lists every recipe in alphabetical order, so you can easily find your favorite recipes.

✓Recipe includes Nutrition Facts and Diabetic Exchanges

✓Recipe includes Nutrition Facts and Diabetic Exchanges

✓Fruit Smoothies, 257
✓Fruity Chicken Tossed Salad, 12
✓Fruity Cooler, 253
✓Fruity Peanut Butter Pitas, 176
Fudge-Filled Brownie Bars, 224

G

Garden Chicken Salad, 132
Garden-Style Beef Lasagna, 268
Garlic Cheese Bread, 49
✓Garlic-Onion Cheese
    Spread, 283
✓Garlic Oregano Zucchini, 92
Garlic Toast Pizzas, 102
German Bratwurst, 48
✓Ginger Salmon Salad, 14
Ginger Sirloin Strips, 202
✓Glazed Carrots, 98
Glazed Kielbasa, 162
Glazed Lamb Chops, 64
Gnocchi with Pesto Sauce, 78
Golden Wheat Bread, 143
✓Golden Sea Bass, 82
✓Grapefruit Spinach Salad, 250
✓Grecian Gold Medal
    Wraps, 259
Greek Garden Appetizer, 304
✓Greek Pork Pockets, 196
Grilled Ham 'n' Jack Cheese, 51
Grilled Jerk Chicken Wings, 281
Grilled Marjoram Corn, 287
Grilled Potato Skins, 31
Grilled Shrimp Fajitas, 28
Grilled Sourdough Clubs, 56
Ground Beef Zucchini Skillet, 247
Guacamole Chicken Salad, 308
Guacamole Chicken Wraps, 109

H

Hacienda Hot Dogs, 182
Ham 'n' Cheddar Corn Bread, 86
Ham 'n' Cheese Lasagna, 135
Ham 'n' Cheese Pasta, 239
Ham and Mango Wraps, 187
Ham and Potato Bake, 243
Ham and Swiss Casserole, 243
Ham Barbecue, 154
Ham Salad Puffs, 309
Ham with Ruby-Red Glaze, 24
Hamburger Hoagies, 65
Hamburger Noodle Bake, 230

Hash Brown Apple Pancake, 57
Hearty Chicken Casserole, 242
Hearty Pasta Soup Mix, 315
✓Hearty Pork Chops, 256
Herb Butter, 296
✓Herb Fish Fillets, 45
✓Herbed Beans and Carrots, 58
Herbed Chicken and
    Tomatoes, 158
Herbed Pork and Potatoes, 139
Herbed Steak Fries, 51
Hole-in-One Eggs, 176
Holiday Snack Mix, 102
Homemade Maple Syrup, 167
Honey Garlic Dressing, 40
✓Honey-Ginger Chicken
    Stir-Fry, 196
Honey-Glazed Drop Biscuits, 149
Honey Pineapple Chicken, 160
Hot Turkey Sandwiches, 105
Hungarian Goulash, 156

I

Italian Beef Sandwiches, 152
Italian Beef with Spaghetti, 134
Italian Cheese Bread, 18
Italian Chili, 41
Italian Meat Loaf
    Sandwiches, 138
Italian Sausage Calzone, 82
Italian Veggie Skillet, 311

J

Jack-o'-Lantern Pops, 33
✓Jalapeno Cheese Spread, 276
✓Jambalaya Skillet, 246
Jazzed-Up French Toast
    Sticks, 176

K

Kielbasa Tortellini Alfredo, 201

L

Lasagna Pizza, 77
Layered Lemon Pie, 291
Layered Salad for a Crowd, 26
Layered Salad Reuben-Style, 181
✓Lazy Days Potato Salad, 65
Lemon Basil Cookies, 313
✓Lemon-Dill Steamed
    Vegetables, 254
✓Lemon Garlic Shrimp, 244

Lemon-Linguine Shrimp
    Salad, 190
Lemon Oat Bars, 221
✓Lemon-Pepper Vegetables, 266
Lemon Poppy Seed Muffins, 144
Lemon Poppy Seed Waffles, 171
Lemon Vinaigrette Salad, 304
Light 'n' Crispy Waffles, 167
✓Light Strawberry Pie, 252
✓Lime Chicken Tacos, 158
Lime Herb Chicken, 76
Linguine with Garlic Sauce, 128
Little Texas Corn Bread, 147

M

Maple Baby Carrots, 64
Maple Butter, 296
Maple Cranberry Chicken, 208
Maple-Glazed Long Johns, 144
Maple-Pecan Pork Chops, 57
✓Marinated Beef Stir-Fry, 228
Mashed Potato Cups, 232
Mashed Red Potatoes, 38
Meatball Stroganoff, 244
Meringue Drops, 293
Mexican Drop Biscuits, 60
Microwave Broccoli Chicken
    Bake, 264
Microwave Potato Salad, 268
Mini Hot Dogs 'n' Meatballs, 155
Mini Spinach Frittatas, 277
Mint Chip Deluxe, 106
Mocha Punch, 233
Mom's Spaghetti Sauce, 157
✓Morning Cinnamon Rolls, 256
Mushroom Green Bean
    Medley, 89
Mushroom Pepper Steak, 152
Mushroom-Swiss Lamb
    Chops, 207

N

Nacho Chicken Pitas, 123
Nectarine Plum Cobbler, 219
Nesting Chicks, 218
Nuts-About-You Cookie Sticks, 22
Nutty Apple Syrup, 174
Nutty Fruit 'n' Cheese Tray, 279
Nutty Salmon, 266

O

Oatmeal Kiss Cookies, 217

✓Recipe includes Nutrition Facts and Diabetic Exchanges

✓Recipe includes Nutrition Facts and Diabetic Exchanges

✓Recipe includes Nutrition Facts and Diabetic Exchanges